Reviewing vertical restraints in Europe

Reform, key issues and national enforcement

Following on from *Concurrences* Journal and the site www.concurrences.com, this collection aims to bring together works in this particularly fast-moving and concrete field of competition law, where several disciplines intersect.

Its prime objective is to cover four categories of works: conferences, and specifically the proceedings of the annual *Concurrences* Journal conference – *New Frontiers of Antitrust / Demain la concurrence* –, monographs on largely professional themes, research works (in particular the winners of the annual Concurrences award), and certain mixed collections.

The Concurrences collection is produced under the scientific supervision of Laurence Idot, Professor at the Université Paris II Panthéon-Assas and editor in chief of *Concurrences* Journal.

Reviewing vertical restraints in Europe

Reform, key issues and national enforcement

Edited by
Jean-François **Bellis** and
José Maria **Beneyto**

Associate editor
Jerónimo **Maillo**

bruylant

For information on our back catalogue and new developments in your
specialist area, go to our website: www.larciergroup.com

© Groupe Larcier s.a., 2012   2ᵉ tirage 2013
Éditions Bruylant
Rue des Minimes, 39 • B-1000 Brussels

ISBN: 978-2-8027-3709-4

PREFACE

This book contains the contributions made by the group of experts who participated in the conference on "Reviewing Vertical Restraints in Europe: Reform, Key Issues and National Enforcement" organized by the CEU San Pablo University in Madrid on 11 and 12 November 2010. One of the interesting features of the conference was that it gathered experts from many different origins: academics, EU Commission and Member State officials, industry representatives and practicing lawyers from several jurisdictions.

The book presents a comprehensive analysis of the 2010 reform of the rules applicable to vertical restraints following the entry into force of Regulation No. 330/2010. It consists of four parts. The first part analyses the reform from a legal and economic perspective with a special focus on the new subjects covered by the new guidelines on vertical restraints, such as, in particular, internet commerce. The second part focuses on three key issues of great practical significance: the notion of agreement in a vertical context, the concept of agency selective/exclusive distribution and franchising as well as parallel trade after the GSK Spain judgments. The third part provides an overview of vertical restraints in two specific markets, namely the energy and automobile markets. Finally, the fourth part discusses the state of national enforcement with respect to vertical restraint in selected Member States, i.e. Spain, Germany, Poland and the Netherlands.

The editors wish to express their appreciation for the contributions made by the authors in an area of competition law which, more than any other, has experienced profound changes over the years, thus making the analysis of Regulation No. 333/2010, the latest in a series of block exemptions on vertical restraints issued since 1967, all the more fascinating.

JEAN-FRANÇOIS BELLIS   JOSÉ MARIA BENEYTO

TABLE OF CONTENTS

INTRODUCTION
A BRIEF HISTORICAL PERSPECTIVE ON EU COMPETITION POLICY WITH RESPECT TO VERTICAL RESTRAINTS

PART ONE
THE REFORM

CHAPTER I
NEW EU COMPETITION RULES FOR SUPPLY AND DISTRIBUTION AGREEMENTS

CHAPTER II

REFORMING THE REFORM: THE NEW RULES FOR VERTICAL AGREEMENTS IN THE EU MARKET SHARE THRESHOLDS AND RESALE PRICE MAINTENANCE

CHAPTER III

THE EC REVIEW OF THE VERTICAL RESTRAINTS POLICY IN THE CONTEXT OF INTERNET COMMERCE

CHAPTER IV

AN ECONOMIC APPROACH
TO THE NEW RULES FOR VERTICAL RESTRAINTS

PART TWO

KEY ISSUES

CHAPTER V

THE NOTION OF AGREEMENT IN A VERTICAL CONTEXT:
PIECES OF A SLIDING PUZZLE

CHAPTER VI

AGENCY, SELECTIVE/EXCLUSIVE DISTRIBUTION AND FRANCHISING AGREEMENTS: BORDERLINES AND IMPACT ON THE QUALIFICATION UNDER COMPETITION LAW

    UNCLEAR BOUNDARIES. 146

    1.1 Is an agent under commercial law and competition law strictly
         the same?. 147
         1.1.1 Authorised representative. 147
         1.1.2 Commission agent. 148
         1.1.3 Deposit agreements. 149

    1.2 The agent in the competition law sense: which definition? 149
         1.2.1 What are the criteria for defining an agency agreement? 149
         1.2.2 Casting light and shade on the risk criterion. 151

    1.3 Agency in the competition law sense and immunity. 152
         1.3.1 Limits to immunity 152
         1.3.2 The difficulty in conciliating the spirit of the commercial
               rules and the residual application of competition law. 152

2. SELECTIVE/EXCLUSIVE DISTRIBUTION, EXCLUSIVE SOURCING AND FRANCHISE:
    ARE THE BOUNDARIES INVULNERABLE WHEN COMPETITION LAW APPLIES?. . . 153

    2.1 Survival of the legal categories 154
         2.1.1 Extent of maintenance of legal categories 154
               a) Maintaining the definitions. 154
               b) The role of the qualification for application
                  of the exemption 155
               c) Role of the qualification for the case by case review
                  of agreements 155
         2.1.2 Uncertainty around certain definitions 156
               a) Has the Commission invented a system of franchise
                  without know-how? 156
               b) The revival of selective distribution? 157

    2.2 Combination of the legal categories 158
         2.2.1 Combination of qualifications widely possible where
               Regulation No. 330/2010 applies. 158
         2.2.2 Limits: the case of selective distribution. 159

PART THREE

AN OVERVIEW OF VERTICAL RESTRAINTS IN SPECIFIC MARKETS

CHAPTER VIII

VERTICAL RESTRAINTS AND ENERGY MARKETS

PART FOUR
NATIONAL ENFORCEMENT

CHAPTER X
NATIONAL EXPERIENCES
IN VERTICAL RESTRAINTS: SPAIN

CHAPTER XI

NATIONAL ENFORCEMENT
OF VERTICAL RESTRAINTS: GERMANY

XI.1 General Courts

CHAPTER XIII

ENFORCEMENT OF VERTICAL RESTRAINTS IN THE NETHERLANDS

LIST OF CONTRIBUTORS

Jean-François Bellis
Partner
Van Bael & Bellis

Constantijn Bakker
Lecturer European Competition Law at the International Business Department Hogeschool van Amsterdam

Helmut Brokelmann
Partner
Martinez Lage, Allendesalazar & Brokelmann Abogados

John Clark
Directorate-General Competition, unit F-2
Directorate General for Competition. European Commission

Paul Csiszar
Director. Market and Cases IV: Basic Industries, Manufacturing and Agriculture.
Directorate General for Competition. European Commission

Andrés Font Galarza
Partner
Gibson, Dunn & Crutcher LLP, Brussels

Marc Greven
Director Legal Affairs
ACEA (European Automobile Manufacturers Association)

Eric Gippini-Fournier
Member of the Legal Service
European Commission

Alejandro Guerrero Pérez
Lawyer and Trainee
Gibson, Dunn & Crutcher LLP, Brussels

Kai Hooghof
Head of Unit, German and European Antitrust Law
General Policy Division of the Bundeskartellamt, Germany

Joaquín López Vallés
Assistant Deputy Director of Industry and Energy
Investigations Division, Comisión Nacional de la Competencia (CNC)

Sandra Marco Colino
Research Assistant Professor
Chinese University of Hong Kong

Luc Peeperkorn
Principal Expert in Antitrust Policy at DG Competition
European Commission

Rafael Piqueras Bautista
General Secretary
ENAGAS, S.A.

Carsten Reimann
Head of External Affairs and Director of Nissan's Brussels Office
Nissan

Hartmut P. Röhl
President
GVA e.V. (Gesamtverband Autoteile-Handel)

Jaroslaw Sroczynski
Founding partner
Markiewicz & Sroczynski

Nikolaos Vettas
Professor, Department of Economics
Athens University of Economics and Business

Joseph Vogel
Founding Partner
VOGEL & VOGEL

Markus Wirtz
Partner
Glade Michel Wirtz: Corporate & Competition

INTRODUCTION

INTRODUCTION

A BRIEF HISTORICAL PERSPECTIVE ON EU COMPETITION POLICY WITH RESPECT TO VERTICAL RESTRAINTS

JEAN-FRANÇOIS BELLIS

Partner

Van Bael & Bellis

Vertical restraints have played a major role in the early development of the EU competition policy. At a time where there existed practically no "competition culture" in Europe, the promotion of single market integration was chosen as one of the main objectives of EU competition policy. Rather than actively prosecuting cartels, which have always been regarded as the most serious antitrust offence by those who see consumer welfare as the main objective of antitrust policy, the Commission chose instead to focus on agreements that tended to keep the Common Market partitioned along national boundaries.

1. The rationale for the prohibition of export restrictions

In this connection, it is interesting to take a close look at a seminal case from the very first years of enforcement of EU competition rules, namely the *Grundig-Consten* case. In that case, the Commission decided that an agreement whereby the German consumer electronics manufacturer Grundig granted absolute territorial protection to its French exclusive distributor, Consten, violated Article 101(1).[1] The Court upheld the Commission decision with respect to the territorial restrictions.[2]

---

1 *Grundig-Consten*, JO 1964, p. 2545.
2 *Consten and Grundig vs. Commission* [1966] ECR 299.

Three basic justifications for the condemnation of territorial protection were put forward in the Commission decision:

(1) The economic goal of encouraging intra-brand competition.

(2) The political goal of achieving an integrated common market.

(3) The social goal of protecting the small parallel trader against the power of the large supplier.

It is interesting to take a close look at these three justifications because they have tended to provide the basis for the EU competition enforcement against vertical restraints until the entry into force of the so-called "modernisation regulation", namely Regulation 1/2003[3].

1.1 Encouragement of intra-brand competition

On the issue of intra-brand competition, the Commission and the Court embarked in *Grundig* on a course which was consistently followed for several decades. The Commission examined only price competition between *Grundig* products and refused to analyse effects on inter-brand competition. The Court upheld the Commission's approach stating that:

'The principle of freedom of competition concerns the various stages and manifestations of competition. Although competition between producers is generally more noticeable than that between distributors of products of the same make, it does not thereby follow that an agreement tending to restrict the latter kind of competition should escape the prohibition of Article 101(1) merely because it might increase the former.'[4]

The Court went on to state that:

'*the absence in the contested decision of any analysis of the effects of the agreement on competition between similar products of different makes does not, of itself, constitute a defect in the decision.*'[5]

Following *Grundig*-Consten, absolute territorial restrictions were considered per se violations of Article 101(1) with no requirement of an analysis of the broader economic effects on competition with other brands.

---

3   Council Regulation No. 1/2003 on the implementation of the rules on competition laid down in Articles 81 and 82 of the Treaty, OJ 2003 L1/1.

4   *Id.*, at p. 342.

5   *Ibid.* The failure of the Commission to examine the effect of the export bans on intra-brand competition was criticised by both the government of Germany in its intervention and Advocate-General Roemer in his opinion. *Id.*, at pp. 325 and 359-360.

1.2 The political goal of achieving market integration

The use of the competition rules to promote the integration of the various Member State markets into a single market has been the most important basis for the prohibition of export bans.[6] In *Consten & Grundig*, the Court stated that, as the agreement had the object of isolating national markets:

> *'It was... proper for the contested decision to hold that the agreement constitutes an infringement of Article 101(1). No further considerations, whether of economic data (price differences between France and Germany, representative character of the type of appliance considered, level of overheads borne by Consten) or of the corrections of the criteria upon which the Commission relied in its comparisons between the situations of the French and German markets, and no possible favourable effects of the agreement in other respects, can in any way lead, in the face of above-mentioned restrictions, to a different solution under Article 101(1).'*[7]

The Commission has tended to reject arguments relating to differences in conditions in national markets. Rather than considering the continuing imperfections in the market, the Commission and the Court, for purposes of condemning territorial restrictions, have treated the market as if it were already integrated and have acted as if the actions of companies operating within the Community were the only barriers to trade. In *Grundig-Consten*, the Commission and the Court failed to consider justifications for price differentials such as differences in transportation costs, customs duties or overheads.

Many of the subsequent cases brought by the Commission proceeded on the assumption that the industry concerned was operating in a truly common market. Yet, very often, this ideal did not correspond to reality. For example, in the *BMW Belgium case*,[8] the Commission and the Court of Justice condemned an export prohibition imposed on Belgian dealers without taking any account of the fact that Belgian price control measures

---

6   In discussing its basic policy on exclusive dealing agreements the Commission stated: 'The attention given to the exclusive dealing agreements was fundamentally due to the fact that such agreements are particularly likely to create obstacles with regard to the integration of national markets into a single market, to the extent that they guarantee to the holder of the concession not only the exclusive right to obtain supplies direct from the manufacturer but also to be the only distributor allowed to introduce the relevant products in to the territory allocated to him'. (*First Report on Competition Policy*, No. 45).

7   *Consten & Grundig vs. Commission* [1966] ECR 299, at p. 343.

8   *BMW Belgium*, OJ 1978 L46/33; on appeal: *BMW Belgium vs. Commission* [1979] ECR 2435.

had caused prices for BMW cars to be lower in Belgium than in Germany, a situation clearly beyond the manufacturer's control. Similarly, in *Distillers*[9] the Commission condemned a dual pricing system as a disguised 'export ban' between the UK and the Continent. Yet, to an economist, the continued existence of differing prices throughout the EU need not mean anything else than that the various markets or regions in the EU are not yet fully uniform, for a variety of reasons (e.g. tax structure, currency changes, standard of living, and distribution pattern).

1.3 The protection of the parallel trader

The Commission also chose to protect the parallel trader himself without any showing that, in fact, the parallel trader was contributing to price reductions or otherwise benefiting the consumer. In his criticism of the Commission's approach in *Grundig-Consten*, Advocate-General Roemer stated:

> '*Thus, for example, it does not seem to be disputed that retail prices are equally high in France for Grundig equipment, whether they are supplied by Consten or by parallel importers. Consequently, the parallel imports, which the Commission considers necessary, do not lead to favourable prices to the consumer; they even have the result, that the consumers are less well served, if, as Consten asserts, it is true (which would have to be proved) that it supplies better benefits through a good guarantee and after-sales service, a comprehensive stock and the provision of supplies to the whole of the French market. It is even possible that if parallel imports were to increase, that is to say, if the market were exploited in a less well organized and less intensive manner than it is by Consten, the development of sales would deteriorate, with corresponding repercussions on the conditions of production and the structuring of the manufacturer's prices.*'[10]

The protection of the parallel trader by the Commission reached extremes in some cases. For example, in an early draft of the block exemption for motor vehicle selective distribution agreements, the Commission set out

---

9   The Distillers Co. Ltd. — Conditions of Sale and Price Terms, OJ 1978 L50/16.
10 Opinion of Advocate-General Roemer in *Consten & Grundig* vs. *Commission* [1966] ECR 299, at pp. 372-373.

in the preamble the following justification for removing the protection for parallel traders when price differentials reach 12 per cent:

> *'it may generally be concluded from observations of imports of motor vehicles through distribution channels other than those established by the manufacturer (parallel imports) that the incentive to engage in parallel imports within the common market increases rapidly where recommendations in different Member States produce price variations of more than 12 per cent of the lowest price.'*[11]

Thus, the Commission was willing to grant protection from parallel traders to official dealers only for as long as it would be uneconomical for them to engage in parallel trade.

In exemptions under Article 101(3), the Commission has allowed limited restrictions on the activities which a distributor may perform outside of its territory. Thus, in agreements falling within the terms of the exclusive distribution block exemption, a distributor can be prevented from soliciting sales or from maintaining stocks outside of its territory.[12]

Another disturbing aspect of the Commission's approach to distribution issues in the early years of EU competition enforcement was the fact that it seemed to be inspired by notions of fairness rather than genuine competition concerns, the notion that the distributor should be protected against the possible greater bargaining power of the supplier.

2. The EU practice with respect to Export Bans

2.1 Export ban within the EU

The Commission has consistently required that export bans be removed from distributor agreements and sales conditions.[13] The only contractual

---

11 Draft Commission Regulation on the application of Article 101(3) of the Treaty to certain categories of motor vehicle distribution and servicing agreements, OJ 1983 C165/2, Recital 29. See also, Van Bael, 'The Draft EU Regulation on Selective Distribution of Motor Vehicles: A Daydream for Free Riders — A Nightmare for industry', (1983) 19 Swiss Rev. Int. Comp. L. 3.

12 Commission Reg. No. 1983/83 on the application of Article 101(3) to categories of exclusive distribution agreements, OJ 1983 L173/1, corrigendum OJ 1983 L281/84, Annex 13 below, Article 2(2) (c).

13 See Kodak, JO 1970 L147/24; Omega, JO 1970 L24/22; WEA Filipacchi Music SA, JO 1972 L303/52; Du Pont de Nemours Deutschland, OJ 1973 L194/27; Bayerische Motoren Werke AG, OJ 1975 L29/1; Goodyear Italiana-Euram, OJ 1975 L38/10; Miller International, OJ 1976 L357/40; Junghans, OJ 1977 L30/10; GERO-Fabriek, OJ 1977 L16/8; Theal Watts, OJ 1977

territorial restrictions which were allowed within the EU were those contained in agreements that were considered to be *de minimis* given the importance of the parties in the market.[14]

Territorial restrictions have been prohibited even if they were not incorporated in a formal written agreement.[15] A company could not successfully defend itself by showing that an export ban in an agreement had not been enforced.[16] Qualifications stating, for example, that an export restriction applied to the extent it is permitted by law would not save an otherwise unlawful export restriction.[17]

In exemptions under Article 101(3), the Commission allowed limited restrictions on the activities which a distributor may perform outside of its territory. Thus, in agreements falling within the terms of the exclusive distribution block exemption, a distributor could be prevented from soliciting sales or from maintaining stocks outside of its territory.[18]

L39/19, BMW Belgium, OJ 1978 L46/33; Kawasaki, OJ 1979 L16/9; Pioneer Hi-Fi Equipment, OJ 1980 L60/21; Johnson and Johnson, OJ 1980 L377/16; Hasselblad, OJ 1982 L161/18; Moët et Chandon (London) Ltd, OJ 1982 L94/7; Polisti /Arbois, OJ L136/9; John Deere, OJ 1985 L35/58; Sperry New Holland, OJ 1985 L376/21; Sandoz, OJ 1987 L 222/28. Bayer Dental, OJ 1990 L351/46; Gosme/Martell, OJ 1991 L185/23; Viho/Toshiba, OJ 1991 L287/39; Viho/Parker Pen, OJ 1992 L33/273.

14 See *Völk vs. Vervaecke* [1969] ECR 295, at p. 302 (paras. 5-7), where the Court said: 'an exclusive dealing agreement, even with absolute territorial protection, may, having regard to the weak position of the persons concerned on the market in the products in question in the area covered by the absolute protection, escape the prohibition Laid down in Article 101(1).' See also the Commission Notice concerning Agreements of minor importance which do not fall under Article 101(1) of the EC Treaty establishing the European Economic Community, OJ 1986 C231/2.

15 See, e.g., *National Panasonic*, OJ 1982 L354/28, at p. 32; *Fisher-Price/Quaker Oats Ltd-Toyco*, OJ 1988 L49/9. *Ford Agricultural*, OJ 1993 L20/1.

16 See *Miller vs. Commission* [1978] ECR 131, at p. 148 (para.7), where the Court stated: 'the fact that the supplier is not strict in enforcing such prohibitions cannot establish that they had no effect since their very existence may create a «visual and psychological» background which satisfies customers and contributes to a more or less rigorous division of the markets.' See also *Sandoz Prodotti farmaceutici SpA vs. Commission* [1990] ECR I-45 (summary publication only).

17 In John Deere, OJ 1985 L35/58, at p. 62, the Commission stated: 'The export ban contained in these sales conditions is qualified by the words «... as far as no contrary legal regulation prevents...». However, the Commission holds that such an Article constitutes an export ban in spite of this saving clause; the Article is worded to read as if exporting is forbidden and imposed without explanation or negotiation by a company that ought to know the law on a multitude of small dealers; such dealers are less likely to know the law and unlikely, in the circumstances, to consult a lawyer; it is most unlikely, therefore, that the dealer would know that an export ban is contrary to Community law and could not consequence of that fact be enforced against intra-Community exports. In other words, and in view of the fact that export bans are illegal within the common market, the drafting of this export ban constitutes a reversal of a general rule of Community law in respect of what should be only a derogation.'

18 Commission Reg. No. 1983/83 on the application of Article 101(3) to categories of exclusive distribution agreements, OJ 1983 L173/1, corrigendum OJ 1983 L281/84, Article 2(2) (c).

2.2 Bans on exports outside the EU

The legality of clauses restricting the ability of a distributor to export a product outside the EU must be determined in light of whether the jurisdictional test in Article 101(1) is met. In several early cases, the Commission held that bans on exports outside of the EU would not affect trade between Member States because, as a result of the accumulation of profit margins and transport costs as well as the obstacle of the Common Customs Tariff, it was deemed to be unlikely that products exported outside the EU would be re-imported into the Community. Even if a product were re-imported, it was considered to be unlikely that the product would be re-exported to another member state since the demand in a member state could be met much more readily and at a more favourable price directly from another member state than from a third country to which the products in demand would be first exported from the EU.[19]

In 1976, the Commission modified its views and ruled that a clause prohibiting exports outside the EU in a distribution agreement for the EU would violate Article 101(1) once the relevant products would no longer be subject to customs duties in trade between the EU and relevant territory.[20]

3. Dual pricing systems and discount practices

Even without formal export restrictions, a company could obtain similar results by charging different prices or by granting different discounts depending upon the destination of the product.[21] In order to prevent pricing practices from being used to isolate markets, the Commission objected to practices that could have such an effect.

The Commission held that a provision whereby customers have to pay the prices applicable in the country of destination, rather than in the territory where the seller is located, was an illegal restriction of competition.[22] It was also illegal for a company to provide a discount to purchasers based on a showing that the product has not been exported to another member

---

19 See *Kodak*, OJ 1970 L147/24; *Goodyear Italiana-Euram*, OJ 1975 L38/10; *Kabelmetal-Luchaire*, OJ 1975 L 222/34.
20 *SABA*, OJ 1976 L28/19, at p. 22.
21 For examples of systems of dual pricing lists see Newitt/Dunlop Slazenger International & Ors, OJ 1992L131/32 and XXIst Report on Competition Policy for 1991, point 123.
22 *Kodak*, OJ 1970 L147/24, at pp. 25-26.

state.[23] More generally, bonus, discount or price schemes which depend on the destination of the sales were likened to export bans and, for that reason, were heavily criticised in the Commission's case law. The following are examples of practices that were condemned by the Commission on that basis:

— the complete abolition of all normal discounts in the case of export sales;[24]

— the imposition of less favourable payment terms for goods known to be exported;[25]

— the imposition of a five per cent surcharge on goods known to be exported;[26]

— the reduction of discounts on exports in order to protect the local exclusive distributor;[27]

— a promotional campaign in Belgium and Luxembourg whereby special terms were offered for a short time on selected car models, but only to residents of Belgium and Luxembourg;[28]

— the requirement of evidence of non-re-export in order to allow a particular sale to be taken into account for the application of a bonus scheme;[29]

— the making of discounts conditional on registration within the territory or on the original purchaser retaining and using the purchased vehicle.[30]

4. Rejection of economic arguments for supporting exclusive distributors

The Commission, in its case law, has not accepted economic justifications for dual pricing systems. In *Distillers*,[31] the Commission objected to an arrangement under which a surcharge was to be paid by wholesalers in the UK whenever the product was exported outside the UK. The differ-

---

23 Pittsburgh Corning Europe-Formica Belgium-Hertel, JO 1972 L272/35, at p. 38; Sperry New Holland, OJ 1985 L376/21, at p. 26; Ford Agricultural, OJ 1993 L20/1.
24 *Gosme/Martell-DMP*, OJ 1991 L185/23, at pp. 28-29.
25 *John Deere*, OJ 1985 L35/38, at p. 61.
26 *Id.*, see also *Ford Agricultural*, OJ 1993 L20/1.
27 Newitt/Dunlop Slazenger International & Ors, OJ 1992 L131/32, at p. 42.
28 Citroën, Eighteenth Report on Competition Policy, point 56.
29 *Sperry New Holland*, OJ 1985 L376/21, at p. 26.
30 *Ford Agricultural*, OJ 1993 L20/1.
31 The Distillers Co Ltd — Conditions of Sale and Price Terms, OJ 1978 L50/16.

ence in price, £5.20 per case of 12 bottles, was said to reflect the considerably higher promotional costs incurred by DCL's sole distributors on the Continent. This in turn was argued to be the result of a major difference between market conditions in the UK and in continental EU countries. In the UK, Scotch whisky is a traditional drink representing more than 50 per cent of the total spirit sales whereas on the Continent, consumer acceptance of Scotch whisky is much lower and, except for Belgium, it must compete against a variety of locally produced spirits, which are often favoured by the relevant tax regime. The UK market could therefore be described as a market which has reached the 'maturity stage' where competition is predominantly based on price and where prices are extremely low as a result of the buying power of the large brewery companies and their retail outlets. In contrast, the continental market was still in the 'expansive phase', facing the competition of cheaper and more popular local products. In such a market emphasis was on promotional activity rather than on price. According to DCL, it was only 'by energetically reminding the public that Scotch whisky is a high-quality, distinctive product for which it is worthwhile to pay the extra tax' that one could hope to lure away customers from tax-favoured local spirits.[32] In essence, DCL claimed that without the protection of the dual price structure UK wholesalers would take a free ride on the promotional efforts and expenses sustained by its sole distributors on the Continent.

Although the Commission recognised that exclusive distributors outside the UK had higher costs than parallel traders arising from their obligation to promote the product, the Commission nonetheless came down firmly on the side of the free riders.[33]

Although the Commission obviously expected the result of its actions to be the lowering of Scotch whisky prices in markets on the Continent, in fact the result was that DCL chose to protect its distributors on the Continent by withdrawing two of their bestselling brands, Johnnie Walker, Red

---

32 *Distillers Company vs. Commission* [1980] ECR 2229, at pp. 2239-2240.
33 In The Distillers Co Ltd — Conditions of Sale and Price Terms, OJ 1978 L50/16, at p. 26, the Commission stated: 'Indeed, sole distributors have higher costs due to their obligations of promoting the spirits. It has been argued that these costs approximate to the difference between the buying price of the parallel importer and that of the sole distributor. However, such differences in the buying price make it distinctly difficult for the DCL United Kingdom trade customers, and even more so, for their subsequent customers to compete with the sole distributors in the other EU Member States or at the very least, render parallel export unattractive.'

Label and Dimple, from the UK market.[34] The confusion resulting from this case has been heightened by the announcement by the Commission that they intended to allow Distillers to re-introduce the dual pricing system in order to recommence selling Red Label on the UK market.[35]

5. Warranty and after-sales service

Even if there is no export restriction, customers could be discouraged from buying products from parallel traders if the manufacturer were to discriminate between products purchased from official distributors and products purchased from other sources with respect to the provision of warranty or after-sales service. The Commission has established the principle that 'a manufacturer's guarantee for the products he distributes must be applicable throughout the Community irrespective of the member state where the product was purchased'.[36] The same principle extends to the provision of after-sales and essential services, including the provision of technical information, in circumstances where the withholding of such services would hinder parallel trade in the products concerned.[37]

The Commission has applied this principle in a series of decisions[38] ensuring that a guarantee given by a manufacturer on branded goods would be provided by any approved dealer and not merely by the dealer from which it was purchased. The court has confirmed the Commission's position in *Hasselblad*[39] *and Swatch*.[40]

It is not necessary for a company to provide the same guarantee service in all parts of the Community. If guarantees vary, then it is permissible for a supplier to provide that guarantee service be provided on the terms

---

34 The Commission Decision on Distillers has been the subject of criticism from Advocate General Warner in his opinion on the appeal and by commentators. See the opinion of Advocate General Warner in *Distillers Co vs. Commission* [1980] ECR 2229; see also *Korah*, 'Goodbye, Red Label: Condemnation of Dual Pricing by Distillers', (1979) 4 E.L.Rev. 1; Baden Fuller, 'Price Variations — The Distillers Case and Article 101 EEC, (1979) ICLQ 128; and Van Bael, 'Heretical Reflections on the Basic Dogma of EU Antitrust: Single Market Integration', (1980) 10 Swiss Rev. Int. Antitrust L. 39.

35 Notice pursuant to Article 19(3) of Council Regulation 17/62, *The Distillers* Co plc, OJ 1983 C245/3.

36 Matsushita Electrical Trading Company, Twelfth Report on Competition Policy, points 77-78; Sixteenth Report on Competition Policy, point 56; Sony, Seventeenth Report on Competition Policy, point 67; Grundig's EC Distribution system, OJ 1994 L20/15.

37 Akzo Coatings, Nineteenth Report on Competition Policy, point 45.

38 *Omega*, JO 1970 L242/22; *Bayerische Motoren Werke AG*, OJ 1975 L29/1; *SABA*, OJ 1976 L28/19; *Zanussi*, OJ 1978 L322/26; *IBM Personal Computer*, OJ 1984 L118/24.

39 *Hasselblad vs. Commission* [1984] ECR 883.

40 *ETA Fabriques d'Ebauches vs. DK Investment* [1985] ECR 3933.

applied where the product is used rather than where it is bought.[41] The Commission has permitted clauses providing that the user must bear the costs of adaptation of a product to local safety standards if it wishes to take advantage of a local guarantee.[42] It is also permissible to require a user to bear the expense of returning a product to the country of origin 'in [a] case where the model concerned is not of the same type as those marketed in the country of use and the spare parts needed for the repair are unavailable'.[43] It would appear that a system according to which the customer pays for the warranty repair in a country other than the country of purchase and obtains a receipt on the basis of which he can reclaim his expenses in the country of purchase is also admissible.[44]

A distributor may provide its own additional guarantee and reserve that guarantee to its own customers. Thus, in *Hasselblad*, the Commission stated that the non-discrimination requirement 'does not mean that a sole distributor is not allowed to provide any additional guarantee services in respect of goods imported and resold by him. However, parallel import products must not be placed at a disadvantage in so far as the manufacturer's guarantee and the sole distributor's guarantee are identical'.[45]

Restrictions on warranty may have the effect of limiting the distribution of a product to certain sales channels. Thus, the Commission objected to a clause in a contract which limited a warranty on plumbing fittings to those which had been installed by plumbers because this would keep consumers from buying products from retailers.[46] On the other hand, restrictions on warranty may be valid within the context of a selective distribution

---

41 See *Zanussi*, OJ 1978 L322/26; see also *ETA Fabriques d'Ebauches* vs. *DK Investment* [1985] ECR 3933.
42 Moulinex, Tenth Report on Competition Policy, point 121; Matsushita Electrical Trading Company, Twelfth Report on Competition Policy, points 77-78.
43 *Ibid.*
44 *Fourteenth Report on Competition Policy, point 70.* The Fiat guarantee system was approved by the Commission subject to the following changes being made: (1) the previous requirement of presenting the replaced parts to the dealer who sold the car was changed so as to only require a check of the documents which show that the work had been done; (2) it was made possible for the customer to obtain reimbursement not only from the original seller but also from the Fiat distribution company issuing the guarantee certificate; (3) the deadline for applying for a refund was extended from one month to two months after payment had been made for the guarantee work; and (4) the customer was given the freedom to make his refund application in his own language.
45 *Hasselblad*, OJ 1982 L161/18, at p. 28. Although the Commission has stated that it was not permissible for the UK Hasselblad distributor to offer faster guarantee service to its own customers, the court stated that it was possible for a distributor to reserve a special 24-hour service to its own customers. *Hasselblad* vs. *Commission* [1984] ECR 883, at p. 905 (para. 34).
46 Ideal Standard's distribution system, OJ 1985 L20/38, at p. 42.

system. In *Metro* vs. *Curtier*,[47] the court held that a manufacturer operating a selective distribution network may refuse to honour guarantees in respect of goods *bought* outside of that system.

Special rules relating to warranty service have been incorporated in the block exemption for automobile selective distribution agreements[48] and in the block exemption on franchise agreements.[49]

6. Resale price maintenance

The Commission and the Court of Justice have recognised that the goal of maintaining a certain minimum price level for a product may be pro-competitive and may serve to improve competition on factors other than price.[50] Nonetheless, the Community authorities have not accepted that resale price maintenance is a legitimate means of guaranteeing such price levels.[51]

---

47 *Metro SB Grossmärkte GmbH* vs. *Cartier*, Case C-376/92, judgment of 13 January 1994 (not yet reported).

48 Commission Regulation 123/85 on the application of Article 101(3) of the treaty to certain categories of motor vehicle distribution and servicing agreements, OJ 1985 L15/16, Article 4(1)(6) and 5(1)(1).

49 Commission Regulation 4087/88 on the application of Article 101(3) of the treaty to categories of franchise agreements, OJ 1988 L359/46, Article 4(b).

50 In *Metro* vs. *Commission* [1977] ECR 1875, at p. 1905 (para. 21), the court stated: 'For specialist wholesalers and retailers the desire to maintain a certain price level, which corresponds to the desire to preserve, in the interests of consumers, the possibility of the continued existence of this channel of distribution in conjunction with the new methods of distribution based on a different type of competition policy, forms one of the objectives which may be pursued without necessarily falling under the prohibition contained in Article 101(1), and, if it does fall thereunder, either wholly or in part, coming within the framework of Article 101(3).
This argument is strengthened if, in addition, such conditions promote improvement of competition inasmuch as it relates to factors other than prices'.

51 'Clarifying its position in the Metro case, the court stated in *AEG vs. Commission* [1983] ECR 3151, at pp. 3196-3197 (para. 42-43): 'A restriction of price competition must however be regarded as being inherent in any selective distribution system in view of the fact that prices charged by specialist traders remain within a much narrower span than which might be envisaged in the case of competition between specialists and non-specialist traders. That restriction is counterbalanced by competition as regards the quality of the services supplied to customers which would not normally be possible in the absence of an appropriate profit margin making it possible to support the higher expenses connected with those services. The maintenance of a certain level of prices is therefore lawful, but only to the extent to which it is strictly justified by the requirements of a system within which competition must continue to perform the functions assigned to it by the Treaty. In fact, the object of such a system is solely the improvement of competition in so far as it relates to factors other than prices and not the guarantee of a high profit margin for approved re-sellers.
AEG was therefore not justified in taking the view that the acceptance of an undertaking to charge prices making possible a sufficiently high profit margin constituted a lawful condition for admission to a selective distribution system. By the very fact that it was authorized not to admit to and not to keep in its distribution network traders who were not, or were no

Resale price maintenance has been considered as being a violation of Article 101(1) both in cases where groups of suppliers agree to impose resale prices on their purchasers (collective resale price maintenance)[52] and in cases where a single supplier agrees with its resellers that they will not supply a product below a certain price.[53] In distribution agreements notified for exemption, the Commission has consistently required that the supplier remove restrictions on resale prices.[54]

The Commission was concerned with protecting the distributor's ability to set its prices freely. Thus, in Hennessy-*Henkell*, the Commission objected to a clause whereby a supplier required that its distributor set its prices between a minimum and maximum price level unless the distributor obtained the supplier's consent.[55]

The prohibition on resale price maintenance does not extend to recommended retail price lists as long as they are non-binding.[56]

In order for resale price maintenance to be found to violate Article 101(1), there must be an effect on trade between member states. The Commission suggested in an early policy statement that purely national systems of resale price maintenance do not fall within the prohibition of Article 101(1) if there is no effect on trade between member states. The Commission stated at that time that 'purely national systems' of resale price maintenance would be a matter of national competition policy.[57]

---

longer, in a position to provide services typical of the specialist trade, it had at its disposal all the means necessary to enable it to ensure the effective application of the system. In such circumstances, the existence of a price undertaking constitutes a condition which is manifestly foreign to the requirements of a selective distribution system and thus also affects freedom of competition.'

52 See, e.g. *VBBB/VBVB*, OJ 1982 L54/36; on appeal: *VBVB/VBBB vs. Commission* [1984] ECR 19; *Publishers Association — Net Book Agreements*, OJ 1989 L22/12.

53 See, e.g. *Deutsche Philips GmbH*, OJ 1973 L293/40.

54 See, e.g. *Omega*, JO 1970 L242/22; *SABA*, OJ 1976 L28/19; *Junghans*, OJ 1977 L30/10; *Hasselblad*, OJ 1982 L161/18; *Yves Rocher*, OJ 1987 L8/49. In *Pronuptia*, OJ 1987 L13/39, at p. 41, the Commission insisted that a clause which required the franchisee not to harm the brand image of the franchisor by his pricing level be removed. See also *XXth Report on Competition Policy*, point 48 and *XXIst Report on Competition Policy of 1991*, point 127.

55 *Hennessy-Henkell*, OJ 1980 L383/11, at p. 16.

56 See *Pronuptia de Paris vs. Irmgard Schillgallis* [1986] ECR 353, at p. 384 (para.27); see also the references to recommended prices in Italian spectacles sector, *Fifteenth Report on Competition Policy*, point 66; the Commission notice concerning Regulation 123/85 on the application of Article 101(3) of the treaty to certain categories of motor vehicle distribution and servicing agreements, OJ 1985 C17/4, at 11(1); Commission Regulation 4087/88 on the application of Article 101(3) of the treaty to categories of franchise agreements, OJ 1988 L359/46, Article 5(e).

57 In the *First Report on Competition Policy*, point 55, the Commission stated: 'Purely national systems of resale price maintenance do not generally come under the Community law prohibiting cartels. To the extent that they are limited to compelling retailers in a Member State to respect certain prices for the resale within that State of products supplied by a manufac-

In subsequent cases, however, the Commission and the Court of Justice have interpreted the requirement of an effect on trade between member states in ways which would make it ill-advised for a company to impose resale price maintenance even in its own country. In *GERO-Fabriek*, the Commission stated that 'the system of retail prices imposed on dealers would be likely to influence trade between member states by deflecting trade flows away from the channels which they would naturally have if prices were fixed freely'.[58]

In *BNIC vs. Clair*, the Court of Justice found an effect on trade despite the fact that the product in question, potable spirits for use in the manufacture of cognac, was not generally traded outside the Cognac region of France. The court stated:

> '*It must be observed in that respect that any agreement whose object or effect is to restrict competition by fixing minimum prices for an intermediate product is capable of affecting intra-Community trade, even if there is no trade in that intermediate product between the Member States, where the product constitutes the raw material for another product marketed elsewhere in the Community. The fact that the finished product is protected by a registered designation of origin is irrelevant.*'[59]

Thus, it would appear that since the 1970 statement, the Community institutions have gradually tended to regard national resale price maintenance as falling within their competence.

One exception to the general trend of the Community institutions to bring national resale price maintenance schemes under their jurisdiction should be noted. Although in the *VBBB/VBVB* case, the Commission and the court found a system of collective resale price maintenance for book prices operating across national borders to be a violation of Article 101(1) which could not be exempted, they made it clear that the proceeding did not relate to the purely national aspects of the resale price maintenance systems.[60]

---

turer established on that market or by a concession holder appointed for that territory, trade between Member States will not, generally, be affected within the meaning of Article 101 of the EU Treaty. That is why the Commission considers that the question of vertical resale price maintenance is essentially a matter of national competition policy. The Commission ensures, however, that intermediaries and consumers are enabled to obtain supplies of the product concerned at the most favourable prices and wherever they choose within the Community.' See also Answer to Written Question No. 247/71, JO 1971 C115/5.

58 See *GERO-Fabriek*, OJ 1977 L16/8, at p. 11.

59 *Bureau National Interprofessionnel du Cognac (BNIC) vs. Clair* [1985] ECR 391, at p. 425 (para. 29).

60 *VBBB/VBVB*, OJ 1982 L54/36; on appeal: *VBVB/VBBB vs. Commission* [1984] ECR 19.

In two cases involving the French law requiring resale price-fixing for books, decided in 1985, the Court of Justice held that:

> '*As Community law stands, the second paragraph of Article 5 of the EU Treaty, in conjunction with Articles 3(f) and 101, does not prohibit member states from enacting legislation whereby the retail price of books must be fixed by the publisher or by the importer and is binding on all retailers, provided that such legislation is consonant with the other specific provisions of the Treaty, in particular those relating to the free movement of goods*'.[61]

These judgments should not be interpreted too broadly, however. In a Community with several different languages and cultures, national rules governing prices of books take on a particular significance relating to the protection of cultural identity. Thus, the court was faced with the politically sensitive problem of reconciling EC competition rules with national rules designed to protect cultural identity that were strongly supported by the French Government.

In *Net Book Agreements*,[62] the Commission prohibited agreements on book prices between British publishers in so far as they applied to intra-Community trade. The Net Book Agreements provided for minimum prices and uniform rules on discounts. According to the Commission, these rules were not indispensable to the improvement of the publication and distribution of books since the parties could have used less restrictive means to achieve the same end. Consequently, the agreements could not be exempted under Article 101(3).

7. Customer restrictions

It is extremely difficult to discover a coherent pattern underlying the Commission's past decisions on the compatibility of customer restrictions with the competition rules. Indeed, in cases decided in 1985, the Commission:

1. granted a negative clearance stating that Article 101(1) does not apply to agreements under which certain suppliers were allowed to sell certain tableware only to hotels and restaurants;[63]

---

61 *Leclerc & Ors vs. Au Blé Vert* [1985] ECR 1 (para. 20); *Saint Herblain Distribution, Centre distributeur Leclerc & Ors vs. Syndicat des Libraires de Loire-Océan* [1985] ECR 2515.
62 Publishers Association — Net Book Agreements, OJ 1989 L22/12.
63 *Villeroy & Boch*, OJ 1985 L376/15.

2. issued a comfort letter stating that the Commission did not intend to take any action regarding an agreement restricting the sale of tyres to authorised dealers and end-users;[64]

3. decided that restrictions on the sale of artificial teeth to dentists, dental technicians, laboratories, universities, hospitals and authorised depots fell within the prohibition of Article 101(1), but were capable of exemption;[65] and

4. required companies to remove from their agreements requirements that eyeglasses be sold only to end-users.[66]

Generally, a restriction that a product be sold only to end-users will be considered a violation of Article 101(1) and not capable of exemption. The Commission considers it to be important for dealers to be able to obtain the product from sources other than the supplier.[67] It is possible to limit a dealer to sell only to other dealers which meet certain requirements within the context of a selective distribution system. Indeed, such restrictions are the essence of a selective distribution system.[68] The Commission, however, has rejected some selective distribution systems because they prevent the product from being sold through other distribution channels.[69]

It was also possible to restrict wholesalers from selling to end-users. In upholding the Commission's decision in SABA,[70] that a restriction on sales by German wholesalers to end-users in Germany did not violate Article 101(1), the court stated that:

> '*The Commission considers that, apart from the fact that this limitation on the activity of wholesalers is in accordance with the requirements of German legislation, it does not constitute a restriction on competition within the meaning of Article 101(1) of the Treaty because it corresponds to the separation of the functions of wholesalers and retailers and because if such a separation did not obtain the former would enjoy an unjustified competitive*

---

64 *Mitsui/Bridgestone*, Fifteenth Report on Competition Policy, point 60.

65 *Ivoclar*, OJ 1985 L369/1.

66 Menrad-Silhouette, Fifteenth Report on Competition Policy, point 64; Rodenstock/Metzler, *id.*, point 65.

67 See 304.

68 See 332.

69 See, e.g. *Ideal Standard's distribution system*, OJ 1985 L20/38, and Grohe's distribution system, OJ 1985 L19/17, which excluded any retailer which was not a plumbing contractor.

70 *SABA*, OJ 1976 L28/19, at p. 22.

advantage over the latter which, since it would not correspond to benefits supplied, would not be protected under Article 101.'[71]

The Commission has permitted customer restrictions when they were found to be justified because of the nature of the product. In *Distillers-Victuallers*, products were supplied on a duty-free basis and the following restrictions were allowed:

> *'(a) not to resell the products supplied except for the purpose of tax and duty-free consumption (in embassies or in aircraft or as ships' stores), and to resell them only to persons or firms which there is no reasonable cause to believe will resell or use such products otherwise than for duty-free consumption;*
>
> *(b) to impose an obligation similar in terms to (a) above on the resale of the products supplied and to use their best endeavour to ensure that the same obligation is accepted by all subsequent purchasers of the products supplied.'*[72]

The Commission found that, in practice, victuallers were unlikely to supply the ordinary (non-duty free) trade and that if they wished to supply such customers, they would be able to obtain products from the suppliers on which duty and taxes had been paid. The Commission stated:

> *'Consequently it may be concluded that, although in theory the standard agreement notified appears to restrict the victualler's freedom to choose his customers and the terms of the sales agreements to be made with them, it does not in practice result in any real restriction on the victualler's freedom of action. It follows that the obligation imposed on victuallers does not have the effect of appreciably restricting competition in the Common Market. Moreover, the agreement notified restricts them in no other way, for it leaves the victuallers free to sell in all countries of the Common Market — and indeed in the world — without restrictions; it does not prevent them from selling other brands of Scotch whisky which are not covered by the agreement, nor does it affect their freedom to determine their resale prices.'*[73]

The Commission adopted similar reasoning in holding that customer restrictions in Villeroy & Boch's specialised sales networks for table-

---

71 *Metro vs. Commission* [1977] ECR 1875, at p. 1908 (para. 28). See also *Grundig's EC distribution system*, OJ 1994 L20/15, at p. 20.

72 *The Distillers Co Ltd — Victuallers*, OJ 1980 L233/43, at p. 44 (para. 6).

73 *Id.*, at p. 45.

ware for hotels and restaurants and for advertising gifts did not violate Article 101(1). According to the Commission, the nature of the resellers' business operations and the nature of the products justified the customer restrictions.[74]

In practice, the Commission was willing to accept customer restrictions which are part of a selective distribution system, or which protect retailers from unfair competition by wholesalers. In addition, the particular nature of a product, such as alcohol labelled 'duty-free', may justify restrictions on the classes of customers which may be served. The Commission will not, however, allow any customer restrictions which completely exclude trade in the product between resellers, such as restrictions that the product be sold only to end-users.

8. Restrictions on use

The Commission and the Court of Justice took the position that it is a violation of the competition rules for a supplier to impose restrictions on the use which its customer may make of a product. In *Société de vente de ciments et betons vs. Kerpen & Kerpen*, the court stated:

> *'clauses in contracts of sale restricting the buyer's freedom to use the goods supplied in accordance with his own economic interests are restrictions on competition within the meaning of Article 101 of the Treaty. A contract which imposes upon the buyer an obligation to use the goods supplied for his own needs, not to resell the goods in a specified area and to consult the seller before soliciting business in another specified area has as its object the prevention of competition within the Common Market.'*[75]

Along the same lines, the Commission condemned in Bayo-n-ox[76] an 'own-use' requirement under which Bayer's customers could only purchase a particular growth promoter (Bayo-n-ox Premix 10 per cent) to cover their own requirements in their own works. The introduction of the own-use requirement must be seen in the context of the expiry of German patent protection for the active substance included in the growth promoter,

---

74 In discussing the restriction on sales to hotels and restaurants in Villeroy & Boch, OJ 1985 L376/15 at p. 19, the Commission stated: 'strictly speaking this entails no restriction of competition since the make-up and appearance of the dinner services are different from those of household dinner services'.

75 *Société de vente de ciments et bétons vs. Kerpen & Kerpen* [1983] ECR 4173, at p. 4182 (para. 6).

76 *Bayo-n-ox*, OJ 1990 L21/71

which triggered a price decrease for the product. Since patent protection remained available in all other Community countries, Bayer feared competition in those countries from cheaper supplies of Bayo-n-ox coming from the German market. Therefore, German customers were offered attractive prices on the condition that they only used the growth promoter in their own works. The Commission characterised the introduction of the own-use requirement as a serious infringement designed to partition the German market from other Community markets and therefore levied a fine of ECU 500,000.

In *Beecham Pharma-Hoechst*, the Commission-objected to clauses in a supply agreement for bulk ampicillin requiring the product to be resold only packaged as medicine for consumers rather than in bulk form, and only for human consumption rather than for veterinary use. The Commission found these restrictions to be unjustifiable, stating:

> '*restrictions on the form in which a raw material may be resold or on the uses to which it may be put are quite as prejudicial to the maintenance of free competition in the Community as geographical market sharing.*'[77]

The Commission was concerned that restrictions on resale of a product in its raw form would mean that purchasers would only be able to obtain the raw product from the original supplier. In several cases, the Commission has objected to clauses imposed by South American coffee suppliers that required purchasers to resell only roasted coffee beans, thus preventing the resale of green coffee beans.[78]

The Commission tended to view such use restrictions as a form of territorial restriction. In *Cafeteros de Colombia*, the Commission said that by including such a clause in its contracts, the supplier:

> '*makes any interpenetration of the Colombian green coffee market very difficult or even impossible. It is able to partition the market into as many isolated units as there are buyers of Colombian coffee, especially as it controls the supply of all Colombian green coffee sold to EU roasting plants.*'[79]

---

77 Beecham Pharma-Hoechst, Sixth Report on Competition Policy, points 129-132. See also, Billiton and Metal & Thermit Chemicals, Seventh Report on Competition Policy, point 131.
78 Marketing Policy of the Instituto Brasileiro do Cafe, Fifth Report on Competition Policy, point 33; Cafeteros de Colombia, OJ 1982 L360/31; Instituto Brasileiro do Cafe (IBC), Sixteenth Report on Competition Policy, point 54.
79 *Cafeteros de Colombia*, OJ 1982 L360/31, at p. 34.

Attacking, under Article 102 of the treaty, a similar clause requiring that bananas sold by United Brands be ripened before being resold, the Commission said:

> 'this requirement also makes it difficult, if not impossible, for trade to be carried on in UBC bananas when green, whether Chiquita or unbranded, either within one member state or between member states. UBC's prohibition on the resale of green UBC bananas therefore amounts to a prohibition on exports and thus maintains an effective market segregation.'[80]

The extent to which safety and public health considerations may justify certain use restrictions must be assessed on a case-by-case basis.

The Commission allowed, by way of a comfort letter, restrictions to be imposed by a supplier of a chemical product on certain uses of the product, and on the resale of the product, when government health regulations required specific approval for such uses of the product.[81] In the European Gas Producers' settlement,[82] the Commission insisted that a prohibition on resale clause be deleted from the standard agreements. If, exceptionally, a supplier wished to include such a clause based on properly justified safety grounds, the contract would have to be notified to the Commission. In 1990 World Cup Package Tours,[83] the Commission had to analyse the allegation that the organisers of the FIFA World Cup in Italy imposed on the authorised travel agencies (and also other officially appointed distribution channels) an obligation not to resell entrance tickets to non-authorised travel agents. The Commission held that for safety reasons it was acceptable for the authorised agencies to be required to resell the entrance tickets only as part of their package tours. Thus, it would appear that for products which could be dangerous to health or which entail safety risks, the Commission could accept that use restrictions are objectively justified and not restrictive of competition, or at least eligible for an exemption pursuant to Article 58(3).

---

80 *Chiquita*, OJ 1976 L95/1, at p. 14.
81 Notice pursuant to Article 19(3) of Council Regulation 17/62 concerning an application for a negative clearance, *Kathon Biocide*, OJ 1984 C59/6.
82 European Gas Producers' settlement of 7 June 1989, press release IP(89) 426. Nineteenth Report on Competition Policy, point 62.
83 Re 1990 World Cup Package Tours, OJ 1992 L326/31.

9. Conclusion: Vertical restraints today

The treatment of vertical agreements under Article 101 has been radically changed since the entry into force in 2000 of the Vertical Agreements Block Exemption[84] and the Vertical Guidelines[85]. In general, these two texts reflect the prevailing view that restrictions imposed in vertical agreements are only liable to have significant anti-competitive effects when they are engaged in by firms with market power. This more liberal approach does not, however, apply to so-called hardcore restrictions, in particular resale price maintenance and overly broad territorial or customer restrictions, which are liable to infringe Article 101(1) even when engaged in with firms whose market shares would otherwise be sufficiently low to benefit from the *De Minimis Notice*[86].

The succinctly drafted Vertical Agreements Block Exemption provides a broadly drawn exemption under Article 101(3) to vertical agreements, which allows parties to such agreements a considerable degree of freedom of contract, provided hardcore restrictions are avoided and the conditions of the Block Exemption are respected. In contrast, the Vertical Guidelines are very lengthy and complex. They provide valuable guidance on the interpretation of the Vertical Agreements Block Exemption. Their main purpose, however, is to identify the principles to be applied in analyzing the application of Articles 101(1) and (3) to vertical agreements outside of the Block Exemption, in particular where the market share threshold is exceeded. The Vertical Guidelines also serve as a tool to assess the risk of an individual agreement being found to restrict competition to an appreciable extent as a result of the cumulative effect of similar vertical restraints applied by competing suppliers.

The emphasis in the Vertical Guidelines is placed squarely on the economic principles that determine whether an agreement should be considered, overall, to be positive or negative for competition. There is, for example, a substantial discussion of the specific types of efficiencies that may be generated by the main types of vertical agreements, which is a key element in the application of Article 101(3). The approach of the Guidelines, however, blurs the distinction between Articles 101(1) and 101(3). It is often not pos-

---

84 Commission Regulation 2790/1999 on the application of Article 101(3) of the Treaty to categories of vertical agreements and concerted practices (the 'Vertical Agreements Block Exemption'), OJ 1999 L336/21.

85 Guidelines on Vertical Restraints (the 'Vertical Guidelines'), OJ 2000 C291/1.

86 Commission Notice on agreements of minor importance which do not appreciably restrict competition under Article 101(1) of the Treaty establishing the Community, OJ 2001 C368/13 (the 'De Minimis Notice').

sible to deduce whether a particular factor identified by the Commission suggests that there is unlikely to be an appreciable restriction of competition under Article 101(1) or, alternatively, whether the factor is only relevant in demonstrating that the criteria for exemption under Article 101(3) are met. Although this is of less importance since the introduction of the direct applicability of Article 101(3) as of 1 May 2004, it is nonetheless a handicap to the practical application of the Guidelines given the substantial difference between the two legal tests[87]. The fact that the relative importance of the many economic factors identified by the Commission will turn on the facts of each particular case is a further barrier to legal certainty under the Vertical Guidelines. This difficulty is exacerbated by the fact that the Guidelines often do not establish a clear hierarchy of principles in analyzing a particular restraint.

In addition to the Vertical Agreements Block Exemption and the Vertical Guidelines, the main source of guidance is the case law of the European Courts and the past decisional practice of the Commission. The case law of the European Courts is relatively sparse in this field, at least outside of single branding and selective distribution. In relying on the Vertical Guidelines, it should be noted that they are not formally binding and they must be read subject to this case law. Caution must be exercised in relying on the Commission's own decisional practice for the period prior to the year 2000, given the significant change in policy that occurred at that time.

---

[87] In particular, efficiencies do not need to be demonstrated in order to avoid an infringement of Article 101(1).

PART ONE

THE REFORM

CHAPTER I

NEW EU COMPETITION RULES FOR SUPPLY AND DISTRIBUTION AGREEMENTS

LUC PEEPERKORN

Principal Expert in Antitrust Policy at DG Competition
European Commission[1]

1. Introduction

On 20 April 2010 the Commission adopted a new Block Exemption Regulation applicable to vertical agreements[2] ("the Regulation"). At the same time it adopted the contents of accompanying Guidelines on Vertical Restraints ("the Guidelines"), which were subsequently formally adopted in all official languages of the Union by Vice-President Almunia on behalf of the Commission on 10 May 2010.[3] Both are applicable since 1 June 2010. The competition rules embodied in these instruments are particularly important in view of the pervasiveness of vertical agreements. Vertical agreements are agreements between firms operating at different levels of the production or distribution chain for the sale and purchase of intermediate products and the purchase and resale of final products. Typical

---

[1] Principal Expert in Antitrust Policy at DG Competition, European Commission. The content of this article does not necessarily reflect the official position of the European Commission. Responsibility for the information and views expressed lies entirely with the author. This text is for a good part based on an article written together with Magdalena Brenning-Louko, Andrei Gurin and Katja Viertiö; *Vertical Agreements: New Competition Rules for the Next Decade*, The CPI Antitrust Journal, June 2010(1) and on *A New (European) Policy in the Field of Verticals*, Luc Peeperkorn, in Current Developments in European and International Competition Law, Carl Baudenbacher (editor), 16th St. Gallen International Competition Law Forum, Basel, 2009.

[2] Commission Regulation (EU) No. 330/210 of 20 April 2010 on the application of Article 101(3) of the Treaty on the Functioning of the European Union to categories of vertical agreements and concerted practices, OJ L 102, 23.4.2010, p. 1.

[3] Guidelines on Vertical Restraints, OJ C 130, 19.05.2010, p. 1.

examples of vertical agreements are distribution agreements between manufacturers and distributors, or supply agreements between a manufacturer of a component and a producer of a product using that component. Because each firm has to purchase certain inputs and most firms need to sell their products to producers further downstream or to distributors, most companies are concerned by these rules.

Vertical restraints are restrictions of competition included in vertical agreements which may foreclose and/or segment markets, soften competition and facilitate collusion. For instance, vertical agreements which have as their main element that the manufacturer sells to only one or a limited number of buyers (exclusive distribution or selective distribution) may lead to foreclosure of other buyers and/or to collusion between buyers and segmentation of markets. Similarly, non-compete obligations which prohibit distributors to purchase and resell competing products may foreclose new manufacturers and rigidify the market positions of incumbent manufacturers.

These rules play an important role in ensuring a consistent approach to vertical restraints under Article 101 of the Treaty on the Functioning of the European Union ("Article 101") as enforcement has mostly been done by the national competition authorities and national courts since the 2004 decentralisation.

This paper does not treat all the aspects of the Regulation and Guidelines, but rather focuses on the novelties and clarifications brought by these recently adopted texts.

2. Background

The Commission published in 1997 a Green Paper on Vertical Restraints in EC Competition Policy, presenting a number of options to improve its policy towards supply and distribution agreements.[4] At the end of the nineties it was clear that the EU was in need of a new competition policy towards supply and distribution agreements. There was a large measure of agreement at the time that the old form-based block exemption regulations adopted in the seventies and eighties — with their long lists of white, grey and black clauses — in combination with the notification procedure of the old Regulation 17, had a straitjacket effect on firms, unnecessarily limiting the latter in their choice between the different commercial options

---

4   COM(96) 721 final.

open to them to distribute their products. At the same time, the form-based approach also carried the risk that situations that did not merit to be block exempted, in particular agreements concluded by firms with significant market power, were covered by the old block exemption regulations. In today's jargon, the form-based approach led at the same time to false positives and false negatives.

The wide ranging public debate that followed the publication of the Green Paper underlined the need to move away from the form-based approach. The Commission subsequently in 1998 outlined the new effects-based approach it favoured in a follow-up to the Green Paper, the Communication on the Application of the EC Competition Rules to Vertical Restraints.[5] In this Communication the Commission recommended *"... a shift from the current policy relying on form-based requirements with sector-specific rules to a system based on economic effects covering virtually all sectors of distribution. ... It proposes to achieve this by means of one wide-ranging block exemption regulation that covers all vertical restraints concerning intermediate and final goods and services except for a limited number of hardcore restraints. It is based mainly on a 'black list' approach, i.e. defining what is not exempt under the block exemption instead of defining what is exempt. This removes the straitjacket effect, a structural flaw inherent in any system which attempts to identify the clauses which are exempt. ... The principal objective of such a wide-ranging and flexible block exemption regulation is to grant companies which lack market power, and most do, a safe harbour within which it is no longer necessary for them to assess the validity of their agreements in the light of the EC competition rules. In order to preserve competition and to limit the benefit of this exemption to companies which do not have significant market power, the future block exemption regulation will make use of market share caps to link the exemption to market power. ... Companies with market shares above the thresholds of the block exemption will not be covered by the safe harbour. It must, however, be stressed that, even in such circumstances, their vertical agreements will not be subject to any presumption of illegality. The market share threshold will serve only to distinguish those agreements which are presumed to be legal from those that may require individual examination."*[6]

Along the lines of the Communication the Commission subsequently adopted in 1999 its first broad umbrella block exemption regulation for

---

5   COM(98) 544 final.
6   XXVIIIth Report on Competition Policy 1998 — SEC (99) 743 final, paragraphs 36-38.

vertical restraints ("the 1999 Regulation")[7] and a few months later in 2000 its first general guidelines on vertical restraints ("the 2000 Guidelines")[8] to accompany the 1999 Regulation.

This marked the start of a dramatic change in the competition policy landscape in the EU. The 1999 Regulation and 2000 Guidelines were the first step in what is now recognised as the introduction of an effects-based approach in EU antitrust policy under Articles 101 and 102. Subsequent steps to introduce an effects-based approach were made with similarly structured block exemption regulations and guidelines for horizontal cooperation agreements and for technology transfer agreements, with an adapted de minimis Notice and with the Article 81(3) Notice. The adoption of Regulation 1/2003 ended the notification system and allowed an effective decentralisation of enforcement to increasingly competent national competition authorities (NCAs), working together with the Commission in the European Competition Network (ECN).[9] More recently, both in the Commission's decisional practice and as set out in the Guidance on Article 82 (now Article 102), the Commission is also promoting a more effects-based approach under Article 102.[10]

Thus, where it was clear at the end of the nineties that the EU was in need of a new competition policy towards supply and distribution agreements, such need for radical change was not obvious for the latest review. This review process was launched in the spring of 2008 in view of the expiry on 31 May 2010 of the 1999 Regulation. The Commission services took stock of enforcement with the national competition authorities within the ECN and a consensus quickly arose that the architecture put in place in 1999 had worked well and only needed some up-dating and clarifications. Experience indicated that overall the rules had enabled the Commission and the NCAs to develop a flexible and meaningful enforcement policy, around the relevant effects of likely foreclosure and softening of competition while taking account of possible efficiencies. At the same time the 1999 Regulation and 2000 Guidelines were considered to have provided, important in this era of required self assessment, a clear analytical framework for companies which contributed to legal certainty. It was thus considered not necessary to have an upheaval of policy as was the case with

---

7   Commission Regulation (EC) 2790/1999 of 22 December 1999 on the application of Article 81(3) of the Treaty to categories of vertical agreements and concerted practices, OJ L 336, 29.12.1999, pp. 21–25.
8   Commission notice — Guidelines on Vertical Restraints, OJ C 291, 13.10.2000, pp. 1–44.
9   See the various regulations and guidelines at: http://ec.europa.eu/competition/antitrust/legislation/legislation.html.
10 See at: http://ec.europa.eu/competition/antitrust/art82/index.html.

the introduction of the effects-based approach but only to refine where necessary the effects-based approach to assess vertical restraints. This was subsequently confirmed by a public consultation that prompted a high response rate. Comments confirmed the general preference 'not to fix what is not broken', i.e. to make changes to the regime only where a need to change could be convincingly argued, also in view of the costs to industry of changing the rules. [11]

While it was decided to maintain the architecture put in place in 1999, it was considered necessary to adapt and update it in light of two major developments since 1999, namely a considerable increase in online sales, and enforcers' increased attention to and experience with the possible anti-competitive effects of buyers' market power. The remainder of this paper focuses on the main novelties and clarifications in the recently adopted Regulation and Guidelines.

3. Scope of the Regulation

3.1 Extension of the 30% Market Share Threshold to Buyers

Introducing a market share threshold to cap the benefit of a block exemption regulation was widely considered by legal commentators at the end of the nineties to be the gateway to hell, a sure way to unsustainable legal uncertainty. The introduction of the 30% market share threshold in the 1999 Regulation was the focal point of opposition to the new approach and many commented that its introduction would fatally undermine the workability of the regulation. With hindsight it can be safely concluded that this opposition was mistaken. The market share cap allowed the Commission to introduce its effects-based approach while at the same time creating a broad safe harbour with the umbrella type block exemption regulation. The use of a market share threshold to cap the benefit of a block exemption seems therefore no longer disputed. Also its level of 30% seems to have been chosen pretty well at the time.

An obvious point in the 1999 Regulation to be improved was to make the benefit of the block exemption dependent on the market share of both supplier and buyer which are party to the agreement and not either the supplier's or the buyer's market share as was the case under that Regulation. The choice to make the benefit of the block exemption dependent on the sup-

---

11   For an overview of the comments received during the public consultation: http://ec.europa.eu/ competition/consultations/2009_vertical_agreements/index.html.

plier's market share only and, in the exceptional case of exclusive supply, on the buyer's market share only, was adopted at the time in the light of the vehement opposition to the introduction of a market share threshold and its supposed practical problems.[12] Since then the Commission, for instance in 2002 in the *de minimis* Notice and in 2004 in the transfer of technology block exemption regulation (TTBER), has adopted the approach that the market share of all parties to an agreement between non-competitors must respect the relevant market share threshold, which in the case of the TTBER has also been set at 30%. It could thus hardly have come as a surprise to those who followed the developments in EC competition policy in the last 10 years, that the Commission proposed to introduce a market share threshold also on the buyer's side when the 1999 Regulation came up for revision.

Extension of the 30% market share threshold to buyers reflects increased recognition and evidence that vertical restraints need not generally be supplier-led: also buyers can have market power that may be used to impose anticompetitive vertical restraints. For instance, an exclusive supply obligation or similar obligation imposed by a powerful buyer (i.e., with a market share above 30%) on small suppliers (i.e., with a market share below 30%) may lead to anticompetitive foreclosure of other buyers, and may therefore harm consumers. The assessment of such an agreement by the relevant national competition authority or national court should not be made more difficult or even impossible[13] because the agreements are benefiting from the block exemption regulation.

It was argued by some that the application of a buyer's market share threshold could and should be limited to certain types of agreements such as exclusive supply agreements, as had been the case under the 1999 Regulation. Under that Regulation the buyer's market share became decisive for the application of the safe harbour in case there was an obligation causing the supplier to sell the contract products to only one buyer inside the Community.[14] However, that solution was obviously flawed as foreclosure and other competition problems on the downstream market can arise not just in case of this extreme scenario of only one buyer for the whole EU, but also, for instance, in case of exclusive distribution with large (national)

---

12 See the 2000 Guidelines, § 21-22.
13 National courts cannot withdraw the benefit of a Commission block exemption regulation. National competition authorities can withdraw the benefit where the agreement has effects which are incompatible with Article 101(3) in their territory or a part thereof and where this territory has all the characteristics of a distinct geographic market. (see recital 14 of the Regulation).
14 See articles 1(c) and 3(2) of the 1999 Regulation.

territories, minimum supply obligations, most favoured customer clauses and most favoured customer plus clauses.[15] Trying to define all such types of agreements would not only reintroduce a form-based approach, it would also be open to circumvention. For instance, under the 1999 Regulation, if an agreement would effectively oblige the supplier to sell to only one buyer in the whole EU, the loss of the benefit of the safe harbour was easily circumvented by appointing one additional very small buyer in, for instance, Malta.

As a result, the main change with regard to the scope of the Regulation is that for all agreements the benefit of the block exemption no longer depends only on the supplier's market share not exceeding 30%, but also on the market share of the buyer not exceeding the same threshold.

In the draft Regulation that was submitted to public consultation the Commission proposed that the market share of the buyer, like that of the supplier, should be assessed in the downstream market(s) in which it (re)sells the products/services as it is in these markets that negative effects on customers are felt. However, many stakeholders voiced concerns about the increased compliance costs for companies, resulting mainly from having to assess the buyer's position on possibly many local downstream markets on which the supplier itself is not present. Others argued that where an intermediate product, such as steel, has multiple uses, the position of the buyer on the upstream market may be more relevant than its position in the downstream market, because it is difficult to see how a buyer with a strong position in a particular downstream market, such as cars, but having only a limited position as purchaser on the steel market, can use its purchasing agreements to foreclose other car manufacturers from having access to the steel market. Making the block exemption dependent on the downstream market share of the buyer would in such cases deny the benefit of the safe harbour where that is not necessary.

To remedy these concerns, the market share of the buyer in the Regulation is assessed on the upstream market where it procures the products/services from the supplier. This market is generally wider than the downstream market (in most cases it will be at least national in scope), it is only one market as opposed to several possible downstream markets, and suppliers will know or be able to reasonably estimate the position of their buyers on this market.

---

15 Most favoured customer plus clauses are clauses requiring the supplier to offer the buyer not just equally favourable terms as offered to other buyers, but to offer better terms which the supplier is not allowed to offer to other buyers.

In most cases the position of the buyer on the upstream market is a good proxy for the buyer's market power in the downstream market and this ensures that the choice for the upstream market share to limit the application of the block exemption is not extending the safe harbour too widely. However, where in an individual case the buyer has only a modest market share on the upstream purchase market, for instance because it is international in scope, while it has a high market share on the (national) market where it (re) sells the contract product, the Commission or NCA may have to withdraw the benefit of the block exemption in case the supply agreement leads to negative effects for consumers and does not fulfil the conditions of Article 101(3).

3.2 Agency Agreements

There is no fundamental change in policy with regard to agency agreements.[16] Intra-brand restrictions, including prices and conditions at which the agent must sell or purchase the goods or services on behalf of the principal, fall outside Article 101(1) if the agent does not bear any contract specific risks, such as financing of stocks, or costs for market specific investments, such as the petrol storage tank of a service station.

The Guidelines however bring the additional clarification that for an agreement to be considered a genuine agency agreement under the EU competition rules (and thus for any intra-brand restrictions to fall outside Article 101(1)), the principal must in addition bear the costs and risks related to other activities it requires the agent to undertake within the same product market where also the agency activity takes place. This change of the Guidelines reflects the Commission's interpretation of the judgment of the General Court in the Daimler Chrysler case.[17] In that judgment the General Court confirmed that the general principle to determine whether an agreement is a genuine agency agreement under the EU competition rules, is whether the costs and risks related to the agency activity are borne by the principal and not by the agent. In that case however there were not only the costs for the sale of new cars, for which the dealers in question operated as agents, but also the costs related to repair activities which the same dealers had to undertake outside their agency contract. The General Court indicated that for the assessment of the agency activity of selling new cars in that case, the costs of the independent repair activity were not

---

16 See paragraphs 12-21 of the Guidelines.
17 Judgment of the Court of First Instance (now General Court) in Case T-325/01 *Daimler Chrysler vs. Commission* [2005] ECR II-3319.

54   BRUYLANT

relevant. While it is not very clear in the judgment whether this was based mainly on the insignificance of these costs in this case or on the fact that they were made for an activity in another product market, the Guidelines clarify that such costs and risks, if made for an activity on another product market, are not relevant for the assessment of the agency activity.

The reason for taking costs incurred for an independent activity on the same product market into account when assessing an agency agreement, is that the conditions imposed on the agent for its agency activity, such as the price at which it has to sell products on behalf of the principal in that product market, will generally influence its incentives and limit its possibilities when selling on the same product market the products that are part of the independent activity. It can be expected that the fixed price imposed for its agency activity products will influence and limit its price setting for the competing products sold as an independent. In that context it is good policy for the purposes of applying Article 101(1) to qualify the agreement not as an agency agreement, but to assess the conditions under Article 101(1), in this case as resale price maintenance. However, it is also obvious that such 'spill-over' of influencing incentives and limiting possibilities will in general not occur where the independent activity takes place on another product market.

Therefore, as an example, a service station operator can be an independent distributor of shop goods or an independent provider of car wash services without this affecting its agency status with regard to petrol retailing. However, to prevent any spill-over effects of intra-brand restrictions (for instance price fixing) between the agency activity and the independent activity, the service station operator cannot be, for the purposes of applying Article 101(1), a genuine agent for one type of petrol and at the same time be an independent distributor for another type of petrol in the same product market.

3.3 Vertical Agreements between Competitors

As a general rule, neither the 1999 Regulation nor the new Regulation cover vertical agreements entered into between competitors. Agreements between competitors, also for the distribution of each others' products, are first and foremost assessed as horizontal agreements.[18] The 1999

---

18 See the Commission Guidelines on the applicability of Article 81 of the EC Treaty to horizontal cooperation agreements, OJ C 3, 6.1.2001, p. 2. A revision of those Guidelines is foreseen to be adopted by the end of 2010.

Regulation however covered a limited number of situations of non-reciprocal vertical agreements between competitors. There are two changes in the Regulation with regard to the coverage of vertical agreements between competitors, both limiting the scope of the Regulation compared to the 1999 Regulation.[19]

Firstly, the 1999 Regulation covered situations in which a producer sold its products to a competing producer that distributed them, providing that the turnover of the latter did not exceed €100 million. This exception to the general rule not to cover agreements between competitors has now been removed, because experience shows that in certain markets a €100 million company can be the main local or national producer and thus an important competitor. In such a case the first concern of a competition authority should be the possible loss of competition between the two parties to the agreement, i.e. a horizontal concern. As a result of this change, such agreements fall outside the scope of the Regulation and will accordingly have to be assessed as horizontal agreements.

Secondly, not only for goods but also for services the coverage by the Regulation of vertical agreements between competitors is now limited to situations of dual distribution, i.e. where the supplier is active at the production and distribution level but the buyer is only active at the distribution level.[20] Under the 1999 Regulation the requirement that the buyer is only active at the distribution level did not apply to services.[21] This meant that the 1999 Regulation also covered non-reciprocal agreements concerning the sale of services between competitors active at intermediate levels, for instance between two software developers, where the first concern of a competition authority should be the possible loss of competition between the two parties to the agreement. By limiting the coverage to non-reciprocal dual distribution agreements, it is expected that the possible competition concerns are limited to vertical concerns such as foreclosure and not a possible loss of competition between the parties. The same is expressed somewhat more cautiously in the Guidelines: *"In case of dual distribution it is considered that in general any potential impact on the competitive relationship between the manufacturer and the retailer at the retail level is of lesser importance than the potential impact of the vertical supply agreement on competition in general at the manufacturing or retail level."*[22] For instance, a brewer's agreements to supply beer to independent pubs fall

---

19 See article 2(4) of the 1999 Regulation compared with article 2(4) of the new Regulation.
20 See article 2(4)(a) and (b) of the Regulation.
21 See article 2(4)(c) of the 1999 Regulation.
22 See paragraph 28 of the Guidelines.

within the scope of the Regulation, also if that brewer at the same time operates its own pubs in the same market. It is considered that the main competition concern, if any, is not the possible loss of competition between the brewer's pubs and the independent pubs supplied by this brewer, but is the possible foreclosure effects at the brewers' level or pubs' level and resulting loss of competition on those markets. The same applies to a franchisor's agreements providing services to its franchisees while also operating its own shops.

4. Hardcore Restrictions

4.1 General Approach to Hardcore Restrictions

Article 4 of the Regulation contains a list of hardcore restrictions, in particular restraints on the buyer's ability to determine its sale price and certain types of (re)sale restrictions. These are considered serious restrictions of competition that should in most cases be prohibited because of their harm to consumers. The consequence of including such a hardcore restriction in an agreement is that the whole vertical agreement is excluded from the scope of application of the Regulation. In addition, in these cases there is a double presumption, namely that the agreement will have actual or likely negative effects and therefore fall within Article 101(1) and that it will not have positive effects in fulfilment of Article 101(3).[23]

This is however rebuttable: in individual cases the parties can bring forward evidence under Article 101(3) that their agreement brings, or is likely to bring efficiencies that outweigh the negative effects.[24] Where this is the case, the Commission is required to effectively assess (rather than just presume) the likely negative impact on competition before making an ultimate assessment of whether the conditions of Article 101(3) are fulfilled. In effect this means that the usual order of bringing forward evidence is inverted in the case of a hardcore restriction.[25] However, the Commission nuances this inversion by adding in a footnote that *"although, in legal*

---

23 See article 4 of the Regulation in combination with paragraph 47 of the Guidelines.

24 See again paragraph 47 of the Guidelines. See also in particular paragraphs 63 to 64 of the Guidelines that provide some examples of a possible efficiency defence for hardcore (re) sales restrictions, paragraphs 106 to 109 that describe in general possible efficiencies related to vertical restraints and Section VI.2.10 on resale price restrictions. For general guidance on this see the Communication from the Commission — Notice — Guidelines on the application of Article 81(3) of the Treaty, OJ C 101, 27.4.2004, p. 97.

25 This was recently again confirmed by the Court in Joined Cases C-501/06 P et al, *GlaxoSmith-Kline*, [2009] ECR I not yet reported, in particular paragraphs 55 and 93 to 95.

*terms, these are two distinct steps, they may in practice be an iterative
process where the parties and Commission in several steps enhance and
improve their respective arguments.*"[26]

4.2 Resale Price Maintenance

Resale price maintenance (RPM), that is, agreements or concerted practices having as their direct or indirect object the establishment of a fixed
or minimum resale price or a fixed or minimum price level to be observed
by the buyer, are treated as hardcore restrictions.[27] However, the practice
of recommending a resale price to a reseller or requiring the reseller to
respect a maximum resale price are not considered hardcore restrictions,
provided that such maximum or recommended prices do not amount to a
fixed or minimum price as a result of pressure from, or incentives offered
by, any of the parties.[28]

The section of the Guidelines that deals with RPM provides a good illustration of the above-mentioned general approach to hardcore restrictions,
because it explains in detail the various ways in which RPM may restrict
competition[29] but also that RPM may, in particular where it is supplier
driven, lead to efficiencies which must be assessed under Article 101(3).[30]

The Guidelines provide a long list of possible negative effects of RPM.
Among the negative effects, RPM may facilitate collusion both between
suppliers (by enhancing price transparency on the market) and buyers (by
eliminating intra-brand price competition) and more generally soften competition between manufacturers and/or between retailers, in particular
when manufacturers use the same distributors to distribute their products
and RPM is applied by all or many of them. It is also recalled that the
immediate effect of RPM is that all or certain distributors are prevented
from lowering their sales price for that particular brand. In other words,
the direct effect of RPM is a price increase. Other negative effects include
a reduction of dynamism and innovation at the distribution level since by
eliminating price competition between different distributors, RPM may
prevent more efficient retailers or distribution formats from entering the
market or acquiring sufficient scale with low prices.

---

26 Footnote to paragraph 47 of the Guidelines.
27 See article 4(a) of the Regulation and paragraphs 48 and 49 of the Guidelines.
28 See article 4(a) of the Regulation.
29 See paragraph 224 of the Guidelines.
30 See paragraph 225 of the Guidelines.

The Guidelines contain three possible positive effects of RPM. Firstly, where a manufacturer introduces a new product, RPM may be helpful during the introductory period of expanding demand to induce distributors to better take into account the manufacturer's interest to promote the product. Indeed, RPM may provide the distributors with the means to increase sales efforts. If the distributors on this market are under competitive pressure, this may induce them to expand overall demand for the product and make the launch of the product a success, also for the benefit of consumers. Secondly, fixed resale prices, and not just maximum resale prices, may be necessary to organise in a franchise system, or similar distribution system applying a uniform distribution format, a coordinated short term low price campaign (2 to 6 weeks in most cases) to the benefit of consumers. Thirdly, in some situations, the extra margin provided by RPM may allow retailers to provide (additional) pre-sales services, in particular in case of experience or complex products. In such a situation, RPM may prevent free-riding and the consequences thereof: indeed, if customers take advantage of these services but then purchase the product at a lower price with retailers that do not provide such services, high-service retailers may reduce or stop providing these services. However, such free riding arguments will not be accepted lightly: *"The parties will have to convincingly demonstrate that the RPM agreement can be expected to not only provide the means but also the incentive to overcome possible free riding between retailers on these services and that the pre-sales services overall benefit consumers as part of the demonstration that all the conditions of Article 101(3) are fulfilled."*[31]

As explained in section 4.1, the hardcore approach means that there is a double presumption: it is presumed that the agreement will have actual or likely negative effects and therefore falls within Article 101(1) and it is presumed that it will not have positive effects in fulfilment of Article 101(3). To overcome this second presumption the parties will have to substantiate that all the conditions of Article 101(3) are fulfilled in case they want the exception to apply to their individual agreement. The parties will have to show in particular that in their situation (1) RPM is likely to induce the distributors to provide extra sales efforts and services, (2) that these extra efforts and services will be beneficial for consumers and (3) that RPM is indispensable to produce the efficiencies.

To start with the third issue, it will be necessary at least to explain why the producer cannot directly contract the extra sales efforts and services.

---

31 See paragraph 225 of the Guidelines.

If directly obliging the distributors to provide specified efforts and services to their customers is a feasible alternative, then RPM is clearly not indispensable. On the first issue, showing that RPM will likely lead to extra sales efforts and services, requires answering the question how efficient, in the market context at hand, the use of RPM is to obtain these efforts and services: is RPM only providing a financial margin to the distributors or is it also providing the incentive to spend this extra margin on the required services? How will RPM overcome the free riding incentive?[32] Is there a free riding problem in relation to the services in question? Lastly, on the second issue, to show that the extra promotion and services will be beneficial for consumers implies answering the question whether many consumers value the extra efforts. In case of new products or complex products this may be more likely, at least for the introduction period, while in case of more mature and simple products and in case of repeat purchases it is probably more likely that most consumers will not benefit from the extra promotion and services and will only suffer as a result of the increased price level.[33]

This approach towards RPM was characterised by some in the public consultation as overly cautious, at least when compared to the current situation in the US. A major shift of policy occurred in the US in 2007, when in the Leegin case the US Supreme Court overturned a century-long policy of treating RPM as a per se illegal restraint.[34]

Prior to Leegin, RPM was per se illegal in the US: the only relevant question that the court or authority had to resolve was whether the agreement, by its form, concerned RPM. As soon as this question was answered positively, the assessment was completed and no further analysis was required.

---

32 In two previous articles I explained my doubts about the effectiveness of RPM as a tool to overcome free riding problems. See *Resale Price Maintenance and its Alleged Efficiencies*, European Competition Journal, Volume 4, Number 1, June 2008, pages 201-212, and *A New (European) Policy in the Field of Verticals*, in Current Developments in European and International Competition Law, Carl Baudenbacher (editor), 16th St. Gallen International Competition Law Forum, Basel, 2009.

33 This issue is described by economists as the different interest of the marginal versus the *infra*-marginal consumers: it may be only the marginal (new) consumers which benefit from the extra promotion, but not the possibly larger group of *infra*-marginal (experienced) consumers which already know what they prefer and which do not benefit from the extra promotion and for whom the extra outlays and the RPM only result in a price increase. The proportion of new consumers may be large where it concerns a new product, but will often be much smaller where it concerns an established product or brand.

34 *Leegin Creative Products, Inc. vs. PSKS, Inc.*, Supreme Court of the United States, 28 June 2007. Of interest is not only the opinion of the court, but also the strong dissenting opinion (the ban on RPM was overturned with a narrow majority of 5 against 4 judges), the arguments brought forward by the various amici curiae and the wider discussion that ensued on the appropriate treatment of RPM, including efforts to restore the *per se* ban.

That is also why, in the Leegin case, the lower courts could not take into account potentially interesting evidence concerning efficiencies submitted by Leegin.

This per se approach differs from the EU hardcore approach. With its double presumption, the EU hardcore approach remains an effects-based approach: companies may bring forward evidence that their agreement brings or is likely to bring efficiencies that outweigh the negative effects and therefore meets the conditions set out in Article 101(3). Each agreement that fulfils the conditions of Article 101(3) is exempted from the prohibition laid down in Article 101(1) and a blank refusal to take into account such evidence would not be possible under the EU approach.

In the US it is not yet clear what the new ("post-Leegin") approach will be. The Supreme Court left it to the lower courts to decide whether a "pure" rule of reason analysis or an analysis circumscribed by presumptions should be applied. Both Assistant Attorney General Varney (US Department of Justice) and Chairman Leibowitz (US Federal Trade Commission) have made public statements, in speeches and US Senate Judiciary Committee Hearings, that they find the opinion of the dissenting judges in the Leegin case (the per se rule was overturned with only a 5 — 4 majority) more persuasive than that of the majority.[35] Chairman Leibowitz also indicated that he supports overturning the Leegin decision. In 2007 in the US Congress senators Kohl, Clinton (now US Secretary of State) and Biden (now US Vice President), introduced a Leegin repealer bill, arguing that abandoning the per se rule against RPM likely leads to higher prices and substantially harms the ability of discount retail stores to compete. This repealer bill, which if adopted would reintroduce the per se approach, passed the Judiciary Committee in both House and Senate, but it is not clear whether it will have sufficient support to be adopted (soon) in view of the sizable opposition. At the state level, a large number of AAGs have declared that they are still in favour of a per se approach and will continue to apply state antitrust laws accordingly. In the public debate in the US some plead for introducing certain negative presumptions to circumscribe the competition analysis while others, in particular economists, plead for the application of a pure rule of reason approach. In view of these divergent opinions,

---

35 Chairman Leibowitz and AAG Varney answering questions on RPM asked by Senator Kohl during a hearing of the Antitrust, Competition Policy and Consumer Rights Subcommittee of the Senate Judiciary Committee, 9th of June 2010. See also the speech of AAG Varney before the National Association of Attorneys General, 7th October 2009, to be found at http://www.justice.gov/atr/public/speeches/250635.pdf.

the EU hardcore approach to resale price maintenance could be suggested as a suitable compromise solution.

The EU presumption-based approach, which is supported by consistent case law, is based on case handling experience at EU Member States and Commission level. A good example is the ending of RPM for books in the UK in 1997. Studies on the UK book sector show that the most significant development in the structure of the UK book retailing after the sector specific RPM laws allowing RPM for books were abolished, has been the accelerated entry and rapid growth of low price internet sellers (notably Amazon) and one-stop grocery supermarket chains (especially Tesco, Asda and Sainsbury) on the book retail market. Initially it was feared that abolition of RPM would make the publishers bring out less titles and would lead to more demand uncertainty and reluctance by retailers to hold stocks. The results do not suggest that this happened. Instead the number of titles grew more than in comparable markets with RPM.[36]

As explained in section 2, the Commission services together with the NCAs took stock of enforcement as part of the review process which led to the adoption of the Regulation and Guidelines. The discussion within the ECN on the RPM cases dealt with since 2000, mainly handled by the NCAs, pointed to the pertinence of a cautious approach towards RPM. In general, companies have been unsuccessful in their attempts to justify RPM. It is considered that extensive recourse to RPM across the EU Member States, many of which have small and concentrated markets, would result in more harm than benefit for the European consumers as a whole.

While economy wide empirical data on RPM are scarce, we have recently witnessed an unwanted natural experiment with RPM in France. The Loi Galland, trying to prevent (large) retailers to sell below cost, effectively allowed since 1997 manufacturers and retailers to enforce RPM. By making pricing below the invoice price illegal, manufacturers and retailers quickly grasped the opportunity to legally agree and enforce RPM: manufacturers charged a high invoice price to retailers and in return gave retailers an end of year discount which, according to the law, could not be used to lower the retail price. This led to an industry wide use of RPM in the retailing sector in France. Empirical studies show that there is strong evidence that the RPM effectively led to the elimination of (or at least an important

---

36 *An evaluation of the impact upon productivity of ending the resale price maintenance on books*, report prepared for the UK Office of Fair Trading by the Centre for Competition Policy at University of East Anglia, February 2008, to be found at: http://www.oft.gov.uk/OFTwork/publications/publication-categories/reports/Evaluating/.

reduction in) intra-brand competition and led to a softening of inter-brand competition. This is said, at least partially, to explain the sharp increase in prices of groceries that occurred after 1997. Price increases in France were 10% higher than in Germany and 5% higher than in the Euro zone in general. Moreover, prices in France became higher than in neighbouring countries such as Germany, Italy, Belgium and Spain.[37] At the same time, service levels did not seem to have improved in French retailing. The negative effects spurred the French NCA to take two prohibition decisions in RPM cases, one concerning school calculators and the other concerning toys, and subsequently led to two amendments of the law, in 2005 and 2008, to end the unwanted experiment.[38] According to the Centre de documentation Économie — Finances, part of the French Ministry of Economics, Industry and Employment, prices of branded products dropped by 4% after the 2005 amendment.[39]

4.3 Resale Restrictions

4.3.1 Hardcore Resale Restrictions

The hardcore resale restrictions relate to market partitioning by territory or by customer group. In general, the Regulation does not cover agreements that restrict sales by a buyer party to the agreement in as far as those restrictions relate to the territory into which or the customers to whom the buyer may sell the contract goods or services. This holds both for restrictions of active sales and for restrictions of passive sales.[40] There are however a series of exceptions to this general hardcore restriction, which are designed to allow suppliers to sell their products efficiently while preventing the risk of harming consumers by partitioning the internal market.

---

37 Patrick Rey, Price Control in Vertical Relations, in The Pros and Cons of Vertical Restraints, Konkurrensverket, 2008; Canivet, G. (2004), Restaurer la concurrence par les prix — Les produits de grande consommation et les relations entre industrie et commerce, report supervised by Documentation francaise. Older surveys for the US, comparing data of before and after 1975 when legislation allowing RPM in certain US states was repealed, provide a similar picture. In his dissenting opinion in the Leegin case Justice Breyer refers to the DoJ reporting at the time that prices as a result of RPM had risen by 19% to 27% and the FTC staff concluding, after having studied numerous price surveys that collectively these surveys indicated that RPM in most cases increased the prices of products sold with RPM.

38 Conseil de la Concurrence, decision 03-D-45 of 25 September 2003 (school calculators) and decision 07-D-50 of 20 December 2007 (toys), both upheld by the Cour d'appel de Paris.

39 http://www.finances.gouv.fr/directions_services/cedef/synthese/loi_galland/synthese.htm.

40 Active and passive sales are described in paragraph 51 of the Guidelines.

A first and novel exception concerns the buyer's place of establishment, one element of active sales. The Regulation now provides for the possibility for a supplier to restrict a distributor's place of establishment whatever the type of distribution system opted for.[41] It can be agreed that the distributor will restrict its outlet(s) and warehouse(s) to a particular address, place or territory. This is designed to facilitate the parallel use of different types of distribution systems in the internal market by providing a possibility of protecting the investments of other than exclusive distributors.

Another exception, that was already contained in the 1999 Regulation, is that it is permissible under the Regulation to prohibit a wholesaler to sell to end users, which allows a supplier to keep the wholesale and retail level of trade separate. Thus, a supplier can require the buyers of its products to "specialise" in the wholesale or retail activity. The novelty here is that it is specified in the Guidelines that this does not exclude the possibility that a "specialised" wholesaler can still sell to certain end users, such as bigger end users, while not allowing sales to (all) other end users.[42]

Another exception already contained in the 1999 Regulation, concerns the restriction of active sales in case of exclusive distribution. Indeed, the Regulation allows a supplier to protect an exclusive distributor from active sales by other distributors in order to encourage that distributor to invest in the exclusively allocated territory or customer group. This is possible, under the block exemption, when the supplier agrees to sell its products only to one distributor for distribution in a particular territory or to a particular customer group and that exclusive distributor is protected against active selling into its territory or to its customer group by all the other distributors.[43] The Guidelines now clarify that the protection against active sales enjoyed by the exclusive distributor does not need to extend to the sales by the supplier itself. This means that exclusive distribution is covered by the Regulation also if the supplier sells directly to customers otherwise exclusively allocated to a particular distributor, i.e. if the exclusivity is shared between the distributor and the supplier.[44] Moreover, and this is again a change compared to the previous regulation, in an exclusive distribution system a supplier can restrict active sales at more than one level of trade. For instance, a supplier can restrict active

---

41 See article 4(b) of the Regulation: "... without prejudice to a restriction on its place of establishment ..." Such a restriction benefitted from the 1999 Regulation only if applied to protect an exclusive distributor or if applied inside a selective distribution system.
42 See paragraph 55 of the Guidelines.
43 See article 4(b)(i) of the Regulation in combination with paragraphs 50 to 54 of the Guidelines.
44 See paragraph 51 of the Guidelines: «... irrespective of sales by the supplier.».

BRUYLANT

sales, into a territory or to a customer group exclusively allocated to a wholesaler, by all other wholesalers and retailers who are parties to an agreement with that supplier.[45] However, to prevent market partitioning a supplier cannot restrict its distributors from making passive sales, which is responding to unsolicited requests from customers and selling to those customers throughout the internal market. Any such restriction of passive sales would be a hardcore restriction of competition.

Selective distribution is another important exception that was already contained in the 1999 Regulation. Under the block exemption, suppliers can implement a selective distribution system which allows them to choose their distributors on the basis of specified criteria and to prohibit any of their sales, both actively and passively, to unauthorised distributors.[46] As the Guidelines now make clear, the Regulation exempts selective distribution regardless of the nature of the product and the nature of the selection criteria.[47] The Regulation covers the prohibition of sales to unauthorised distributors in the territory reserved by the supplier to operate selective distribution. A supplier can restrict an appointed distributor from selling, at any level of trade, to unauthorised distributors located in any territory where selective distribution is currently operated or, as is now clarified in the Guidelines, where the supplier does not yet sell the contract products.[48] Other restrictions of the authorised distributors' freedom regarding where and to whom they may sell are generally considered hardcore restrictions. Thus, an authorised distributor should be free to sell to any final consumer and to supply and/or get supplies from any other authorised distributors.[49] The reason for protecting this freedom of authorised distributors to sell to other authorised distributors (freedom of cross supplies) and to end users is that selective distribution would otherwise involve a high risk of market partitioning because, as explained above, in that system a supplier is allowed to restrict active and passive sales to unauthorised distributors, thereby preventing in particular arbitrage by parallel traders.

What this leads to if a supplier wants to combine selective distribution in one part of the EU with other forms of distribution elsewhere in the EU

---

45 See article 4(b)(i) in combination with article 1(1)(i) of the Regulation, which make it clear that all buyers party to the agreement can be restricted in their active sales.

46 See article 1(1)(e) in combination with article 4(b)(iii) of the Regulation. See also paragraph 55 of the Guidelines.

47 See paragraph 176 of the Guidelines. However, the nature of the product and selection criteria will of course play a role in case an individual assessment under Article 101 is made; see in particular paragraphs 175 and 176 of the Guidelines.

48 See paragraph 55 of the Guidelines.

49 See article 4(c) and (d) of the Regulation.

is made clear with the following example. Assume a supplier, currently active in two countries A and B, wants to use, because of differences in the available infrastructure and/or consumer preferences for services, a selective distribution network in country A and an exclusive distribution network in country B. In both territories distributors may have to undertake important investments which are worth protecting against 'free riding'. The exclusive distributors in country B can and — in order to benefit from the block exemption — have to be protected against active sales by the other exclusive distributors in country B and by the distributors in country A. On the other hand, the exclusive distributors in country B can be prohibited to open a shop in country A, to avoid free riding on the shop and services of authorised distributors in country A. However, any other restrictions on the distributors' active sales from country B into country A, including active sales over the internet, continue to be treated as hardcore restrictions.

The example shows that it remains difficult to operate a closed selective distribution system in one part of the EU while selling through other formats elsewhere in the EU, at least if transport costs are low compared to the price difference between areas. In order to benefit from the block exemption, the distributors elsewhere should remain free to sell passively and, except for the location clause, also actively in the part where selective distribution is applied, both to end users and unauthorised distributors. At the same time the authorised distributors from the part where selective distribution is applied should remain free to sell passively and, if no exclusive distribution is used in the other part of the EU, also actively to end users and distributors in this other part. The example indicates that the Commission is (still) very concerned about the negative effects of market partitioning and price discrimination.[50]

4.3.2 Restrictions on the Use of the Internet

The general rules explained in the previous section apply to offline and online sales. Since the internet allows distributors to reach different customers and different territories, restrictions of the distributors' use of the

---

50 It can of course be argued that a supplier can avoid most of these problems by applying a (more or less) uniform price across the EU. For an assessment of the effects of price discrimination, see Luc Peeperkorn, *Price Discrimination and Exploitation*, in International Antitrust Law & Policy, Barry E. Hawk (editor), Annual Proceedings of the Fordham Competition Law Institute, 2009. A more technical analysis, but reaching similar conclusions, can be found in *Monopoly Price Discrimination and Demand Curvature*, Iñaki Aguirre, Simon Cowan and John Vickers, American Economic Review 100, September 2010.

66   BRUYLANT

internet are generally considered as hardcore resale restrictions. In principle, every distributor must be allowed to use the internet to sell products. As in the offline world, under the block exemption, a supplier can restrict active sales into exclusively allocated territories or customer groups while passive sales should remain free. The Guidelines contain a careful delineation of active and passive sales, aimed at allowing the internet to continue contributing to cross-border trade in the internal market while preserving the efficiency of exclusive distribution.[51] The general principle is that if the distributor has a website and a customer visits the web site and contacts the distributor (without being solicited) and if such contact leads to a sale, including delivery, then that is considered passive selling. The same is true if a customer opts to be kept (automatically) informed by the distributor and it leads to a sale. The Guidelines also clarify that any obligations on distributors to automatically reroute customers located outside their territory, or to terminate consumers' transactions over the internet if their credit card data reveal an address that is not within the distributor's territory, are hardcore restrictions of passive selling. Similarly, any obligation that dissuades distributors from using the internet, such as a limit on the proportion of overall sales which a distributor can make over the internet, or the requirement that a distributor pays a higher purchase price for units sold online than for those sold offline ("dual pricing"), is also considered a hardcore restriction of passive selling.[52]

In contrast, any efforts by distributors to be found specifically in a certain territory or by a certain customer group are active selling into that territory or to that customer group. For example, paying a search engine or online advertisement provider to have advertisements displayed specifically to users in a particular territory is active selling into that territory. Territory-based banners on third party websites are also a form of active sales into the territory where these banners are shown. However, offering different language options on the website does not, of itself, change the passive character of such selling.[53]

Since suppliers can appoint the exclusive distributor of their choice or implement a selective distribution system which allows them to freely choose their distributors on the basis of specified criteria and to prohibit

---

51 See in particular paragraphs 51-53 of the Guidelines.
52 Dual pricing should not be confused with price discrimination. In case of dual pricing, the same distributor is charged a different price depending on how or to whom it resells the supplier's product. In case of price discrimination, the supplier charges different prices to different distributors.
53 See in particular paragraphs 51-53 of the Guidelines.

any of their sales to unauthorised distributors, the block exemption covers a requirement by the supplier that its distributors have one or more brick and mortar shops or showrooms as a condition for becoming a member of its distribution system.[54] In other words, under the Regulation the supplier may choose not to sell its product to internet-only distributors. To ensure an efficient operation of the brick and mortar shops, a supplier can also require from a distributor that it sells at least a certain absolute amount (in value or volume) of the products offline. This absolute amount of required offline sales can be the same for all buyers, or determined individually for each buyer on the basis of objective criteria, such as the buyer's size in the network or its geographic location. A supplier can also pay a fixed fee to its distributor to support the latter's offline sales efforts.[55] However, as explained earlier, under the Regulation a supplier cannot restrict in general the online sales of its appointed distributors — for instance by dual pricing or limiting the proportion of overall sales that can be made over the internet — since such is a hardcore sales restriction. Similarly, a supplier cannot use the brick and mortar requirement to "punish" a distributor for selling successfully over the internet (in particular in the territories where the supplier/other distributors charge higher prices).[56]

More in general, under the block exemption, the supplier may require quality standards for its distributors' online sales, just as the supplier may require quality standards for offline sales. However, agreeing criteria for online sales which are not overall equivalent to the criteria agreed for the sales from the brick and mortar shop(s) and which dissuade distributors from using the internet is a hardcore restriction.[57] This does not mean that the criteria agreed for online sales must be identical to those agreed for offline sales, but rather that they should pursue the same objectives and achieve comparable results and that the difference between the criteria must be justified by the different nature of these two distribution modes.[58] Similarly, if a distributor wants to distribute contract products via third party platforms, a supplier may require that its distributor uses third party platforms only in accordance with the standards and condi-

---

54 See in particular paragraph 54 of the Guidelines.
55 See paragraph 52 of the Guidelines.
56 See paragraph 54 of the Guidelines, in which it is clarified that the requirement to have one or more brick and mortar shops can be applied flexibly and may change over time, but not if these changes "have as their object to directly or indirectly limit the online sales by the distributors."
57 See paragraph 56 of the Guidelines.
58 Paragraph 56 of the Guidelines provides some examples of quality standards for online/offline sales which are not identical, but which are overall equivalent.

tions agreed between the supplier and its distributor for the distributor's use of the internet. For instance, where the distributor's website is hosted by a third party platform, the supplier may require that customers do not visit the distributor's website through a site carrying the name or logo of the third party platform.[59]

4.3.3 Individual Justifications of Hardcore Resale Restrictions

As for RPM, the parties can bring forward evidence in an individual case that their agreement containing hardcore resale restrictions may fall outside the scope of Article 101(1) or may fulfil the conditions of Article 101(3). The Guidelines contain some concrete examples of such individual justifications of hardcore resale restrictions.[60]

Hardcore restrictions may be objectively necessary in exceptional cases for an agreement of a particular type or nature[61] and therefore fall outside Article 101(1). However, such a defence based on objective necessity of the restriction will only be valid in rare circumstances. For example, although a hardcore restriction could be objectively necessary to ensure that a public ban on selling dangerous substances to certain customers for reasons of safety or health is respected, it is normally the task of public authorities to set and enforce public health and safety standards.[62]

Where substantial investments by a distributor to start up and/or develop a new market are required, restrictions of (active and) passive sales by other distributors into such a territory or to such a customer group, if necessary for the distributor to recoup those investments, generally fall outside the scope of Article 101(1) during the first two years that the distributor is selling the contract goods or services in that territory or to that customer group. This justification relates to a genuine entry of the supplier on the relevant market, where there was previously no demand for that type of product in general or for that type of product from that supplier.[63] In case of such genuine entry the Guidelines do not acknowledge a general need for resale restrictions beyond the first two years, but in an individual case

---

59 See paragraph 54 of the Guidelines.
60 See paragraphs 60-64 of the Guidelines.
61 See paragraph 18 of the Communication from the Commission — Notice — Guidelines on the application of Article 81(3) of the Treaty, OJ C 101, 27.4.2004, p. 97.
62 See, for instance, Case T-30/89 *Hilti vs. Commission* [1991] ECR II-1439, paragraphs 118-119; Case T-83/91 *Tetra Pak International vs. Commission* (Tetra Pak II) [1994] ECR II-755, paragraphs 83, 84 and 138.
63 See paragraph 61 of the Guidelines.

such a need for a longer period can, depending on the specific situation, be argued under Article 101(3).

In the case of genuine testing of a new product in a limited territory or with a limited customer group and in the case of a staggered introduction of a new product, the distributors appointed to sell the new product on the test market or to participate in the first round(s) of the staggered introduction may be restricted in their active selling outside the test market or the market(s) where the product is first introduced. This restriction falls outside the scope of Article 101(1) for the period necessary for the testing or introduction of the product.[64]

A restriction of active sales imposed on wholesalers within a selective distribution system may be necessary to solve a possible "free riding" problem and therefore may fulfil the conditions of Article 101(3) in an individual case, that is when wholesalers are obliged to invest in promotional activities in "their" territories to support the sales by appointed retailers and it is not practical to specify in a contract the required promotional activities.[65] Similarly, in some specific circumstances, an agreed dual pricing policy may fulfil the conditions of Article 101(3) that is when online selling by distributors leads to substantially higher costs for the supplier than their offline sales and when a dual pricing policy allows the supplier to recover those additional costs. For example, where offline sales include home installation of a technical product by the distributor but online sales do not, the latter may actually lead to more customer complaints and warranty claims for the manufacturer.[66]

5. Conclusion

The newly adopted rules mark an evolution and refinement of the effects-based approach the Commission introduced in 1999/2000. While the rules are adapted to recent market developments, in particular regarding online sales, they are based on the same effects-based philosophy. There is thus a large measure of continuity in the approach embodied in the Regulation and Guidelines, but they give more attention to buyer power issues and online resale restrictions.

The rules do not aim to impose or favour certain distribution formats. Instead of forcing manufacturers and distributors to offer all or certain

---

64 See paragraph 62 of the Guidelines.
65 See paragraph 63 of the Guidelines.
66 See paragraph 64 of the Guidelines.

distribution models, the rules allow a large measure of freedom for manufacturers to agree with distributors how they want their products to be distributed. Consumers can then make their choice based on these offers, thereby rewarding the best available options and stimulating business to adapt to what consumers want and ensure that European supply and distribution remain globally competitive.

CHAPTER II

REFORMING THE REFORM: THE NEW RULES FOR VERTICAL AGREEMENTS IN THE EU MARKET SHARE THRESHOLDS AND RESALE PRICE MAINTENANCE

SANDRA MARCO COLINO

Research Assistant Professor
Chinese University of Hong Kong.

1. Introduction: the context of the 're-reform'

Anyone who has followed the regulatory developments in vertical restraints in the EU over the course of the years is bound to have cherished the exciting developments of the last decade. Already in the late nineties, the many critics of the European Commission's policy towards these restrictions saw a light at the end of the tunnel when the institution finally acknowledged the unworkability of its approach, and announced its intention to make amends in the 1997 Green Paper on Vertical Restraints. Of course, it was not that DG COMP failed to understand the complexities of vertical relationships prior to the publication of the Green Paper. More often than not, cynics have been too quick to blame the Commission for all the woes of a system which had become obsolete as the unprecedented process of integration transformed the context of its application. A rigid and centralised exemption system for agreements between firms operating at different levels of production may have been acceptable — one might even say necessary — in a Community of six Member States, more so considering the countries' limited prior experience applying competition law. However, by the mid nineties the European Union comprised no less than fifteen members, and further accessions were already on the horizon. The EU had somewhat become a victim of its own success; the progressive widening of the Union's territory multiplied the amount of agreements the Commission had to scrutinise, and it was incapable of keeping up with the workload.

The block exemptions adopted to alleviate the burden of the Commission were more formalistic than pragmatic, but provided a temporary way out of the unsustainable situation.

The result of the reform announced by the Green Paper was a new concept of block exemption which materialised in the adoption of Regulation 2790/99 and the 2000 Guidelines on Vertical Restraints. The changes transformed the legal arena for businesses. Rather than focusing on the form of agreements, the exemption now depended on market power, and those situations in which the market share of the supplier did not exceed 30 per cent would be afforded an automatic presumption of legality. This rebuttable presumption would vanish in the presence of the hardcore restrictions listed in the Regulation. Indeed, minimum resale price maintenance and absolute territorial protection would rule out the application of the block exemption, leaving the legal exception of 101(3) TFEU as the only lifeline for agreements falling within the scope of Article 101(1) TFEU. The overhaul of the exemption system was followed by similarly groundbreaking changes in the procedural rules in May 2004. Coinciding with the accession to the EU of ten new Member States, the 'Modernisation Package' planted the seed for decentralised enforcement of EU competition law by giving direct effect to Article 101(3) TFEU, and increasing the role of national competition authorities and courts in the application of EU antitrust rules.

On 31 May 2010 Regulation 2790/99 expired, prompting the Commission to embark upon a review of the functioning of the rules and to point towards any remaining problems that ought to be addressed. It came as no surprise that the Commission concluded that the rules were generally working well, and advocated only for what appeared to be minor changes. This 're-reform' came in the shape of Regulation 330/2010 and the 2010 Guidelines on Vertical Restraints, which entered into force on 1 June 2010. It would be accurate to say that, in practice, the new rules prolong the essence of the effects-based approach of the previous regulation. The shadow of the major overhaul introduced by the preceding revision has left the changes introduced by the current regime largely overlooked, yet there are important modifications which deserve particular attention. This paper focuses on two specific aspects of the reform: the novelties introduced in respect of market share thresholds, and the clarifications on the legality of resale price maintenance. With regard to the former, it is now both parties to the agreement — seller and buyer — that must observe the 30 per cent cap for the exemption to apply. This rather unfortunate novelty undoubtedly limits the scope of the regulation, and leads to relative uncertainty for the contracting parties, who need to be aware of each other's market positions before entering into a contract — an oftentimes complicated endeavour. The potential advantages of the new threshold are discussed in order to determine whether they are solid enough to compensate for these woes. As for resale price maintenance, fixing minimum prices is still considered a hardcore restriction in the Regulation, although the Guidelines refer to specific scenarios in which it may be lawful. This elucidation makes clear that EU hardcore restrictions are different from US per se illegal clauses, despite an all too frequent tendency to equate the two. Article 101(3) TFEU can, in principle, apply to all kinds of restrictions on competition; in theory, per se illegality has never applied in the European context, and public and private enforcers of EU competition law may always weigh the anti-competitive effects of a restriction against the potential benefits. At the same time, the Guidelines describe scenarios where a recommended price can turn into a fixed price, and where a maximum threshold can actually be a disguised minimum price that buyers are virtually forced to observe. Very much in line with the leading case law, the Guidelines stress the importance of ensuring that such impositions are also caught by 101(1) TFEU when they have the object or effect of restricting competition.

Underlying the analysis is the question of whether it was adequate to opt for maintaining the block exemption system. A substantial number of theorists whose work has focused on the nature of vertical restraints would argue that there is a strong case for doing away with the block exemption system altogether, at a time when there is a general consensus that such restrictions of competition are nearly always pro-competitive. Moreover, block exemption regulations were originally enacted as a solution to the procedural chaos of the centralised enforcement system in place prior to 2004, which has now been replaced. The following pages will look at potential alternatives, and in particular whether the interplay between the prohibition of 101(1) and the legal exception of 101(3) would suffice to exert an adequate control over potentially harmful restrictions of competition in vertical relationships.

2. Regulation 330/2010 and the 2010 Guidelines on Vertical Restraints in a nutshell

Broadly speaking, the changes introduced by the new block exemption and accompanying Guidelines appear to respond to two priorities. The first has been expressly referred to by the Commission, while the other manifests itself somewhat tacitly in the new rules. Firstly, the resilience of certain problems and the emergence of others, according to the Commission, required further action. In this sense, the institution openly highlighted the priorities of the reform in order to tackle these issues. Secondly, the policy changes of other jurisdictions could not be ignored, and particularly the developments in US case law which finally extended the rule of reason analysis to all forms of vertical price restraints. Each of these lines of action is assessed in this section.

2.1 The response to new challenges and resilient problems

It was in July 2009 — eight months prior to the expiration of Regulation 2790/99 — that the Commission launched a public consultation to complete the due review of the block exemption for vertical agreements, only days after the publication of a new draft block exemption and guidelines. In stark contrast to the self-criticism of Green Paper that had announced a thorough reform of the system some 12 years earlier, this time it was the Commission's view that the rules introduced in 2000 were functioning adequately. Nonetheless, the momentum for reform would not be squandered, and some changes were suggested to address remaining problems and to adapt the regulation to new emerging challenges. In particular, the increase of power at the retailing level and the proliferation of the Internet as a forum for sale transactions were taken into consideration. To this end, proposals for reform included the establishment of a 30 per cent cap on the market share of the buyer for the exemption to apply — one of the central issues addressed in this paper — and a more detailed clarification of the distinction between online active and passive sales in the draft Guidelines.

The consequences of the double market share threshold (on the seller and the buyer) are addressed in detail in the next section; suffice it to say here that a certain coherence has been achieved by applying the same cap on the buyer and the seller, particularly since this was already the approach followed in the De Minimis notice. However, the restrictive impact it has had on the scope of the block exemption appears to be anachronic at a time of growing tolerance towards these restrictions. As for the additional explanations regarding Internet sales, it is important to note that there is an acknowledgment that, in some cases, tolerance towards selling in areas beyond the distributor's allotted territory may unduly exacerbate free-riding. It is for this reason that some exceptions to the hardcore restrictions of the block exemption are referred to in paragraphs 54 and 55 of the Guidelines. As a consequence, manufacturers may demand that distributors meet certain quality standards in order to engage in online reselling, and a brick and mortar showroom can also be required of dealers in selective distribution systems. Online sales may even be prohibited altogether in such scenarios, thus giving the manufacturer a broader margin for establishing limits without losing the benefit of the block exemption. While this may, in some cases, restrict the possibilities for expansion of online retailers, it would appear that the manufacturer ought to have solid reasons for introducing such limitations on the resale of its goods or services. If dealers engage in novel cost-cutting distribution methods that will increase sales, in principle this will benefit the producer, who will make larger profits with the boost.

The clarifications made with regard to online active and passive sales, and the restrictions that may be imposed on online (and catalogue) resellers are one of the many manifestations of the Commission's attempt to clarify the real nature of hardcore restrictions. These are not, as will be seen when addressing the changes in attitude towards resale price maintenance, per se illegal. They simply prevent the application of the block exemption, without prejudice to the legal exception of Article 101(3) TFEU. This aspect of the reform will be discussed in detail in section 3.

2.2 The influence of other jurisdictions: keeping up with the Joneses?

The final version of the new rules retains most of the features of the draft presented back in July 2009. Importantly however, in the new Guidelines there is an additional attempt to shed light on the distinction between hardcore restrictions and per se illegality which manifests itself in the approach towards resale price maintenance. Commentators have inevitably linked this clarification to the recent developments in US antitrust, and particularly the US Supreme Court's decision in Leegin, which in 2007 removed the per se illegal rubric from minimum resale price maintenance.

Since the landmark judgment in Dr. Miles, vertical restraints had been considered per se illegal. Leegin culminated the progressive expansion of the rule of reason to vertical restraints which started in the late 1970s when, coinciding with the boost of the ideas of the Chicago School, Sylvania discarded the per se ban in respect of non-price restrictions. It took another twenty years for the Supreme Court to tamper with the per se illegality of price restraints, and it was not until 1997 that Khan extended the rule of reason to maximum resale price maintenance. It thus took almost a century to completely overrule the precedent set in Dr. Miles that minimum resale price maintenance should be subject to a per se rule. Broadly speaking, the Supreme Court in Leegin recognised that, in the absence of market power, minimum resale price maintenance may indeed not be contrary to Section 1 of the Sherman Act. It may however still be considered to violate some state laws, but courts will now be able to determine on a case-by-case basis whether or not the Sherman Act is infringed, following the application of the rule of reason.

In practice, this change does not quite fulminate the (rather accurate) premise that minimum resale price maintenance is, in most cases, harmful for competition. Nonetheless, over the years economic theory has progressively built a strong case for recognising benefits of vertical price fixing in specific circumstances, under which it would appear that consumer welfare is in fact enhanced. For instance, establishing a price floor may indeed ensure the survival of full-service retailers. They possess the expertise and the infrastructure to provide customers with additional assistance that they may well be willing to pay for; however, such retailers may not be able to survive if stores who cut costs by not offering expert services are able to sell at a cheaper price, sometimes free riding on the investments of the investments of full-service outlets. Moreover, it has been suggested that fixing a retail price may force retailers to look for cost-cutting initiatives and increase their efficiency, thus indirectly correcting potential market failures. These arguments clearly stem from Chicago School principles, but the disappearance of the per se rule ought not to be interpreted as the mere assumption of the premises of the famous school of thought. For one thing, the removal of the rule of reason does not imply per se legality, but merely opens the door to case-by-case analysis by the courts. Most importantly, the potential benefits purported by resale price maintenance are substantiated by a wealth of practical examples in everyday business life as well as more recent and elaborate doctrinal postulates.

Following Leegin, speculation arose in Europe as to whether the change in position would bear an impact on the European legislation regarding minimum resale price maintenance, particularly in the light of the expiration of the rules for vertical restraints. Would this lead to the disappearance of Article 4(a) of Regulation 2790/99, which prevents the application of the block exemption to agreements that impose on the buyer a minimum resale price? In fact, such a change did not take place, and Regulation 330/2010 maintains this hardcore restriction. However, this modification was not necessary, as per se illegality has never existed in EU competition law. The black list of Article 4 simply implies that such restraints will not be exempted en bloc. Nothing precludes, however unlikely, that an agreement may indeed not be considered to fall within Article 101(1) in the first place (in which case it needs not be exempted). Moreover, provided that it is considered to be prohibited, the legal exception of 101(3) TFEU may still render such a restriction lawful, as demonstrated by the case law. The legality of minimum resale price maintenance is nonetheless the exception rather than the general rule. This does neither contradicts the current position of the US Supreme Court — which has merely opened the door for a potential judicial assessment of the effects of such restrictions in the specific circumstances of each case —, nor is it incoherent with predominant economic theory. One must not forget that, in most scenarios, minimum resale price maintenance has been proven to be notoriously harmful. Therefore, the possibility of declaring it lawful if this is not the case must not be mistaken with what would be an unjustified predisposition to its legality.

In light of the frequent confusion as to the nature of hardcore restrictions, the new Guidelines on Vertical Restraints clarify those circumstances under which resale price maintenance (as well as those clauses granting absolute territorial protection that are also blacklisted) may be lawful. Furthermore, paragraph 48 of the Guidelines also describes those circumstances under which recommended and maximum resale prices, which are a priori exempted, in fact amount to illegal price fixing and must thus fall outside the scope of the Regulation. Such a premise had already been laid down by the European Courts. The intricacies of these clarifications — both in the case law and the new legislation — are discussed below.

3. Market share thresholds: limiting the scope of the exemption

The application of the 30 per cent market share cap to both the seller and the buyer follows a relatively convincing logic. The reasons as to why it only applied to one of the parties to the contract under Regulation 2790/99 — which was the first to introduce market share thresholds — were somewhat unclear. Moreover, considering only the market power of the buyer was incoherent with the system laid down in other pieces of legislation. The De Minimis Notice in particular establishes a recommendation that vertical agreements where 'the market share held by each of the parties to the agreement does not exceed 15 per cent on any of the relevant markets affected' be considered incapable or restricting competition, and should therefore fall outside the scope of Article 101(1) TFEU. Besides this added consistency, the Commission has argued that the new approach will allow authorities to investigate a higher number of potentially anti-competitive practices.

Unfortunately, the double market share threshold has the inevitable effect of reducing the scope of the exemption, which seems contrary to the spirit of the reform of the late 1990s. The cap was introduced following a recognition that vertical restraints are necessary and generally pro-competitive in the absence of market power, and that authorities need to focus on serious threats to competition such as horizontal price fixing or market-sharing agreements. This appears to be put aside in the 're-reform', and the gains to be obtained from the change remain unsatisfactorily explained. Furthermore, the relevance of considering the buyer's market share has been questioned beyond exclusive supply agreements, where naturally the concern is whether competitors of the seller are precluded from competing for customers. Having to look at the buyer's power in other scenarios will not be exempt from difficulties; sellers are forced to try to determine the position of their customers on the relevant market before entering into an agreement if they want to ensure that they will be entitled to the benefit of the block exemption. Such an endeavour will often be extremely complicated, if not impossible. The uncertainty for the parties stemming from the extended threshold is evident.

In addition to these woes, the very market share threshold system as introduced in Regulation 2790/99 is riddled with uncertainties and problems that ought to be borne in mind, some of which the author has previously emphasised elsewhere. Market power is not easily defined; market share thresholds are too formalistic to measure such an intricate phenomenon and oftentimes too complex to be determined. The essential process of defining the relevant market is anything but straightforward, and national courts and authorities are not always position to engage in such a complex endeavour. The first question that arises is why the cap was set at 30 per cent, as it has been described as a somewhat arbitrary figure. Fortunately the system allows for other factors to be additionally considered to determine the existence market power. As a consequence however, the extent to which market share thresholds have 'simplified' the economic analysis is more than dubious. Going back to that magic number of 30 percent and the quest for the reasoning behind the choice to set the threshold at this level, it would appear that this was purely a Solomonic decision. When Regulation 2790/99 was drafted, a two-tier threshold was proposed which would have established a 40 per cent cap for what were considered 'less serious restraints', and a 20 per cent limit on serious restrictions. While having a single market share threshold may be more straightforward at first sight, one cannot help but feel that the limit is somewhat low, particularly when agreements include only those 'less serious' restraints' discussed in the draft of the previous reform.

The author has frequently voiced her preference for a 40 per cent threshold, which would be very much in accordance with the prevailing tolerant position on vertical restraints. Moreover, EU competition law rules ought to aim at creating a coherent framework of analysis of potentially anti-competitive practices. Under this light, and looking beyond the rules applicable to agreements, it is worth bearing in mind that, when it comes to dominance, the Guidance Paper on Article 82 (now Article 102) establishes a soft harbour of 40 per cent. When a company's market share is below this threshold, it is considered that it will be unlikely to be in a dominant position. It would have seemed logical to have used that same market share cap in the context of agreements, particularly in the context of vertical restraints. This would have led to a more lenient approach and an extension of the scope of the block exemption which would have somewhat made up for the limitations introduced by the new double threshold. Unfortunately, this increase of the cap has not taken place in the 're-reform'. Consequentially, the general conclusion with regard to the changes introduced in respect of market share thresholds are disappointing, and seem to have overlooked the direction in which the previous reform process had pointed out.

4. Resale price maintenance: a 'soft' rule of reason?

4.1 Situations in which minimum resale price maintenance may be lawful

As discussed above, minimum resale price maintenance remains in the black list of hardcore restrictions of the block exemption. Nonetheless, the new Guidelines on Vertical Restraints provide a detailed explanation as to how the clauses listed in Article 4 of the Regulation should be interpreted. In particular, paragraph 60 explains that '[h]ardcore restrictions may be objectively necessary in exceptional cases for an agreement of a particular type or nature and therefore fall outside Article 101(1).' Two are the keys to the legality of such restraints under the block exemption. On the one hand, the restriction must be 'objectively necessary'; on the other hand, the agreement must be of a 'particular type or nature', in which case it need not be exempted as it will not fall within the scope of the prohibition laid down in the Treaty. Although the intricacies of these elements are not described in detail, the Guidelines provide some examples as to when the presence of hardcore restrictions will not prevent the application of the block exemption. Importantly, in the case of minimum resale price mainte-nance, paragraph 225 describes a specific scenario of legality:

> 'However, RPM may not only restrict competition but may also, in particular where it is supplier driven, lead to efficiencies, which will be assessed under Article 101(3). Most notably, where a manufacturer introduces a new product, RPM may be helpful dur-ing the introductory period of expanding demand to induce dis-tributors to better take into account the manufacturer's interest to promote the product. RPM may provide the distributors with the means to increase sales efforts and if the distributors on this market are under competitive pressure this may induce them to expand overall demand for the product and make the launch of the product a success, also for the benefit of consumers. Simi-larly, fixed resale prices, and not just maximum resale prices, may be necessary to organise in a franchise system or similar distribution system applying a uniform distribution format a coordinated short term low price campaign (2 to 6 weeks in most cases) which will also benefit the consumers. In some situations, the extra margin provided by RPM may allow retailers to provide (additional) pre-sales services, in particular in case of experi-ence or complex products. If enough customers take advantage from such services to make their choice but then purchase at a lower price with retailers that do not provide such services (and hence do not incur these costs), high-service retailers may reduce or eliminate these services that enhance the demand for the sup-plier's product. RPM may help to prevent such free-riding at the distribution level. The parties will have to convincingly demon-strate that the RPM agreement can be expected to not only provide the means but also the incentive to overcome possible free riding between retailers on these services and that the pre-sales services overall benefit consumers as part of the demonstration that all the conditions of Article 101(3) are fulfilled.'

Such an analysis is based on the Commission and the Courts' experience in applying Article 101 and the block exemption to vertical restraints. In this sense, the new Guidelines confirm that acquired understanding of mini-mum resale price maintenance. While its inclusion in the Guidelines does not imply a shift in position, it is praiseworthy in that it certainly goes a step further towards achieving legal certainty. Nonetheless, it raises ques-tions about the need for such specific soft legislation, which somewhat jeopardises the very spirit of competition law rules. Assessing this aspect in detail is beyond the intention of this paper, but it is the intention of the author to further develop this premise in subsequent research.

4.2 Illegality of maximum and recommended resale prices?

The hardcore restriction contained in Article 4(a) of Regulation 330/2010 makes reference to maximum and recommended prices. These are frequent in the business world and deemed to be within the scope of the block exemption, 'provided that they do not amount to a fixed or minimum sale price as a result of pressure from, or incentives offered by, any of the parties.' 'Pressure' or 'incentives' are therefore the two factors that could affect the nature of these apparently non binding recommendations and maximum prices, and it is not sufficient that a dealer merely respects price guidelines established by the manufacturer. In the Regulation, no details are given as to what is to be understood to be pressure or incentives, but paragraph 48 of the Guidelines explains certain scenarios in which resale price maintenance is indirectly achieved:

> 'Examples [...] are an agreement fixing the distribution margin, fixing the maximum level of discount the distributor can grant from a prescribed price level, making the grant of rebates or reimbursement of promotional costs by the supplier subject to the observance of a given price level, linking the prescribed resale price to the resale prices of competitors, threats, intimidation, warnings, penalties, delay or suspension of deliveries or contract terminations in relation to observance of a given price level. Direct or indirect means of achieving price fixing can be made more effective when combined with measures to identify price-cutting distributors, such as the implementation of a price monitoring system, or the obligation on retailers to report other members of the distribution network that deviate from the standard price level. Similarly, direct or indirect price fixing can be made more effective when combined with measures which may reduce the buyer's incentive to lower the resale price, such as the supplier printing a recommended resale price on the product or the supplier obliging the buyer to apply a most-favoured-customer clause. The same indirect means and the same "supportive" measures can be used to make maximum or recommended prices work as RPM. However, the use of a particular supportive measure or the provision of a list of recommended prices or maximum prices by the supplier to the buyer is not considered in itself as leading to RPM.'

The examples referred to in the Guidelines are clearly based on the wealth of case law that has clarified these concepts over the years, and has specified when price recommendations may become unlawful resale price maintenance. One of the most recent cases is *Pedro IV vs. Total*, in which a service station agreement between with an exclusive supply obligation was challenged before the Spanish courts. The contract had a duration of 20 years, and Total, a supplier of petroleum-based products, worked out a recommended retail price to be charged by Pedro IV, the service station operator. It did so by adding a distribution margin to the price Pedro IV had to pay for Total's products. When the case reached the Court of Justice via a preliminary ruling, the Court insisted it was for the national court to decide whether there are constraints imposed on the reseller that turn the recommendation into a virtually binding resale price. It made clear that clauses relating to retail price may indeed benefit from the exemption provided that it is 'genuinely possible' for the reseller to decide on that price. If such clauses lead, 'directly or by indirect concealed means, to fixing of a retail price or the imposition of a minimum sale price by the supplier', they are not exempted. Importantly however, the Court emphasised that such clauses are only illegal when they breach Article 101(1) TFEU (i.e when they have the object or effect of harming competition and affect trade between Member States).

The emphasis placed by the European Courts on the need to breach Article 101(1) before condemning any form of resale price maintenance has often diverged from the position of Commission, particularly when the issue of the protection of parallel trade has arisen. A famous example is that of the General Court's decision in JCB Service, in which the manufacturer imposed a 'service support fee' on distributors selling outside their allotted territory, which had to be paid to the distributor in charge of that area. According to the producer, the purpose of the fee was to compensate the latter for any costs incurred during the warranty period. While the Commission saw that this was a clear attempt to prevent parallel imports and harmonise retail prices, since the fees were unrelated to the alleged costs, the General Court did not find there was sufficient evidence to conclude that there had indeed been such an intention. Moreover, the Commission's allegation that bonuses were not granted to those distributors who intended to export the machinery purchased was also set aside by the Court, who pointed out that the withdrawal appeared to be related to whether or not the goods were being sold to end users. The Court of Justice subsequently upheld these arguments.

Importantly, it is when horizontal price-fixing effects are felt that competition authorities are less tolerant towards indirect resale price maintenance. One clear example is the severe fine recently imposed on bitumen producers Repsol, Cepsa and British Petrol by the Spanish competition authority, the Comisión Nacional de Competencia. In 2009, a penalty of nearly 8 million euro was imposed on the three companies for effectively fixing retail prices in their gas stations. The way they achieved this was establishing a uniform price at which their dealers were to purchase the fuel, and subsequently also setting their commissions via contractual clauses. As a consequence of these agreements, each operator was de facto ensuring control of the retail prices of those independent gas stations that sold its products. Similar restrictions were also imposed on those stations operated by the companies themselves. However, these are not forbidden under Article 101(1) as they are considered unilateral conduct. The resulting system did not only threaten intrabrand competition, but also interbrand competition since the three major operators had similar arrangements. National courts subsequently confirmed the fine.

5. Conclusion: Assessing the merits of the re-reform

After a careful reflection on the outcome of the changes, to say that, as of 2010, there are brand new rules governing vertical agreements in the EU would appear to be like an optimistic inaccuracy. Indeed, formalistically a new block exemption and a new set of Guidelines have been established, and some relevant modifications have been introduced in respect of the previous legislation. However, in practice the spirit and style of Regulation 2790/99 and its accompanying Guidelines lives on in the new rules. In this light, the re-reform is somewhat part of the 'pebble effect' of the stone that was thrown into the sea of competition law ten years earlier — it is by no means a new pebble.

The absence of radical changes is nonetheless understandable considering the success of the previous reform on the one hand, and the difficulty in engaging in such doctrinal ruptures on the other. Furthermore, there was a general feeling that a major overhaul was not currently needed, which contrasts with the clamour for change of the late 1990s. While the feeling of contempt may hold true regarding the substance of the rules, it is more questionable that the form would not have benefitted from a more adventurous and less complacent attitude to the expiration of the previous regime. In earlier works, the author raised the issue of whether the time has indeed come to rethink the entire EU block exemption system, which — despite the enhanced flexibility introduced in progressive reforms — reflects a level of specificity that seems contrary to the essence of competition law regimes. The ever increasing case law that has frequently addressed the particulars of the application of the Treaty's competition provisions can be said to be sufficient to fill in the majority of the uncertainties that may have been cause for concern for the businesses potentially affected by the rules. In fact, it would appear that the courts would be in a better position to develop these principles than the legislator — in this case the Commission. The merits of such a drastic reform need to be closely considered more carefully in the future. It would certainly appear that vertical restraints would be a good starting point to begin the transition given the widely — recognised benefits of said restrictions.

For the time being, and focusing now on what is currently on the table, the modifications introduced leave one with a feeling of dissatisfaction. The specifications regarding the nature of hardcore restrictions in general and legality of resale price maintenance in particular are doubtlessly helpful, and ought to put an end to the misguided view that hardcore restraints are to understood as per se illegal. In this sense, the clarification included in the Guidelines that, in certain scenarios, hardcore restrictions may not be contrary to Article 101(1) is a mere reinstatement of what has been common practice in the EU, and not — as some have interpreted — a reaction to the US Supreme Court's decision in Leegin. The fact that redemption is the exception is not surprising given their overwhelmingly negative effects in the majority of circumstances. Importantly as well, it is highlighted that recommended and maximum prices are not automatically legal, as they may hide threatening forms of price vertical and horizontal price fixing. However, they only confirm what the case law of EU and national courts has repeatedly demonstrated. The examples contained in the Guidelines serve to illustrate some of the most frequent scenarios outside the general rule, but given the many forms of vertical restrictions the list is by no means comprehensive. Again, it is the courts and authorities who remain crucial in determining when resale price maintenance may be lawful.

After the adoption of an umbrella block exemption in 2000, with a much wider scope of application than its predecessors, it is even more discouraging that the new reform takes a step back and limits the reach of the Regulation by establishing a new double market share threshold. Valuing market shares is certainly necessary to ensure an effects-based approach to the application of competition law. Yet the inconveniences inherent to a market share cap system cannot be overlooked. In the specific context of the reform, the difficulties the parties will face in determining each other's market shares (and in particular for a seller to know the share of the buyer) are bound to lead to legal uncertainty as to whether or not their arrangements are entitled to benefit from the block exemption. Increasing the threshold from 30 to 40 per cent ought to have been considered to grant coherence with the 'soft harbour' for dominance of the Article 102 Guidance Paper: if, in principle, a market share of between 30 and 40 per cent does not mean that a company is in a dominant position, it would seem wise to allow that company to benefit from the block exemption in the absence of hardcore restrictions.

To conclude, despite the value of retaining rules that have worked well in practice, overall one cannot help but feel that the reform could have gone further and tackled important pending issues. Once again the author finds herself longing for the next set of changes to see if the Commission finally takes the bull by the horns. Unfortunately Regulation 330/2010 expires in 2022 — we are clearly in for a long wait.

CHAPTER III

THE EC REVIEW OF THE VERTICAL RESTRAINTS POLICY IN THE CONTEXT OF INTERNET COMMERCE

Andrés Font Galarza

Partner
Alejandro Guerrero Pérez. Lawyer and Trainee
Gibson, Dunn & Crutcher LLP, Brussels

1. Introduction

In 2009, initially surprising to some, one of the hottest issues in the competition policy discourse turned out to be the review of Commission Regulation (EC) No. 2790/1999 on the application of Article 81 (3) EC Treaty to certain categories of vertical agreements (the original Vertical Restraints Block Exemption Regulation or "original vBER") and the respective Guidelines. With the original vBER expiring on 31 May 2010, the Commission was believed to seek only a slight refinement as "(t)he Commission's preliminary assessment of its application, based on experience and feedback from stakeholders, found that the current rules have worked well in practice." However, what had first appeared to be a routine review of an existing, well functioning legal framework proved to be more controversial in the end and led to impressive amount of written contributions from all sorts of stakeholders.

Leaving minor changes aside, the Commission had sought to adapt the vBER against the backdrop of the rise of the internet as a sales channel and of increased buyer power due to continuing concentration in the retail market. At the time of the inception of the vBER, in the 1990s, internet players such as Google, eBay or Amazon were yet to unleash their market potential and thus the Commission had made only few references to online sales in the vBER. Ten years later, after the internet revolution, the Commission seems keen to push the development of the internet further for it is perceived as a tool to finally complete the internal market with substantial cross — border sales resulting in added competition and lower prices for consumers. Finding the right balance between this goal and the economic freedom of manufacturers turned out to be a highly complex task. This article will examine the Commission's updated Regulation and updated Guidelines with a focus on main issues, i.e. amendments reflecting concerns on buyer power and provisions relating to the internet.

2. The vBER and the review process

2.1 The original vBER's scope and selective/ exclusive distribution systems

As the original vBER stated, a safe harbour on the basis of Art. 101 (3) TFEU is provided for vertical agreements, most notably distribution agreements, exempting them from the application of Art. 101 (1) TFEU as "(f) or most vertical restraints, competition concerns can only arise if there is insufficient inter-brand competition." The basic precondition for the exemption was that the supplier's market share would not exceed 30% and that certain vertical restrictions (i.e., those considered "hardcore") would not be used. In 1999, this resulted in a major change for businesses and the safe harbour has since provided the opportunity to assess oneself the antitrust relevance of vertical agreements and increased legal certainty for all market participants.

2.2 The 2010 regime: Buyer power — A new market share threshold

The most important change that the Commission made to the Regulation is the introduction of a market share threshold for the buyer side of agreements. Until now, only the supplier's market share had to stay within 30%, which now applies to the buyer as well. On various public occasions, Commission officials stressed that this is to take account of an increasing concentration in the retail market that has been ongoing for the last two decades. This is certainly true in certain sectors in Europe.

A large number of comments submitted during the Commission's public consultation on the proposed vBER dealt with this particular amendment, questioning its overall justification and emphasising practical difficulties it engenders.

First of all, the change presents a volte-face in the Commission's consideration of certain agreements that have so far been exempted but might not be so in future. In cases where the supplier had a market share below 30%, alleged anticompetitive effects of vertical restraints were deemed negligible or at least outweighed by efficiency gains. Since the block exemption does not apply if either party exceeds the threshold, the updated Regulation may adversely affect the agreements that have hitherto been exempted. The updated Regulation will not apply for a transitional period of one year (i.e., until 31 May 2011) to the agreements that were exempted under the original vBER. Beyond this date the clauses should in principle still be covered by Art. 101 (3) TFEU but in case of a dispute the supplier would see a reversal of the burden of proof compared to the block exemption where an antitrust conformity is assumed a priori. Additionally, there have been no major cases involving vertical restraints where the buyer side was discovered to use its strong negotiation position to impose anticompetitive contractual clauses. Suppliers are therefore bound to hesitate more, given the reduced degree of legal certainty in such situations.

Secondly, when it comes to the practical implications of this amendment there are a myriad of unsolved questions. To begin with, many suppliers stated that they have no reliable data on the market share of their retailers. Obviously, observers of the discussions on the original vBER can point to similar concerns in the 1990s (made in relation to the supplier's market share) that subsequently turned out to be less problematic in practice than initially anticipated. However, the present concerns should be put into context: there is indeed less data on retailers' market shares compared to the supplier side. Furthermore, the market share information available might not be ready to use for a specific category of products.

Finally, to complicate matters even more, the geographic market for retailers can be regional or even local, and in some cases the level of analysis might not necessarily be self-evident due to overlaps of and connections between markets. However, the buyer's market share will be calculated upstream i.e. at the contract market. Calculations at the contract market level are in principle easier as regards the value of the sales but the geographic market definition may change, normally the market definition should be broader, adding difficulty to the exercise. In practice, where suppliers have separate agreements with each of their retailers they would have to first inquire the exact market share (or at least estimate it) and subsequently reassess and possibly adapt the contracts as some clauses might no longer be exempted due to too high market shares. Leaving the additional administrative burden aside for a moment, the question is whether retailers would accept in some situations having diverging contracts. Furthermore, there might be an increased risk of information exchanges. The ultimate result might be that the supplier abstains completely from using certain vertical restraints — knowing that he loses certain advantages that would have been antitrust compliant but for the added threshold test.

2.3 The internet as a distribution channel in the vBER

2.3.1 Online sales provisions in the original vBER

The vBER along with the accompanying Guidelines have helped companies to develop their business models while relying on official legal guidance. This is particularly the case for selective and exclusive distribution systems. These distribution arrangements, where the supplier chooses its retailers according to qualitative and/or quantitative requirements, are a vital instrument in the development and preservation of brands. Most branded goods producers (and certainly those in the upper market segment) would like to ensure that the investments in their brands are not undermined and, therefore, have an interest in a retail environment that supports the development of their brands. The Guidelines allow suppliers to set standards when it comes to the location of their retailers, the staff's professional training, certain customer services and other quality requirements. With the development of the internet into a complementary sales channel, questions arise as to how free suppliers are to restrict online sales.

As promising as the rise in online sales is at first sight, there are manufacturers with specific products that for obvious business reasons might not want online sales of their products which would not be subject to certain qualitative safeguards. Those manufacturers that operate selective or exclusive distribution systems to preserve and develop their brands are concerned about commoditization of their products. While for their physical points of sales they insist — legitimately so, according to the vBER — on a number of qualitative and quantitative requirements, it is not evident that certain products can be merely sold through the internet without any kind of adaptation to the online channel. Indeed, there are products that may not be fully suitable for online sales or only under certain carefully designed conditions. This is particularly true of certain products that require professionally trained personnel to provide guidance during the purchase or where tasting, touching or smelling is essential to ensure that the consumer is satisfied with the purchased good. The original Guidelines contained only a brief reference to internet sales — the basic provision was contained in Paragraph 51 and read as follows:

> *"(51) Every distributor must be free to use the internet to advertise or to sell products. A restriction on the use of the internet by distributors could only be compatible with the Block Exemption Regulation to the extent that promotion on the internet or sales over the internet would lead to active selling into other distributors' exclusive territories or customer groups. In general, the use of the internet is not considered a form of active sales into such territories or customer groups, since it is a reasonable way to reach every customer. [...]".*

This gave only limited guidance on internet related restrictions; indeed, there have been diverging court rulings in the European Union and even within Member States on the suppliers' rights in this regard. It appears to be clear for the Commission and some National Competition Authorities that at least a total ban on the use of the internet is not permissible but even this is under question in a pending French case before the Court of Justice.

In its attempt to clarify such questions, the Commission introduced internet related language in the updated Guidelines, but not in the updated Regulation itself.

2.4 The 2010 regime: The passive nature of online sales

Following the approach taken in the original Guidelines, the internet continues to be regarded as a passive means of sale. This means that customers who visit websites online are treated as though they were visiting physical (offline) outlets and are deemed to not have been solicited through, for example, targeted e-mails. The Commission considers internet advertising as "reasonable general advertising" and thus not targeted. Given the recent and potential future technological developments it is doubtful whether this assessment of internet sales remains justified. The general rule is that:

> *"General advertising or promotion is considered a reasonable way to reach such customers if it would be attractive for the buyer to undertake these investments also if they would not reach customers in other distributors' (exclusive) territories or customer groups."*

Consequently, the Commission defines targeted advertising forms as opposed to general advertising:

> *"[...] the Commission considers online advertisement specifically addressed to certain customers a form of active selling to these customers. For instance, territory-based banners on third party websites are a form of active sales into the territory where these banners are shown. In general, efforts to be found specifically in a certain territory or by a certain customer group is active selling into that territory or to that customer group. For instance, paying a search engine or online advertisement provider to have advertisements displayed specifically to users in a particular territory is active selling into that territory."*

Yet, while the Commission elaborates on advertising efforts that it deems to constitute target advertising it states that, "(o)ffering different language options on the website does not, of itself, change the passive character of such [online] selling." This is surprising, in that, for example, a Polish website that offers an independent German language version, most probably targets German customers living in Germany, rather than German citizens living in Poland. If, furthermore, different language versions are found under the same generic ".com" top-level domain ("TLD"), rather than under a country-specific TLD (i.e., ".pl" for Poland), and even though this language version is likely to appear in German search engine results, the website would not be deemed to target German customers. In this respect, it is significant that the Commission has not taken advantage of the review process to question some of the initial decisions taken 10 years ago. Even though in the 1990s the internet had admittedly been a rather passive means of sale — comparable to catalogue sales — it does not mean that this continues to be valid into the current millennium; given the rapid pace of technological developments, it might be even less valid in 5 or 10 years from now. Trying to fit the internet into the policy grid intended for fundamentally different sales channels might ultimately have even a counterproductive effect. In fact, the single market objective applied to a policy vision of internet commerce has prevailed over other economic, technological or legal considerations.

2.5 The 2010 regime: internet sales-related hardcore restrictions

In its updated Guidelines, the Commission continues to strengthen the retailer's right to use the internet, this time going into more detail. Considered as hardcore restrictions are the following measures:

"(a) an agreement that the (exclusive) distributor shall prevent customers located in another (exclusive) territory from viewing its website or shall automatically re-route its customers to the manufacturer's or other (exclusive) distributors' websites. This does not exclude an agreement that the distributor's website shall also offer a number of links to websites of other distributors and/ or the supplier;

(b) an agreement that the (exclusive) distributor shall terminate consumers' transactions over the internet once their credit card data reveal an address that is not within the distributor's (exclusive) territory; "

The intention the Commission had with the introduction of these hardcore restrictions is evident: promoting further market integration — one of the aims of competition policy. However, first of all, the question is whether these issues are actually to be solved with a competition soft law instrument rather than with EU or national measures in the field of consumer policy or internal market policy where the E-Commerce Directive sets the basic framework for online transactions. Secondly, using the concept of hardcore restrictions — that are often perceived by businesses as per se prohibitions or at least almost impossible to rebut — might be going too far. There can be situations where legitimate legal or economic reasons exist not to deliver products from one country to another, e.g. differing consumer laws or creditworthiness concerns. At the very least, a more nuanced approach leaving room for objective justifications would have been welcome.

Two more internet related hardcore restrictions concern the degree of freedom a supplier has over limiting online sales. Considered as hardcore are:

"(c) an agreement that the distributor shall limit its proportion of overall sales made over the internet. This does not exclude the supplier requiring, without limiting the online sales of the distributor, that the buyer sells at least a certain absolute amount (in value or volume) of the products offline to ensure an efficient operation

of its brick and mortar shop (physical point of sales), nor does it preclude the supplier from making sure that the online activity of the distributor remains consistent with the supplier's distribution model (see paragraphs (54) and (56)). This absolute amount of required offline sales can be the same for all buyers, or determined individually for each buyer on the basis of objective criteria, such as the buyer's size in the network or its geographic location;

(d) an agreement that the distributor shall pay a higher price for products intended to be resold by the distributor online than for products intended to be resold offline. This does not exclude the supplier agreeing with the buyer a fixed fee (that is, not a variable fee where the sum increases with the realised offline turnover as this would amount indirectly to dual pricing) to support the latter's offline or online sales efforts."

These provisions again underline the Commission's policy in favour of online commerce. They are particularly relevant for suppliers whose products necessitate selective or exclusive distribution systems and who want to have a say on online sales for business strategic reasons. Here, the fundamental concern for most suppliers is the potential for free-riding: suppliers fear that online shops could free-ride on physical outlets' investments in presentation and service, selling online without facing these costs, ultimately reducing incentives for making these investments. To a certain degree the Commission has taken account of this issue, recognising that suppliers may require a physical outlet to be opened before establishing an online presence.

However, this does not prevent a retailer from concentrating its business activities online, making only basic investments offline. Therefore, some manufacturers may like to retain the right to impose limits to online sales, which the Commission generally rejects. It is also worthy of note that the German Federal Court permitted fixing a percentage ratio between online and offline sales. Acknowledging the manufacturers' concerns, the Commission would allow for a fixed fee to support retailers in physical stores and having a minimum sales volume. It is still unclear, however, how these should be applied in practice and where the thin line between a fee and price discrimination between online and offline sales will be drawn.

Finally, to touch upon one of the fundamental questions raised in the beginning of this paper, the Commission also elaborates on how the selective distribution requirements translate from offline to online sales:

"[...] the Commission considers any obligations which dissuade appointed dealers from using the internet to reach a greater num-

ber and variety of customers by imposing criteria for online sales which are not overall equivalent to the criteria imposed for the sales from the brick and mortar shop as a hardcore restriction. This does not mean that the criteria imposed for online sales must be identical to those imposed for offline sales, but rather that they should pursue the same objectives and achieve comparable results and that the difference between the criteria must be justified by the different nature of these two distribution modes."

In the course of the review debate, even more controversial formulations had been on the table, asking for "the same criteria for online and offline sales" or "criteria that are not more onerous for online sales." The above mentioned equivalence test might therefore constitute a compromise acceptable for all stakeholders. Since there is ample room for interpretation this test increases legal uncertainty for suppliers using these clauses who might ultimately bear the burden of proof in case of a dispute. This could potentially lead to more lawsuits being filed across Europe, with an added risk of diverging results in the Member States.

3. Some Case-law examples regarding selective distribution systems of luxury products and the implementation in practice of the principle of overall equivalence in internet sales

Certain business models, in particular those launched and developed by luxury product manufacturers, must now take note of the Commission's purposes of achieving a high number of online transactions by 2015. These suppliers, that which have established brick and mortar selective distribution networks to market their goods, would like to keep an efficient balance between brick and mortar and online sales to preserve the economic integrity of their network and their business model. As mentioned above, the updated Guidelines try to offer solutions by allowing restrictions of two kinds. First, the manufacturer may request the retailer to execute a certain absolute amount of sales through the brick and mortar shop and may also agree with the retailer a fixed fee to support the offline sales. Both of this these measures may allow the retailer to strengthen the viability of the physical store and to avoid the most serious free-riding issues. Second, the supplier may request the retailer's website to comply with certain high qualitative standards, including service standards, that standards that shall be equivalent to the criteria imposed on physical stores, in order to achieve the targeted objectives.

Notwithstanding the above, the retailer still holds the right to use the internet to market and sell products; hence, the question shifts to how the Commission or the national jurisdictions will enforce selective distribution networks against improper online marketing. National courts across the EU have recently adopted several rulings regarding the said distribution networks under Trademark protection — which constitutes the former's essential core — and unfair commercial practice law. Although the majority of the rulings adopted concern online distribution through unauthorised retailers, the guidance offered by the national courts may be useful to assess the balance that shall be achieved within the authorised distribution networks too.

In 2007, the Territorial Court of Valencia (Spain) adopted the reasoning of its analogous Court in Zaragoza, confirming that the properties of luxury products include, besides their material characteristics, the specific perception that consumers have of the said products. This perception and the 'aura of luxury' is simultaneously dependant on other factors, such as their presentation and their status of as luxury products that they hold in society. Therefore, "trademarks covering this kind of products also cover the former's image of luxury; accordingly, those actions or omissions regarding specific aspects of its commercialization which damage the said image of luxury and prestige of the branded products will without any doubt represent a damage of the trademark itself."

In 2008, the Territorial Court of Alicante (Spain) deepened and developed this reasoning in order to apply the abovementioned assertions to online commerce. The Court confirmed that marketing conditions constitute, in many cases, an authentic "quality Trustmark projected in an immediate and direct manner on the trademark". Consequently, conditions regarding the sales of goods may be imposed on retailers obeying "certain criteria, as well as regarding their capacity to manage the said products and to protect and defend the trademark's image". This would justify that trademark owners base their claims on Article 13(2) of the Community Trademark Regulation and national implementations of Article 7(2) of the Trademark Directive; trademark exhaustion does not apply when the marketing conditions established by the trademark owner within a selective distribution network are being infringed.

If the objective of establishing a selective distribution network is to protect and improve the branded product's status by establishing certain criteria on the retailer stores, which would be the equivalent criteria applicable to online stores? In the case that pended before the Territorial Court of Alicante, regarding an unauthorised retailer that sold selective products in the internet, the Court of first instance had ruled that the conditions imposed by the manufacturer on off-line sales were not applicable to online sales. However, in the appeal, the Territorial Court confirmed that this reasoning would lead to admit that "exemptions exist in the compliance of the specific rules according to the kind of commerce engaged". On the other hand, "it wouldn't be acceptable to directly admit the infringement of the distribution conditions because of the exercise of a certain modality of electronic commerce." Accordingly, the Territorial Court asserted that electronic commerce channels involve a series of mechanisms and allow a variety of activities, to which the conditions established by the supplier may be applied to a certain extent. This was asserted without the Territorial Court pronouncing the word 'equivalence', later adopted by the Commission in its Guidelines. In this case, the Territorial Court confirmed that "no efforts have been made by the defendant to differentiate some products from others, one range from others, and to offer, regarding each specific range, a specific service. It offers telephone assistance but not a specialized service. Products are ranked, within each category, in alphabetical order, in a setting where equality is the chosen criteria over any other, despite the distribution contract specifies that the retailer is bound not to market any other product that may affect the brand image." In consequence, the unauthorised retailer had clearly violated the conditions set in the selective distribution system.

Without willing to replace the law or to create any de facto test on how conditions initially conceived for off-line commerce apply to online commerce, the Territorial Court actually offered some guidance on how the principle of equivalence may apply. The ruling concerned mainly (i) the absence of differentiation and the context of the trademark display, and (ii) the absence of specialized personal service. The first criteria had already been dealt with by the European Court of Justice in *Parfums Christian Dior vs. Evora*, where the controversial marketing channel was not the internet but advertising through leaflets. Similarly, the Court of Appeal of Paris (France) asserted that the classification of luxury perfumes within the "hygiene" section of an online sales website contributed inter alia in damaging the brand status. The second criteria referred to the quality of the personal service offered on the phone. As selective distribution agreements usually contain a clause regarding the academic background and experience required to market and attend customers, this condition was easily adapted to the online commerce by requiring specialized online or telephone personal services.

In addition to the abovementioned criteria, it may be analyzed analysed if the Commission or the national courts could make in the future a more extensive development of the principle of equivalence. Indeed, applying this principle means that online sales shall pursue the same objectives and achieve comparable results. In practice, selective product suppliers may support broader monitoring on the retailers' activities in the internet based on three non-negligible reasons.

3.1 Convenience of homogenised designs from the marketing perspective

Marketing theory emphasizes the importance of design homogenization. Maintaining throughout the marketing process the same design and colour scheme makes a product easily identifiable by the consumer, and therefore enhances the possibility of being remembered, targeted and consumed again. If this is true with every day products such as soft drinks (e.g., Pepsi Cola and blue colour), it also applies to a larger extent to luxury brands. The latter does not mean that the same brand sections hosted by different authorised retailers should be absolutely equal, but rather that the same overall structure and conditions may be followed. It also means that design quality standards shall be enhanced in the online channel in order to be equivalent to physical quality standards applied to brick and mortar shops.

In regard to the above, analysis of administrative precedents on physical stores may be useful, especially since the Commission has accepted proportional and objective provisions contained in distribution agreements by virtue of which the supplier "intends to meet the objective of ensuring that the products covered by the contract are presented in an enhancing manner". These criteria includes the ability of the manufacturer to evaluate if a retailer is qualified to act as an authorised reseller based on "(t)he location, name and fittings of the retail outlet [...]. In particular, the quality of the outlet is assessed by reference to the nature, standing and external appearance of the other shops in the immediate neighbourhood and the facade, shop window size and decoration, sales area, lighting, floor, furniture, fixtures and fittings of the shop. If another activity is carried on in the retail outlet, the eligibility of the application for the opening of an account is also assessed in the light of the scale of such other activity, the external and internal presentation and separation of the two activities and the competence of the staff allocated to the sale of Yves Saint Laurent products." The supplier's right to determine de facto a large number of the appearance-related elements of the retail store was largely backed by the Court of First Instance in its judgments, as long as the principles of proportionality and objectivity were respected.

Accordingly, the online counterparts of the abovementioned criteria shall be identified and targeted as lawful criteria. The most clarifying example may be found in the Guidelines, where it is stated that by obliging the retailer not to show the third party platform's logo hosting the former's website, the manufacturer is establishing a lawful quality standard. Considering that this condition is the online counterpart of the criteria governing the area surrounding the retail outlet and its location, and taking into account that the latter was found not to be "inherently covered by Article (101(1)) of the Treaty inasmuch as its purpose is to ensure that such products are not sold in totally unsuitable premises", all other conditions regarding interior design, external appearance, or the sale of other goods should be considered as not causing major competition concerns.

3.2 Brand content and designs developed by product suppliers

Online marketing often implies the use of technical and virtual brand content and designs developed by the product manufacturer that may be transferred to and used by authorised retailers in their websites under license. Like physical store requirements (e.g., location, lighting, etc.), website or brand section designs can be modified to match these suppliers' standards; brand content implementation might take for instance the form of a brand owner directly developing an average website from a path URL and transmitting it entirely — including sub-path URLs, links, etc. — to the authorised retailers. Both principles of objectivity and proportionality will have to be respected in order to find the appropriate balance in the license agreement giving access and allowing the use of the brand content to the retailer.

The purpose of this reasoning is to identify the main advantages that a retailer can obtain by complying with the standards and the designs made by the supplier. Firstly, it may be asserted that by adopting the manufacturer's standards and designs, the authorised retailer will introduce its website store into the list of authorised websites that may be identified as so by the user. This includes sharing the same structure, quality images and text, official high-quality pictures, and other material of interest. Secondly, and by doing so, the authorised retailer is taking advantage of all the effort and investments carried out by the manufacturer on marketing and promotion, and adopts the results in order to achieve more sales. Third, the manufacturer's structure enhances the website as a whole, and its design or display may inspire other sections managed by the retailer.

Consequently, some authorised retailers may consider the benefits of sharing with other authorised retailers a common and easily recognizable interface that ensures a high quality experience.

3.3 Benefits to consumers

Finally, it must be recalled that quality standards set on online commerce may create similar benefits as standards set on off-line commerce, already accepted by the Commission. Firstly, in order to ensure consumers the choice between mass and luxury of their wish, which entails that "the luxury product will not become an everyday product as a result of a downgrading of its image", the product supplier shall take account of the essential characteristics of a retailer's online store. It shall be borne in mind that product commoditization may not only be caused by mass sales made through undesired channels in physical stores, but can also overcome due to mass online sales carried out through non-specialized or unsuitable websites. In this regard, marketing a luxury product through a second-hand website may have similar commoditizing effects as selling the same product in an unequipped and bad poorly located retail store; the average consumer understands so.

Secondly, the Commission observed that selective distribution systems have "the effect of focusing on factors of competition other than the price, such as the provision of an advisory service for customers and the constant availability of the essential products in the ranges [...]." Needless to say that these factors can and shall be transposed to the online commerce sector in order to ensure the consistency of selective distribution networks. Moreover, other factors of competition that benefit consumers may be included to in this list, such as the implementation of a security payment tool to conclude online transactions, or the creation of subject-specific web pages within a brand site to explain the background and history of a determined product.

4. Conclusion

While formulating the updated regime on Vertical Restraints, the Commission has taken a strong pro-internet stance. Some of the provisions regarding online sales certainly require further clarification; also, more thought should have been given to the question whether the Guidelines are the right legal instrument for regulating some of the abovementioned issues.

By allowing retailers to market their products online, it is certain that undertakings will want to establish more elaborate qualitative standards regulating this channel. Consequently, some more extended guidance of the Commission in its Guidelines as to how the principle of overall equivalence shall be applied by undertakings and the authorities would have been welcomed. The latter may well come from the enforcement at European National level and the European Competition Network Policy. The overall equivalence principle, although ambiguous, might be a workable and long-standing legal concept in this field that authorities and judges can modulate and enforce. A thorough analysis of the means through which quality monitoring could take place proves it to be proportionate, feasible and highly rewarding to both retailers and consumers. Nevertheless, the scope of interference of suppliers into the retailer's website may be regarded by the authorities as being too high. Technological developments might also change the outcome of legal interpretations.

Given that there are a number of amendments to the original vBER, companies will in any case have to review and reassess their existing distribution contracts. Against the background of the new hardcore restrictions and uncertainties surrounding some of the other amendments, the updated vBER might actually be a challenge requiring sophisticated planning for businesses which take a careful antitrust approach but want to also benefit from the competitive efficiencies involved in some vertical restrictions.

CHAPTER IV

AN ECONOMIC APPROACH
TO THE NEW RULES FOR VERTICAL RESTRAINTS

Nikolaos Vettas

Professor, Department of Economics
Athens University of Economics and Business

1. Introduction

Vertical relations refer to all types of relations among firms that act relative to one another as buyers and sellers of goods or services. These may be relations between wholesalers and retailers, or relations that involve the sale of inputs or intermediate products or services that are, in turn, transformed into final goods. Such vertical relations can be classified into two main categories, the first being vertical integration, or in other words vertical mergers (including vertical acquisitions), and the second being vertical agreements (or "restraints") between otherwise independent firms. In this article we examine vertical agreements, not vertical mergers.

Although our focus is on agreements between independent firms, one of our main arguments in this article is that thinking of vertical agreements within the more general context of vertical relations is a very fruitful way to position the issue, since most — if not all — types of vertical agreements are incomplete forms of vertical integration. We argue, therefore, that the treatment of vertical agreements in the law should recognize this fact, rather than following a more formalistic approach that would tend to view such agreements as dangerous unless proven otherwise. Emphasis is also given to the fact that such vertical agreements often tend to lead to significant efficiency gains, as they occur between trade partners (and not between competitors, like horizontal agreements). We also argue that an economics approach should be followed in the analysis of vertical agreements, emphasizing that any such agreement (or the absence thereof) modifies the "rules of the game". In other words, such agreements are expected to change how firms compete with one another, their equilibrium profit levels and the implications for the final consumer and for social welfare in the market.

Our particular focus is on agreements that fall within Article 101 of the Treaty on the Functioning of the European Union (TFEU), that is, agreements where the 'upstream' and the 'downstream' firms involved do not need to have a dominant position in their markets. We discuss the revision of the relevant Block Exemption Regulation (BER), applicable to vertical agreements, which was adopted by the European Commission on June 1, 2010, and the new Guidelines that accompany the revised BER. We do not present the details of the revision since there are now some high quality presentations of the main changes, including several articles in the present volume.

Our attention is mainly given to a discussion of these changes from the viewpoint of an economic analysis. We also place the recent revision within the context of the overall framework for vertical agreements, as it has been developed in the last years. We argue that the revision has moved in the right direction, providing some clearly needed simplifications of the framework and various clarifications that will improve the applicability of the law in the future and help avoid possible complications. However, we also argue that the revision could have been more drastic, and should have recognized that it is extremely unlikely that any type of vertical agreements among small enough firms will be harmful for competition. Taking also into consideration that vertical agreements may often also have significant pro-competitive effects, when all the firms involved have a small enough market share one could essentially favour a *de minimis* approach that would include any vertical agreement. Perhaps, such an approach can be adopted in a possible future revision of the BER.

The article is structured as follows. Section II offers an introduction to the basic economic analysis behind vertical relations, explaining some positive and negative implications for competition policy. Section III focuses on the related legislation and the new Block Exemption Regulation (BER) applicable to vertical agreements in the EC and the revised accompanying Guidelines. In Section IV, we discuss in some more detail the new BER, examining both its positive aspects and areas where additional improvement relative to the old Regulation could have been possible and where perhaps further improvement may be possible in the future. Section V concludes.

2. An introduction to the economics of vertical relations

It is useful to start by reviewing briefly some of the basic economic arguments in the area of vertical agreements and in that of vertical relations more generally. Along a "vertical chain" we view the vertically linked firms as the producer and the retailer, or the buyer and the seller, or more abstractly as the 'upstream' and the 'downstream' firm. Vertical chains differ in many ways: whether there are two or more stages before reaching the final consumer, whether firms are vertically separated (independent) or vertically integrated (one firm that operates both upstream and downstream, with the goal of maximizing its joint profit), and whether trade is exclusive (with an exclusive supplier or exclusive buyer or both) or more than one firm is actively trading at each stage.

Trade between vertically linked firms may take a simple form, where a single price per unit of quantity sold is arranged, that is, we have 'linear pricing' or the relationship may be a more complex one, in which case the need arises in competition policy to study more carefully these 'vertical agreements'. These include 'nonlinear' pricing schemes, such as two-part tariffs, quantity discounts, royalty payments and rebates and also other forms of 'vertical restraints', such as Resale Price Maintenance (RPM), dictating the price at which the buyer will sell the good further down the vertical chain and various types of exclusivity.

Under vertical separation and linear pricing, that is when we have a constant price for each additional unit sold, vertical separation leads to higher final product prices than those we would have under vertical integration (VI). This is a key result in the economics literature, known formally since Spengler (1950). To see this point let us consider a simple vertical market structure with one upstream firm (U) and one downstream firm (D). Firm U's product is sold to firm D, which in turn (re)sells to the final consumers (possibly after some further processing). Let us assume that the U firm sets the price when it sells its product to firm D and that the D firm sets its price when it sells to the final consumers.

This fundamental double marginalization argument relies on the assumption that each firm is independent from the other, in the sense that it seeks to maximize its own profit and not that of the entire chain. The key result that one obtains when working out the equilibrium pricing decision by all parties in this model, a central result in the vertical relations literature, is that this process of double marginalization leads to prices for the final consumers that are ever higher than the prices that would emerge under a vertically integrated monopoly. In this sense, two monopolies, one at each stage, produce a worse outcome than a single, vertically integrated, monopoly. Given that the monopoly profit is by definition the maximum profit attainable in any market arrangement, it also follows that with independent sellers at each stage of the vertical chain, in other words under vertical separation, the aggregate profits (the sum of profits of firm D and firm U) will be strictly below the profit in the vertically integrated case. Thus, in this case, vertical separation with linear pricing hurts both the consumers and the firms, while vertical integration will benefit all parties involved in this market. The main logic behind this result is that independent firms fail to internalize the vertical externality that exists in their pricing — in particular, the U firm does not internalize the impact that an increase in its own price will have on the final price for the consumers.

As should be apparent from the above discussion, one possible solution to this "double marginalization problem" would be vertical integration. This would improve the situation, moving the market back to a simple, single stage monopoly that covers both stages of the market. Importantly, however, the double marginalization problem can also be eliminated (or in any event, greatly diminished) if alternative, "nonlinear", pricing schemes are used instead of linear pricing, like two-part tariff arrangements. Under such arrangements, if for example the per-unit price is set at the competitive level (cost) and the fixed fee is set a little lower than the total monopoly profit, the exact monopoly solution can be recovered, without having formally a vertical integration arrangement. Another way to solve the double marginalization problem in this case would be some vertical restriction, in particular RPM that would fix the final market price at the monopoly level.

Also note that the double marginalization situation changes if we allow the D firm to have all the price-setting power, or bargaining power, against both the final consumers and the U firm. In such a setting, only one profit margin can be applied and there is no additional distortion (relative to the standard monopoly one). Finally, when the D firm is able to participate in setting the price at which it transacts with the U firm, the formal or informal bargaining procedure that is expected to take place between the U and the D firm would restrict the market power of the U firm and would lead to the internalization, at least partially, of the final market price considerations. As a result, the final price will be lower in the equilibrium of the game when the bargaining power is balanced between the U and the D firm, or when the D firm is more powerful than the U firm.

In most real world markets, of course, one encounters much richer vertical structures than the simple vertical one-supplier- one-distributor chain. As a result, in addition to the basic vertical double marginalization effect discussed above, we may also have horizontal externalities, arising in the competition among several wholesalers, or several retailers within a single vertical chain, a phenomenon that we could call 'intra-brand' competition. This emerges when one or more suppliers trades with more than one distributor. In such cases, it is not only the vertical strategic interaction between suppliers and distributors that matters, but also all the horizontal relations.

In cases where only intra-brand competition downstream is important, nonlinear pricing schemes or other vertical restraints could be effective in 'softening' the competition in the final market and maximizing the suppliers' (upstream) profits. In the case of a two-part tariff, the wholesale price level may control the horizontal externality and soften competition between the distributors, while profit may be shorted upstream in the form of a fixed fee. RPM, or other resale restrictions set by the supplier, such as restrictions on the retailers' discretion to set a price, or restrictions imposing that each retailer only deals with a part of the final demand, in a territorial or other sense, could also lead to higher downstream prices and higher profit for the entire chain.

The analysis becomes even more complicated, and the final market outcome harder to predict, when there is both 'intra-brand' and 'inter-brand' competition. In such cases, when there are two or more suppliers trading with two or more distributors, some of the trading agreements can be exclusive, either in one or in both directions of trade, and others not. In such setups, controlling the horizontal externality among its own distributors may not be as important a consideration for a supplier, as competition with the rival supplier. Figure 1 presents a typical such scenario, where we assume that there are two large upstream and two large downstream firms. In the particular situation presented, U2 sells exclusively to D1, D2 buys exclusively from U1, however, U1 sells to both retailers and D1 buys from both suppliers.

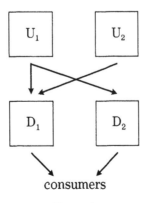

consumers

Figure 1.

It is also important to note that final consumers do not only care about the prices at which they buy the products, but also about the ease of access, quality and variety of these products. These other aspects typically depend on actions taken by all parties involved along the vertical chain. Ensuring a particular level of quality or variety typically requires the effective collaboration of all these parties, upstream and downstream. If such collaboration cannot be ensured, product quality will be below the optimal level, not only from the viewpoint of the final consumers, but also from that of the vertical chain. Related effects may be particularly important for products, the sale of which depends on a high quality reputation. When a manufacturer seeks to establish a strong 'brand name', but can only reach the final consumer via a set of retailers, then it is reasonable that both price and non-price aspects of the entire distribution system may have to be appropriately controlled. 'Spillovers' or informational externalities play a crucial role here. As the cost associated with assuring high quality is not fully 'internalized' by each independent distributor, the market will tend to provide in general sub-optimal quality. Strict rules for controlling the behaviour of retailers that collaborate with the seller may have to be set for each product sold, and resale may have to be controlled through a selective or otherwise restrictive distribution system.

A closely related issue is that of specific investments by suppliers or by distributors. The effective supply of a product or service to the final consumer often requires investments that are specific to the particular transacting pair of supplier and distributor, offering again a rationale for vertical integration or vertical restrictions to neutralize the threat of 'opportunistic' behaviour or 'hold-up' by either party. The key point about specific investments is that their market value tends to be significantly lower than their value for the given pair of trading buyer and seller. Since vertical integration may be an extreme and costly solution, especially due to high administrative or other managerial costs, other appropriate measures will have to be taken to solve the problem, specified in vertical agreements. A comparison between the pros and cons of vertical integration would effectively determine the vertical boundaries of the firm.

Resale price maintenance (RPM) is a common vertical restraint which has received much attention in competition policy. The economics literature has concluded that there are both anti-competitive and pro-competitive effects from the use of RPM. We provide such an analysis in the EAGCP 2010 report Hardcore restrictions under the Block Exemption Regulation on vertical agreements: An economic view, by Massimo Motta, Patrick Rey, Frank Verboven and Nikolaos Vettas, Economic Advisory Group in Competition Policy, submitted to the EC, DG-Competition. On the one hand a possible anti-competitive effect could be related to the solution of the 'commitment problem' of a monopolist, which would impede even a monopolistic supplier from enjoying full monopoly profits, because this supplier would have the temptation to reduce the wholesale price set to one distributor to allow that distributor to expand its market share, even when this hurts rival distributors of the same product. A market-wide RPM if it is credible to all parties could solve this problem because it could prevent this opportunistic behaviour on the part of the supplier. RPM may also possibly soften competition when two or more suppliers sell their products to two or more distributors ('interlocking relationships'). RPM might also facilitate collusion, either among suppliers or among distributors. In particular, collusion among suppliers may be easier to achieve because RPM can help offer a superior monitoring of deviations from the collusive agreement. On the other hand there may be also significant pro-competitive effects, since RPM may help protect necessary specific investments by preventing opportunistic or free-riding behaviour among distributors. It may also help with signalling the quality of products, or help to establish a price reputation and the overall brand image for the supplier's product.

Resale restrictions may be used to limit, geographically or otherwise, the markets in which a certain distributor can operate. These are often essential for a supplier to implement a price discrimination strategy across markets or groups of consumers, so that the supplier can charge different prices at markets where there are different elasticities of demand (in other words, markets across which consumers' willingness to pay differs significantly). This is because, more generally, in order to price discriminate across consumers, firms need to prevent arbitrage, in other words to prevent buying in parts of the market where prices are low and reselling where the prices are high. Thus, to study the effects of territorial or other resale restrictions, one has to study the implied price discrimination. The literature has shown that price discrimination has ambiguous effects on welfare, and that the final net effect depends on various parameters, such as the relative importance of the different types of consumers and the product characteristics. Also, allowing rival oligopolistic firms to price discriminate typically leads to more intense competition among them. As a result, territorial or other resale restrictions have mixed welfare results, from an economics point of view.

In general, we should emphasize that vertical relations in markets refer to completely different economic phenomena than horizontal relations, that is, relations between firms operating in the same market. Along a vertical chain all trading firms have to cooperate with each other, in order for the goods or services to reach the final consumer. In other words, horizontal relations are between firms that sell substitute products, whereas vertical relations are between firms that sell complementary products. Horizontal agreements take place among competitors; thus, it is reasonable to start the analysis from the presumption that competition will be likely harmed, and often significantly so, at least on impact. Vertical agreements, in contrast, do not take place among competitors in the same market and, therefore, there cannot be a presumption that competition will be harmed, except under specific sets of circumstances. One such condition for vertical agreements to be harmful is that at least some of the firms involved already possess some significant market power. The adverse effects for competition emerge indirectly, either through foreclosure of rivals, or because the change in the form or terms of the vertical relation adversely affects the horizontal behaviour of firms in a market.

3. The treatment of vertical agreements in EC competition policy

The early treatment of vertical restrictions in the law, starting in the U.S. and then in Europe, was focused on form and assumed the rather simplistic view that restraints of all types reduce independence in the market, foreclosing seller access to customers or seller access to key inputs. This formalistic approach, dominating the debate at least until the late 1960s, could be simply described as taking the view that as long as a restriction was imposed on market transactions, it reduced the freedom of the market participants. Such a restriction on competition, according to the same logic, could not be desirable. The conclusion of this logic was that these restraints should not be allowed. Very little attention was given to the fact that these vertical agreements are, by their nature, agreements among firms collaborating in the markets and acting in a complementary manner, and not among competitors. For example, the imposition of minimum price RPM by an upstream firm was viewed as almost the same as horizontal price fixing, a view that had not been formally overturned in the U.S. case law until recently.

Since the 1960s the 'Chicago School' approach significantly changed the overall competition policy debate, again starting from the US. As a result the formalistic approach started to become weaker, albeit only gradually. By applying neoclassical economic theory, the 'Chicago School' approach has brought some economic 'discipline' to the overall competition policy analysis. This was particularly true for the treatment of vertical agreements. Competition takes place within markets and not across markets, and as a result it is only horizontal agreements and not vertical ones that can reduce it. The implication for vertical restraints like RPM is that the focus of competition policy should be on protecting and promoting inter-brand competition rather than being preoccupied with intra-brand competition. In addition, when vertical restrictions reduce the choices of a wholesaler or retailer, the benefits from achieved efficiencies must exceed the costs from reduced competition, for that firm to be willing to accept these restrictions in the first place.

The more modern approach to competition policy has been developed in parallel to the emergence of game theory as the language for industrial organization analysis in the 1980s. Contrary to the Chicago view, it has been shown that vertical integration or contractual restrictions could indeed have anticompetitive outcomes, by 'changing the game', in other words by changing the strategies available to the firms and in particular their commitment power. Foreclosure, that is when access to some buyers or suppliers becomes impossible as a result of a merger, an agreement or other action that changes the game, became a central issue in the discussion about vertical relations. Thus, starting from an early stage when vertical restraints were viewed as harmful (the formalistic approach), and then another stage when they were viewed as not harmful (the Chicago school approach), the current status of the academic and policy debate generally recognizes that vertical restraints may be harmful, but only under a particular set of circumstances that should be explicitly described. It is also important to note that whereas a particular vertical agreement may influence adversely a competitor, the impact on competition and on the final consumers may be positive.

An extreme way in which two vertically linked firms can agree to 'cooperate' is a merger between them. The matter of vertical mergers, like other mergers (or acquisitions; more generally 'concentrations') is dealt with by the EC Merger Regulation (Regulation 139/2004). It is important to note that the formal 'Non-Horizontal Merger' Guidelines were only issued in November 2007, following a substantial debate as to whether it was really advisable or even possible to issue such guidelines, due to the complexity and variety of non-horizontal mergers. These Guidelines clearly state that horizontal and vertical mergers are to be approached very differently.

Vertical agreements represent a looser form of vertical cooperation relative to a merger (note that every type of behaviour that is supported by an agreement could also be replicated within a merger). Since such agreements represent a less drastic change in the market structure, they cannot be equally harmful as a corresponding merger. Vertical agreements may involve firms that have a dominant position in the market, upstream or downstream. Then, Article 102 of the Treaty on the Functioning of the European Union (TFEU), ex Article 82 EC Treaty, becomes applicable. Vertical agreements, however, may be subject to legal restrictions, even when they do not involve a firm with a dominant position in its markets. Then Article 101 TFEU, ex Article 81 Treaty EC, becomes applicable.

The 'Modernization of Article 81', has responded to a number of growing concerns, which could be summarized as the view that the Commission should move away from treating vertical restrictions as restrictions to economic freedom, and towards focusing on the efficiency effects of the practices under consideration. The publication of the Commission Regulation No. 2790/1999, on the application of Article 81(3) of the Treaty to certain categories of vertical agreements and concerted practices (Official Journal L 336, 29.12.1999, pp. 21-25), was an important development in the area of vertical relations. This 'Block Exemption Regulation' (BER) was intended to provide a 'safe harbour' to firms with less than a 30% market share and was accompanied by the relevant Guidelines on Vertical Restraints (Official Journal C 291, 13.10.2000, pp. 1-44). The BER has been viewed as the first of a new generation of block exemption regulations and guidelines, inspired by an effects-based approach, and it has been followed by similar reforms in other areas of competition policy. The core of this approach is that, in order to reach an assessment about a given vertical agreement, the precise potential effects of the agreement on the market should be analysed, thus moving away from the old formalistic approach.

The 1999 BER established that article 81(1) does not apply to vertical agreements in which the supplier does not hold more than 30% market share. Since vertical agreements are likely to harm welfare only if the firms using them possess substantial market power, Competition Authorities should not use their scarce resources to monitor vertical agreements entered into by firms with small market power. Such firms should benefit from a safe harbour which guarantees legality of their vertical agreements. The BER (in its Article 4) also stated that the exemption should not apply to some vertical agreements that the Commission considered harmful. These 'black-listed' — or 'hardcore' — clauses include in particular RPM (more precisely resale price fixing and minimum resale price) and vertical clauses which aim at restricting 'active' sales from one territory to the other. Vertical agreements containing such hardcore restrictions were not exempted from the application of Article 81(1), even if the firms concerned had an arbitrarily small market share, since the *de minimis* Notice (2001/C 368/07) does not apply to such hardcore restrictions. Moreover, according to the 1999 Guidelines, paragraph 46, "Individual exemption of vertical agreements containing such hardcore restrictions is also unlikely", thus implying a regime which is in practice very close to *per se* prohibition for these black-listed restrictions.

With the BER bound to expire in May 2010, the Commission proceeded to a review and revision process. Along with the new Guidelines on Vertical Restraints (2010/C 130/01), the new BER came into force on June 1, 2010 and will be valid until 2022, with a one-year transitional phase. As it was judged that the old BER had worked reasonably well overall, there were no drastic changes in the new BER. The revisions could be described as proceeding to a 'modernisation' of the Regulation where that was appropriate, as well as offering some needed clarifications.

The most significant change in the new BER is that it is no longer enough (for a vertical agreement to fall under the block exemption) that the seller's relevant market share does not exceed 30%, but also that the market share of the associated buyer does not exceed 30% in the same market. This change reflects the increased recognition that vertical contracts are not determined by the sellers alone. In a market where there is a strong buyer, this buyer may possess market power which could be used to impose certain types of vertical agreements that could have an anticompetitive effect.

Additional revisions, which in general can be viewed as positive, include the following. The rule that an agreement would be exempt, under the BER, when the turnover of a competitor who acted as a distributor was below EUR 100 million has been changed.

Also, the requirement of 'dual distribution' (i.e. the requirement that the buyer is active only in the distribution market) for an agreement to be exempt under the BER has now been extended to services markets, whereas previously this requirement was only applicable to product markets. Also for agency agreements to be considered genuine and therefore to fall outside Article 101(1), the 'principal' in the trading relation must bear the costs and the risk not only of the specific agreement, but also the ones related to other activities that it requires the 'agent' to undertake in the same market.

Like in its old version, the new BER contains a list of restrictions that are 'black-listed'. The black list includes RPM and other (that is, non price) resale restrictions. These are viewed as hard-core violations that represent serious restrictions of competition and the view is taken that there should be a presumption in the EC law that they should be prohibited. Specifically, according to Paragraph 47 of the Guidelines, if an agreement contains a 'black listed' restriction, then there are two consequences: the agreement presumptively falls within the scope of prohibited agreements under Article 101(1) as having actual or likely negative effects; and it presumptively does not satisfy the justification standards of Article 101(3). This means that once a hardcore restriction is established, the agreement is presumptively both anticompetitive and unjustifiable. Still, it is recognized that this double presumption is rebuttable and the parties can bring forward evidence that the positive effects of the agreement under examination outweigh the presumed negative effects.

Regarding minimum price and fixed price RPM, in particular, the new Guidelines offer a detailed exposition about evidence that could be put forward in RPM cases. Specifically, Paragraph 224 of the Guidelines describes various possible ways in which RPM may restrict competition, whereas Paragraph 225 states that justifications will be considered and that the possible efficiencies will be assessed under Article 101(3). Similar to RPM, regarding Resale Restrictions, the BER generally does not cover agreements that restrict the buyer's ability to sell in some territories or to some consumers the goods or services that the agreement refers to. However, there are a number of important exceptions, where such restrictions are not considered hard-core, like in the old BER. The two most important ones are systems of 'exclusive distribution' and 'selective distribution'. Regarding exclusive distribution, a supplier is allowed to protect an exclusive distributor from active sales by other distributors in those specified as exclusive territory or consumer groups. The new Guidelines also clarify that the exclusive distribution is covered by the BER, even when the supplier itself is also selling directly to the customers in the territory or consumer group otherwise treated as exclusive for some distributors. However, a restriction on passive sales, that is responding to unsolicited requests from customers outside the specified territory or consumer group, would be considered a hard-core restriction. Regarding selective distribution, the BER allows suppliers to have a selective distribution system, where distributors are selected according to some specified criteria.

4. Discussion of the 2010 revision of the Block Exemption Regulation and Guidelines

As discussed above, the overall logic of the BER is correct. For vertical agreements, in contrast to horizontal ones, there cannot be in general a presumption that they harm competition. This is because vertical agreements do not occur among competitors, but among firms that in any event have to collaborate in the market for the products or services to reach the final consumers. The 2010 revision has rightly maintained the general structure of the previous BER, offering a modernization and some useful clarifications and simplifications. The fundamental logic of the BER, to allow firms with a market share that is not too high to use vertical agreements as they wish, has appeared to be working well enough and is not expected to create problems in the future. Keeping the relevant market share threshold at 30% also appears satisfactory, since not only firms with a market share high enough to be considered dominant, but also firms with sizeable market power do not automatically benefit from an exemption. At the same time, it ensures that firms with low market power enjoy legal certainty which is important for the overall planning of their business strategies.

From an economics viewpoint, the main aspects of the 2010 revision of the BER can be classified in two categories. First, the new BER offers a clarification and a modified approach to particular issues of competition policy implementation that had emerged. Second, it has moved more decidedly ahead, better acknowledging the efficiency gains that could arise from all types of vertical restraints.

First, the most important of the implementation-type changes is that the benefit of the block exemption no longer depends only on the supplier's market share, but also on the buyer's market share: neither of these two market shares can now exceed 30% for the exemption to apply. This approach seems to be in the right direction, given that in practice the buyers can often be as powerful as sellers, or even more powerful. Vertical restraints need not generally be imposed by the suppliers: strong buyers can also use their market power to impose anticompetitive vertical restraints. From a practical viewpoint, of course, we can expect some problems when it comes to implementation. Accurately calculating the market share of a buyer may not always be easy or even feasible for a seller, and of course the accuracy of market definition becomes even more crucial than before.

Another change is about restrictions on the use of the Internet for trade. This change also seems in the right direction and both the BER and the Guidelines now describe in more detail how one can distinguish between 'active' and 'passive' sales in the case of Internet sales. Thus, assuming that one does wish to distinguish between active and passive sales, the revision appears useful since online sales have become increasingly more important, since the old BER was initially enacted. One could argue however that, from the viewpoint of an economist, it is not really clear why active and passive sales should be treated differently in the law, since both have the same effect: more uniform prices across markets. Furthermore, whether in a particular market price uniformity or price discrimination implies higher consumer welfare, depends crucially on the market conditions, including the actions and reactions of other firms. As a result, it may be more appropriate in the future to move away from the active versus passive sales distinction, which may be too formalistic and to some extent arbitrary. Instead, it may be preferable to use a more 'effects-based' approach, according to which the treatment of firms that use territorial restrictions would depend on the market share they hold and the possible efficiency justifications associated with such restrictions.

Second, the new BER better acknowledges the efficiency gains that possibly result from all types of vertical restraints, including these in the hard-core list. The language in the Guidelines generally appears now more supportive of the view that firms should be free to select their own distribution strategies, including the use of various kinds of vertical agreements, and that consumers can benefit from these, especially when firms do not have high market power. This is also a step in the right direction.

One could, however, make some remarks regarding aspects of the revision that have not been as drastic and clear as perhaps they should have been. These refer both to the specific treatment of the 'black listed' or 'hard-core' restraints, but also to its more general logic. Let us start the discussion from the specifics of Article 4. Regarding RPM, and relative to the old one, the new BER makes a step towards more fully acknowledging the potential efficiency gains that can follow from this practice, somewhat similar to the recent trend in the U.S. However, the BER continues to place in the 'black list' a number of vertical restraints that are considered 'hard core', including minimum and fixed price RPM and other resale restrictions. It would have been a good idea to consider a change in this policy that would allow small enough firms when trading with other small firms to use any type of vertical agreement. Regarding RPM, economic analysis has shown that it could have both anti-competitive and pro-competitive effects. For the anti-competitive effects to be possible, the suppliers should be endowed with considerable market power. Therefore, it is likely that such effects could be overlooked if suppliers and their buyers have small enough market shares. Such a *de minimis* treatment of all vertical agreements appears appropriate.

More generally, it also appears appropriate that EC competition policy and law now moves still further and more decisively away from the old formalistic approach that would view various types of vertical restraints as suspicious. The idea here is that, contrary to the old view, according to which any restriction would be considered harmful for competition, since by definition it would be restricting the actions of some market participants (sellers or buyers), a more modern approach should be effects-based and not form-based. Careful analysis should indicate what would be the precise type of harm caused by any type of vertical restriction used. Restrictions modify the 'game' played among oligopolistic firms and the strategies available to them — as a result, the equilibrium properties of such a game could be significantly modified if some restriction could or could not be used. Of course that would have significant implications for profit levels, prices and consumer welfare.

It would also be useful to recognize that vertical agreements are incomplete forms of vertical integration. Every type of behaviour that is supported by an agreement could essentially also be replicated within a merger between the two parties involved. It remains a question, if two parties can be allowed to have a vertical merger why they cannot have any type of vertical agreement between them. Take an example where a supplier and retailer each have such a small market share and small enough overall market power that it would not even be conceivable to block a vertical merger between them. If a merger has taken place, and given that the merged entity is not in a dominant position, then the vertically integrated firm could sell anywhere and at any price it chooses, with no restrictions in its behaviour whatsoever. If the two firms have remained independent entities, why would it be a good idea to view any agreement between them as presumably anti-competitive?

Let us consider RPM as a leading example for the discussion just above. As discussed earlier, the economics literature has shown that the use of RPM could have either positive or negative competitive effects, depending on the overall market conditions. Despite the progress made in the revision, in both the old and the new version of the BER, RPM is viewed by the Commission as detrimental for competition, enough so that it should be treated as a hard-core restriction and that the usual order in bringing forward evidence should be reversed. The Commission here appears to be following a form-based approach, stating that since fixed or lower price RPM restricts the ability of retailers to sell at a lower price than the one dictated by the RPM, this represents an obvious way in which consumers are harmed, by facing higher prices in the market.

Certainly, RPM could have serious enough anti-competitive effects (even when the parties involved are not dominant). However, such a position, by essentially focusing on protecting intra-brand competition independently from inter-brand competition, does not appear to be fully taking into consideration how changes in the overall strategies of the firms involved, could possibly affect consumer welfare, directly or indirectly. In other words, a much preferable approach would be to study the overall effect of using RPM in a particular market. To make this point clearer, since the prices (upstream and downstream), the quality and the other product characteristics are decided endogenously by the competing firms, it is possible that removing the ability of some firms to use RPM will lead to an inferior overall market outcome. For instance, it may be that the use of RPM by small firms is essential for their ability to penetrate markets otherwise dominated by stronger competitors. Also, it may be that the wholesale prices that will prevail in the market when RPM cannot be used are higher than the wholesale prices when RPM is possible and, as a result, the final (retail) prices may be lower under RPM. In addition, of course, even if RPM may lead to higher prices, it may also allow the provision of greater variety and higher quality of products in the markets, for instance through the provision of better services.

5. Conclusion

In this article we have discussed the new (2010) vertical agreements Block Exempt Regulation that exempts from Article 102 TFEU most types of vertical agreements between firms that do not have too high a market share. We take an economics view in our analysis and make a number of specific points. These can be summarised as follows. First, the overall logic of the BER is correct; for vertical agreements, in contrast with horizontal ones, there cannot be, in general, a presumption that they harm competition, since they do not occur among competitors. The revision is also in the right direction; it has offered clarifications and simplifications in areas where they were needed and it has also taken overall a more positive stand relative to various types of agreements.

However, we also argue that the revision could have gone further in various respects, in particular to recognize that even some types of currently 'black-listed' restraints (like RPM and other resale restrictions) cannot be expected to have a negative net impact on competition, unless one or more of the parties involved has a large enough market share. Thus, a *de minimis* approach can be justified, even for such restraints, and such an approach could be considered in future possible revisions. Second, the overall approach of this BER, by its nature, appears to be a legacy of the old formalistic approach to competition policy, where certain types of restraints were viewed as suspicious and presumably anticompetitive. The general logic of the modernization could be pushed further, so that economic analysis is used to establish that harm can be expected, before some type of a vertical restraint can be viewed as suspicious. Vertical agreements are incomplete forms of vertical integration and may have a positive or a negative effect, depending on the market conditions. To reach a conclusion, an analysis would be needed that would take into account how the strategic incentives of the firms and the overall market equilibrium would change as a result of the use of a given agreement.

PART TWO

KEY ISSUES

CHAPTER V

THE NOTION OF AGREEMENT IN A VERTICAL CONTEXT: PIECES OF A SLIDING PUZZLE

ERIC GIPPINI-FOURNIER

Member of the Legal Service
*European Commission**

The *summa divisio* between horizontal and vertical agreements attends to the existence or lack of a direct competitive relationship between the undertakings participating in the agreement. As is usually the case with theoretical distinctions, reality does not always fit neatly in one of the ready-made boxes. Undertakings may at the same time be competitors and be in a vertical relationship, or may change roles over time. Nevertheless, for the purposes of our discussion the issues can be simplified. A vertical agreement, typically between a manufacturer and its distributors, brings together firms active at different levels of the same chain of production, distribution and/or service.

The question as to the existence of an "agreement" has traditionally presented itself differently in horizontal and vertical relationships. Horizontal cartels practically always raise issues of proof of facts which participants strive to keep secret. In typical vertical cases the facts are comparatively less clandestine and the issues, if any, concern the boundaries of the very notion of an agreement as opposed to purely unilateral conduct.

---

* Member of the Legal Service, European Commission; Lecturer, Université de Tours. I thank Ewa Drewniak for helpful research assistance. The views expressed are personal and not those of the European Commission or its Legal Service. Mistakes and omissions are the author's own.

1. General considerations on the notion of agreement

1.1 The case law

The Court of Justice has held that, for there to be an agreement within the meaning of Article 101(1) TFUE, it is sufficient for the undertakings in question to have expressed their joint intention to conduct themselves in the market in a particular way.[2]

An agreement does not have to be made in writing; no formalities are necessary, and no contractual sanctions or enforcement measures are required. Article 101 has been applied to agreements which were written, but not signed by the parties;[3] to standard agreements which had not been individually negotiated;[4] to "gentleman's agreements";[5] to purely oral agreements.[6] The fact of agreement may be express or implicit in the behaviour of the parties. This does not mean that a concerted practice will also constitute an agreement, nor is there any confusion with the notion that a restrictive agreement may have had an "effect" on the market. It simply means that, in case of doubt, the actual behaviour of the parties may be an element of proof of the existence of an agreement or its exact meaning.[7]

The legal status of the agreement is irrelevant. In order to constitute an agreement within the meaning of Article 101 it is sufficient that a provision is the expression of the intention of the parties, without its being necessary

---

2   Case 41/69, *Chemiefarma vs. Commission*, [1970] ECR 661, paragraph 112; Cases 209 to 215 and 218/78, *Van Landewyck vs. Commission*, [1980] ECR 3125, paragraph 86; Case T-7/89 *Hercules vs. Commission* [1991] ECR II-1711, paragraph 256; Case T-208/01, *Volkswagen vs. Commission*, [2003] ECR II-5141, paragraph 30.

3   Commission Decision (79/934/EEC) of 5 September 1979(IV/29.021 — BP Kemi-DDSF), O.J. L 286, of 14.11.1979, p. 32, paragraph 27.

4   Commission Decision (70/332/CEE) of 30 June 1970 (IV/24055 — Kodak), O.J. L 147, of 7.07.1970, p. 24, paragraph 14; Commission Decision (77/66/EEC) of 22 December 1976 (IV/24.510 — GERO-fabriek), O.J. L 16, of 19.01.1977, p. 8, point II.a.2.

5   See e.g. the Quinine cartel case, *Chemiefarma vs. Commission*, *supra* note; Case T-141/89, *Tréfileurope Sales SARL vs. Commission*, [1995] ECR II-791, paragraph 96; Commission Decision (2000/118/EC) of 26 October 1999 (IV/33.884 — Nederlandse Federatieve Vereniging voor de Groothandel op Elektrotechnisch Gebied und Technische Unie (FEG and TU)), O.J. L 39 of 14.2.2000, p. 1, paragraph 100.

6   See Commission Decision (77/129/EEC) of 21 December 1976 (IV/28.812 Theal/Watts), O.J. L 39, of 10.02.1977, p. 19, and Case 28/77, *Tepea vs. Commission*, [1978] ECR 1391, paragraphs 11, 17.

7   See e.g. Commission Decision (95/477/EC) of 12 July 1995 (Case IV/33.802 — BASF Lacke+Farben AG, and Accinauto SA), O.J. L 272, of 15.11.1995, p. 16, paragraph 71, confirmed by the Court of First Instance in Case T-176/95, *Accinauto SA vs. Commission*, [1999] ECR II-1635, paragraphs 63, 64 et seq, 83-93.

for it to constitute a valid and binding contract under national law.[8] This applies not only to contract law, but also to other provisions of national law having a bearing on the validity or enforceability of the agreement.[9] Indeed, if the agreement falls foul of the prohibition of Article 101(1) and does not fulfil the conditions of Article 101(3), its legal status will always be that provided for in Article 101(2): automatically void. The *goals* sought by the arrangement are also irrelevant to its qualification as an agreement.[10] Even litigation settlements may be subject to scrutiny under Article 101.[11] This may include also settlements approved by a national court to make them enforceable.[12] The extent to which the agreement is applied, or even whether it is actually applied at all, does not exclude its qualification as an agreement.[13]

1.2 The blurry boundary with the other elements of Article 101(1)

In borderline cases, the notion of agreement cannot comfortably be dissociated from the other conditions of application of article 101 TFEU. It is not enough to say that an "agreement" involves a "concurrence of wills". In difficult cases, passing judgment on the existence of an "agreement" often requires a complete view on *whose* wills are involved and *what* has been agreed. These are in theory the domain of other conditions of Article 101: the notion of undertaking and the restriction of competition.

---

8   Case C-277/87, *Sandoz vs. Commission*, [1990] ECR I-45, paragraph 13; *Van Landewyck vs. Commission, supra* note.

9   See Case C-376/92 Cartier [1994] ECR I-15, paragraph 24; Case C-41/96, V*AG-Händlerbeirat eV vs. SYD-Consult*, [1997] ECR I-3123, paragraphs 11-15, and the Opinions of Advocate General Tesauro in both Cartier, at paragraphs 11-23, and VAG, at paragraph 11. These cases concerned the issue whether the 'Imperviousness' (Lückenlosigkeit) of a distribution system as a precondition for its enforceability against third parties under German case-law had any bearing on the applicability of Article 101. See R. Kovar, Le dernier métro — L'étanchéité des réseaux de distribution: un réseau peut être ouvert ou fermé, in La Semaine Juridique — Édition Entreprise, 1994, Suppl. No. 4, p. 2 et seq., contra Bechtold, Ende des Erfordernisses der Lückenlosigkeit, in Neue Juristische Wochenschrift, 1994, p. 3211 et seq.

10 See e.g. Joined Cases 96/82 to 102/82, 104/82, 105/82, 108/82 and 110/82 *IAZ and Others vs. Commission* [1983] ECR 3369, paragraph 25.

11 Case 65/86, *Bayer vs. Sülhöffer*, [1988] ECR 5249, paragraph 15 ("[i]*n its prohibition of certain "agreements" between undertakings, Article [101] (1) makes no distinction between agreements whose purpose is to put an end to litigation and those concluded with other aims in mind*").

12 See Case 258/78, Nungesser, [1982] ECR 2015, paragraphs 80-89.

13 See e.g. Commission Decision 2000/627/EC of 16 May 2000 (IV/34.018), Far East Trade Tariff Charges and Surcharges Agreement (FETTCSA), O.J. L 268, of 20.10.2000, p. 1, paragraph 135.

An agreement is only relevant for competition law purposes where it involves a commitment as to future behaviour, whether explicit or implicit, legal or moral. Agreements matter because they "tie down the future".[14] EU competition law is concerned only with agreements which result in a commitment to future market conduct,[15] i.e. those where one party binds itself, whether expressly or tacitly, to act on the market in the future in a certain manner, or to abstain from acting in a certain manner, restricting its choices in future dealings with third parties. This is why a spot transaction, for example where a seller agrees to provide a product and the buyer agrees to pay a given price, is typically outside the scope of Article 101. Such commercial transactions do not bind the parties in any manner as to their future market behaviour in dealing with others.

The notion of "commitment to future action or abstention" is not the end of the story. An undertaking's commitment must relate to its own offer of goods or services on the market, which I call its *own market function* for lack of a better expression.[16] An internet retailer such as Amazon may contract with transport companies to deliver its products. A furniture store may hire independent contractors to transport and mount cupboards and desks at the customers' premises, and cash the price upon delivery on behalf of the store. Obviously, the suppliers expect –and demand– the carrier to deliver to the designated customer at the price specified, and not to somebody else who is ready to pay more or who costs less to deliver to. There is no question that the carrier is an autonomous undertaking and that he has agreed to deliver the product to a specific customer and collect a fixed amount of money. Yet, we don't call this customer allocation or vertical price fixing, and for good reason. The reason is that the carrier implements a specific function in a specific market, and reselling is not part of it. The carrier is active in the market for transport services, not in the retail sales market. Instructions from the supplier as to the price to collect or the customers to serve do not concern the carrier's economic activity, but the supplier's.

The Court has tackled this issue in the context of agency relationships, and its recent case law has resolved them through recourse to the notion

---

14 O. Odudu, The Boundaries of EC Competition Law — The Scope of Article 81 (2006), p. 82.

15 See e.g. Cases C-7/95 P, *John Deere Ltd vs. Commission*, [1998] ECR I-3111, paragraph 88; C-194/99 P, *Thyssen Stahl AG vs. Commission*, [2003] ECR I-10821, paragraph 89; T-49/02 to T-51/02, *Brasserie nationale vs. Commission*, [2005] ECR II-3033, paragraph 101.

16 There are undoubtedly exceptions to this principle, as shown by Cases T-99/04, *AC-Treuhand vs. Commission*, [2008] ECR I-1501, paragraphs 122-127, and T-29/05, *Deltafina vs. Commission*, [2010] ECR II-not yet reported. A fuller discussion would exceed the scope of the present contribution.

of "undertaking". In CEES[17] and CEPSA/Tobar,[18] the ECJ had to deal with contracts between petrol stations and their suppliers, which contained clauses concerning resale prices. The Court approached the question by inquiring whether such clauses could be considered as "agreed" between two undertakings. The Court explained that, in a principal-agent relationship, certain clauses should be considered as "instructions" from the principal as to how to conduct business on its behalf; the agent's compliance with such clauses is not to be viewed as the expression of the will of an independent undertaking, since the agent does not act as such when conducting transactions for the principal. While the distinction between a "genuine agent" and an independent distributor is not always clear-cut, the Court implicitly approved the criteria proposed by the Commission in its Vertical Guidelines.[19] These criteria seek to establish whether the supposed "agent" bears the risk of the transactions. The Court enumerated as relevant criteria the ownership of the goods, the contribution to the costs linked to their distribution, their safe-keeping, liability for any damage caused to the goods or by the goods to third parties, and the making of investments specific to the sale of those goods. In the Court's construction, examination of these criteria should provide the answer to the question whether the service-station operators were independent undertakings in relation to the price clauses in the contracts.

This approach is a valid, although slightly artificial, solution to the problem. One may also approach such situations as involving two undertakings but not a true "agreement" because, although there are two undertakings, there are not two independent "wills" to be expressed in relation to price or choice of customer. Since it is the content of the agreement that makes it clear that the "restraints" are not within the scope of Article 101, these agreements may also be viewed as not restricting "competition" in any meaningful sense,[20] the agent not being a competitor in the retail market. The question may be entirely theoretical, as suggested by AG Kokott.[21] Nevertheless, it illustrates how difficult it is sometimes to disentangle the notion of "agreement" from the rest of Article 101, and the need, in vertical

---

17 Case C-217/05, Confederación Española de Empresarios de Estaciones de Servicio, [2006] ECR I-11987, paragraphs 41-46, 60-62, 65. See also the opinion of AG Kokott, paragraphs 43-67.
18 Case C-279/06, CEPSA, [2008] ECR I-6681, paragraphs 35, 40-42, 44.
19 The judgment refers to the previous version of the Vertical Guidelines. Currently, these criteria appear in Commission notice — Guidelines on Vertical Restraints, O.J. C 130 of 19.05.2010, p. 1, paragraphs 12-21.
20 See e.g. the case law cited in footnote above.
21 Opinion of AG Kokott in Case C-217/05, Confederación Española de Empresarios de Estaciones de Servicio, paragraph 51.

relationships, to take a holistic view of the situation, rather than a reductionist one.

The Commission seems to have taken a pragmatic approach and incorporates in its analysis the notions of "commitment to future action of abstention on the market" and "own market function" without ascribing them specifically to one or another of the conditions of Article 101. The Article 101(3) Guidelines state that

> "The type of co-ordination of behaviour or collusion between undertakings falling within the scope of Article [101](1) is that where at least one undertaking vis-à-vis another undertaking undertakes to adopt a certain conduct on the market or that as a result of contacts between them uncertainty as to their conduct on the market is eliminated or at least substantially reduced"[22]

The Regulation on Vertical Restraints defines a "vertical agreement" as one

> "entered into between two or more undertakings each of which operates, for the purposes of the agreement or the concerted practice, at a different level of the production or distribution chain, and relating to the conditions under which the parties may purchase, sell or resell certain goods or services"[23]

These statements, in my view, take a more transparent meaning when considered against the notions of "commitment to future action of abstention on the market" related to the undertaking's "own market function".

2. "Apparently unilateral" measures in vertical relationships

2.1 Traditional case law

It will often be difficult to establish that a "meeting of the minds" has taken place between the distributors and the manufacturer in order to limit sales outside the distribution network, outside an exclusive territory, or as regards resale prices, if these stipulations have not been expressly

---

22 Guidelines on the application of Article 81(3) of the Treaty [now Article 101 TFEU], O.J. C 101, 27.04.2004, p. 97, point 15.

23 Commission Regulation 330/2010 of 20 April 2010 on the application of Article 101(3) of the Treaty on the Functioning of the European Union to categories of vertical agreements and concerted practices, O.J. L 102, 23.4.2010, p. 1 (emphasis added).

formulated in writing. The intrinsic difficulty of proof is compounded by the fact that actual behaviour of the distributors on the market may not always be a reliable indicator, because such restrictions are primarily in the interests of the supplier. Hence the distributors may often attempt not to abide by the agreement.

The Court of Justice has held that sales conditions systematically reproduced on the back of invoices, orders and price lists constitute an "agreement between undertakings" within the meaning of Article 101.[24] When the existence of an "invitation" or "call" by the supplier is established, the remaining issue is the acceptance or "acquiescence" by the distributor. It is sufficient that the reseller accepts, at least tacitly, the restraint which the supplier imposes on him. It has been said that in such a context, an agreement may be found to exist if one party (usually the supplier) sufficiently communicates to the other parties its expectations as to a particular form of conduct and the other parties recognize the consequences of failure to observe the agreement from their own experience, from the experience of others, or from an explicit threat.[25]

Thus, in *Sandoz*, the systematic dispatching by a supplier to his customers of invoices bearing the words "export prohibited" constituted an agreement, and not unilateral conduct. The tacit acceptance by the customers of the conduct adopted by the supplier was attested by renewed orders placed without protest on the same conditions.[26] Similarly, in *Dunlop Slazenger*, unilateral statements by the supplier and subsequent renewal of orders by the customers on identical terms indicated the existence of an agreement.[27] In these cases and many others, even in the absence of an explicit agreement, a tacit agreement can be inferred from unilateral action inserted within the context of continued contractual relationships. Invoices, recommendations, circular letters or instructions, and other commercial correspondence between the supplier and its customers may establish the existence of a tacit agreement. In *Volkswagen*, the Court of

---

24 Joined Cases 32/78, 36/78 to 82/78 *BMW Belgium vs. Commission* [1979] ECR 2435, paragraphs 28-30; Joined Cases 25 and 26/84, *Ford vs. Commission*, [1985] ECR 2725, paragraph 21; Case 75/84 *Metro vs. Commission* ('Metro II') [1986] ECR 3021, paragraphs 72-73; *Sandoz vs. Commission, supra* note, paragraphs 7-12; Case C-70/93, *BMW vs. ALD* [1995] ECR I-3439, paragraphs 16-17.

25 L. Ritter, W. Braun, F. Rawlinson, European Competition Law. A Practitioner's Guide, 2nd ed. 2000, p. 85.

26 Commission Decision (87/409/EEC) of 13 July 1987 (IV/31.741 — Sandoz), O.J. L 222, of 10.08.1987, p. 28, paragraphs 25-28; confirmed in this regard by the Court in *Sandoz vs. Commission, supra* note. See also Case C-279/87 *Tipp-Ex vs. Commission* [1990] ECR I-261.

27 Case T-43/92, *Dunlop Slazenger International Ltd vs. Commission* [1994] ECR II-441, paragraphs 54-55, 60-61.

First Instance restated the law in broad terms. According to the Court, "It is settled law that a call by a motor vehicle manufacturer to its authorised dealers is not a unilateral act which falls outside the scope of Article [101(1)] of the Treaty but is an agreement within the meaning of that provision if it forms part of a set of continuous business relations governed by a general agreement drawn up in advance".[28] The Court then applied this case law to the case at hand and accepted the existence of an agreement on the grounds that the unilateral measures by the supplier aimed at influencing the distributors in the execution of their contracts.

The judgment of the Court of Justice in *Ford* contained a similarly broad interpretation of the notion of "agreement" in the context of vertical relationships. The typical contract stated that Ford would sell "all its products" to the distributors, who remained free to sell them to final buyers everywhere in the Community. Subsequently, Ford decided to cease supplies of right-hand drive vehicles to its German distributors. The Court stated that "such a decision on the part of the manufacturer does not constitute, on the part of the undertaking, a unilateral act which [...] would be exempt from the prohibition contained in [Article 101(1) TFEU]. On the contrary, it forms part of the contractual relations between the undertaking and its dealers."[29]

2.2 The Significance of the Bayer case law

In *Volkswagen*,[30] the ECJ conveniently summarised the issues involved in finding "agreement" in vertical cases. "The will of the parties may result from both the clauses of the dealership agreement in question and from the conduct of the parties, and in particular from the possibility of there being tacit acquiescence by the dealers in a call from the manufacturer".[31] When the supposed agreement arises from an "invitation" or "call" by one of the parties, typically the supplier, to the other party to behave in a certain manner, the Court seemed to envisage two possibilities to prove the will of the distributors: either the calls at issue were "provided for or authorised by the clauses of the dealership agreement", or else there needs to be dis-

---

28 Case T-62/98, *Volkswagen AG vs. Commission*, [2000] ECR II-2707, paragraph 236.
29 *Ford vs. Commission, supra* note, paragraph 21.
30 Case C-74/04 P, Volkswagen AG, [2006] ECR I-6585.
31 *Id.*, paragraph 39.

crete proof of "the dealers' explicit or tacit acquiescence to the measure adopted by the [supplier]".[32]

The Court of Justice rejected a "legality" criterion posited by the Court of First Instance, which had practically established a presumption that there is no agreement every time the agreement may turn out to be contrary to Article 81. The Court held that "the Court of First Instance erred in law in finding [...] that clauses which comply with the competition rules may not be regarded as authorising calls which are contrary to those rules" (ECJ, paragraph 43).

While *Volkswagen* provides useful clarifications, the truly seminal precedents in relation to the notion of agreement in vertical cases are the judgments of the Court of First Instance and the Court of Justice in the case of Bayer AG (Adalat). In its *Adalat* decision,[33] the Commission found that Bayer had changed its delivery policy, and ceased fulfilling in full of the increasingly large orders placed by wholesalers in low-price countries (Spain and France), clearly in order to limit the volume of parallel imports of its products. Although the wholesalers were not required to refrain from exporting the products acquired, the restriction of supply by Bayer made it more difficult for them to engage in parallel trade because of the limited quantities available after supplying their home market. Some of the wholesalers demanded additional quantities and some may have attempted to mislead Bayer into believing that the additional supplies were not intended for parallel trade. The Commission established the existence of an agreement on the basis of the continuation of commercial relations between the manufacturer and the wholesalers.

The Court of First Instance annulled the decision,[34] considering that the Commission had failed to prove that Bayer had demanded or negotiated the adoption of any particular line of conduct on the part of the wholesalers concerning the destination for export of the packets of Adalat which it had supplied, and that it penalised the exporting wholesalers or threatened to do so. According to the Court:

> *"The proof of an agreement between undertakings within the meaning of Article [101(1)] of the Treaty must be founded upon the direct or indirect finding of the existence of the subjective element that characterises the very concept of an agreement, that is to say*

---

32 *Id.*, paragraphs 40-48, in particular 46 and 48.
33 Commission Decision (96/478/EC) of 10 January 1996 (IV/34.279 — Adalat), O.J. L 201, of 9.08.1996, p. 1.
34 Case T-41/96, *Bayer AG vs. Commission*, [2000] ECR II-3383.

> *a concurrence of wills between economic operators on the imple-*
> *mentation of a policy, the pursuit of an objective, or the adoption*
> *of a given line of conduct on the market, irrespective of the man-*
> *ner in which the parties' intention to behave on the market in*
> *accordance with the terms of that agreement is expressed [...] The*
> *Commission misjudges that concept of the concurrence of wills*
> *in holding that the continuation of commercial relations with the*
> *manufacturer when it adopts a new policy, which it implements*
> *unilaterally, amounts to acquiescence by the wholesalers in that*
> *policy, although their de facto conduct is clearly contrary to that*
> *policy." [...] contrary to what the Commission appear[s] to main-*
> *tain, the right of a manufacturer faced [...] with an event harmful*
> *to his interests, to adopt the solution which seems to him to be the*
> *best is qualified by the Treaty provisions on competition only to*
> *the extent that he must comply with the prohibitions referred to*
> *in Articles [101 and 102]. Accordingly, provided he does so with-*
> *out abusing a dominant position, and there is no concurrence*
> *of wills between him and his wholesalers, a manufacturer may*
> *adopt the supply policy which he considers necessary, even if, by*
> *the very nature of its aim, for example, to hinder parallel imports,*
> *the implementation of that policy may entail restrictions on com-*
> *petition and affect trade between Member States."*[35]

It is important to underline that in *Bayer*, *both* "expressions of will" were in dispute: no manufacturer's "invitation" or "call" to the dealers to behave in a certain way was apparent and, unsurprisingly, there was precious little evidence to show "acquiescence" by the dealers to a "call" that had not been shown to exist. I submit that the absence of an invitation or "call" was a crucial issue, rightly leading the Court to reject the finding of an agreement.

I am more sceptical with the relevance given by the Court of First Instance to the *de facto* behaviour of some distributors, contrary to the manufacturer's policy. This does not appear to be a solid test. Not only because it appears difficult to reconcile with settled case law,[36] but also for reasons specific to vertical relationships. Characteristically, distributors never

---

35 *Id.*, paragraphs 173, 176.
36 See Case T-347/94, Mayr-Melnhof, [1998] ECR II-1751, paragraph 65 ("it is sufficient that the undertakings in question should have expressed their joint intention to conduct themselves on the market in a specific way [...] the question whether the undertakings in question consid-ered themselves bound — in law, in fact or morally — to adopt the agreed conduct is there-fore irrelevant").

have a *direct* interest in vertical restraints, such as export bans or minimum resale prices which limit their business options. Dealers do not draw any immediate benefit from these limitations. Their interest is to remain free to disregard them if this helps increase their revenue. The distributors' interest in vertical restraints is only an *indirect* one: they have an interest in abiding by them only to the extent that the same restraints are imposed on other distributors in the network, because they protect them against intrabrand competition.

This difference in incentives is particularly visible in a case concerning export restrictions like Bayer, where the interests of distributors in low-price countries are, almost by definition, directly opposed to those of the manufacturer. Export sales increase the distributor's business with little risk of negative side-effects, since products from high-price countries will not be imported into low-price ones. Therefore, it is only natural that, in such a situation, distributors will often attempt to circumvent export bans, whether express or covert. Although it is clear that not every restriction that a manufacturer attempts to impose on its distributors qualifies as an agreement, it appears from the case-law prior to Bayer that the apparent acquiescence of the distributors to a condition newly imposed by the manufacturer should suffice to find an agreement. The distributors' external reaction to the restraint imposed upon them should matter more than their covert attempts to defeat the manufacturer's policy. As a factual issue, however, it seems clear that in Bayer the Commission lacked convincing evidence even of such external reactions[37] and, more importantly, of any "call" or "invitation" by the manufacturer for dealers to behave in a certain way or lend assistance with the goal to limit parallel imports.

While the judgment of the Court of First Instance remains confusing, the subsequent judgment of the Court of Justice in *Bayer (Bundesverband der Arzneimittel-Importeure)*[38] does appear to bring a workable clarification of the boundary between unilateral behaviour and "agreement" in the context of vertical relationships. First, the Court states that

> *For an agreement within the meaning of Article [101(1)] of the Treaty to be capable of being regarded as having been concluded by tacit acceptance, it is necessary that the manifestation of the wish of one of the contracting parties to achieve an anti-com-*

---

37 *Bayer, supra* note 33, see e.g. paragraph 122.
38 Joined cases C-2/01 P and C-3/01 P, Bundesverband der Arzneimittel-Importeure, [2004] ECR I-23.

petitive goal constitute an invitation to the other party, whether express or implied, to fulfil that goal jointly. [39]

Nevertheless, the Court adds "and that applies all the more where, as in this case, such an agreement is not at first sight in the interests of the other party, namely the wholesalers". [40] For the reasons explained above, I would not attach much significance to this *obiter dictum*, which may be interpreted as drawing attention to the difference between vertical agreements and horizontal cartels (where the convergence of interests among the participants and the immediate advantage each of them derives from the agreed course of action are much more obvious).

But the more important contribution of *Bayer (Bundesverband der Arzneimittel-Importeure)* to the clarification of the notion of "agreement" lies elsewhere. The Court states that

> "*an agreement cannot be based on what is only the expression of a unilateral policy of one of the contracting parties, which can be put into effect without the assistance of others*". [41]

I submit that this is the crucial aspect of the judgment. Despite appearances, and despite what the judgment of the Court of First Instance may have suggested, Bayer should not be viewed as a case concerned with proof of the "acquiescence" of wholesalers with a unilateral policy of their supplier. The essential point, and the one where the Commission had gone a step too far, concerned the absence of an expression of will by the supplier that would have required *any acquiescence at all* to be implemented. All that Bayer did was to restrict supplies to its wholesalers. Whether it shared with them the reasons for doing so, and whether the wholesalers found those reasons agreeable, is of little relevance. What matters is that Bayer's policy did not rest, for its implementation, on the wholesalers behaving in any particular way. Wholesalers were not required to refrain from exporting or to agree to limit their orders to national requirements. Bayer did not *need* any agreement or acquiescence from the wholesalers, and it can be taken for granted that the (exporting) wholesalers, who saw their supply restricted, would *not*, and *did not*, share Bayer's desire to restrict exports. On these facts, their acquiescence or not with the goal of limiting parallel

---

39 *Id.*, paragraphs 101-103.
40 *Ibid.*
41 *Id.*, paragraph 101 (emphasis added). See also paragraph 123 ("Bayer's unilateral policy, *the implementation of which did not depend on their* [the wholesalers'] *cooperation*") (emphasis added). See also paragraph 104 (distinguishing *Sandoz*).

trade could not be relevant. In these conditions, it is right to demand serious evidence before finding a tacit agreement.

An intriguing issue in the *Bayer (Bundesverband der Arzneimittel-Importeure)* judgment concerns the extent to which it represents an overruling of *Ford* and *Sandoz*. The Court stated that

> *The mere concomitant existence of an agreement which is in itself neutral and a measure restricting competition that has been imposed unilaterally does not amount to an agreement prohibited by that provision. Thus, the mere fact that a measure adopted by a manufacturer, which has the object or effect of restricting competition, falls within the context of continuous business relations between the manufacturer and its wholesalers is not sufficient for a finding that such an agreement exists.* [42]

The scope and practical implications of these general statements remain uncertain. On the one hand, they seem to contradict previous judgments such as *Ford*, *AEG*, or *Sandoz*. Yet, the Court in *Bayer* appears to confirm the continued validity of these judgments and purports to distinguish the case on factual grounds. [43]

Concerning *Sandoz*, the distinction rests on the explicit *invitation* by the manufacturer (present in *Sandoz*, absent in *Bayer*) and the fact that, in *Sandoz*, the wholesaler's cooperation was necessary to implement the manufacturer's policy. Sandoz had required specific future market behaviour from its customers: to refrain from exporting. In distinguishing *Sandoz*, the ECJ does not address the element of *acquiescence* by the buyers or their subsequent behaviour, which confirms that this point is of secondary importance. [44] As regards *Ford* and *AEG*, the Court distinguished those cases by saying that the existence of an agreement had "already been

---

42 *Id.*, paragraph 141.
43 *Id.*, in particular paragraphs 104, 106-109, 144.
44 *Id.*, paragraph 104 ("... it is undisputed that, in [*Sandoz*], the manufacturer had sought the cooperation of wholesalers in order to eliminate or reduce parallel imports, their cooperation being necessary, in the circumstances of that case, in order to attain that objective. In such a context, the insertion by the manufacturer of the words 'export prohibited' on invoices amounted to a demand for a particular line of conduct on the part of the wholesalers. That is not the case here.") and paragraph 142 ("The existence of a prohibited agreement in [*Sandoz*] rested not on the simple fact that the wholesalers continued to obtain supplies from a manufacturer which had shown its intention to prevent exports, but on the fact that an export ban had been imposed by the manufacturer and tacitly accepted by the wholesalers"). In *Sandoz*, as the Court reminds in the previous sentence, the "acquiescence" had been established on the basis of "[t]he repeated orders of the products and the successive payments without protest"; it seems therefore clear that the only remaining distinguishing factor was the express "invitation" by the manufacturer and the fact that the wholesaler's cooperation was necessary to implement the manufacturer's policy.

established", and "the Court was able to confine itself ... to examining the question whether measures subsequently adopted by the manufacturer formed part of the agreement in question".[45]

Personally, I find that *Sandoz* and *AEG* can be effectively distinguished from *Bayer*. Indeed, *Sandoz*, because of the express invitation by the supplier to implement a policy which required, unambiguously, the cooperation of the distributors. *AEG*, both for similar reasons and for those explained in the next section.

By contrast, *Ford* appears more difficult to reconcile with *Bayer*. Neither the supplier's "invitation" nor the buyers' acquiescence was any more obvious in *Ford* than it was in *Bayer*. The manufacturer in *Ford* did not need to rely on, or expect, any behaviour by the distributors to implement its policy. All it needed to do, and all it did, was to cease supplying right-hand drive vehicles to its German dealers.

The Court in *Bayer* (*Bundesverband der Arzneimittel-Importeure*) attempted to distinguish *Ford* on the fact that the central issue there concerned the granting or withdrawal of an exemption under Article 101(3).

It is true that this was the question raised in *Ford*, and that the Commission had taken into account Ford's decision to cease supplies of right-hand drive cars to German dealers as part of the economic context relevant to its exemption decision; the Commission actually had more or less accepted that Ford's action was unilateral.[46] Nevertheless, the Court in *Ford* appeared to believe that the question whether the decision by Ford was "unilateral" or in fact agreed with its distributors was inescapable. It stated that "such a decision on the part of the manufacturer does not constitute [...] a unilateral act [...] on the contrary, it forms part of the contractual relations between the undertaking and its dealers. Indeed, admission to the Ford AG dealer network implies acceptance by the contracting parties of the policy pursued by Ford with regard to the models to be delivered to the German market".[47]

Given that Ford's decision to discontinue supplies required no behaviour from the German dealers, it is difficult to see why their "acceptance" would be relevant. Perhaps the specificities of organised distribution networks

45 *Id.*, paragraph 109.
46 Commission Decision (83/560/EEC) of 16 November 1983 (IV/30.696 — Distribution system of Ford Werke AG), O.J. L 327, 24/11/1983 p. 31, at recital 36 ("unilateral measures which as such do not constitute agreements or practices within the meaning of Article 85 (1) may have to be considered in deciding whether an exemption can be given [...] a unilateral act may be taken into account by the Commission even if it is not directly caused by the agreement because the Commission must consider an agreement in the economic context in which it has been applied.").
47 *Ford vs. Commission, supra* note, paragraph 21.

(see next section) may still justify the holding in *Ford*. Nevertheless, if *Ford* is still good law after *Bayer*, the least that can be said is that it had a close shave.

2.3 Dealer approval and termination in selective distribution networks

Where the manufacturer distributes its products through an exclusive or selective distribution network, contractual stipulations concerning the approval of distributors constitute an "agreement between undertakings" within the meaning of Article 101.[48] But the most interesting feature of restricted distribution networks is whether an agreement may be found in refusals to supply or approve additional dealers, or in decisions to terminate (or threats to terminate) dealers unwilling to comply with certain manufacturer's policies, when those policies do not appear expressly as conditions in the distribution contract.

The "unilateral" termination of a dealer is not itself an "agreement", but it may *prove* the existence of an underlying agreement. Through the manufacturer's approval and termination decisions, it can be shown that an apparently "unilateral" policy is part of the contractual relations between the supplier and *existing* or "compliant" distributors. In the context of distribution networks, the relationship is typically a "triangular" one. The agreement, whether express or tacit, is the one between the supplier and "compliant" or "docile" dealers who expect to be protected against "non compliant" dealers in respect of resale prices or territorial restrictions. The circumstances surrounding dealer terminations, interruptions of supplies or refusal to admit dealers into the network may provide *proof*, a "negative image" of the conditions that have been tacitly accepted by authorized distributors when those conditions are not express.

Thus, dealer termination has tended to be seen as reflecting an implicit understanding between manufacturer and dealers as to the circumstances that would trigger termination, a "meeting of the minds" satisfying the definition of "agreement." In *AEG-Telefunken* the ECJ categorically stated that

> "*[a refusal by a manufacturer to approve distributors who satisfy the qualitative criteria of his system of selective distribution] does not constitute [...] unilateral conduct which [...] would be*

---

48 Joined Cases 56 and 58/64 *Consten and Grundig vs. Commission* [1966] ECR 299.

exempt from the prohibition contained in article [101](1) TFEU]
[...]. On the contrary, it forms part of the contractual relations
between the undertaking and resellers. Indeed, in the case of the
admission of a distributor, approval is based on the acceptance,
tacit or express, by the contracting parties of the policy pursued
by AEG which requires inter alia the exclusion from the network
of all distributors who are qualified for admission but are not
prepared to adhere to that policy.

The view must therefore be taken that even refusals of approval
are acts performed in the context of the contractual relations with
authorized distributors inasmuch as their purpose is to guaran-
tee observance of the agreements in restraint of competition which
form the basis of contracts between manufacturers and approved
distributors. Refusals to approve distributors who satisfy the
qualitative criteria mentioned above therefore supply proof of an
unlawful application of the system if their number is sufficient
to preclude the possibility that they are isolated cases not forming
part of systematic conduct."[49]

This case law needs to be carefully checked against the ruling in Bayer,
which drew the line of "unilateral" policies where those can be "put into
effect without the assistance of others." A policy is not unilateral where a
party needs to rely on the behaviour of another to fulfil its goal and issues
a "manifestation of [...] wish" constituting "an invitation to the other party,
whether express or implied, to fulfil that goal jointly."[50] To remain consistent with Bayer, the "policy" of the manufacturer must be one that requires
implementation by the dealers. This was clearly the case in AEG, where the
policies in question related to minimum resale prices and export prohibitions.[51] Termination or non-approval of dealers by a manufacturer having
invited its network to abide by conditions such as a minimum resale price
or refraining from sales outside a certain territory is therefore considered
as resting on a tacit agreement. The 2010 Vertical Guidelines unambiguously construes dealer termination scenarios as "indirect" means to agree

---

49 Case 107/82, *Allgemeine Elektrizitäts-Gesellschaft AEG-Telefunken vs. Commission*, [1983]
    ECR 3151, paragraphs 38-39 (emphasis added).
50 Bundesverband der Arzneimittel-Importeure, *supra* note, paras. 101-102.
51 AEG had refused to approve (or threatened to terminate) dealers, or interrupted supplies on
    various grounds related to failure to comply with retail prices or "minimum" profit margins,
    procuring contract goods from other countries or selling outside allocated territories. See the
    discussion of individual occurrences in paragraphs 79-136 of the judgment in *AEG-Telefunken
    vs. Commission, supra* note. All these required market behaviour to be implemented by the
    dealers.

on resale prices.[52] Nevertheless, as illustrated by AEG, isolated acts may not suffice to establish agreement. Absent direct proof that termination is linked to a refusal to comply with an "invitation" by the supplier, proof will have to rely on indicia and a pattern of terminations or threats.

It is unclear whether *Ford* fits into this picture. Even assuming that it does not, it may be argued that the theory of "incorporation in a pre-existing contractual relationship" makes sense in the case of pre-established distribution agreements, where the dealer ties itself to a given manufacturer and invests resources for this purpose. Such dealers incur in sunk costs which may make it difficult to object to apparently "unilateral" policies subsequently decided by the supplier, which may be construed as changing the original understanding between the parties (for example, as to which products or which quantities would be supplied).

2.4 GlaxoSmithKline

In truth, the *GlaxoSmithKline* case[53] raised few issues in relation to the existence of an "agreement". Glaxo had announced a change in its general conditions of sale to Spanish wholesalers. According to the new general conditions, its products would be sold at two different prices ("clause 4A" and "clause 4B" prices), according to the subsequent destination of the product. Wholesalers were expected to pay the cheaper price only for products to be distributed in Spain for uses reimbursed by social security, and the higher price if the product was to be resold for any other use (in practice, for export). These general conditions were sent to wholesalers, who had to accept and countersign them as a condition of continued supply. Most wholesalers did.

The Court of First Instance was satisfied that an agreement had been proved. It stated that an agreement may be proved by "direct evidence, taking the form, for example, of a written document ... or, failing that, indirect evidence, for example in the form of conduct".[54] In this case, the Court found that the Commission had evidence in the form of an "exchange of documents showing, beyond all possible doubt that GW had proposed to the Spanish wholesalers that they conduct themselves on the market in the

---

52 See Guidelines on Vertical Restraints, O.J. C 130 of 19.5.2010, p. 1, at paragraph 48 (listing "threats, intimidation, warnings, penalties, delay or suspension of deliveries or contract terminations in relation to observance of a given price level"). See also paragraph 50.

53 Case T-168/01, *GlaxoSmithKline Services Unlimited vs. Commission*, [2006] ECR II-2969.

54 *Id.*, paragraph 83.

manner specified in the General Sales Conditions and that most of them had agreed to that proposal."[55]

Nevertheless, it would be wrong to think that the significant difference between GlaxoSmithKline and Bayer was the formal existence of a signed contract. The truly significant difference was the subject matter of the supposed agreement, which in GlaxoSmithKline unequivocally required specific future conduct from the dealers, related to their own market function. The dealers were required to maintain two separate resale channels, and not to sell for export a product purchased at the price that the manufacturer intended to reserve to the national market.

GlaxoSmithKline shows that, when the agreement is one that relies on the dealers' conduct for its implementation, their acquiescence may be grudging, or even coerced. Whether the dealers de facto comply with the agreement or not is, at best, of secondary importance. The Court referred in this regard to case law on cartel "cheating", and the comparison is indeed apposite. More than that, the solution is *a fortiori* more justified in vertical situations such as that in *GlaxoSmithKline*, because the incentives and interests of the parties are even more resolutely in conflict than in cartel cases. In a horizontal cartel, all participants stand to benefit directly from the agreement, even if they individually retain an incentive to "cheat". In a vertical case such as *GlaxoSmithKline*, the Spanish dealers drew no benefit whatsoever from the agreement. It was to be expected that they would protest and accept the new sales conditions only under threat. As underlined above, when the dealers' interests are not convergent with those of the manufacturer, it should be of little relevance that these dealers attempt to circumvent or disobey the agreement in their own interest. An agreement grudgingly entered into, even with mental reservations, and even with the intention of "cheating", is no less an agreement.

Indeed, the Court found specifically that "it is true that a number of [wholesalers] exported medicines purchased from GW at the Clause 4A price. However, it is also apparent from the case-file that they eventually agreed, at GSK's request, to pay the invoices corresponding to the difference between that price and the Clause 4B price. In any event, those facts concern only a few wholesalers and it cannot be concluded that they all distanced themselves from the agreement which they had previously concluded with GW".[56] The fact that a number of wholesaler associations whose members included signatories of the General Sales Conditions com-

---

55 *Id.*, paragraph 84.
56 *Id.*, paragraph 87.

plained to the competition authorities was also considered insufficient to discard the existence of an agreement.[57]

One may go one step further and wonder what the answer would have been in GlaxoSmithKline if the new sales conditions had merely been announced unilaterally by the manufacturer without requiring a signature. Contrary to the situation in Bayer, the conditions clearly required, for their implementation, specific conduct on the part of the wholesalers. It is submitted that in such a situation, the conditions for the application of standard case law would have been fulfilled, and an agreement could be found if GlaxoSmithKline had ceased supplying noncompliant wholesalers. The situation would have been similar to that of Sandoz or AEG. A good test for the existence of an agreement in such circumstances would be to approach the case from the civil law perspective and the application of Article 101(2). Had GlaxoSmithKline attempted to enforce its sales conditions (e.g. claim the difference between the low and the high price upon learning that a wholesaler had exported products bought at the cheaper price), a civil judge would, in all circumstances, need to find an agreement, whether to uphold the new sales conditions or to declare them void.

3. Conclusion

This contribution illustrates how the notion of "agreement" cannot be considered in a vacuum. The different requirements of Article 101 interact with each other like pieces of a sliding puzzle, to the extent that they sometimes seem interchangeable. To solve the puzzle, one needs to have the pieces and be aware of the interactions between them.

The case law, in particular the judgment of the Court of Justice arising from the Bayer litigation, has done a reasonable job of clarifying the key points that govern the interpretation of the notion of agreement. The requirement in Bayer that an agreement relates to a policy which requires "the assistance of others" to be put into effect ties well with the related notions that an agreement involves a "commitment to future action of abstention on the market" given by one undertaking to another, and that this commitment typically relates to the undertaking's "own market function". These pieces are not an infallible beacon to guide individual decisions in borderline cases -and there will always be borderline cases. The pieces do not *solve* the puzzle; they *are* the puzzle.

---

57 *Id.*, paragraph 88.

CHAPTER VI

AGENCY, SELECTIVE/EXCLUSIVE DISTRIBUTION AND FRANCHISING AGREEMENTS: BORDERLINES AND IMPACT ON THE QUALIFICATION UNDER COMPETITION LAW

JOSEPH VOGEL

Founding Partner
VOGEL & VOGEL

The evolution of the relationship between competition law and the qualification of distribution agreements is well known. First was the golden
age of legal categories for agreements. The classic block exemption regulations were by definition specific to an agreement or block of agreements;
they defined those categories of agreement and even the types of clauses
that were presumed either to contravene Article 85(1) or to benefit from
exemption under Article 85(3). Second came Regulation No. 2790/99[1]
which marked the decline of the legal categories. According to Recital 3
of Regulation No. 330/2010[2], successor to Regulation No. 2790/99: *"For the
application of Article 101(3) of the Treaty by regulation, it is not necessary to define those vertical agreements which are capable of falling
within Article 101(1) of the Treaty"*. The method of analysing agreements
is now focused on their economic effects; the Commission considers that a
distribution agreement does not have the same effect as another agreement
belonging to the same category if it falls within a different economic context. The Regulation states, *"In the individual assessment of agreements
under Article 101(1) of the Treaty, account has to be taken of several factors, and in particular the market structure on the supply and purchase*

---

1 Commission Regulation (EC) No. 2790/1999 of 22 December 1999 on the application of
Article 81(3) of the Treaty to categories of vertical agreements and concerted practices.
2 Commission Regulation (EU) No. 330/2010 of 20 April 2010 on the application of Article 101(3)
of the Treaty on the Functioning of the European Union to categories of vertical agreements
and concerted practices, Official Journal L 102, 23/04/2010 P. 0001 — 0007.

side". If we confine ourselves to the Regulation, the nature of a distribution agreement is no longer of any relevance in respect of the competition rules: the block exemption applies to all vertical agreements with the categories defined very broadly as it includes not only distribution agreements, but all contracts relative to buying and selling conditions[3]; where the block exemption does not apply, only economic criteria would have to be taken into account.

Should we, however, consider that there are now no boundaries between the main categories of distribution agreements? From the viewpoint of commercial law there clearly are some: the rights and obligations of the parties differ depending on the type of contract concluded. Distinctions also remain under competition law. Heads of networks are caught between two opposing imperatives; on the one hand, through increasingly complex and dense contractual arrangements they try to control as far as possible the conditions of the distribution of their products, including ultimately their resale price, and on the other, they want to limit their distribution costs. Here is the first boundary; agency agreements are the only contracts outside the limits of application of competition law; a lot may be imposed but that power comes at a cost (I). Where competition law applies, the boundaries between distribution agreements are blurred although they do not disappear (II).

1. Agency: Contracts outside the limits of competition law but with unclear boundaries

The principle that competition law does not apply to representation agreements was laid down long ago by the Commission[4] and reiterated by the Court of Justice. According to the ECJ, "*If such an agent works for his principal, he can in principle be regarded as an auxiliary organ forming an integral part of the latter's undertaking bound to carry out the principal's instructions and thus, like a commercial employee, form an economic unit with this undertaking*"[5]. As he has no commercial autonomy, the agent

---

3   Article 1(a) of BER No. 330/2010: "vertical agreement" means an agreement or concerted practice entered into between two or more undertakings each of which operates, for the purposes of the agreement or the concerted practice, at a different level of the production or distribution chain, and relating to the conditions under which the parties may purchase, sell or resell certain goods or service".

4   See EC Commission Notice of 24 December 1962, OJ 24/12/1962 (known as the "Christmas Message").

5   ECJ Case 40/73 *Suiker Unie and others vs. Commission* [1975] ECR 1663, at point 539.

cannot be regarded as an undertaking; therefore, between the agent and his client there can be no meeting of minds between *independent* undertakings, which is the condition for application of Article 101 TFEU.

Regulation No. 330/2010 does not address the issue of agency agreements and before that there was no specific regulation for that category of agreement; this is logical as those agreements do not need to be exempted. The new Guidelines on Vertical Restraints do however address the question[6], basically reiterating the terms of the previous guidelines and integrating certain rules stemming from the case law.

Because it means escaping the prohibition on restrictive agreements and being able to control prices and selling conditions, agency agreements are extremely sought after. However, opting for this type of agreement involves a series of constraints for the supplier: first of all the classification as agent in the sense of commercial agent as per Directive No. 86/653 of 18 December 1986[7] and as an agent within the meaning of the rules on competition are largely the same (A); the qualification as an agent within the meaning of competition law means that the supplier bears the commercial risks of the distributor (B); and finally, the immunity from which the agency contract benefits is not total (C).

1.1 Is an agent under commercial law and competition law strictly the same?

1.1.1 Authorised representative

Is an agent within the meaning of competition law the same as an agent under commercial law? The definitions of agency agreement provided in Directive No. 86/653 and the Guidelines on Vertical Restraints are similar. According to the Directive, a commercial agent is a self-employed intermediary who has continuing authority to negotiate the sale or the purchase of goods on behalf of another person or to negotiate and conclude such transactions on behalf of and in the name of that person (Article 1(2)). According to the Guidelines (point 12), "*An agent is a legal or physical person vested with the power to negotiate and/or conclude contracts on behalf of another person (the principal), either in the agent's own name or in the name of the principal, for the purchase of goods or services by*

---

6   Guidelines on Vertical Restraints, 2010/C 130/01, OJEC C 130, 19 May 2010.
7   Council Directive 86/653/EEC of 18 December 1986 on the coordination of the laws of the Member States relating to self-employed commercial agents, OJ L 382, 31.12.1986, p. 17–21.

the principal, or sale of goods or services supplied by the principal". In a great number of cases, an authorized representative will therefore be an agent under both Directive No. 86/653 and competition law.

1.1.2 Commission agent

However, we can pose the question of whether competition law goes even further than commercial law: according to the Vertical Restraints Guidelines, an agent may act "in his own name"; an agent could therefore, within the competition law meaning, be a commission agent; the Guidelines specify moreover that it is irrelevant how an agreement is defined by the parties or by the national law for the definition of agency within the meaning of competition law (point 13). By opting for a commission agreement, a supplier can thus combine the advantages of the two sets of rules: immunity from fines for interfering in the commission agent's running of his operation and no indemnity for termination of contract. The solution could be contested based on point 16 of the Guidelines which state: *"For the purpose of applying Article 101(1), an agreement will thus generally be considered an agency agreement where property in the contract goods bought or sold does not vest in the agent".* Could the fact that the intermediary acts in his own name lead to loss of the status as agent in the competition law sense? The issue has not been resolved by the relevant authorities in matters of competition and is thus open to debate. Nevertheless, various arguments can be put forward in response: reading between the lines of point 16 of the Guidelines leads to the question of whether title in the ownership of the goods sold passes directly from the principal to the third-party co-contracting party or does it pass via the commission agent. French judicial case law has ruled in favour of the direct transfer of title from the principal to the third-party buyer. Certainly for tax purposes (VAT) and in respect of the invoicing rules, the commission agent is treated as a buyer-reseller but there is nothing to stop an operator from invoicing on behalf of others. Ultimately to qualify the intermediary as an "agent", care must be taken to ensure that such risks are not borne by the agent but by the principal. The Court of Justice stated: « *as regards the risks linked to the sale of the goods, it is likely that the service-station operator assumes those risks when he takes possession of the goods at the time he receives them from the supplier, that is to say, prior to selling them on to a third party"* [8]. By contrast, it can be deduced that, in any

---

8 ECJ, 14 December 2006, Case C-217/05, *Confederación Española de Empresarios de Estaciones de Servicio vs. Compañía Española de Petróleos SA.*

event, even if title is considered to pass to the commission agent, if the ownership of the goods is momentary and only occurs when resale to a third party actually takes place, the commission agent would not, in practice, bear any risk linked to its capacity as "momentary" owner and could therefore be considered to be an agent within the meaning of competition law as long as he bears no other risk.

1.1.3 Deposit agreements.

Other hypotheses are possible where the combination of classifications can be precluded, as demonstrated in a recent decision of the French Competition Authority relating to distribution agreements of the Spanish clothing brand *Mango*[9]. This case clearly shows how imaginative operators can be when trying to make the best of the cumulative legal regulations: the agreement excluded the status for commercial agents; the distributor was simply a depositary of the goods with no commercial autonomy and never acquired ownership of them. The French Competition Authority, whilst taking care to point out that it would not take a stand in respect of the legal qualification under commercial law, found that it was an agency agreement. The French judicial courts hold that an intermediary with no possibility of negotiation and who cannot in any way modify the tariffs and conditions fixed by the principal is not an agent within the meaning of the Directive[10]. A deposit agreement, such as the contract for the distributors of the ready-to-wear brand, could escape both the prohibition on restrictive agreements and the end-of-contract indemnity applicable to the status of commercial agent. And, at least according to the French courts, the same could apply for agents or authorised representatives with no power of negotiation.

1.2 The agent in the competition law sense: which definition?

1.2.1 What are the criteria for defining an agency agreement?

Even if a supplier manages to avoid conferring a commercial agency status, immunity from Article 101 TFEU will still be at a price; he would bear

---

9 French Competition Authority decision No. 09-D-23, 30 June 2009, relative to practices implemented in the women's ready-to-wear clothing and accessories distribution sector.
10 Cass. Com., 15 Jan. 2001, No. 06-14.698, *Radio Communication Equipements (SA) vs. SFR (SA)*.

the burden of the commercial risks related to the activity carried out by the agent. For the Commission, this criterion is the *"determining factor"* (point 13) for defining an agency agreement and indeed appears to be the only criterion it is concerned with. In the *DaimlerChrysler case*[11], the CFI restated that: *"an agent can lose his character as independent economic operator only if he does not bear any of the risks resulting from the contracts negotiated on behalf of the principal* and *he operates as an auxiliary organ forming an integral part of the principal's undertaking"*. The test used by the Commission does not touch upon the question of the agent's ability to determine his own commercial strategy, as evoked in DaimlerChrysler where the Tribunal states that the agent operates as part of the principal's undertaking, and only considers the risk criterion. In a subsequent decision, the Court said *"It follows that the decisive factor for the purposes of determining whether a service-station operator is an independent economic operator is to be found in the agreement concluded with the principal and, in particular, in the clauses of that agreement, implied or express, relating to the assumption of the financial and commercial risks linked to sales of goods to third parties. As the Commission rightly submitted in its observations, the question of risk must be analysed on a case-by-case basis, taking account of the real economic situation rather than the legal classification of the contractual relationship in national law"*[12]. However, the Court has not ruled out other factors being taken into account. The French Competition Authority, for its part, has recently stated that *"the applicable test is based on a series of factors in two parts"*[13]. The French Competition Authority, for its part, devotes three pages of analysis to the entrepreneurial capacity of the agent in the Mango decision, underlining that: *"The ability of a distributor to determine his own commercial strategy depends on a certain number of factors. He must in particular be able to freely decide on the location of the site of the business, the lay-out of the sales outlet, the promotion of the activity, the supply of its sales outlet and on the determination of prices and commercial terms to customers. All of these factors contribute to establishing the entrepreneurial capacity of the distributor as an autonomous economic entity"*. It is true that recourse to the integration criterion has been criticised by legal commentators, with some noting that it leads to the taking into account of the constraints borne by the agent in

---

11 Case T-325/01 *DaimlerChrysler vs. Commission* [2005] ECR II-3319.
12 Case C-217/05, 14 Dec.2006, *Confederación Española de Empresarios de Estaciones de Servicio vs. Compañía Española de Petróleos SA.*
13 The expression comes from the *Mango* case, cited above — French Competition Authority.

order to assess whether those same constraints should escape application of Article 101 TFEU[14]. It is equally true that it can be sometimes difficult to distinguish what is part of the risk and what relates to the agent's entrepreneurial capacity: e.g. the question of ownership of the goods for the Commission is related to the risk and for the French Competition Authority is part of the entrepreneurial capacity. This point, which was not raised in the decisions of the Court, would be worth clarification by the EU courts.

1.2.2 Casting light and shade on the risk criterion

The approach taken by the Commission to the financial or commercial risk is characterised by a number of features; first of all, a certain pedagogy, that is even more marked than in the previous Vertical Restraints Guidelines. The Commission lists the types of risk taken into account: risks relative to contracts concluded, market-specific investments, the agency agreement with the principal and — only since the *DaimlerChrysler* judgment — the risk related to other activities undertaken on the same market (point 14). Another new development is that the Commission lists the risks in order of importance with contract-specific risks prevailing over the others (point 17). Like the previous Guidelines, a list of indicators provide a measurement of the risk borne by the agent: contributions to the costs relating to transportation of goods, maintaining a stock, responsibility towards third-parties and customers, sales promotions, investments (point 16). There is also a certain severity: the agreement is only qualified as an agency agreement if the agent *"does not bear any, or bears only insignificant, risks"* (point 15); and the scrutiny carried out by the Commission is very far-reaching; if the agent does not incur contract-specific risks, then it is necessary to continue assessing the risks related to market-specific investments; and if the agent does not incur any risks related to market-specific investments, the risks related to other required activities within the same product market may still have to be considered (point 17). Ultimately, we can ask ourselves whether in the eyes of the Commission there are actually any agents at all; despite the pedagogical stance of the Guidelines, it is extremely difficult to define the risk. What are the *"risks related to other required activities within the same product market"*? When are they insignificant and at what point do they become significant? Would del credere clauses — traditionally regarded as legitimate since it is up to the agent to select and to provide creditworthy customers to the principal — cause the agreement to lose its status as an agency agreement, as

---

14 M. Waelbroeck and A. Frignani, *Commentaire Megret, T. IV, Concurrence*, esp. No. 624.

the Commission seems to consider[15]? This definition issue, together with the Commission's harsh treatment of the matter, makes the benefit of the status as an agency agreement very aleatory.

1.3 Agency in the competition law sense and immunity

1.3.1 Limits to immunity

Assuming that the criteria identified by the Commission are met, the supplier will still not be immune from prosecution. The Commission identifies two separate markets: i) the market where the products of the supplier are offered, and where the benefit of the immunity applies; ii) the market on which the agent offers its services to suppliers. On that market, immunity does not come into play. This was confirmed by the Court[16]. Although the Commission considers that exclusive agency provisions will not in general lead to anticompetitive effects, it does find that non-compete provisions may do so if they lead to or contribute to a cumulative foreclosure effect (point 19 Guidelines).

1.3.2 The difficulty in conciliating the spirit of the commercial rules and the residual application of competition law

Going beyond the problems involved in characterising a cumulative foreclosure effect (the difficulties of the question are not limited to this field), certain issues arise when we attempt to clarify the principles stemming from the Guidelines and those coming from Directive No. 86/653. It has

---

15 The Commission states that the contract will be an agency agreement within the meaning of competition law if the intermediary « (d) *does not take responsibility for customers' non-performance of the contract*" (point 16 Guidelines). When a *del credere* clause is included, the agent is liable for the customer's failure to pay.

16 Case C-217/05, 14 Dec.2006, *Confederación Española de Empresarios de Estaciones de Servicio vs. Compañía Española de Petróleos SA*. "Nevertheless, it must be pointed out that, in such a case, only the obligations imposed on the intermediary in the context of the sale of the goods to third parties on behalf of the principal fall outside the scope of that article. As the Commission submitted, an agency contract may contain clauses concerning the relationship between the agent and the principal to which that article applies, such as exclusivity and non-competition clauses. In that connection it must be considered that, in the context of such relationships, agents are, in principle, independent economic operators and such clauses are capable of infringing the competition rules in so far as they entail locking up the market concerned." (§62). See also Judgment in case C-279/06, 11 sept. 2008, *CEPSA Estaciones de Servicio SA vs. LV Tobar e Hijos SL* (§41).

been pointed out[17] that the supplier wishing to include a non-compete clause in its agency agreements and to avoid any competition law issue must make a choice: either limiting the duration of the agreement to five years so it may be exempted in application of Article 5(1)(a) of Regulation No. 330/2010, but taking the risk that the end of the contract will automatically give rise to a right to an indemnity for the agent, or limiting the duration of just the non-compete clause to five years with the correlated risk that the agent will start to represent the principal's competitors after the term has been reached. More generally, Directive No. 86/653 places a specific loyalty obligation on the agent (Article 3(1)), and the French legislator has for example interpreted this such that the agent may not represent competitors without the consent of his principal (Article L. 134-6 of French Commercial Code). Conciliating the rules of competition law and the spirit of the commercial rules is far from clear.

As attractive as the agency agreement may be, the decision to opt for this type of contract translates, for the supplier, into a series of constraints with the conditions of application of that status being aleatory. The supplier can expect both the best (non-application of the prohibition of restrictive agreements and of the agent status arising from Directive No. 86/653), and the worst (application of the ban on restrictive agreements and the Directive). The use of conventional distribution contracts may allow the supplier to avoid having to pay an end-of-contract indemnity (in the Member States excluding end-of-contract indemnities for distribution agreements), without having to assume the commercial risks of its distributor. It remains to be reviewed where the boundaries between these contracts should be drawn.

2. Selective/exclusive distribution, exclusive sourcing and franchise: are the boundaries invulnerable when competition law applies?

With Regulation No. 330/2010, and mainly its predecessor Regulation No. 2790/99, the four major legal categories concerned by the previous regulations and the case law, i.e. franchise, selective distribution, exclusive distribution, and exclusive purchase, give way to the wider concept of vertical agreement. However, one must be careful — those categories

---

17 F. Bortolotti and N. Genty, Contrat d'agence et interdiction des ententes: les critères distinctifs des lignes directrices entre «vrais» et «faux» agents sont-ils réellement applicables?, Concurrences, n° 3-2010.

remain and their qualification remains an essential step (A). One of the major issues at stake for the supplier is whether he can use those qualifications concurrently and how (B).

2.1 Survival of the legal categories

2.1.1 Extent of maintenance of legal categories

a) Maintaining the definitions

Two types of contract are defined in Regulation No. 330/2010: firstly selective distribution, which is defined as a "distribution system where the supplier undertakes to sell the contract goods or services, either directly or indirectly, only to distributors selected on the basis of specified criteria and where these distributors undertake not to sell such goods or services to unauthorised distributors within the territory reserved by the supplier to operate that system" (Article 1(1)(e)); and then exclusive purchase by means of the definition of the non-compete obligation: "non-compete obligation" means any direct or indirect obligation causing the buyer not to manufacture, purchase, sell or resell goods or services which compete with the contract goods or services " (Article 1(1)(d) [18]. The Commission has not forgotten the other categories though: they are defined in the Guidelines. Exclusive distribution refers to a contract in which "the supplier agrees to sell its products to only one distributor for resale in a particular territory" (point 151). The fact of keeping those definitions, whether in the Regulation or in the Guidelines, is of relevance: the characteristic obligation within the meaning of commercial law of each of those categories of agreement, or at least the obligation that distinguishes it from other types of distribution agreement, is a potential restriction of competition. Competition law cannot ignore this. In matters of distribution, the approach will always consist of referring to the three main categories of agreement (exclusive distribution, exclusive purchase and selective distribution) in order to qualify a vertical agreement and determine the system it falls under in competition law, both when the Regulation applies and when it does not.

---

18 Which includes within the definition "any direct or indirect obligation on the buyer to purchase from the supplier or from another undertaking designated by the supplier more than 80% of the buyer's total purchases of the contract goods or services and their substitutes on the relevant market, calculated on the basis of the value or, where such is standard industry practice, the volume of its purchases in the preceding calendar year".

b) The role of the qualification for application of the exemption

The block exemption, which creates a safety zone for a number of agreements, depends on two considerations: one purely economic — the market share of the supplier and the buyer — and the other legal: defining the agreement with respect to certain clauses restricting sales. Why is this? Because the rules governing certain restrictions of competition regarding black and red clauses (respectively Articles 4 and 5 of the Regulation) depend on the qualification of the agreement. At times, the Regulation relaxes the applicable rules for a given type of contract. Restrictions of sales into a specific territory would normally give rise to loss of the exemption but they are lawful if in the context of an exclusive distribution agreement (Article 4 (b)(i)). Benefit of the exemption is removed for restrictions of sales to professionals but such restrictions are lawful in the context of a selective distribution agreement (Article 4(b)(iii)). Elsewhere, on the other hand, the Regulation is more severe in respect of the rules applying to a given type of contract: in the context of selective distribution there is no possibility of restricting active sales or cross-supplies (Article 4(c) and (d) of the Regulation): exclusive purchase agreements are only exempted if their duration does not exceed five years (Article 5(1)(a)). The conditions governing exemption of restrictions of competition therefore refer implicitly, but necessarily, to the qualification of the agreement and that qualification will therefore be essential for the application of the competition rules.

c) Role of the qualification for the case by case review of agreements

The individual review on a case by case basis depends mainly on economic considerations of an essentially structural nature and on a counterfactual test (what would happen if the agreement or restriction under consideration did not exist?). These considerations are decisive today and make up a large part of the review. However, just like in the past, economic considerations will come once the agreement has been defined in terms of the known categories of the distribution agreement: the nature of the agreement is the first of the factors cited in the Vertical Restraints Guidelines to be taken into account to assess the situation under competition law (point 111); The Guidelines look at each category of agreement to see how the common economic criteria used to measure the effect of the restriction envisaged can play in each specific case. There is no surprise there since, as we have seen, the characteristic obligation of each agreement in relation to another distribution agreement is a potential restriction of competition, the effects of which must be measured.

2.1.2 Uncertainty around certain definitions

There is possibly one exception to this assertion relative to franchise agreements. The definition of franchise — like that of selective distribution but for different reasons — raises certain issues.

a) Has the Commission invented a system of franchise without know-how?

Regulation No. 330/2010 does not provide a definition of franchise. Here too, the definition is provided by the Guidelines (point 189). Nonetheless, when the new legislation was adopted some commentators wondered if the Commission had not made up a system of franchise ignoring know-how, which is the factor that they considered to be the main subject matter of such an agreement. In Regulation No. 330/2010, a franchise is still described as *"a package of non-patented practical information,. resulting from experience and testing by the supplier, which is secret, substantial and identified"* — but the definition of the word "substantial" has changed. It provides that *"the know-how is significant and useful to the buyer for the use, sale or resale of the contract goods or services"*, whereas the previous regulation used the term *"indispensable"* (compare Articles 1(g) of both texts). Insofar as the Regulation only covers agreements of which intellectual property rights are not the main subject matter (see Article 2(3) of Regulation), it is an either/or situation: either franchise agreements are no longer covered by the exemption or the transfer of know-how is only a secondary aspect of the contract[19]. From that point of view, a distinction must be made. The BERs are not really concerned with franchise agreements in an absolute sense, but with franchise agreements for the distribution of products, insofar as they can contain vertical restraints. From that viewpoint for the application of competition law, the main subject matter of a distribution franchise is the distribution of products[20]. The Commission therefore logically considers that *distribution* franchise agreements are still covered by the exemption if they con-

---

19 See Guy Gras, Réflexion sur la qualification du contrat de franchise au regard du règlement n° 330/2010, Concurrences n° 3-2010.

20 This was also clear in the definition provided by Regulation No. 4087/88 of 30 November 1988 on categories of franchise agreements: *'franchise' means a package of industrial or intellectual property rights relating to trademarks, trade names, shop signs, utility models, designs, copyrights, know-how or patents,* **to be exploited for the resale of goods or the provision of services to end users;** *'franchise agreement' means an agreement whereby one undertaking, the franchisor, grants the other, the franchisee, in exchange for direct or indirect financial consideration, the right to exploit a franchise* **for the purposes of marketing specified types of goods and/or services"** (our emphasis).

tain vertical restraints (Guidelines point 44). Franchises stand out in that regard from the three major categories i.e. selective distribution, exclusive distribution and exclusive supply: for franchises the characteristic element of the distribution agreement (which distinguishes it from other distribution agreements) is not a potential restriction of competition. The transfer of know-how is not restrictive of competition, which is why the Commission is relatively indifferent to such matters. Commercial courts however will necessarily be interested in the consideration provided for the royalties paid by the franchisee: where there is no transfer of know-how, such payment is without justification. There is therefore no cause to fear a weakening of the concept due to the new definition in the Regulation: even though practitioners are accustomed to referring to the definitions in block exemption regulations — that Commission jurists themselves developed by looking at the actual practice — the transmission of know-how will remain an indispensable element of the qualification of such an agreement under commercial law. And it will continue to be used in competition law in the context of case by case examinations of vertical restraints; according to the Guidelines, the more important the transfer of know-how is, the more likely it is that the restraints create efficiencies and that the vertical restraints fulfil the conditions for exemption (point 190).

b) The revival of selective distribution?

Under competition law two types of selective distribution were distinguished: purely qualitative selective distribution, this qualification being reserved for selection systems where selection was justified by the nature of the products, was based on the objective criteria required by the nature of the products and applied uniformly without going beyond what was necessary; in such a configuration and since the *Metro* judgment, Article 101 TFEU was not applicable. Anything further was considered as indirectly limiting the selection of resellers and the benefit of the exemption was only granted under very strict conditions, even where the criterion in question only indirectly limited the number of potential resellers. This approach is still current where the exemption does not apply and the Vertical Restraints Guidelines still distinguish purely qualitative selective distribution and quantitative selective distribution (points 175 et seq.) However, when the exemption applies, if we refer to the definition in Regulation No. 330/2010, the selection criteria should only be subject to one requirement — they must be defined[21]. A supplier should therefore be able to use selection criteria that directly limit the number of resellers, selection criteria that indirectly limit them, whether justified and objective or not and regardless of whether they are strictly necessary and even of whether they are applied in a discriminatory manner. The new Vertical Restraints Guidelines — unlike previous Guidelines — now expressly acknowledge that: "*the Block Exemption Regulation exempts selective distribution regardless of the nature of the product concerned and regardless of the nature of the selection criteria*" (point 176). Of course, the Commission has set up a number of safeguards against a totally arbitrary use of selective distribution; the Vertical Restraints Guidelines specify for instance that the benefit of the exemption could be withdrawn if the characteristics of the product do not require the use of such a system or in the event of abusive requirements for distributors to have brick and mortar outlets, for cases, we assume, where that system would be used to limit online sales (ibid). The opportunity is worth seizing, especially for sectors such as perfume distribution where only purely qualitative selective distribution was traditionally accepted and used, whereas it may be in the interests of suppliers of the most prestigious brands to limit the number of their distributors or upgrade their criteria without subjecting themselves to the scrutiny of the courts in respect of the necessity and proportional nature of the criteria posed.

2.2 Combination of the legal categories

2.2.1 Combination of qualifications widely possible where Regulation No. 330/2010 applies.

It may be in the interest of the supplier to combine the possible restrictions of competition, and therefore the qualifications. This possibility is widely available when the exemption applies. According to the Guidelines, exclu-

---

21 This issue has raised an important debate in French case law. French Courts have often be tempted to control the justification of selective quantitative criteria, even in the case of distribution systems under the 30% threshold. According to a judgment of the French Supreme Court (28 June 2005, *Grémeau vs. Daimler Chrysler*, Lawlex2005000663JBJ), it seemed that the Courts should control whether the quantitative criteria were not only precise but also objective. This led the European Commission to intervene in the procedure as amicus curiae to deny such control of the objectivity of quantitative criteria. In the meanwhile, French case law seems to admit that quantitative criteria used within an exempted selective distribution system only have to be precise (Paris Court of Appeal, 2 December 2009, *Land Rover vs. Auto 24*, Lawlex200900003589JBJ; Paris Court of Appeal, 17 December 2008, Renault/Billiar, n° 05/17984; the appeal against this judgment has been denied by Cass. Com., 2 February 2010).

sive distribution can be combined with exclusive purchasing and a non-compete obligation limited to five years (point 152). For a franchise, the scope of possibilities is even wider than under Regulation No. 4087/88: that regulation allowed the combination of a franchise agreement and exclusive distribution; however, it only allowed recourse to selective distribution if this was necessary to protect the intellectual or industrial property rights or to maintain the common identity and reputation of the franchised network[22]. A franchising agreement can now be combined with a non-compete obligation, selective distribution or exclusive distribution (point 190). Despite this extensive deregulation, some combinations can give rise to conflicts.

2.2.2 Limits: the case of selective distribution.

Two examples can be drawn from selective distribution. Restrictions of cross-supplies between network members give rise to removal of the benefit of the exemption (Article 4(d) of the Regulation). It is therefore not possible to combine selective distribution and exclusive purchasing. The Guidelines state that it is possible to combine selective distribution with a non–compete obligation (point 176), but for the supplier this only means that he will be able to impose the purchase of his brand, he cannot require distributors to obtain the products directly from him. Another example is the combination of selective and exclusive distribution. The possibility of banning active sales outside the contract territory is inherent to exclusive distribution; it is incompatible with the prohibition on the restriction of active sales in selective distribution arrangements. The possibility of banning sales outside the network is inherent to selective distribution; it is incompatible with the prohibition of restrictions of sales (subject to sales outside the territory) in exclusive distribution arrangements. This incompatibility between the conditions for exemption of a combined agreement means either relinquishing the combination or getting rid of the clauses constituting hardcore restrictions present in one of the two systems. The

---

22 Commission Regulation (EEC) No. 4087/88 of 30 November 1988 on the application of Article 85 (3) of the Treaty to categories of franchise agreements, Official Journal L 359, 28/12/1988 P. 0046 — 0052: article 2 *"The exemption provided for in Article 1 shall apply to the following restrictions of competition: ... (b) an obligation on the master franchisee not to conclude franchise agreement with third parties outside its contract territory"*; article 3 1. *"Article 1 shall apply notwithstanding the presence of any of the following obligations on the franchisee, in so far as they are necessary to protect the franchisor's industrial or intellectual property rights or to maintain the common identity and reputation of the franchised network: ... (e) to sell the goods which are the subject-matter of the franchise only to end users, to other franchisees and to resellers within other channels of distribution supplied by the manufacturer of these goods or with its consent".*

Guidelines suggest withdrawing the possibility of bans on active sales outside the territory[23] and this has been validated by the French Competition Authority[24]. Even with a part missing, this combination is the way forward for suppliers, as they will be able to concurrently ban sales outside the network, control the number of sales outlets and their location and, if need be, impose a non-compete obligation.

Within the new system — at least as long as the exemption applies — the opportunities open to network heads are wide-ranging and the stranglehold effect of the old regulations has disappeared. However, the fact that Regulation No. 330/2010 requires, in the situations we have described, that a choice be made between the distribution models or that aspects be cut out from one of them is a very clear illustration of the continuing need to qualify distribution agreements when dealing with vertical restraints of competition.

---

23 §176 "Qualitative and quantitative selective distribution is exempted by the Block Exemption Regulation as long as the market share of both supplier and buyer each do not exceed 30%, even if combined with other non- hardcore vertical restraints, such as non-compete or exclusive distribution, provided active selling by the authorised distributors to each other and to end users is not restricted"; §152: "A combination of exclusive distribution and selective distribution is only exempted by the Block Exemption Regulation if active selling in other territories is not restricted."

24 Decision No. 07-D-25 of 25 July 2007 relative to referrals by the *Conseil national des professions de l'automobile* (CNPA) against certain motorcycle manufacturers concerning the conditions of distribution of their products.

CHAPTER VII

PARALLEL TRADE AFTER THE GSK SPAIN JUDGMENTS

HELMUT BROKELMANN

Partner

Martinez Lage, Allendesalazar & Brokelmann Abogados [1]

1. The Problem of Parallel Trade in the Pharmaceutical Sector

Unlike most competition regimes outside the EU, European competition law does not only pursue the classical objective of enhancing consumer welfare, but also the objective of creating an internal market among the Member States of the EU (which, eventually, will also enhance consumer welfare). This is why vertical restrictions of competition have traditionally been treated differently in EU competition law, since they are liable of compartmentalizing the internal market along national boundaries –e.g. through the grant of absolute territorial protection-, thus reversing the market integration sought by Article 3(3) of the Treaty on European Union, Article 3(1)(b) of the Treaty on the Functioning of the European Union, Protocol 27 and their predecessor the EC Treaty (Articles 2 and 3(1) (g) EC).

A specific concern of the European authorities in their competition policy concerning vertical restraints has been the promotion of parallel trade. Parallel trade is so important for the EU's single market imperative because it fosters the interpenetration of national territories and acts as a corrective to excessive price differentials between Member States. One could therefore say that parallel trade has been, and still is, a "sacred cow" of EU competition policy.

---

[1] The author was partner at Howrey Martinez Lage, which was co-counsel to GSK in the proceedings before the European Commission and both Community Courts.

While these policy aims are, as a matter of principle, completely legitimate to pursue in any industrial sector (e.g., tennis balls[2]), in the pharmaceutical sector, parallel trade has raised specific issues that put the European Commission's policy into question. In the pharmaceutical sector, parallel trade stems from structural differences in the price of pharmaceutical products as a result of different national legislations which fix the prices of pharmaceuticals to a larger or lesser extent. The origin for parallel trade in this sector is therefore not the policy of pharmaceutical companies of setting different prices in various territories, but State intervention in the determination of the price which the public health systems of the different Member States are prepared to reimburse to pharmaceutical companies.

This fact allows the questioning of the legitimacy of parallel trade in this specific sector and explains why pharmaceutical companies have, since the seventies, tried to oppose parallel imports of their products from other Member States in which the intervened price of the same product is much lower than in the country of destination.

While the benefits of parallel trade in pharmaceuticals for consumers in the country of import is limited because exporters usually pocket as a windfall profit the advantage in terms of price which parallel trade may entail, parallel exports lead to shortages of supply in the country of export and reduce the ability of pharmaceutical companies to invest in R&D.

2. Parallel Trade and the Free Movement of Goods

The first route tested by pharmaceutical companies to oppose parallel imports of their products was the Treaty's provisions on the free movement of goods. The companies attempted to oppose such imports on the basis that their intellectual property rights (patents or trademarks) had not been exhausted by marketing the same product in a lower-priced Member State in which there was no patent protection[3].

The European Court of Justice (ECJ), however, refused to limit the fundamental freedom of the free movement of goods (Art. 34 of the Treaty on the Functioning of the European Union, TFEU) in such circumstances and

---

2 See Case T-43/92 *Dunlop Slazenger International Ltd/Commission* [1994] ECR II-441 and Commission Decision 94/987/EC of 21 December 1994 relating to a proceeding pursuant to Article 85 of the EC Treaty (IV/32.948 — IV/34.590 *Tretorn and others*), OJ L 378/45 of 31.12.1994.

3 Case 187/80 *Merck/Stephar* [1981] ECR 2063.

held that the exhaustion doctrine applied fully, irrespective of any price intervention or differing patent protection regimes[4].

In the *Centrafarm/Sterling Drug* case, Sterling Drug had tried to argue that price differences resulting from State price control measures should permit the holder of a patent for the product in question to oppose parallel imports, although such opposition would normally be contrary to the exhaustion of rights principle (i.e. the "exhaustion" of the right to invoke national intellectual property legislation in order to prevent parallel imports if the product in question has been put onto the market in the Member State of exportation by the right holder himself or with his consent). The Court, however, rejected the parties' arguments to apply Article 36 of the Treaty contrary to the exhaustion of rights principle.

This case law was again confirmed in the 1996 Merck/Primecrown judgment[5] in which the Court declared that "although the imposition of price controls is indeed a factor which may, in certain conditions, distort competition between Member States, that circumstance cannot justify a derogation from the principle of free movement of goods. It is well settled that distortions caused by different price legislation in a Member State must be remedied by measures taken by the Community authorities and not by the adoption by another Member State of measures incompatible with the rules on free movement of goods" (para. 47).

Thus, the Court does not consider the fact of a Member State fixing the price of certain products as sufficient to justify a restriction on imports under the terms of Article 36 (that is, the undertaking harmed by such imports cannot oppose those imports by invoking a national intellectual property right recognised under Article 36 as an exception to the free movement of goods). Pharmaceutical companies could not justify the application of national trademark or patent laws to oppose parallel imports of their products on the basis of Article 36 TFUE.

3. Parallel Trade and the Competition Rules

After it had become clear in the *Merck/Primecrown* judgment of 1996 that the free movement of goods provisions did not provide a solution to the problem of parallel trade, GlaxoSmithKline (GSK) decided to pursue a new route by justifying restrictions of parallel trade in the context of

---

4   Case 15/74 *Centrafarm/Sterling Drug* [1974] ECR 1147 and case 187/80 *Merck/Stephar* [1981] ECR 2063.

5   Joined cases C-267/95 and C-268/95. *Merck/Primecrown*, [1996] ECR I-6285.

the competition rules. The Court's above-mentioned *Centrafarm/Sterling Drug* ruling provided the basis for this novel approach. In this judgment the Court held that:

> *"This question requires the Court to state, in substance, whether the patentee can, notwithstanding the answer to the first question [which dealt with the free movement of goods provisions], prevent importation of the protected product, given the existence of price differences resulting from governmental measures adopted in the exporting country with a view to controlling the price of that product.*
>
> *It is part of the Community authorities' task to eliminate factors likely to distort competition between Member States, in particular by the harmonisation of national measures for the control of prices and by the prohibition of aids which are incompatible with the common market,* in addition to the exercise of their powers in the field of competition."

3.1 Article 101 (1) TFEU

Following this indication from the Court, in 1998, GSK Spain (then still Glaxo Wellcome) notified the European Commission of new sales conditions for its pharmaceutical products in Spain. Clause 4 provided for a system of differentiated prices: While the price set by the Spanish health authorities would apply to medicines funded by the National Health System and dispensed in the Spanish territory under the applicable Pharmaceutical Act[6], GSK would freely set a different (higher) price for any other medicine, in particular those to be exported. GSK never disputed that this clause was adopted for the purpose of limiting parallel exports of its products from Spain to other Member States. Nonetheless, in its notification GSK argued that the clause did not restrict competition or, alternatively, deserved an exemption under the then Article 81(3) EC (currently Article 101(3) TFEU). In a decision adopted in 2001[7], the Commission eventually rejected GSK's request for negative clearance or individual exemption arguing that GSK's

---

6   Article 100 of Act 25/1990, of 20 December.
7   Commission Decision of 8 May 2001 relating to a proceeding pursuant to Article 81 of the EC Treaty Cases: IV/36.957/F3 Glaxo Wellcome (notification), IV/36.997/F3 Aseprofar and Fedifar (complaint), IV/37.121/F3 Spain Pharma (complaint), IV/37.138/F3 BAI (complaint), IV/37.380/F3 EAEPC (complaint) (notified under document number C (2001) 1202). *OJ L 302, 17.11.2001, pp. 1-43.*

sales conditions amounted to a dual pricing scheme and to an export ban that restricted competition by "object" and therefore did not qualify for an exemption under the third paragraph of Article 101.

GSK appealed and the then Court of First Instance (CFI, today the General Court) in its ruling of 27 September 2006[8] partially annulled the Commission's decision insofar as it denied the requested individual exemption without sufficient analysis. On appeal, the European Court of Justice (ECJ, today Court of Justice) confirmed the CFI's judgment[9], although the ECJ dissented with the lower court on the issue of whether a limitation of parallel trade restricted competition "by object", as will be explained below.

The CFI not only annulled the Commission's rejection of the individual exemption sought by GSK, but also disagreed with the Commission as to whether the sales conditions restricted competition by "object" within the meaning of Article 101(1) of the Treaty. The Court held that it was necessary to take into account the specific legal and economic context of the pharmaceutical sector, in which the coexistence of different national legislations distorted competition. The Court confirmed that *"the price of medicines reimbursed by the national health insurance schemes is not determined as a result of a competitive process throughout the Community but is directly fixed following an administrative procedure in most Member States and indirectly controlled by the other Member States"* (para. 125). Hence, *"the differences between the applicable national provisions are a structural cause of the existence of significant price differentials between Member States"* (para.127) and *"those price differentials are themselves the cause of parallel trade in medicines in the Community"* (para. 129).

Furthermore, the Court declared that exporters usually keep the advantage of parallel trade in terms of price, so that consumers do not benefit from price reductions in the countries of destination and that parallel traders *"are the vectors of artificial competition and not of effective competition within the meaning of Article 3(1)(g) EC and Article 81 EC"* (para. 146).

Thus, the Court concluded that *"the prices of the products in question, which are subject to control by the Member States, which fix them directly or indirectly at what they deem to be the appropriate level, are determined at structurally different levels in the Community and, unlike the prices of other consumer goods to which the Commission referred in its written submissions and at the hearing, such as sports items or motor*

---

8 Case T-168/01 *GlaxoSmithKline Services vs. Commission* [2006] ECR II-2969.
9 Joined cases C-501/06 P, C-513/06 P, C-515/06 P and C-519/06 P, *GlaxoSmithKline Services vs. Commission* [2009] ECR I-9291.

cycles, are in any event to a significant extent shielded from the free play of supply and demand.

That circumstance means that it cannot be presumed that parallel trade has an impact on the prices charged to the final consumers of medicines reimbursed by the national sickness insurance scheme and thus confers on them an appreciable advantage analogous to that which it would confer if those prices were determined by the play of supply and demand. (paras. 133/134).

Consequently, the Court rejected that GSK's undisputed intention to limit parallel trade with its new sales conditions restricted competition by object, since it could not be taken for granted that parallel trade tends to reduce the prices set by the public authorities and thus to increase the welfare of final consumers.

In spite of disagreeing with the Commission on the existence of a restriction by object, the CFI nevertheless upheld the Commission's finding that the sales conditions restricted competition within the meaning of Article 101 (1) TFEU because of their anti-competitive effect.

Although the CFI declared that an agreement limiting parallel trade does not necessarily restrict competition, it could do so if parallel trade contributes to price competition. In the case at hand GSK's sales conditions barely had an appreciable effect on competition because intrabrand competition between exporting wholesalers and distributors in the country of destination was "limited" and pressure on prices resulting from parallel trade was "marginal" given that parallel traders would not pass the price differences on to consumers in those countries. Nevertheless, the Court understood that Clause 4 of GSK's sales conditions could contribute to reinforcing pre-existing price rigidity, affecting, by network effect, a significant number of products and national markets, and therefore concluded that it had the effect of restricting competition.

On appeal, however, the ECJ disagreed with the CFI's conclusion that the sales conditions did not restrict competition by "object". Although the higher Court acknowledged that it was necessary to take into account the legal and economic context to assess whether an agreement aimed at restricting parallel trade had as its object to restrict competition, it rejected the CFI's conclusion that an agreement aimed at limiting parallel trade restricted competition by object only if it may be presumed to deprive final consumers of the advantages of effective competition in terms of supply or price. According to the ECJ, this conclusion is not supported by the wording of Article 101 nor the case law since Article 101 protects not only interests of competitors or consumers, but also the structure of the market and, in so doing, competition as such.

The ECJ's discrepancy with the CFI is surprising for three reasons. First, because the ECJ actually did not analyse the legal and economic context, after declaring that such an analysis was necessary. Second, because in our view there should be no contradiction between the analysis of whether an agreement restricts "competition" and the analysis of whether an agreement harms consumers. Article 101 protects the structure of the market since it presumes that the competitive functioning of the market generates benefits for consumers.

Third, because the ECJ's finding of a *per se* infringement arguably contradicts its *GSK Greece* judgment[10] on the compatibility of limitations of parallel trade with Article 102 TFUE. In that preliminary ruling, the Court held that restrictions of parallel trade resulting from a so-called supply quota system (by which the manufacturer unilaterally –and thus without infringing Article 101 TFEU because there is no "agreement"[11]- limits the amounts supplied to wholesalers to the needs of the national market) do not *per se* constitute an abuse since even a dominant manufacturer is entitled to protect its commercial interests. Thus, if the amounts requested by wholesalers are out of all proportion to those previously sold by the same wholesalers to meet the needs of the national market, a dominant company may limit the amounts it supplies to such wholesalers without infringing Article 102 TFEU. In other words, the refusal to meet orders that are out of the ordinary because they are disproportionate as compared to the quantities previously sold by wholesalers to meet the needs of the domestic market do not infringe Article 102 TFEU.

The conclusion to be drawn from this judgment is that, if a limitation of parallel trade by a dominant undertaking does not *per se* constitute an abuse of a dominant position pursuant to Article 102 TFEU, it should neither constitute a restriction "by object" under Article 101 TFEU.

3.2 Article 101 (3) TFEU

Both the judgment of the General Court and that of the Court of Justice confirm that an agreement that restricts parallel trade –and thus, according to the ECJ, competition "by object" within the meaning of Article 101(1)

---

10 Joined Cases C-468/06 to C-478/06 *Sot. Lélos kai Sia* [2008] ECR I-7139.
11 Case T-41/96 *Bayer vs. Commission* [2000] ECR II-3383 and Joined Cases C-2/01 P and C-3/01 P *BAI and Bayer vs. Commission* [2004] ECR I-23.

TFEU- may nonetheless benefit from an exemption pursuant to the third paragraph of Article 101 if it fulfils the four cumulative conditions established in that provision, i.e. if it creates efficiencies, benefits consumers, the restriction is indispensable and it does not eliminate competition on the market. Both judgments include important statements as to the possible fulfilment of these conditions.

3.2.1 Efficiencies

As regards the first condition of Article 101 (3), both Courts acknowledged that an agreement that restricts parallel trade may generate efficiencies by allowing pharmaceutical companies to increase their investment in R&D. The CFI annulled the Commission's refusal to grant an exemption on the grounds that it had failed to undertake a rigorous examination of GSK's arguments concerning the loss of efficiency caused by parallel trade —the decrease of its ability to invest in R&D — and the gain in efficiency resulting from GSK's sales conditions — the possibility of increasing investment in R&D- and to weigh up the advantages and disadvantages of the sales conditions as required under the balancing test of the first limb of Article 101 (3).

The Court of Justice, for its part, reminded that for an agreement to entail an appreciable objective advantage it is sufficient that such an advantage is "sufficiently likely" and that it was not necessary that *all* additional funds recovered by GSK by limiting parallel trade are invested in R&D. This was one of the Commission's main battlegrounds, which argued that pharmaceutical companies could also limit other budgetary items, instead of limiting parallel trade, to have more funds to invest in R&D and therefore denied that there was a casual link between parallel trade and R&D spending. The Court of Justice also confirmed that to determine whether an agreement generates efficiencies, it may be necessary to take into account the nature and specific features of the sector concerned.

On the basis of these indications from the Courts, in our view it would seem "sufficiently likely" that a restriction of parallel trade generates efficiencies taking into account the nature and specific features of the pharmaceutical sector. Due to the intense interbrand competition based on innovation, pharmaceutical companies have every interest in reinvesting part of the funds recovered by limiting parallel trade in R&D. Taking into account the importance of interbrand competition as compared to the limited role of intrabrand competition, the advantages of a limitation of parallel trade for interbrand competition are likely to exceed the disadvantages that such limitation entails for intrabrand competition between parallel traders and distributors in the country of destination.

3.2.2 Benefits to consumers

The CFI found that the Commission had not replied to GSK's arguments that pharmaceutical companies had every interest in reinvesting additional benefits in R&D, thus increasing interbrand competition.

It seems clear that any increase in R&D investment leading to the development of new pharmaceutical products constitutes a clear benefit for consumers (i.e. patients). Furthermore, and due to the existence of an intense competition based on innovation, pharmaceutical companies are likely to invest a not insignificant part of the funds recovered by limiting parallel trade in R&D.

3.2.3 Indispensability

Neither the CFI nor the Court of Justice provided indications as to how to assess the fulfilment of the indispensability requirement in Article 101 (3) TFEU.

This criterion should be applied on a case by case basis and the issues to be analysed probably would be the level at which prices should be set to ensure the profits necessary for the optimum financing of R&D and whether it is sufficient to limit or necessary to prevent parallel exports altogether.

3.2.4 No elimination of competition

In respect of the negative condition of Article 101(3) TFEU, the CFI held that: "[...] *the fact that Clause 4 of the General Sales Conditions prevents the limited pressure which might exist, owing to parallel trade from Spain, on the price and the cost of medicines in the geographic markets of destination must be related to the facts, put forward by GSK and not disputed by the Commission, that competition by innovation is very fierce in the sector and that competition on price exists in another form, although by law it emerges only when, upon expiry of the patent, manufacturers of generic medicines are able to enter the market. In those circumstances, it was still necessary, in accordance with the case-law cited at paragraph 109 above, to assess what form of competition must be given priority with a view to ensuring the maintenance of effective competition sought by Article 3(1)(g) EC and Article 81 EC.*"

In our view it seems clear that priority must be given to the enhancement of interbrand competition over the very limited — "marginal" in the words of the CFI- intrabrand competition between exporting wholesalers and distributors in the country of destination. The latter is irrelevant because parallel traders typically do not pass on to consumers in the country of destination the price difference between both markets but rather keep that difference to a great extent for themselves. Furthermore, competition is never eliminated altogether because there is usually competition from generics upon expiry of the patent. As regards interbrand competition — which is always more relevant than intrabrand competition in the analysis of a vertical restraint-, the decisive parameter of competition between pharmaceutical companies is R&D since prices are usually intervened by the public authorities of the Member States.

3.3 Conclusion

The result of the appeal proceedings before both EU Courts was that the Commission's decision was confirmed as regards the finding that GSK's sales conditions restricted competition "by object". However, the Commission's refusal to grant an individual exemption under Article 101(3) TFEU was annulled.

It is therefore not definitively settled whether the four conditions of Article 101(3) are fulfilled by a system of differentiated prices that seeks to limit parallel exports of pharmaceuticals from a country which fixes the prices of these products for dispensation on the national territory. There are, however, encouraging indications from both Courts that such a system may fulfil the four requirements of the third paragraph of Article 101 TFEU in view of the specific circumstances –i.e. the intervention of prices- governing the pharmaceutical sector in Europe.

4. The Aftermath in Spain

While the European Commission's policy priorities in the pharmaceutical sector switched from parallel trade to patent-related issues, particularly during the period between the CFI's and ECJ's judgments in the *GSK Spain* case, parallel traders continued to bring complaints before national competition authorities and national courts.

In Spain, these complaints gave rise to a number of decisions by the National Competition Commission (CNC), all of which rejected the parallel traders' claims. Interestingly, the CNC attached special importance to the legal context of the practices complained of and, in particular, to Article 90 of the Pharmaceutical Act[12] which reserves the application of

---

12 Law 29/2006, of 26 July 2006, on Guarantees and Rational Use of Pharmaceutical and Sanitary Products.

the regulated prices fixed by the Spanish authorities to products that are financed with public funds and dispensed in Spain.

4.1 Laboratorios Farmacéuticos

In the *Laboratorios Farmacéuticos*[13] case, the CNC dismissed a complaint by two wholesalers (SEDIFA and GRUFARMA) concerning an alleged concerted or consciously parallel practice between several pharmaceutical companies to terminate their supply agreements with the complainants contrary to Article 1 of the Spanish Competition Act (LDC).

In its decision, the CNC made reference to the judgment of the *Juzgado de Primera Instancia* of Alcobendas[14] that dismissed the action brought by the same wholesalers to obtain supplies by PFIZER, holding that there is no obligation under the (pharmaceutical) legislation in force for pharmaceutical companies to supply their products upon request by any wholesaler.

The CNC found no evidence of the alleged concerted or consciously parallel practice. It held that the coincidence in the dates of termination by the various pharmaceutical companies of their supply agreements with the complainants could be explained by the entry into force of the new Pharmaceutical Act 29/2006 which provides in Article 90 that the regulated price, fixed by Spanish authorities, applies to products financed with public funds and dispensed in Spain. According to the CNC, to apply this Article, pharmaceutical companies need to know where their products are dispensed. This can be more easily done if the number of wholesalers is reduced, which could explain, in the case at hand, why pharmaceutical companies terminated all of their existing agreements with wholesalers and concluded new agreements with a smaller number of wholesalers, chosen on the basis of objective criteria.

4.2 Spain Pharma

An example of the decreasing interest of the European Commission in parallel trade cases in the aftermath of the GSK case is the *Spain Pharma* case.

---

13 Decision of the CNC of 25 September 2008 in case S/0030/07 *Laboratorios Farmacéuticos*.
14 Judgment of the *Juzgado de Primera Instancia* of Alcobendas in case n° 660/2006, upheld on appeal.

The Spanish wholesaler Spain Pharma lodged a complaint before the European Commission in relation to an alleged agreement between PFIZER and the association of wholesalers COFARES whereby PFIZER would ensure supplies to the members of the association subject to the latter undertaking not to export.

The European Commission informed the CNC of the complaint, indicated that in its opinion the CNC was the authority best placed to deal with the complaint and finally rejected Spain Pharma's complaint for lack of Community interest[15].

The CNC found no evidence of the alleged agreement between PFIZER and COFARES[16].

In the same decision, the CNC also rejected Spain Pharma's complaint against the agreements entered into by PFIZER and its wholesalers, which according to Spain Pharma established a "double pricing" system. The CNC found that these agreements were covered by the then applicable Vertical Block Exemption Regulation[17]. Moreover, the CNC held that these agreements did not establish a "double pricing" system. According to the CNC, the application of a "free price" by PFIZER was a unilateral decision of PFIZER based on the Pharmaceutical Act. PFIZER only set one "free price", which was replaced by law by the regulated price set by Spanish authorities pursuant to Article 90 of the Pharmaceutical Act (and Article 100(2) of the former Pharmaceutical Act[18]) for those products fulfilling the conditions established in this Article. In this respect, the CNC referred to the judgment of *Juzgado de Primera Instancia* of Valencia of 27 April 2007[19] which confirmed that the application of the regulated price is conditional upon the fulfilment of the two requirements of public financing and dispensation of the product at issue in Spain.

The CNC also invoked Recommendation VI of the "G10 High Level Group on innovation and provision of medicines in the European Union" of 7 May 2002, pursuant to which *"the Commission and Member States should secure the principle that a Member State's authority to regulate prices in the EU should extend only to those medicines purchased by, or reim-*

---

15 Case 39.184 *SP/PFIZER*.
16 Decision of the CNC of 21 May 2009 in case 2623/05 *Spain Pharma*.
17 Commission Regulation (EC) No. 2790/1999 of 22 December 1999 on the application of Article 81(3) of the Treaty to categories of vertical agreements and concerted practices, OJ L 336/21 of 29.12.1999.
18 Law 25/1990, of 20 December.
19 Judgment of *Juzgado de Primera Instancia* of Valencia of 27 April 2007 in case 567/2003.

bursed by, the State. Full competition should be allowed for medicines not reimbursed by State systems or medicines sold into private markets"[20].

4.3 *EAEPC* vs. *Laboratorios Farmacéuticos*

In the *EAEPC* case[21], the CNC rejected a complaint by the European Association of Euro-Pharmaceutical Companies (EAEPC) against several pharmaceutical companies in relation to their "double pricing" systems which, according to EAEPC, infringed Articles 1 LDC and 81 EC (now Article 101 TFEU).

EAEPC had already lodged a complaint against PFIZER for the same facts before the European Commission, which dismissed it for lack of Community interest[22].

As in the above mentioned *Spain Pharma* case, the CNC distinguished between "double pricing" and "free pricing" systems. According to the CNC, pharmaceutical companies fix just one price that is replaced by the regulated price fixed by the Administration when the conditions for the application of the latter (public financing and dispensation in Spain) are fulfilled. The CNC held that the regulated price is fixed in view of the public interest of the Spanish State -in that it relates to products financed with public funds- and cannot be extended to exported products. It also found that pharmaceutical companies need to know the place of dispensation of their products to be able to apply the regulated price and that, consequently, information systems whereby wholesalers should provide information as to dispensation in Spain do not affect competition.

Furthermore, the CNC discarded a possible concertation between pharmaceutical companies to apply their "free price" systems. Again, the CNC stated that the establishment by these companies of information systems as to dispensation in Spain can be explained by the need to comply with Article 90 of the Pharmaceutical Act.

Finally, the CNC rejected EAEPC's allegations relating to the foreclosure of wholesalers. The CNC found no evidence of such foreclosure and held that pharmaceutical companies are free to determine the size of their distribution networks.

---

20 http://ec.europa.eu/health/ph_overview/Documents/key08_en.pdf
21 Decision of the CNC of 14 September 2009 in case S/0017/07 *EAEPC* vs. *Laboratorios Farmacéuticos*.
22 Decision of 8 August 2006.

4.4 FEFE

In the *FEFE* case[23], the CNC again rejected a complaint -this time by the Spanish Federation of Pharmacists (FEFE)- against so called "double pricing" systems applied by several pharmaceutical companies and other instrumental conducts (foreclosure of wholesalers, information systems as to dispensation in Spain, shortages of supply, application of the distribution margin in direct sales by pharmaceutical companies to pharmacies).

As in previous cases, the CNC differentiated between "double pricing" and "free pricing" systems. Invoking the judgment of the Court of Justice in the *GSK Spain* case, it added that, pursuant to EU case law, "double pricing" systems could be justified in that they generate efficiencies (by an increase of investment in R&D) to the benefit of consumers.

The CNC also found that the conducts complained of by FEFE did not in themselves infringe competition law since they were instrumental to the application of the free pricing system nor did they constitute a de facto implementation of a double pricing system.

4.5 SEDIFA y GRUFARMA

In the *SEDIFA y GRUFARMA* case[24], the CNC rejected a complaint by these two wholesalers against several pharmaceutical companies for an alleged abuse of a dominant position contrary to Article 2 of the Spanish Competition Act, namely for a refusal to supply to the complainants and their discrimination vis-à-vis other wholesalers.

The complaint related to the same facts already analysed by the CNC in the above mentioned *Laboratorios Farmacéuticos* case, where the same two wholesalers contended that the termination by several pharmaceutical companies of their supply agreements with them was the result of a restrictive agreement contrary to Article 1 LDC. The two wholesalers had also brought an action before the ordinary courts in relation to the same facts alleging inter alia an infringement of Articles 1 and 2 LDC, which shows the Spanish wholesalers' firm determination to challenge this kind of conduct using all available avenues.

23 Decision of the CNC of 17 February 2010 in case S/0038/08 *FEFE vs. Laboratorios y Almacenistas Farmacéuticos*.
24 Decision of the CNC of 9 June 2010 in case S/0176/09, *SEDIFA y GRUFARMA*.

However, SEDIFA and GRUFARMA were not successful; neither before the ordinary courts nor the CNC.

The CNC confirmed its finding in *Laboratorios Farmacéuticos* that the decision by the pharmaceutical companies to terminate their existing agreements with wholesalers and conclude new agreements with a reduced group of wholesalers (selected on the basis of objective criteria) had to be seen in the context of the entry into force of the new Pharmaceutical Act 29/2006 which partially liberalized the price of pharmaceutical products and modified wholesale margins, which in turn led pharmaceutical companies to restructure their distribution networks to reduce costs and increase efficiency.

The CNC concluded that, even assuming that the pharmaceutical companies enjoyed a dominant position — which had not been proved — their conduct could not be deemed abusive.

First, their conduct could not be deemed an abusive refusal to supply since there was no indication that it restricted competition in the wholesale market contrary to consumer interest and, in any event, it was objectively justified by the need or aim of restructuring distribution networks to increase efficiency. In this respect, the CNC invoked the judgment of the *Juzgado de lo Mercantil* n° 2 of Barcelona[25] that rejected the action brought by SEDIFA and GRUFARMA in relation to the same facts on the grounds that the alleged refusal to supply was objectively justified. The CNC also found that the *GSK Greece* judgment was not relevant in the case at hand, since that judgment related to a refusal to supply with the object of restricting exports.

Secondly, the CNC held that the conduct complained of could not be deemed an abusive discrimination of the complainants as compared to other wholesalers with whom the pharmaceutical companies concluded new supply agreements. As in the *Laboratorios Farmacéuticos* case, the CNC invoked the judgment of the Juzgado de Primera Instancia n° 6 de Alcobendas to confirm that pharmaceutical companies — even if they are dominant — are not under any obligation to supply to all wholesalers placing an order with them, especially when, as in the case at hand, wholesalers that receive supplies are selected on the basis of objective criteria.

---

25   Judgment 56/10 of the *Juzgado de lo Mercantil* n° 2 of Barcelona of 24 February 2010.

5. Conclusion

After the two rulings delivered by the Court of First Instance and, on appeal, the European Court of Justice in the GSK Spain case it has become clear that the solution to the distortions of competition caused by parallel trade in pharmaceuticals is to be found in the third paragraph of Article 101 TFEU.

Although both Courts have acknowledged that there is a distortion of genuine competition due to the fact that the prices of these products are fixed by various Member States — a circumstance that makes parallel exports from low-priced to higher priced countries possible in the first place-, the ECJ has nonetheless concluded that any limitation of parallel trade, also in such intervened products, restricts competition "by object" within the meaning of Article 101(1) TFEU.

It is also clear from the CFI's judgment that *"the conduct consisting in establishing, by contract, a system of differentiated prices prohibiting the Spanish wholesalers dealing with GW from purchasing at that price (the Clause 4A price) medicines which they will resell in other Member States, and obliging them to purchase those products at a higher price (the Clause 4B price), is not imposed by the Spanish regulations"* (para. 73). Article 101 TFEU therefore fully applies to such a system of differentiated prices even if the prices of reimbursable medicines are fixed wholly independently by the Spanish authorities and are binding.

This is why the solution of the problem created by parallel trade in a product with intervened prices can only be found in the third paragraph of Article 101 TFEU.

Although the GSK case has not definitively settled whether a system of differentiated prices fulfils the four requirements of Article 101(3) TFEU, there are indications in the judgments of both Community Courts that these four conditions may be fulfilled, bearing in mind the specific circumstances of the pharmaceutical sector.

Both rulings show that the decade-long discussion in the GSK case about the merits of parallel trade in products with fixed prices eventually has convinced competition authorities in Europe that such parallel trade does not merit protection. This can be seen in decisions of the Spanish competition authority delivered in the aftermath of the GSK case. *In the EAEPC case the CNC held that "it would make no sense to extend the fixing of prices by the Spanish State according to public interest criteria to other territories or that products for exportation were affected by the inter-*

vened prices determined in Spain, limiting in an unjustified manner the [fundamental] *freedom of producers* [to set their prices]".

As the CFI expressed it in its GSK judgment, in the pharmaceutical sector parallel traders "*are the vectors of artificial competition and not of effective competition within the meaning of Article 3(1)(g) EC and Article 81 EC*" *(para. 146)*.

PART THREE

AN OVERVIEW OF VERTICAL RESTRAINTS IN SPECIFIC MARKETS

CHAPTER VIII

VERTICAL RESTRAINTS AND ENERGY MARKETS

Rafael Piqueras Bautista

General Secretary
ENAGAS, S.A.

1. Introduction

The achievement of an Internal Market for Energy has become one of the
main concerns of the European Union during the last years. The *"Internal
Market for Energy"* and *"Competition"* are closely linked concepts, given
that such an internal market needs full competition to exist. The achievement of full competition in the energy market requires specific measures as
is shown by the different Directives of common rules for the internal markets of gas and electricity produced by the European Commission during the
last years. Such measures (third party access to common infrastructures,
activities unbundling...), specific to the energy sectors, differ from those
addressed to defend Competition in general, the vertical restraints regime
being among them. Nonetheless, general rules on Competition are applicable to energy activities as well. Certainly, specific actions in the energy
sectors try "to improve" competition in them while the general Competition
regime "defends" it in any sector. However, the boundaries between both
kinds of measures are becoming weaker every day. In this context, some
integrated gas Companies in Germany and other countries have recently
been forced to comply with the so-called "ownership unbundling" of the gas
transmission grid –a specific measure for the gas and electricity markets
included in the *"Third Package"* of common rules for the energy internal
market- as a way of avoiding the consequences of antitrust proceedings
opened by the European Commission against grid owners for abusing their
dominant position. So, in May 2008, RWE agreed to sell its German gas
grid in settlement of the antitrust proceedings that the EU Commission
initiated against it in April 2007. RWE Transportnetz Gas GmbH had been
suspected of unlawfully blocking access to the German gas transmission

system. In December 2008, RWE submitted a formal undertaking to sell its gas transmission system to an independent third party. In March 2009, the EU Commission declared this to be legally binding and thereupon dropped its investigations. Although RWE took the view that the accusations were unfounded, it agreed to the proposed settlement to avoid protracted litigation. The relevant operations were transferred to Thyssengas GmbH, a subsidiary which was prepared for sale in the course of 2010. The EU Commission dropped its investigations of RWE's operations in the electricity sector in October 2009, having been unable to find any evidence of misconduct on its part. To underscore its commitment to an independent electricity transmission grid, however, RWE opted for the "third way" envisaged by the EU's package of proposals for a Single Energy Market, and in September 2009 transferred its electricity transmission grid operations to Amprion GmbH, a new company with 850 employees based in Dortmund, Germany. Although a 100 percent subsidiary of RWE, Amprion has been set up as a completely self-sufficient company and is fully independent of the other companies in the Group; it reports directly to the Board of RWE AG. The establishment of Amprion ensures the independent, non-discriminatory and reliable electricity transmission that the EU demands.

Examples of both kinds of actions in energy sectors will be commented on here. Vertical restraints have been considered in Spain as a threat to competition in the distribution of oil products. In other energy sectors, like gas, resale price maintenance has not been considered as a vertical restraint, but instead it has been the imposition of "destination clauses" by some non-EU suppliers of gas that has caught the authorities' attention. Finally, vertical integration of gas and electricity Companies, including transmission grids, is considered a barrier for Competition in both sectors and it has been paid special attention in the *"Third Package"*.

This *"Third Package"*[1] of common rules for the energy internal market for

---

1   The "Third Package" of measures adopted by the Commission will ensure that all European citizens can take advantage of the numerous benefits provided by a truly competitive energy market. Consumer choice, fairer prices, cleaner energy and security of supply are at the centre of the third legislative package, adopted by the Commission on 19 September 2007. In order to reach those goals, the Commission proposed: to separate production and supply from transmission networks; to facilitate cross-border trade in energy; more effective national regulators; to promote cross-border collaboration and investment; greater market transparency on network operation and supply; and increased solidarity among the EU countries. The new legislative measures were published on OJ L 211, 14 August 2009 and include:
    – Regulation (EC) No. 713/2009 of the European Parliament and of the Council of 13 July 2009 establishing an Agency for the Cooperation of Energy Regulators;
    – Regulation (EC) No. 714/2009 of the European Parliament and of the Council of 13 July 2009 on conditions for access to the network for cross-border exchanges in electricity and repealing Regulation (EC) No. 1228/2003;

gas and electricity was published last year (this means that there has been a first, 1996-1998[2], and a second package, 2003[3]). These measures include, among others, the "ownership unbundling" of certain activities because the vertical integration of such activities is considered "per se" a barrier to competition without the need for an effective abuse as in the case of the regulations about vertical restraints.

Of course, the existence of special rules for an internal market for energy does not mean that general rules on competition are not applicable to energy sectors.

Therefore, I will refer here, first of all, to a case of application of the regulation on vertical restraints, relating to resale price maintenance, in the retail Spanish sector for petrol products.

Secondly, I will explain a case of vertical restraints, relating to "destination clauses" in the gas market in which vertical restraints regulations have not been applicable because non-EU suppliers were involved. The European Commission has happily solved this conflict.

And finally, but briefly, I would like to comment on the limitations imposed on the vertical integration of gas and electricity undertakings by the Third Package of measures on the internal market for energy.

- Regulation (EC) No. 715/2009 of the European Parliament and of the Council of 13 July 2009 on conditions for access to the natural gas transmission networks and repealing Regulation (EC) No. 1775/2005;
- Directive 2009/72/EC of the European Parliament and of the Council of 13 July 2009 concerning common rules for the internal market in electricity and repealing Directive 2003/54/EC;
- Directive 2009/73/EC of the European Parliament and of the Council of 13 July 2009 concerning common rules for the internal market in natural gas and repealing Directive 2003/55/EC;
- Directive 2009/72/EC and Directive 2009/73/EC, have been object of several "Interpretative Notes" published by the Commission on 22 January 2010.

2   Directive 96/92/EC of the European Parliament and of the Council of 19 December 1996 concerning common rules for the internal market in Electricity and Directive 98/30/EC of the European Parliament and of the Council of 22 June 1998 concerning common rules for the internal market in natural gas.

3   Directive 2003/55/EC of the European Parliament and of the Council of 26 June 2003 concerning common rules for the internal market in natural gas and repealing Directive 98/30/EC and Directive 2003/54/EC of the European Parliament and of the Council of 26 June 2003 concerning common rules for the internal market in electricity and repealing Directive 96/92/EC.

2. Vertical restraints in the distribution of oil products

2.1 The different contractual formulas
to operate a petrol-station

After being produced from a well and traded, crude oil is refined and converted into different products ready to be consumed (automobile gasoline and gas oil, heating gas oil, aviation kerosene, liquefied petroleum gas as butane and propane, fuel-oils and finally asphalts and other heavy condensates). Each product is commercialized through the appropriate channel and, as is known, automobile gasoline and gas oil are distributed in petrol-stations in roads and streets. However, anytime consumers stop at a petrol-station to refill the tank of their cars, they are totally unaware of the complex commercial and legal framework that lies underneath the brand and the corporate image of a well known Oil Company which they assume is the owner and operator of the station.... but this is not always the case.

Different contractual alternatives are possible:

COCO (Company Owned-Company Operated) contracts. Petrol-station facilities are owned and operated by a wholesale distributor of oil products, usually a large vertically integrated Oil Company that develops upstream activities (exploration and production), that trades internationally crude, that owns refineries to obtain the products and that commercializes them through different channels, including their own petrol-stations. This contractual formula, the most desirable one for Oil Companies, does not represent any risk of vertical restraints to Competition, given that vertical integration of undertakings, by itself, is not considered a threat as in the gas or the electricity sectors. Selling prices are freely and directly fixed by the Oil Company.

DOCO (Dealer Owned-Company Operated) contracts. Petrol-station facilities are owned by a third party who contractually transfers its operation to the Oil Company. The effect is similar to COCO contracts, the only difference being the temporal limitation that results from the lease of the station. The Oil Company directly fixes sales prices with no incidence to vertical restraints.

COCO and DOCO contracts represent approximately 17% of the total of petrol-stations in Spain, while Oil Companies (REPSOL, CEPSA and BP mainly) are still trying to increase that share.

CODO (Company Owned-Dealer Operated) contracts. The petrol-station facilities are owned or leased by the Oil Company which contractually transfers the operation to a third party (the dealer).

DODO (Dealer Owned-Dealer Operated) contracts. The petrol-station is owned by a third party who also operates it through a contract with an Oil Company.

In both cases, the Oil Company becomes the exclusive wholesale supplier of the dealer and provides the dealer with its brand and corporate image, as well as its technical and commercial support. Other conditions such as reselling prices could be agreed upon in the case of "agency agreements".

In CODOs and DODOs, not being the Oil Company, but the operator of the petrol-stations, risks of vertical restraints appear, and Commission Regulations[4] and Guidelines[5] on Vertical Restraints become applicable. In both cases, the dealer can act in the market as an "agent" of the Oil Company or as a "reseller".

If the dealer acts as an "agent" it must be under the conditions for the "agency agreements" described in paragraphs 12 to 21 of the current Guidelines. Therefore, the dealer should not bear one or more of the relevant financial or commercial risks in relation to the activities for which it has been appointed as an agent by the principal. The Guidelines include, among the risks that a real agent should not assume, making *"market-specific investments in equipment, premises or training of personnel, such as for example the petrol storage tank in the case of the petrol retailing...*[6]*"*.

---

4 Commission Regulation (EU) No. 330/2010 of 20 April 2010 on the application of Article 101(3) of the Treaty on the Functioning of the European Union to categories of vertical agreements and concerted practices (OJ L 102, 23 of April 2010).

5 Guidelines on Vertical Restraints (OJ C 130, 19 of May 2010).

6 "(13) The determining factor in defining an agency agreement for the application of Article 101(1) is the financial or commercial risk borne by the agent in relation to the activities for which it has been appointed as an agent by the principal.) In this respect it is not material for the assessment whether the agent acts for one or several principals. Neither is material for this assessment the qualification given to their agreement by the parties or national legislation.
(15) For the purposes of applying Article 101(1), the agreement will be qualified as an agency agreement if the agent does not bear any, or bears only insignificant, risks in relation to the contracts concluded and/or negotiated on behalf of the principal, in relation to market-specific investments for that field of activity, and in relation to other activities required by the principal to be undertaken on the same product market. However, risks that are related to the activity of providing agency services in general, such as the risk of the agent's income being dependent upon its success as an agent or general investments in for instance premises or personnel, are not material to this assessment.
(16) For the purpose of applying Article 101(1), an agreement will thus generally be considered an agency agreement where property in the contract goods bought or sold does not vest in the agent, or the agent does not himself supply the contract services and where the agent: ... (f) does not make market-specific investments in equipment, premises or training of personnel, such as for example the petrol storage tank in the case of petrol retailing or specific software to sell insurance policies in case of insurance agents, unless these costs are fully reimbursed by the principal; (17) This list is not exhaustive. However, where the agent incurs one or more of the risks or costs mentioned in paragraphs (14), (15) and (16),

In case of a real "agency agreement", the Oil Company, as principal, takes the risks relating to selling and purchasing the oil products, and therefore it is in a position to determine the commercial strategy. That is why some obligations on the agent's part will be considered to form an inherent part of an agency agreement, such as limitations on the territory in which the agent can act, limitations on the customer to whom the agent can sell the products and "the prices and conditions at which the agent must sell or purchase these goods or services"[7]. On the contrary, if the contracts between the Oil Company and dealer –CODOs and DODOs do not fulfil the requirements of being considered "agency agreements", those limitations, being the price of selling among them, may be considered as vertical restraints to Competition, and could not be imposed on the dealer by the Oil Company.

It is easy to guess that a correct qualification of the contracts is essential to determine the obligations that Oil Companies can impose on the dealers and that, in practice, such qualifications have caused a number of controversies with the Spanish Competition Authorities for Oil Companies in Spain.

---

the agreement between agent and principal will not be qualified as an agency agreement. The question of risk must be assessed on a case-by-case basis, and with regard to the economic reality of the situation rather than the legal form. For practical reasons, the risk analysis may start with the assessment of the contract-specific risks. If contract- specific risks are incurred by the agent, it will be enough to conclude that the agent is an independent distributor. On the contrary, if the agent does not incur contract-specific risks, then it will be necessary to continue further the analysis by assessing the risks related to market-specific investments. Finally, if the agent does not incur any contract-specific risks and risks related to market-specific investments, the risks related to other required activities within the same product market may have to be considered". Paragraphs 13, 15 and 16 of the Guidelines.

7   In the case of agency agreements as defined in section 2.1, the selling or purchasing function of the agent forms part of the principal's activities. Since the principal bears the commercial and financial risks related to the selling and purchasing of the contract goods and services all obligations imposed on the agent in relation to the contracts concluded and/or negotiated on behalf of the principal fall outside Article 101(1). The following obligations on the agent's part will be considered to form an inherent part of an agency agreement, as each of them relates to the ability of the principal to fix the scope of activity of the agent in relation to the contract goods or services, which is essential if the principal is to take the risks and therefore to be in a position to determine the commercial strategy: (a) limitations on the territory in which the agent may sell these goods or services; (b) limitations on the customers to whom the agent may sell these goods or services; (c) the prices and conditions at which the agent must sell or purchase these goods or services. Paragraph 18 of the Guidelines.

2.2 The Spanish retail market
of oil products in petrol-stations

World War I showed the strategic importance of mechanized vehicles and, consequently, of petrol. The development of the automobile industry after the War made clear the economic importance of oil products that could also be the object of high taxation by States. All that led to a good number of States establishing public monopolies on the activities related to oil (importation, refining, storage, transport and distribution). Spain did so in 1927 and all those activities were developed by CAMPSA, a specific Company, State-owned, that, with the condition of a leaser, operated a monopoly until its dismantlement with Spain's entry into the Common Market in 1986. During the time of the monopoly, petrol-stations were operated by CÁMPSA itself or by third parties under a concession regime. In the years following Spain's European Union entry, the motor fuel market was gradually liberalised; the former monopoly of CAMPSA was dismantled and restrictions on the building of new service stations were removed. Accordingly, Spain, which had a very low number of petrol-stations per inhabitant compared to other EU markets, witnessed a large-scale construction and refurbishment of petrol-stations. CODOs and DODOs were subscribed to, most of them as agency agreements, according to which the dealer sells the oil products to the final consumer on behalf of the Oil Company, at the price and the conditions fixed by the Oil Company, but with the possibility of providing price discounts against the agent's own commission.

A particular form of CODO was used at that time. Some owners of bare land or of old service station buildings entered into long-term contracts with the main suppliers of fuel at the time, in particular Repsol. According to the contracts signed with Repsol, land owners granted a "right in rem" for a long period (from 25 to 40 years) to Repsol on their land or on their land and building. Repsol would then finance the construction or refurbishment of the station, rent the station back to the owner and, for the duration of the "right in rem", be the exclusive supplier of motor fuel to the station. Around 500 similar contracts signed by Repsol were in force at that time.

Only a small part of CODOs and DODOs have been, more recently, subscribed to under the modality of a "resale agreement," under which the dealer assumes the risk of its activity, acts on its own and not on behalf of the Oil Company, and determines the sales price, generally referring to the international price of each product according to "Platt's Oilgram" (Platts is a provider of energy and metals information and a source of benchmark price assessments in the physical energy markets; Platts has provided information since 1909) without prejudice to the possibility of the supplier imposing a maximum sale price.

During a first period, the now-extinguished *Tribunal de Defensa de la Competencia* (the Spanish Competition Authority), in light of EC Regulation 1984/83[8], considered that CODOs and DODOs in Spain were real "agency agreements" that did not represent a risk to Competition. Despite this, since the end of the 1990s, petrol-station dealers have been trying to obtain the cancellation of their contracts with the various suppliers involved (REPSOL and others) before national courts, on the grounds that these contracts infringed Spanish competition rules, which mirror EC rules. More precisely, the station operators often argued before national courts that the duration of the contracts were contrary to competition rules, and that REPSOL was fixing retail prices although the operators were not real agents of REPSOL.

When Commission Regulation (EC) 2790/1999[9] of 22 December 1999 on the application of Article 81(3) of the Treaty to categories of vertical agreements and concerted practices came into force and the Guidelines on Vertical Restrictions were published by the Commission on 13 October 2000 the situation changed.

According to Regulation 2790/1999, Repsol was not covered by the block exemption established in it. At that time the motor fuel market was highly concentrated. Major players were Repsol (which had a market share of around 40%) Cepsa, BP and Shell. All of Repsol's competitors had a market share below 10%, except Cepsa, which had a market share that was around half of Repsol's share (i.e. 20%). Vertical integration in the market was very high: around half of all petrol-stations in Spain were owned by the wholesale suppliers and, contrary to other Member States' markets, the Spanish market had not experienced an increase in the number of "white stations" (unbranded stations) or of stations owned by supermarkets.

All the Oil Companies operating in Spain, except Repsol, held a share that did not exceed 30% of the market, so their contracts were under the exemption of paragraph 2 of the Regulation 2790/1999. On the contrary, Repsol's contracts did not benefit from such an exception. Therefore, in December 2001, REPSOL notified, pursuant to the Regulation, all its supply agreements to the Commission, with a view to obtaining a negative clearance or, subsequently, an individual exemption under Article 81.3 of the Treaty. On

---

8   EC Regulations 1984/83 of 22 June 1983 (OJ 173, 30 June 1983).
9   OJ L 336, 29 December 2009.

12 April 2006[10], the Commission adopted a decision based on Article 9 of Regulation EC 1/2003 of 16 December 2002[11] on the implementation of the rules on competition laid down in Articles 81 and 82 of the Treaty.

The Commission's investigation showed that access to the market was rather difficult because of its structure and in particular because of vertical integration of all operators. Exclusivity contracts signed between the operators and the remaining independent petrol-stations tied these stations for long periods of time to the operators, further hindering competition. The contracts signed by Repsol, in particular the long-term contracts which were based on "rights in rem" owned by Repsol, particularly contributed to the foreclosure of the market. This ultimately diminished the pressure to reduce prices and improve quality, to the detriment of consumers. In a first stage, REPSOL committed to offering to dealers the possibility of 'buying back' the "right in rem" before the scheduled expiry of the agreement. This option could in principle have been exercised at any time after the date when the agreement had only 12 years left to run. The exercise of the option would have involved paying REPSOL compensation equal to the value of the "right in rem" in question.

Additionally, Repsol took on a number of other commitments that should be implemented before 31 December 2011. First of all, Repsol committed to not conclude any new supply contracts with a duration exceeding 5 years with service stations. Repsol also committed not to purchase any independent station that was not supplied by Repsol during the first two years following the Commission's decision. Finally, Repsol committed to ensuring that all service stations within its network would be able to provide discounts on the price recommended by Repsol; those discounts should also be applicable in those stations where they only act as agents of Repsol (in such cases, the station would be able to share its commission with the client in order to reduce the price for the client).

However, neither the block exemption applicable to Cepsa and other Oil Companies, nor the favourable, although subject to conditions, Decision of the Commission obtained by Repsol, improved their position from the point of view of vertical restraints. In particular, in 1999 the Spanish Competition Authorities opened formal proceedings against Repsol and Cepsa for vertical restraints in their contracts with petrol-stations dealers. As a consequence of such proceedings, the *Tribunal de Defensa de la Compe-*

---

10 OJ L 176, 30 June 2006.
11 Council Regulation (EC) No. 1/2003 of 16 December 2002 on the implementation of the rules on competition laid down in Articles 81 and 82 of the Treaty (OJ L 1, 4 January 2003).

tencia stated on 30 of May and 11 of July 2001 (Decisions n. 490/2000 and 493/2000) that Cepsa and Repsol had committed in a breach of the Spanish Competition Law. The TDC considered that some of the contracts signed under the modality of "agency agreement" were not real agency agreements. According to these agreements, the dealer, the supposed agent, assumed product risks vis-à-vis third parties and also assumed financial risks, since it paid for the product supplied in nine days after its supply, even before selling it. Therefore, neither Cepsa nor Repsol could fix the resale prices according to the TDC's decisions, as they were doing at that moment. In this regard, the TDC considered that the possibility given by Repsol to its dealers to apply discounts with charge to their commissions was not enough to justify a real capability of dealers to fix prices. Cepsa was fined for an equivalent 1,2 million Euros and Repsol for the equivalent to 1,8 million Euros, and both were obliged to cease the anticompetitive practice of resale price fixing.

Repsol alleged that it had obtained a "comfort decision" from the Commission regarding its contracts (the aforementioned Decision of 12 of April 2006). However, the TDC declared that the Commission's decision did not interfere with the execution of what had been resolved by TDC. Cepsa and Repsol appealed against those TDC decisions before the Spanish courts but they confirmed the above-mentioned TDC decisions.

Very recently, the *Tribunal Supremo de Justicia* (Spanish High Court) in a *Sentencia* (Judgement) issued on 17 November 2010 has confirmed the previous judgement of the *Audiencia Nacional* rejecting the court appeal of Repsol against the TDC decision. On the contrary, another recent *Sentencia* of the *Tribunal Supremo de Justicia*, issued on 10 November 2010, has considered that some other contracts subscribed to among Repsol and oil station dealers were properly "agency agreements", declaring according to law the way Repsol acted.

It seems that, in spite of these decisions, Oil Companies in Spain may have persisted in some anticompetitive practices in their vertical relations with dealers that operate petrol-stations. The *Tribunal de Defensa de la Competencia*, on 30 of July 2009, produced a new decision (Expte. 662/07 REPSOL/CEPSA/BP) that declared that Repsol, Cepsa and BP had committed a breach of Spanish Competition Law and paragraph 81.1 of the EC Treaty, fixing prices to non-agent dealers, restraining competition among the stations of their respective networks and all other petrol-stations. The arguments of this decision are similar to those of 2001. However, a new argument appears in this decision. The TDC considered that the renalified vertical anticompetitive practices also had a horizontal effect, since they made the alignment of prices easier between competitors (i.e. stations and Oil Companies).

The Spanish Competition Authorities concluded again that the risks assumed by the dealers made them resellers and not real agents. As a consequence, Repsol was fined 5 million Euros, Cepsa 1,8 million euros and BP 1,1 million Euros.

The decision of 30 of July 2009 has been adopted in line with Commission Regulation (EC) 2790/1999 of 22 December 1999 not in force yet. However, new Commission Regulation EU 330/2010 of 20 April 2010[12] on the application of Article 101 (3) of the Treaty on the Functioning of the European Union to categories of vertical agreements and concerted practices and the new Guidelines on Vertical Restraints[13] made public on 19 of May 2010 will make the application of vertical restraints to competition in the energy sector (such as those detected in the contracts CODO and DODO so far in Spain) even more difficult.

3. Vertical restraints in the supply of natural gas

There is another case in the energy sector of vertical restraints that is worth mentioning here. It is an issue of vertical restraints not related to price, but destination markets, imposed by non-EU undertakings to EU undertakings.

Natural gas is produced from wells, associated or not to condensate oil. It is transported from the production points to the consumption markets through pipelines, when geographically possible, or by ship in liquefied form to be re-gasified again and transported and distributed through pipelines for consumption. Natural gas has, nowadays, an outstanding role in the energy structure given that it is one of the most efficient "raw energies" to produce electricity thanks to the Combine Cycle Gas Turbine (CCGT) technology.

Even though the maturity of the market has allowed more "spot contracts", international natural gas suppliers have traditionally sold their gas under long term contracts (around 20 years) with "take or pay clauses"[14] as a way

---

12 OJ L 102, 23 April 2010.
13 OJ C 130, 19 May 2010.
14 Take-or-pay contracts are written agreements between a buyer and seller that obligate the buyer to pay regardless of whether or not the seller delivers the good or service. Generally, this obligation to pay does not involve the full amount due for the product, and protects the seller in the event that the buyer refuses to accept the good or service when delivery is attempted.

to secure the recovery of the investments incurred to commercialize their gas. These contracts usually include a "destination clause". In gas supply contracts between a gas producer and a gas wholesaler, territorial restrictions (also called "destination clauses") prevent the buyer/importer from reselling the gas outside a certain geographic area (normally a Member State). Alternatively to territorial restrictions clauses, contracts included "profit sharing mechanisms" that oblige the buyer/importer to share a certain part of the profit with the supplier/producer if the gas is sold on by the importer to a customer outside the agreed territory or to a customer using the gas for another purpose than the one agreed upon, have been used as an alternative to territorial restrictions clauses.

The Commission expressed its concerns relating to the anti-competitive nature of such clauses (*"an important obstacle for the creation of a single EU-wide market in gas"* to the European buyers/importers. However European buyers/importers, as the weakest party in the supply contracts in the face of non-EU companies, had scarcely any chance to change the clauses as the Commission required of them. Therefore, the Commission set up negotiations with the main non-EU suppliers (the Rusian "Gazprom", the Nigerian "Nigeria LNG Ltd" and the Algerian "Sonatrach"). A common understanding was reached with each of them (the last one, with Sonatrach, was announced by the Commission on 11 July 2007). The common understanding reached can be summarised as follows:

— Deletion of territorial restriction from all existing contracts and no insertion in future contracts.

— Profit sharing mechanisms (so called "PSMs") only to be applied in LNG (Liquefied Natural Gas) contracts under which the title of the gas remains with the seller until the ship is unloaded (in practice, sales under DES terms). Consequently, Sonatrach is aiming to transform the remaining FOB and CIF existing LNG contracts to sales under DES terms.

— No PSMs in future LNG contracts under which the title of the gas passes to the purchaser at the port of loading (in practice, for sales under FOB and CIF terms).

— No PSMs in existing or future pipeline gas supply contracts.

In conclusion, there were vertical restraints due to "destination clauses" in the international market for natural gas that could affect the Internal Market. A "diplomatic" action of the European Commission satisfactorily solved the issue.

4. Vertical "disintegration" in the common market for energy

As has been said before, general rules on competition coexist with the specific regime to achieve a "common market on energy". The internal market in natural gas and electricity, which has been progressively implemented throughout the Community since 1999, aims to deliver real choice for all consumers of the European Union, be they citizens or businesses, new business opportunities and more cross-border trade, so as to achieve efficiency gains, competitive prices, and higher standards of service, and to contribute to security of supply and sustainability. The freedoms which the Treaty guarantees the citizens of the Union — inter alia, the free movement of goods, the freedom of establishment and the freedom to provide services — are achievable only in a fully open market, which enables all consumers freely to choose their suppliers and all suppliers freely to deliver to their customers.

The process of liberalisation in the gas and electricity sectors has relied on the "third party access" concept that entitles gas undertakings to pass their gas through the transmission grid owned by other gas undertakings in equal, fair and transparent conditions.

Directive 2003/55/EC of the European Parliament and of the Council of 26 June 2003 concerning common rules for the internal market in natural gas and Directive 2003/54/EC of the European Parliament and of the Council of 26 June 2003 concerning common rules for the internal market in electricity made a significant contribution towards the creation of such an internal market for both sectors. However, at present, there are obstacles to the sale of electricity and gas on equal terms and without discrimination or disadvantages in the Community. In particular, non-discriminatory network access and an equally effective level of regulatory supervision in each Member State do not yet exist.

The Communication of the Commission of 10 January 2007 entitled *"An Energy Policy for Europe"* highlighted the importance of completing the internal market in natural gas and of creating a level playing field for all natural gas undertakings established in the Community. The Communications of the Commission of 10 January 2007 entitled *"Prospects for the internal gas and electricity market"* and *"Inquiry pursuant to Article 17 of Regulation (EC) No. 1/2003 into the European gas and electricity sectors (Final Report)"* showed that the present rules and measures do not provide the necessary framework for achieving the objective of a well-functioning internal market.

As a result of that process, the *"Third Package"* of measures for a common market on energy was approved: The Third Package encompasses:

— Regulation (EC) No. 713/2009 of the European Parliament and of the Council of 13 July 2009 establishing an Agency for the Cooperation of Energy Regulators.

— Regulation (EC) No. 714/2009 of the European Parliament and of the Council of 13 July 2009 on conditions for access to the network for cross-border exchanges in electricity and repealing Regulation (EC) No. 1228/2003

— Regulation (EC) No. 715/2009 of the European Parliament and of the Council of 13 July 2009 on conditions for access to the natural gas transmission networks and repealing Regulation (EC) No. 1775/2005

— Directive 2009/72/EC of 13 July 2009 concerning common rules for the internal market in electricity and repealing Directive 2003/54/EC

— Directive 2009/73/EC of July 2009 concerning common rules for the internal market in gas and repealing Directive 2003/53/EC

Both Directives promote the vertical disintegration of gas and electricity undertakings through the "ownership unbundling" of transmission networks of gas and electricity granting the independence in their operation relating to the interest of vertically integrated companies. Acting in this way, Commission has considered vertical integration (or "disintegration") as a key issue for the energy internal market and has regulated it when defining the structure itself of that market.

According to the Gas Directive (both Directives are very similar) Member States shall ensure that from 3 March 2012 each undertaking which owns a transmission system acts as a transmission system operator and that:

a) the same person or persons are entitled neither:

— directly or indirectly to exercise control over an undertaking performing any of the functions of production or supply, and directly or indirectly to exercise control or exercise any right over a transmission system operator or over a transmission system; nor

— directly or indirectly to exercise control over a transmission system operator or over a transmission system, and directly or indirectly to exercise control or exercise any right over an undertaking performing any of the functions of production or supply;

b) the same person or persons are not entitled to appoint members of the supervisory board, the administrative board or bodies legally representing the undertaking, of a transmission system operator or a transmission system, and directly or indirectly to exercise control or exercise any right over an undertaking performing any of the functions of production or supply; and

c) the same person is not entitled to be a member of the supervisory board, the administrative board or bodies legally representing the undertaking, of both an undertaking performing any of the functions of production or supply and a transmission system operator or a transmission system.

The rights referred to in points (a) and (b) shall include, in particular:

— the power to exercise voting rights;

— the power to appoint members of the supervisory board, the administrative board or bodies legally representing the undertaking; or

— the holding of a majority share.

Where on 3 September 2009, the transmission system belongs to a vertically integrated undertaking a Member State may decide not to apply the "ownership unbundling" as described. In such case, the Member State concerned shall either:

— designate an independent system operator in accordance with Article 14 of the Directive (the *Independent System Operator* Model), or

— comply with the provisions of Chapter IV (the *Independent Transmission Operator* model)

Regarding the Spanish model, the "ownership unbundling" of the electricity and gas transmission grids has been a fact for a good number of years. In the electricity sector, when created in 1985 Red Eléctrica de España S.A. took over the transmission grid and the operation of the Spanish power system, well before the recent world-wide trend towards the segregation of activities, establishing transmission as a separate activity from generation and distribution. This marked a radical change in how the Spanish power sector operated and served as a model for other countries when liberalising their power sectors. The Electricity Sector Act 54/1997 confirmed the role of Red Eléctrica as Transmission System Operator. This law created a wholesale power market which required an effectively-managed transmission grid to work properly and a coordinated operation of the generation-transmission system, to ensure that demand would be satisfied at all times. Act 17/2007 of 4 July amended the previous law to adapt it to European Directive 2003/54/EC which established the common guidelines for the internal power market. This law has resulted in the definitive consolidation of Red Eléctrica's TSO Model (Transmission System Operator). In this regard, Red Eléctrica, as the system operator, guarantees the continuity and security of the power supply and the proper coordination of the production and transmission system, performing its functions based on the principles of transparency, objectiveness and Independence. In addition, Red Eléctrica is the manager of the transmission grid and acts as the sole transporter on an exclusive basis.

In the gas sector, as a consequence of the important growth in energy consumption and the existing forecasts in Spain, at the beginning of the 70s, Spanish authorities decided to spread the use of natural gas to the entire national territory. With the objective of creating a network of gas pipelines in the Iberian Peninsula, the Ministry of Industry published a Decree on 23 March 1972, creating the *Empresa Nacional del Gas* (National Gas Company, Enagás, S.A.). The State considered that it was important to take part in this newly created company through the National Industry Institute (I.N.I.). In the first years following its creation, Enagás concentrated on carrying out planning analyses and technical studies necessary to develop gas infrastructure. On November 13 1975, the Official State Gazette published the first Gasification Plan, which included the administrative licence granted to Enagás for the construction of the gas infrastructure network in Spain. In 1981, Enagás became a part of the National Institute for Hydrocarbons (I.N.H.).

In June 1994 I.N.H. sold 91% of Enagás' share capital to Gas Natural SDG, with the remaining 9% being sold in October 1998. In this way the main gas vertically integrated undertaking became the owner of gas transmission grid. Anticipating unbundling tendencies, the Spanish Government by Royal Decree-Law 6/2000 of June 23, appointed Enagás as Technical Manager of the Gas System, including among its main functions the commitment of guaranteeing continuity and safety in natural gas supply and the correct coordination of access points, storage, transport and distribution. According to this Royal Decree Gas Natural SDG was obliged to disinvest up to 65% of its stake in Enagás. Therefore, on June 2002, Enagás started to be quoted on the stock exchange.

According to Law 62/2006 of 30 December, Gas Natural SDG was obliged to reduce its stake to 5% and finally, with occasion of merging with Unión Fenosa, was obliged to sell such remaining 5% according to the decision of the *Comisión Nacional de Competencia* 11 February 2009 ("Exp. 0098/08 GAS NATURAL/UNION FENOSA").

Law 12/2007, published on 2 July 2007, modifies Law 34/1998 in the hydrocarbons sector in order to adapt it to Directive 2003/55/EC of the European Parliament and Council of 26 June 2003, on community standards for the internal market of natural gas. This Law established, in addition to the current 5% maximum limit on shareholdings, a 3% limit on the exercise of voting rights. Any physical person or legal entity, involved in the gas sector and those which directly or indirectly participate in its capital over 5% will not be able to exercise voting rights in the Technical System Operator over 1%. These limitations will not be applicable to the direct or indirect participation corresponding to the public Administration.

In addition, with the objective of strengthening its independence as the Technical System Operator, the Company has separated the activities that it carries out as the Technical Operator of the system from those that it carries out as a carrier and network manager. Therefore, Enagás has created a specific unit responsible for the Technical System Operator.

Royal Decree Law 6/2009, dated 30 April, designated Enagás with the condition of Transmission System Operator for the high pressure gas network.

Enagás is currently the technical manager of the gas system and common carrier for the high pressure gas network in Spain. Its facilities include more than 9,000 km. of high-pressure gas pipeline over all of the Spanish territory, two underground natural gas storages, Serrablo (Huesca) and Gaviota (Vizcaya) and three regasification plants: Barcelona, Cartagena and Huelva. These plants have a total emission capacity of 4,650,000 m³/hr, and a total storage capacity of 1,437,000 m³ of LNG. Also, in September 2009, the Company signed a contract for the purchase of 40% of the regasification plant of Bilbao. To guarantee the security of the Gas System, Enagás works to develop new infrastructures and to extend the existing ones. As for the still outstanding projects, they are the new regasification plant of Gijón and an underground natural gas storage in Yela (Guadalajara).

CHAPTER IX

MOTOR VEHICLES: IS THERE STILL ROOM FOR SECTOR-SPECIFIC TREATMENT AS REGARDS VERTICAL RESTRAINTS?

JOHN CLARK

Directorate-General Competition, unit F-2
Directorate General for Competition. European Commission

PAUL CSISZAR

Director of Market and Cases IV: Basic Industries, Manufacturing and Agriculture.
Directorate General for Competition. European Commission[1]

2010 was not only the year in which the Commission's general regime for vertical restraints was updated; it also marked the end of the review of the motor vehicle block exemption[2] and the entry into force of a new regime for the sector. This is an important area as regards vertical agreements, since they regulate many thousands of relationships between vehicle manufacturers and their dealers and repairers. It has also historically been viewed as a sector with particular characteristics that distinguished it from others: so much so that it justified an entirely separate block exemption.

This sector-specific regulation has been reviewed and modified three times, with each renewal witnessing a tug-of war between various categories of actor. The latest review was particularly keenly fought, and saw the claimed need for continued sector-specific treatment subjected to vigorous scrutiny. This chapter looks at the results of the process, and the implications.

---

1   The views expressed in this article are those of the authors and not necessarily those of the European Commission.
2   Commission Regulation (EC) No. 1400/2002 of 31 July 2002 on the application of Article 81(3) of the Treaty to categories of vertical agreements and concerted practices in the motor vehicle sector. Official Journal L 203, 01.08.2002, pages 30-41.

1. A glance in the rear-view mirror

The Commission's evaluation report in 2000[3] was fairly scathing about the effectiveness of the previous sector-specific block exemption Regulation 1475/95[4]. This old-style regime had failed to reach its objectives, and moreover was out of line with an "economic" approach to vertical restraints. Perhaps the most obvious policy response would have been to let the Regulation lapse, thereby bringing the sector within the scope of Regulation 2790/1999[5], and the general guidelines on vertical restraints ("General Guidelines")[6]. For several reasons, the Commission chose not to take this line.

Firstly, it was under intense pressure from consumers and Member States to produce a strict set of rules to deal with competition issues particular to the sector[7]. Consumers had frequently complained that they were unable to take advantage of high price differentials between Member States. The Commission had brought four cases against vehicle manufacturers for impeding parallel trade,[8] and imposed substantial fines.

Secondly, it was concerned that an ongoing merger wave could harm inter-brand competition and that it was therefore necessary to introduce special measures to protect both inter- and intra-brand competition between dealers.

Finally, the wholesale move to the general regime might have proven disruptive to a sector that had until then been used to using the block exemption as a template for drafting vertical agreements. In 2002, the Commis-

---

3   Report on the evaluation of Regulation (EC) No. 1475/95 on the application of Article 85(3) [now 81(3)] of the Treaty to certain categories of motor vehicle distribution and servicing agreements 15.11.2000 — COM(2000)743.
4   Commission Regulation (EC) No. 1475/95 of 28 June 1995 on the application of Article 85(3) of the Treaty to certain categories of motor vehicle distribution and servicing agreements, Official Journal L 145, 29.06.1995, pages 25-34.
5   Commission Regulation (EC) No. 2790/1999 of 22 December 1999 on the application of Article 81(3) of the Treaty to categories of vertical agreements and concerted practices
6   Commission Notice — Guidelines on Vertical Restraints Official Journal 2000/C 291/01.
7   See the speech by Mario Monti, Commissioner for Competition Policy « Who will be in the driver's seat? » Forum Europe Conference Brussels, 11 May 2000 — SPEECH/00/177
8   Commission Decision of 28 January 1998 relating to a proceeding under Article 85 of the EC Treaty (Case IV/35.733 — VW) (1) Official Journal L 124, 25.04.1998, pages 60-108 Commission Decision of 20 September 2000 relating to a proceeding under Article 81 of the EC Treaty (Case COMP/36.653 — Opel) (notified under document number C(2000)2707) Official Journal L 59, 28.02.2001, pages 1-42.
    Commission decision of 10 October 2001 relating to a proceeding under Article 81 of the EC Treaty (notified under document number C (2001) 3028) (Case COMP/36.264 — Mercedes-Benz) SEP et autres / Automobiles Peugeot SA (case COMP/36623) Summary version of the decision in all languages. Official Journal L173, 27.06.2006, p. 20.

sion therefore chose to adopt a new sector-specific Regulation that can be seen as a kind of hybrid, following the economic lines of Regulation 2790/1999, but taking on board many of the clauses of Regulation 1475/95, as well as a number of additional measures.

When Regulation 1400/2002 was itself reviewed in 2008[9], the Commission concluded that although it had brought certain improvements, the regime that it laid down was less than optimal. Many of the detailed sector-specific rules concerning vehicle distribution agreements had been ineffective or even counter-productive, had caused confusion and prompted a large number of spurious complaints relating mainly to contractual disputes between dealers and vehicle manufacturers rather than to breaches of the competition rules. Moreover, the Evaluation Report and the subsequent Communication of July 2009[10] found that there were no significant competition shortcomings in the EU which would justify sector-specific treatment for this market.

In contrast, the rules relating to the aftermarkets were too lax, and needed to be tightened up to deal effectively with failures to grant access to technical repair information and with new forms of abuse. Although this result could be partially achieved by applying to such agreements the requirements for exemption of Regulation 330/2010, including the market share threshold of 30%, thus leaving the vast majority of these agreements outside the safe harbour, this would not in itself fulfil the Commission's aims.

2. The chosen option

The option eventually chosen was to apply the general regime to both the primary and aftermarkets, but with a number of sector-specific elements.

— Firstly, the Commission gave operators on the primary market a three-year delay, during which time Regulation 1400 would continue to apply, in order to allow for the amortisation of investments made pursuant to that regulation.

— Secondly, three hardcore clauses from Regulation 1400/2002 were retained. These relate exclusively to the distribution of spare parts.

---

9 Commission Evaluation Report on the operation of Regulation (EC) No. 1400/2002 concerning motor vehicle distribution and servicing, http://ec.europa.eu/competition/sectors/motor_vehicles/block_exemption.html hereinafter "Evaluation Report".

10 Communication from the Commission — The Future Competition Law Framework applicable to the motor vehicle sector (Text with EEA relevance) {SEC (2009) 1052} {SEC(2009) 1053} -COM/2009/0388 final.

— Thirdly, the Commission adopted a set of highly-detailed supplementary Guidelines for the sector, to be read in conjunction with the General Vertical Guidelines. Unlike the Explanatory Brochure that accompanied Regulation 1400/2002, these are a Commission document, and bind the institution. They cover both the primary and the secondary markets and provide clarification as to how to assess various restraints both above and below the threshold for exemption.

On the face of it, this new framework implies more textual complexity. Until 2013, the primary market will be subject to Regulation 1400/2002 and the accompanying Explanatory Brochure, while the aftermarkets will be governed by Regulation 330/2010 together with the Vertical Guidelines, supplemented by Regulation 461/2010 and the Supplementary Guidelines. From June 2013, both the primary and aftermarkets will be subject to Regulation 330/2010 and the General Guidelines, supplemented by Regulation 461/2010 and the Supplementary Guidelines. However, the greater number of applicable texts masks a greater commonality between the rules applicable to motor vehicles and those applying to other sectors. There are no longer any sector specific conditions, and the number of hardcore clauses applicable to vertical agreements in the sector has been reduced from thirteen to eight.[11]

More fundamentally, the new competition law framework for the motor vehicle sector reflects the differing competitive conditions on the markets and draws a basic distinction between agreements for the sale of new motor vehicles and agreements for repair and maintenance services and for spare parts distribution.

3. Sale of new vehicles

Regulation 1400/2002 was highly detailed as regards the types of clause that manufacturers could put into their agreements with dealers if they wished to benefit from the block exemption. It contained conditions relating to contractual protection for the weaker party, and did not exempt either location clauses or single-branding obligations.

In its 2008 Evaluation Report, the Commission found that these provisions had had no pro-competitive effect, and instead had limited contractual

---

11 See John Clark and Stephan Simon: The New Legal Framework for Motor Vehicle Distribution: A Toolkit to Deal with Real Competition Breakdowns, Journal of European Competition Law & Practice (2010) 1(6): 478-490 first published online October 6, 2010.

freedom and increased distribution costs. The application of the general vertical block exemption to dealer agreements from 1 June 2013 will mean that these provisions will not be carried forward.

There will also be more markets in which networks of motor vehicle distribution agreements will not benefit from the block exemption, thanks to the move to a unified market share threshold of 30% for exemption. The consequences of this change are explained in the Supplementary Guidelines[12].

3.1 Contractual protection

Unlike Regulations 2790/1999 and 330/2010, Article 3 of Regulation 1400/2002 contained measures designed to promote the independence of dealers from their suppliers, mainly by attempting to safeguard their sunk costs. These provisions, which had been present in one form or another in all motor vehicle block exemptions dating back to 1985, were flanking measures to encourage pro-competitive conduct[13]. In 2002, there had been a number of instances of manufacturers intimidating dealers in order to prevent them from granting discounts[14], or selling to consumers from other Member States[15]. The "contractual protection" provisions in Regulation 1400/2002 relate to contract duration, periods of notice for termination or non-renewal, the giving of reasons for contract termination, and the transfer of dealership contracts between the members of the same network. Not surprisingly, these clauses are dear to the heart of dealers, who fought tooth and nail to have them maintained. Car manufacturers, on the other hand, saw them as holding up network reorganisation, and interfering with their contractual freedom.

Modern thinking is that such clauses have no place in competition law, and belong instead to the domains of commercial fairness and national contract laws. The Commission recognised this in the context of the modernisation of the antitrust rules that led to the adoption of Regulation 1/2003. After this point, the days of Article 3 were quite clearly numbered. It is notable in this respect that in its Resolution of 5 May 2010 on the draft motor vehicle block exemption, the European Parliament called on the Commission to ensure that also distributors such as car dealers could

---

12 See para. 56.
13 See Recital 9 of the block exemption.
14 See footnote 4 above.
15 See footnote 6 above.

benefit from the contractual protection currently granted to commercial agents pursuant to Directive 86/653/EEC.[16]

The experience of the contractual protection provisions also illustrates their futility. According to Article 3(3), for example, dealer agreements can only be exempted if the dealer has the right to transfer the dealership to another distributor within the network of the same brand without the consent of the manufacturer. As the recitals to Regulation 1400/2002 explain, the idea was to facilitate the emergence of dealer groups with a European footprint, thereby fostering market integration[17]. The outcome, however, was that few dealers entered into such transactions with dealers in other Member States, and the only effect seems to have been to facilitate the growth of large national dealer groups, which can hardly be said to have had a positive effect on competition.

Other clauses have simply been outpaced by developing commercial conditions in the sector. Article 3(5), for instance, requires that indefinite duration contracts contain a clause requiring two years' notice to be given in case of termination, in order to protect dealers' sunk costs. However, investments required by vehicle manufacturers are now so great that even a two-year notice period is not sufficient to amortise them. Extending this period still further would be out of the question, for one thing since it would mean that newcomers would have fewer opportunities to build up their networks because dealers could not easily transfer from one brand to another.

It is therefore not surprising that the Commission did not carry Article 3 forward. However, by recognising the beneficial effects of transparent contractual relations, it did not entirely leave dealers out in the cold.[18] In particular, it underlined that Codes of Conduct were a valid means of achieving greater transparency. The Guidelines state that such codes may *inter alia* provide for notice periods for contract termination, which may be determined in function of the contract duration, for compensation to be given for outstanding relationship-specific investments made by the dealer in case of early termination without just cause, as well as for arbitration as an alternative mechanism for dispute resolution. If a supplier incorporates such a Code of Conduct into its agreements with distributors and repair-

---

16 Resolution of the European Parliament on the Motor Vehicle Block Exemption Regulation of 5 May 2010 (PE: B7-0245/10).

17 See Recital 10 of Regulation 1400/2002.

18 Supplementary guidelines on vertical restraints in agreements for the sale and repair of motor vehicles and for the distribution of spare parts for motor vehicles, OJ C 138 of 28 May 2010, pp. 16-27, para. 7.

ers, makes it publicly available, and complies with its provisions, this will be regarded as a relevant factor for assessing the supplier's conduct in individual cases.[19]

3.2 Single-branding obligations

Prior to the adoption of Regulation 1400/2002, the sector was in the middle of a merger wave[20] that was expected to continue, leaving vehicle production in the hands of a few competitors. Had these few vehicle manufacturers resorted to single branding obligations, this could have foreclosed of new entrants from Korea, China and India. The Commission therefore decided to diverge once more from the general model by introducing a condition and a definition in Regulation 1400/2002 removing single-branding obligations from the scope of the exemption, and defining them at 30% of total purchases.[21] It also attempted to promote a particular form of multi-branding consisting of selling the brands of more than one manufacturer within the same showroom.

In any event, the feared concentration wave did not emerge, and new Asian makes were able to establish themselves in the European market, mostly without needing to access the éxisting dealer networks. Moreover, the form of multi-branding characterised by displaying competing brands in the same showroom which had been promoted by Regulation 1400/2002 did not meet with any significant success.[22] The expansion of multi-branding applauded by some commentators simply reflects the growth of large multi-brand dealer groups or includes instances where a single dealer sells brands from the same manufacturer group.

As well as being unnecessary and ineffective, the provision on multi-branding also had unwanted side-effects. In order to prevent brand dilution and preserve the image of their brand, vehicle manufacturers increased the qualitative standards required of dealers, particularly those related to brand and corporate identity. This in turn led to an increase in costs of around 20%.[23]

---

19 The main associations of motor vehicle manufacturers (ACEA, JAMA) have recently agreed to propose a Code of Conduct with provisions derived from Regulation (EC) No. 1400/2002.
20 See Commission Evaluation Report on the Operation of Regulation (EC) No. 1400/2002 concerning motor vehicle distribution and servicing, Annex 2, page 10.
21 See Recital 27 of Regulation 1400/2002, Articles 1 (1) b and 5 (1).
22 See "Do we need a Motor Vehicle Block Exemption?" Report by ESMT CA, June 2009, page 5.
23 Commission Evaluation Report on the operation of Regulation (EC) No. 1400/2002 concerning motor vehicle distribution and servicing (2008), p. 14.

The Commission therefore decided to do away with the sector-specific multi-branding provisions in Regulation 1400/2002, and to follow the approach set out in Regulation 330/2010[24]. These rules set the definition of single-branding at 80% instead of 30% and exempt such clauses for up to five years. They therefore represent an implicit acceptance that both multi-brand and mono-brand distribution systems have their own advantages and disadvantages. Dealers which focus on one brand are better positioned to communicate its specific values and advantages, with consequent positive effects on inter-brand competition. In addition, a manufacturer is more likely to step in and financially support ailing dealers if those dealers only distribute its brands. As to multi-brand distribution, this allows a dealer to spread costs and risk. These factors are likely to outweigh the advantages of single-branding where it represents only brands with a low market share or where the dealer is located in a remote location. This is exactly where one tends to find multi-brand sites in the EU.

The supplementary Guidelines also contain safeguards to make it plain that it is not entirely for the vehicle manufacturer to determine when a dealer may multi-brand. The degree of freedom that they enjoy in this respect is dependent upon many things, including their market power.

Firstly, and perhaps most obviously, single-branding obligations will not be block exempted where the vehicle manufacturer's brands have a combined market share of over 30%. This is often the case in vehicle manufacturers' home markets.

Secondly, vehicle manufacturers with a market share of 30% or less may use single-branding obligations with a maximum duration of five years, following which dealers must be free to terminate the tie. The general Guidelines state that no obstacles must exist that hinder a dealer from effectively terminating the non-compete obligation at the end of the five year period.[25] The Guidelines make it plain that the block exemption will not cover vehicle manufacturers seeking to impose single-branding for a longer duration by indirect means: for instance by threatening to impose a second five-year period of single-branding before the dealer has been able to amortise the relationship-specific investments made in respect of the additional brand that he proposes to take on.[26] Based on these principles, if a car dealership undertakes relationship-specific investments during the five-year period the dealer will not be truly free to decide whether or not to

---

24 Article 1(1)(d).
25 Vertical Guidelines, para. 66.
26 Guidelines, para. 26.

accept a second five-year non-compete obligation unless these investments can be fully amortised by the end of that period, or unless the vehicle manufacturer agrees in advance to compensate the dealer if these investments are lost upon contract termination[27].

Thirdly, the block exemption does not cover single-branding obligations that amount to a boycott of an existing brand. This would be the case if the obligations in question had the effect of excluding defined brands from a vehicle manufacturer's network.[28]

Fourthly, below the 30% market share threshold, if the widespread use of single-branding obligations has a cumulative effect that leads to the foreclosure of competing brands, competition authorities may withdraw the benefit of the block exemption on an individual basis pursuant to Article 29 of Regulation 1/2003 or entirely from a market pursuant to Article 6 of Regulation 461/2010.

3.3 Location clauses

Location clauses oblige dealers to operate from a given site and prevent them from establishing additional sales or delivery outlets at other locations, including in other Member States. Location clauses in selective distribution agreements for new motor vehicles will usually bring efficiency benefits in the form of more efficient logistics and predictable network coverage, and are exempted under the general regime for vertical restraints. However, Article 5(2) of Regulation 1400/2002 excludes location clauses in selective distribution agreements concerning new passenger cars or light commercial vehicles from the benefit of the block exemption. The aim was to protect intra-brand competition and stimulate parallel trade by encouraging dealers to sell directly into high–priced markets. The provision was highly controversial at the time, with opponents arguing that it removed an essential element of quantitative selective distribution, made it difficult for carmakers to match supply to demand, and would destabilise distribution networks in Member States[29] where prices were high. As a consequence, the Commission delayed the entry into force of Article 5(2) until 1st October 2005.

---

27 Guidelines, para. 7.
28 Guidelines, para. 27.
29 CECRA Position paper number 2004-250 strongly criticises the end of the exemption of such clauses. See http://www.cecra.eu/en/publications/publications.php.

In any event, very few dealers opened extra outlets[30], probably due to the commercial risks that such a move would entail, and to the fact that price differentials between Member States continued to decline over the period of validity of the block exemption, thereby reducing potential profits. Dealer growth occurred mainly through the expansion of groups absorbing smaller firms, rather than the hoped widespread opening of additional outlets. Article 5(2)(b) can therefore be seen as an unsuccessful divergence from the general rules.

As with the multi-branding provisions, Article 5(2)(b) of Regulation 1400/2002 may have caused a defensive reaction that pushed up distribution costs; it seems likely that the potential for network destabilisation caused vehicle manufacturers to raise qualitative standards across the board. These additional costs were borne by all dealers, and not just those that might hypothetically have taken advantage of Article 5(2)(b).

After 31 May 2013, the general regime will apply, implying the exemption of location clauses where the carmaker and the dealer have market shares below 30%. Above this level, it may be questioned whether such clauses can satisfy the conditions laid down in Article 101(3) of the Treaty[31].

3.4 Vehicle specifications and showroom-only dealerships

Regulation 1400/2002 also had two other peculiarities compared to the general regime, which were dropped almost without protest from the new legal framework.

The first was the so-called availability clause, which is a relic of earlier sector-specific block exemptions. Article 4(1)(f) of the Regulation specifies that it is a hardcore restriction for agreements to restrict a distributor's ability to obtain vehicles with specifications current in other Member States. The purpose of this clause is to allow dealers to fulfil orders from foreign final consumers. For the Commission, this restriction is implicitly covered by the definition of territorial restrictions contained in Article 4(1)(b) which expressly applies to all direct and indirect restrictions on the

---

30 Evaluation Report, p. 6.

31 Supplementary guidelines on vertical restraints in agreements for the sale and repair of motor vehicles and for the distribution of spare parts for motor vehicles, OJ C 138 of 28 May 2010, pp. 16-27, para. 56.

territory in which and the customers to whom the dealer may sell cars: an interpretation that is backed-up by case-law from the Court of Justice.[32]

A final sector-specific clause (Article 4(1)(g)) lists as a hardcore restriction any provision which restricts a dealer's ability to operate vehicle sales businesses without also having to carry out repair and maintenance services. With the benefit of hindsight, it is easy to say why this clause did not enjoy any success among dealers, whose profits are generated by their after-sales business, and who make very narrow margins on car sales.

4. Repair and maintenance and spare parts

As already outlined, the automotive aftermarkets are less competitive than the primary markets for vehicle sales. For one thing, the authorised networks commonly have market shares in excess of 50%: the remainder being in the hands of the fragmented independent garage sector. For another, authorised outlets have direct access to technical information and captive spare parts that their independent competitors cannot obtain elsewhere.

Independent repairers exert valuable competitive pressure due to their different business model, which generally results in lower costs. Prices charged are on average 15-20% lower than those of the authorised repair networks.[33] Independent repairers are particularly important for the owners of older vehicles, who are more price-sensitive and less concerned with maintaining vehicle value through a "full dealer service record"[34].

4.1 The overall framework

Given the risks[35], it might seem strange that Regulation 1400/2002 treated the aftermarkets more leniently than did the general regime, by setting a specific 100% threshold for the exemption of qualitative selection. This meant that the second set of measures had to take the form of hardcore clauses to claw back the exemption if the agreements had the effect of

---

32 Judgment of 28 February 1984, joined cases 228 and 229/82 *Ford of Europe Inc. and Ford-Werke Aktiengesellschaft vs. Commission* ECR (1984) 1129.
33 Attwood, Daniel: Carmakers fight to control fleet cars. In: Fleet News, February 4, 2010, S. 1; Hyundai has calculated 27% higher costs on average for authorised repair shops, see Pohmer, Frank: Auswirkungen der GVO auf das Händlernetz und die Profitabilität der Händler /Servicepartner. Speech given at the 11th PraxisForum Kfz-Vertrieb, Cologne, 20 Mai 2010.
34 i.e. a full set of stamps from authorised repairers in the vehicle's warranty booklet.
35 For a more detailed description of how the Commission perceived these, see article by John Clark and Stephan Simon, referenced at footnote 10 above.

foreclosing independent operators. It also meant that the Commission might be drawn into awkward analyses of whether a given restriction was qualitative or quantitative in nature, and therefore exempted or not; this was less of a problem under Regulation 2790/1999, which applied a uniform 30% threshold to both qualitative and quantitative selection.

The reason for the 100% threshold was both historical and political. Previous block exemptions for the sector had not only exempted quantitative selective distribution without market share limitation; they had also made exemption conditional on linking sales and after-sales activities, meaning that one could only become an authorised garage if one also agreed to sell new cars of the brand in question. In this light, removing the exemption entirely from agreements between vehicle manufacturers and authorised garages was seen as a step too far. Moreover, the higher threshold for qualitative selective distribution gave a strong message in favour of this form of agreement.

By setting the market share threshold for the exemption of quantitative selection at 30%, the Commission ensured that those car manufacturers wishing to benefit from the block exemption had to appoint standalone authorised garages to their networks, so long as these met qualitative criteria. The aim was to reverse the decline in authorised garages which had occurred as a result of the downsizing of the dealer networks. Decline in repairer network density has a greater impact that a similar decline in sales network density, since consumers are not prepared to travel far to have their vehicles repaired. The Commission's analysis showed that the impact of this measure was broadly positive, as numbers of authorised repairers (and thereby intra-brand competition) rebounded strongly after the entry into force of Regulation 1400/2002.[36]

However, experience taught the Commission the limits of granting exemption irrespective of market share and then relying on a hardcore list to protect competition between authorised and independent repairers. Firstly, this approach was by nature limited in scope to types of abuse that were foreseen in 2002, and could not deal effectively with new areas of concern such as the use of warranties as a means of steering trade towards the authorised networks. Secondly, a problem relating to a little-known recital in Regulation 1400/2002 arose in the context of the four cases that the Commission brought against car manufacturers in 2007 for failing to release

---

36 LE study, page 138.

technical information[37]. The clause in question, Recital 26, allowed car manufacturers to withhold any safety- and security- related information.

4.2 Access to authorised repair networks

The application of the general market share threshold of 30% removes the exemption from the vast majority of authorised repair agreements, and vehicle manufacturers must therefore rely upon general principles, and indeed case-law[38], to assess whether their agreements comply with the rules. However, the new supplementary guidelines underline that agreements that oblige all authorised repairers to also repair new cars will not normally benefit from Article 101(3). This is a clear message that the Commission will not tolerate a mass backslide to the pre-2002 landscape. Nonetheless, in certain rare circumstances such a tie may have pro-competitive effects.[39] Car dealers make most of their money from vehicle repair and spare parts, and it may be difficult for a car manufacturer new to the market to recruit dealers if it cannot promise them that for a limited period no other authorised repairers will be appointed in their geographical area of responsibility. However, in all other circumstances, the restriction that such a tie would involve as regards the repair markets would outweigh any risk to the stability of the vehicle sales networks.

4.3 Access to technical repair information

It is striking that although in 2002, carmakers did not contest the need to provide technical information to independent operators, this proved in practice to be a particularly thorny issue. The Commission was called upon to bring four cases in 2007[40] against car manufacturers that had not respected their obligations.

The increased complexity of the latest generation of cars also brought the issue of technical information increasingly to the fore, with new types of technical information emerging, along with new methods of delivery.

---

37 Cases Comp/39.140 — 39.143 DaimlerChrysler, Fiat, Toyota and GM — Press release IP/07/1332 of 14.09.2007. See also market test notices concerning the commitments proposed by the four firms — Official Journal C 66, 22.3.2007, pp. 18-29.
38 Volkswagen and Audi to conclude agreements with repair shops for the provision of after-sales services. Press Release — IP/03/80, 20.1.2003.
39 Guidelines, para. 71.
40 See footnote 7 above.

Because of this technical complexity, there are clear arguments that this area should be dealt with through technical regulation, rather than through the application of the competition rules. The four competition cases definitely gave momentum to the Commission's efforts in the regulatory field, culminating in the adoption of the EURO5/6 Regulation 715/2007 and 595/2009, which place an obligation on vehicle manufacturers to release all technical information on models launched after 2008. This implies that more and more of the vehicle park will progressively fall within the regulatory sphere. This has clear advantages, because there are limits to what can be achieved by applying Article 101 to agreements between repairers and vehicle manufacturers[41].

The four cases also taught the Commission the limits of its overall approach to the aftermarkets, which coupled a high market share threshold with a series of hardcore "clawback" clauses. The Commission's aim in lowering the threshold for exemption was to remove authorised repair agreements from the safe harbour, and make it easier to subject them to individual scrutiny in case of abuse. This would also make the hardcore provision in Article 4(2) of Regulation largely[42] redundant. However, when the draft Regulation was published in December 2009, certain associations of independent aftermarket operators, such as FIGIEFA and the Right to Repair Campaign[43] saw the proposed change as a weakening of the Commission's approach, and campaigned to maintain the hardcore clause. This is most probably because they had not been witness to the travails that the Commission had faced when applying the rules in the four cases that it brought.

From the Commission's point of view, it seemed obvious that Article 4(2) had had little, if any, dissuasive effect, since the IKA study[44] of 2004 had shown that vehicle manufacturers continued to withhold information, and enforcement action had been necessary in order to convince the sector that the Commission meant business. The Commission had also seen how vehicle manufacturers could stretch the notion of security or safety-related information, and was aware of how difficult it would be to carry forward Article 4(2) without the corresponding recital 26.

---

41 See Clark and Simon, referenced at footnote 10 above.
42 Except in certain cases where there is no separate aftermarket.
43 http://www.r2rc.eu/.
44 Do motor vehicle suppliers give independent operators effective access to all technical information as required under the EC competition rules applicable to the motor vehicle sector? Study on access to technical information in the car sector. Report by Institut für Kraftfahrwesen, RWTH Aachen, 2004.

The Commission's chosen approach was therefore to do away with the hardcore clause, and to give very detailed clarification in the supplementary Guidelines as to how withholding technical information will be dealt with in the context of Article 101, drawing inspiration from the four cases which were resolved through commitments in 2007. The supplementary Guidelines point out by reference to the relevant case-law that qualitative selective distribution networks will be caught by Article 101(1) if they do not leave any space for other forms of distribution.[45] They then go on to apply this principle to the specific case of technical information:

> *"Qualitative selective distribution agreements concluded with authorised repairers and/or parts distributors may be caught by Article 101(1) of the Treaty if, within the context of those agreements, one of the parties acts in a way that forecloses independent operators from the market, for instance by failing to release technical repair and maintenance information to them."*

The other problem with the approach under Regulation 1400/2002 was that the definition of technical information was basic, fixed, and did not keep pace with technological progress. In contrast, the supplementary Guidelines give a full description of what constitutes technical information, and the actors to whom it should be provided. To ensure that the concept evolves with technical progress, the text makes cross-reference to the provisions of Regulation 715/2007 and its implementing regulations, which will be updated as need arises.

Unlike under Regulation 1400/2002, any attempt to justify withholding certain elements of technical information must be made in the context of Article 101(3), and will therefore need to demonstrate consumer benefit and that equivalent protection could not be achieved by less restrictive means.

4.4 Misuse of warranties

The other advantage of lowering the threshold for exemption of qualitative selective distribution agreements is that it will now be easier for the

---

45 "Purely qualitative selective distribution systems may nevertheless restrict competition where the existence of a certain number of such systems does not leave any room for other forms of distribution based on a different way of competing. This situation will generally not arise on the markets (...) for repair and maintenance, as long as independent repairers provide consumers with an alternative channel for the upkeep of their motor vehicles. See for example Case T-88/92 *Groupement d'achat Édouard Leclerc vs. Commission* [1996] ECR II-1961".

Commission to act against other forms of behaviour likely to foreclose independent repairers.

The low profit margins on the primary market are driving vehicle manufacturers and their authorised repairers to derive alternative revenue streams from other stages of the vehicle lifecycle. Moreover, increasing choice in many segments naturally leads carmakers to seek novel means of distinguishing their products through finance deals, extended warranties and servicing packages. The vast majority of this innovation is pro-competitive, and brings considerable benefits to the consumer. Given the high cost of vehicle repair, offering increasingly longer warranties has proven to be an effective means for manufacturers to attract customers to their products. However, the Commission has become aware that some such schemes have been used as an illegitimate means of reserving all repair and maintenance work to the authorised network during a substantial period of a vehicle's life, and of ensuring that only carmaker-branded parts are used. Plainly this can cause considerable harm, particularly to the owners of newer vehicles.

Paragraph 69 of the supplementary Guidelines therefore stipulates that agreements may be caught by Article 101(1) if, for instance, the manufacturer's warranty is made conditional on the end user having repair and maintenance work that is not covered by warranty carried out only within the authorised repair networks. The same applies to warranty conditions which require the use of the manufacturer's brand of spare parts in respect of replacements not covered by the warranty terms. The supplementary Guidelines further explain that selective distribution agreements containing such practices are unlikely to benefit from the exception in Article 101(3) of the Treaty.

4.5 Spare parts

There are few consumer goods for which spare parts play such an important role, and there are none which have such a major impact on the average consumer's wallet. There are also obvious barriers to free competition on these markets, most notably in the form of design protection and upstream arrangements that prevent components producers from supplying to the aftermarket.

The outcome of the review process as regards spare parts distribution demonstrates that the Commission did not see the process as a preconceived simplifying crusade, as some appear to have believed. Rather, each element of the block exemption was examined to see whether sector-specific treatment was merited, and if so, in what form — i.e. clause in a regulation, or Guidelines. Plainly both instruments have their advantages and disadvantages. The Commission was also aware that the general vertical block exemption, Regulation 330/2010 (and previously Regulation 2790/1999), contains no provisions relating specifically to spare parts.

In the end, it was the issue of market definition that convinced the Commission that hardcore clauses were the right approach. Although vehicle manufacturers have a very high share of overall spare parts provision, it might be possible to define markets on which the 30% threshold for exemption was not exceeded, meaning that in the absence of hardcore clauses, different rules would apply to some spare parts than to others.

Regulation 461/2010 therefore contains three hardcore provisions on spare parts. The first of these, Article 5(1)(a) provides that the exemption shall not apply to agreements which have as their object

> "(a) the restriction of the sales of spare parts for motor vehicles by members of a selective distribution system to independent repairers which use those parts for the repair and maintenance of a motor vehicle; "

This article is intended to tackle the problem of carmakers preventing independent repairers from getting hold of captive parts — i.e. parts that are only available through the authorised networks. These will include parts that are not replaced very often, as well as parts such as body panels and interior trim that are design protected in many Member States. This has not generally proved to be an issue over the lifetime of Regulation 1400/2002, but there is plainly a potential for vehicle manufacturers to seek to withhold, say, security-related parts, and thereby prevent independent repairers from carrying out a wide variety of repair jobs.

The second hardcore restriction provides that the exemption shall not apply to agreements which have as their object

> "(b) the restriction, agreed between a supplier of spare parts, repair tools or diagnostic or other equipment and a manufacturer of motor vehicles, of the supplier's ability to sell those goods to authorised or independent distributors or to authorised or independent repairers or end users;"

This clause was aimed at ensuring that alternative channels for non-captive parts and tools remain open, thereby placing competitive pressure on the vehicle manufacturer's own distribution channel. Article 4(1)(b) was, however, misunderstood by certain actors, who perceived it as a blanket prohibition on any arrangement preventing them from supplying the after-market directly. This is obviously false, since no block exemption clause, whatever its nature, has any relevance when agreements are not caught by Article 101(1) of the Treaty.

A particular issue in point is that of so-called tooling arrangements. These are arrangements in which the vehicle manufacturer pays for all or part of a tool used to produce components and then forbids the components manufacturer from using the tool to produce spare parts to supply the aftermarket. Plainly, where this can be characterised as a sub-contracting arrangement, it will not be caught by Article 101(1)[46]. However, as the Guidelines explain, in other circumstances it will be so caught, and will need to be analysed under the block exemption, or examined to see if the agreement can benefit from Article 101(3).

The final hardcore relates to

> "(c) the restriction, agreed between a manufacturer of motor vehicles which uses components for the initial assembly of motor vehicles and the supplier of such components, of the supplier's ability to place its trade mark or logo effectively and in an easily visible manner on the components supplied or on spare parts."

This provision allows repairers to source parts manufactured by original equipment suppliers which are sold directly to the aftermarket rather than being sold under the vehicle manufacturer's brand. Matching an individual vehicle to the correct replacement part is a key problem facing repairers, and the logo or trademark allows them to determine the manufacturer of the original component or replacement part.

One of the hardcore provisions in Regulation 1400/2002 was not carried over to the new block exemption, since it was seen as a rephrased clause on non-compete obligations, and better dealt with as a condition for exemption. Article 4(1)(k) of Regulation 140/2002 related to:

> "(k) the restriction of a distributor's or authorised repairer's ability to obtain original spare parts or spare parts of matching quality from a third undertaking of its choice and to use them for the repair or maintenance of motor vehicles, without prejudice to the ability of a supplier of new motor vehicles to require the use of original spare parts supplied by it for repairs carried out under warranty, free servicing and vehicle recall work;"

---

46 Commission notice of 18 December 1978 concerning its assessment of certain subcontracting agreements in relation to Article 85 (1) of the EEC Treaty.

5. Conclusion

The outcome of the review of the motor vehicle block exemption can be seen as an endorsement of the general rules, in that only three out of all of the sector-specific clauses in Regulation 1400/2002 survived. Although the supplementary Guidelines are on the face of it sector-specific, they simply represent the application of general principles to provisions commonly found in vertical agreements in the sector. It may therefore be asked whether the Supplementary Guidelines may be used to assess agreements in other similar sectors. The text is ambiguous on this point (our italics):

> *"These Guidelines do not apply to vertical agreements in sectors other than motor vehicles, and the principles set out herein may not necessarily be used to assess agreements in other sectors."*[47]

Plainly, for instance, if lack of the technical information provision threatens to foreclose independent repairers of agricultural vehicles, this document could provide useful guidance over and above what can be found in the General Guidelines on vertical restraints. Just as the motor vehicle sector has provided much useful case-law in the fields of parallel trade, resale price maintenance, and access to qualitative selective distribution networks, the supplementary Guidelines may sometimes serve as an illustrative example the Commission's overall policy for vertical restraints.

---

47 Supplementary Guidelines, para. 3.

COMMENTS ABOUT THE IMPACT
AND ASSESSMENT OF THE NEW RULES

Marc Greven

Hartmut P. Röhl

Carsten Reimann

1. Comments by Marc Greven [1]

1.1 Overall assessment

Overall, European automobile manufacturers make a positive assessment of the EU rules that apply/will apply to agreements regarding the distribution of motor vehicles, after-sales service and spare parts.

In particular, they welcome the greater alignment between the rules applicable to the motor vehicle sector (Regulation 461/2010) and those applicable to all other sectors (Regulation 330/2010) and the removal from the legislation of various provisions that had proven to be ineffective (contractual provisions, multi-branding, additional sales outlets).

The greater freedom that the new Regulations provide to the industry to design its distribution policy and structure its networks should lead to greater efficiency, lower costs and more competition.

Vehicle manufacturers regret that the Commission decided to establish a longer than usual transitional period with regard to motor vehicle sales agreements and postpone the application of Regulation 461/2010 to 1 June 2013 while applying the new rules for agreements regarding after-sales service and parts already as from 1 June 2010. This creates unnecessary delay and complexity.

---

1 Director Legal Affairs, ACEA (European Automobile Manufacturers Association).

Also, they find that the Commission's view that the market for after-sales service and spare parts is brand-specific, and that consequently vehicle manufacturers can generally be presumed to have a market share of more than 30%, will decrease legal certainty since this implies that they would not be able to avail themselves of the benefit of the Block Exemption.

1.2 Motor vehicle sales

This is the area that appears to have undergone the most important changes. In particular, vehicle manufacturers will have the right to make the opening of additional sales and delivery outlets conditional on their consent and they will have more opportunities to restrict multi-branding initiatives.

They welcome this development because they feel that the provisions of the current Block Exemption Regulation 1400/2002 regarding multi-branding are unrealistic (selling competing brands in the same showroom is rarely the best option for anyone), ineffective (this type of multi-branding is not very widespread) and even counterproductive (as it caused defensive reactions in the form of increased showroom standards making distribution more expensive).

1.3 Contractual provisions

Vehicle manufacturers welcome the removal from the Block Exemption Regulation of all provisions relating to contractual issues. They have always held that such provisions belong in national contract law rather than in EU competition law. This applies in particular to provisions regarding the minimum duration of fixed-term contracts, the provision of reasons for termination and the transfer of dealerships.

At the same time, however, manufacturers believe that it can make perfect business sense to agree with their dealer networks on the use of an alternative dispute resolution mechanism and set minimum periods of notice that will apply when agreements are terminated. This is why ACEA had adopted a code of good practice regarding these matters. The adoption of this code implies that the member companies of ACEA will include the corresponding provisions in their new agreements with their networks.

1.4 Service and parts

At first sight, this area appears to have undergone few changes. The provisions regarding spare parts laid down in Regulation 461/2010 are a simple copy/paste of Regulation 1400/2002. Arguably, the accompanying guidelines contain some new elements with regard to issues such as subcontracting, access to repair and maintenance information and warranties.

The main issue in this area is that vehicle manufacturers will not be able to benefit from the Block Exemption if the Commission maintains its assessment that their market share exceeds 30%. It can be questioned, however, whether this assessment is valid in all cases. There would seem to be good reasons for considering that sales and after-sales service form only one market with respect to heavy commercial vehicles, for example. Indeed, the buyers of these products are professionals for whom the total cost of ownership (including repair and maintenance) is the decisive factor. In all likelihood, this would bring manufacturers' market shares below the 30% threshold in many cases.

Another remaining issue in this area is the risk of additional rules regarding access to repair and maintenance information being adopted within the context of the EU type-approval legislation. This is happening currently with regard to the issue of parts identification data ("raw data"). This adoption of competition rules "by the backdoor" is a worrying development.

1.5 Outlook

Vehicle manufacturers do not expect the new Block Exemption Regulations to have a major impact on their dealer networks. The continued fall in motor vehicle registrations in the EU (15% for passenger cars since 2007) is likely to be a more important factor in this respect.

While motor vehicle distribution will not change fundamentally in the short term, some new developments or experiments might take place with regard to the sale of electric vehicles or "mobility" packages.

2. Comments by Hartmut P. Röhl[2]

2.1 Foreword[3]

Following the expiry of the Block Exemption Regulation (BER) No. 1400/2002 on 31st May 2010, the European Commission has introduced a new competition law framework for the automotive sector focusing on aftermarket issues.

Whereas the first Automotive Block Exemption Regulation (EU) 123/85 was almost exclusively dealing with the contractual conditions of new car sales, in the successor BERs (EU)1475/95 and (EU) 1400/2002 an ever increasing importance was given to the automotive aftermarket culminating in BER (EU) 461/2010 dealing exclusively with the automotive aftermarket.

Applied in the market since 1st June 2010, these new rules are enacted in four key legal instruments:

— the Automotive Block Exemption Regulation (EU) No. 461/2010;

— the sector-specific Guidelines on vertical restraints in agreements for the sale and repair of motor vehicles and for the distribution of spare parts for motor vehicles;

— the Vertical Restraints Block Exemption Regulation (EU) No. 330/2010;

— the general Guidelines on vertical agreements.

These rules will apply until 31st May 2023. They cover the trade in spare parts for and the repair and maintenance of all self propelled vehicles with more than 3 wheels (e.g. passenger cars, light commercial vehicles and heavy duty vehicles). While the new rules are particularly important to illustrate what vehicle manufacturers may or may not do, they also affect the agreements concluded between independent aftermarket operators.

This text is addressed to all the actors of the aftermarket chain: independent and authorised repairers, parts suppliers and parts distributors, publishers of technical information, tools and garage equipment manufacturers, roadside rescue services, as well as all the many other independent operators who contribute to the efficient repair and maintenance of motor vehicles across Europe.

---

2 President, GVA e.V. (Gesamtverband Autoteile-Handel). Member of the Board of FIGIEFA (International Federation of Automotive Aftermarket) Distributors, Brussels.

3 The author has undertaken measures to ensure the correctness of the representations made in this text. It should, however, be noted that the explanations given herein are of a general nature. As any individual case may bear different characteristics, they are not meant to replace specific legal advice.

2.2 The mechanism behind the rules

Since 1st June 2010, four key texts designed to ensure effective competition apply in the automotive aftermarket. Two of these contain sector specific rules, whereas the two others contain general rules applicable to all industry sectors:

The sector-specific rules:

— The Automotive Block Exemption Regulation (EU) No. 461/2010.

— The sector-specific Guidelines on vertical restraints in agreements for the sale and repair of motor vehicles and for the distribution of spare parts for motor vehicles.

The generic rules:

— The Vertical Restraints Block Exemption Regulation (EU) No. 330/2010.

— The general Guidelines on vertical agreements.

2.2.1 The Block Exemption Regulations (BERs)

Block Exemption Regulations exempt an entire category of agreements (block exemption) from the normal application of competition law. Based on the prerequisite that neither the market share of the supplier, nor of the purchaser, exceed 30%, the Block Exemption Regulations confer a "safe harbour" within which companies can be certain that their agreements comply with the requirements of competition law. Of course, the beneficiaries of the exemption must abide by specific provisions contained in the Regulations.

This is particularly true for the so-called "hardcore restrictions" or "black clauses" — **these should be observed regardless of market shares, as violations can only be justified in the most exceptional circumstances.**

For the automotive sector, the Block Exemption Regulations are complementary. Companies hoping to benefit from the "safe harbour" will need to comply with the requirements of the general rules on vertical restraints, as well as the sector-specific rules. This applies to agreements with vehicle manufacturers, as well as to parts distribution agreements in the aftermarket.

2.2.2 The general rules on vertical restraints

The general Vertical Restraints Block Exemption Regulation contains essential rules that need to be considered by anyone trading in goods or services. It provides for several hardcore restrictions, i.e. clauses that should be avoided in distribution agreements, as they would give rise to issues under competition law. A vehicle manufacturer selling parts to authorised repairers will need to observe these limits, as well as a parts supplier selling its products to an independent wholesaler.

Most notably, the general Vertical Restraints Block Exemption Regulation states that a supplier may not normally require its customer to resell the product at a fixed or minimum price. As a general rule (to which few exceptions apply), the customer may determine the resale price on its own, without being pressured by the supplier. The supplier may however issue non-binding recommendations.

Similarly, the general Vertical Restraints Block Exemption Regulation describes limits on customer and territory allocation, the ability of the supplier to require the distributor to operate out of an agreed place of establishment, or the right of members of a distribution system to cross-sell goods between them.

2.2.3 The sector-specific Guidelines
a) The strength of the Guidelines

The Guidelines complete the set of competition law instruments for the automotive sector. By complementing the general guidelines on vertical restraints, the sector-specific Guidelines serve to explain the Automotive Block Exemption Regulation and convey the Commission's view on competition law as applied to the sale of new vehicles, the distribution of spare parts and the repair of motor vehicles. These are not mere explanations of the content of the Automotive Block Exemption Regulation 461/2010, as it was the case for the Explanatory Brochure on the application of the Motor Vehicle Block Exemption Regulation 1400/2002. In practice, **Guidelines are very important**. Although technically they are only binding upon the European Commission (and on the National Competition Authorities) no undertaking can afford to ignore them: they interpret, explain and somehow expand the provisions of binding regulations. In case of litigation, courts of law will take them into account. The European Court of Justice has on numerous occasions pointed out the importance of Guidelines: they are part of the "acquis communautaire" and they shape essential Union policies and consequently the development of the European Union itself.

b) The Guidelines applied to the Automotive Aftermarket

For the aftermarket, they explain in detail 1) how to understand the provisions of the Block Exemption Regulations and 2) how to ensure effective competition in situations falling outside the scope of the Block Exemption Regulations, notably in light of the above-mentioned 30% threshold above which no exemption will be granted.

2.3 Trade in spare parts and equipment

2.3.1 Original parts and parts of matching quality
a) Definitions

Ensuring effective competition in the markets for spare parts and equipment is the primary aim of the definitions of "original parts" and "parts of matching quality" contained in the Guidelines.

According to the wording adopted by the European Commission, **"original parts or equipment"** are parts or equipment manufactured according to the specifications and production standards provided by the vehicle manufacturer for the production of parts or equipment for the assembly of its vehicles.

This means that **"original parts"**, if they fulfil the above conditions, may be:

— parts produced "in-house" by the vehicle manufacturers

— parts manufactured by parts producers and which are supplied to the vehicle manufacturers for the assembly of vehicles or for distribution as spare parts to the members of their authorised networks.

— parts manufactured by independent parts producers and which are supplied to the independent aftermarket, provided that they are manufactured according to the vehicle manufacturer's specifications. This might happen for example when a parts producer is or was manufacturing parts for a vehicle manufacturer. These parts only bear the parts producer's trademark.

Vehicle manufacturers supply their authorised network with their own branded spare parts. Although most of the time these are produced by original equipment suppliers. In such cases, the spare parts producer, however, may not be hindered from placing its own trademark on the part (either exclusively or in parallel as "double branding").

In order to be considered as being of "matching quality", parts must be of a sufficiently high quality that their use does not, according to the EU Commission, "endanger the reputation of the authorised repair network". The burden to prove that a part does not fulfil this requirement falls upon the vehicle manufacturer who must bring evidence to that effect in case it wants to discourage authorised repairers from using such parts.

Following this new definition, a part of matching quality does not refer per se to the quality of the part originally fitted into the vehicle. It may match the quality of the spare parts of a specific range supplied by the vehicle manufacturers to its authorised network, including spare parts from a vehicle manufacturer's "economy line".

b) Certification requirements

The members of the vehicle manufacturers' authorised network have the obligation to use parts that are at least of matching quality. It is worth noting that independent repairers, as they are not members of the 'franchised' network, are of course not subject to such obligations. As explained above, if vehicle manufacturers want to contest the use of a specific part by the members of the authorised repair network, they have to prove that the spare part used does not fulfil the requirements of the definitions of "original part" or "part of matching quality". Even though vehicle manufacturers bear this burden of proof, in order to facilitate sales from independent distributors to the members of the authorised networks and to avoid possible legal challenges from the vehicle manufacturers, parts suppliers are invited to issue — on demand — a (self-) certificate for the quality of their parts (e.g. in the packaging, as a separate declaration, or a notice on the Internet).

2.3.2 Freedom to supply spare parts and equipment to the aftermarket

a) The concept

Following the former Block Exemption Regulation 1400/2002, the new competition law framework confirms that vehicle manufacturers may not hinder their original equipment suppliers from also supplying their products as spare parts to independent distributors or directly to independent or authorised repairers.

As a direct consequence, and for logistic efficiency, independent parts distributors are of course free to supply independent and authorised repairers with the parts supplied by the parts suppliers.

To satisfy consumer demand, part producers may also supply the independent aftermarket with spare parts of higher quality than the original equipment, or with parts fit for purpose and adapted to the age of the vehicle; these should of course fulfil all legal requirements, notably those contained in the product safety and environmental legislations.

b) The new regime on "tooling arrangements"

In its evaluation of the functioning of the former MVBER 1400/2002, the European Commission found that on many occasions vehicle manufacturers abused their bargaining power to restrict the ability of their original equipment manufacturers to sell the parts in the independent aftermarket, thus rendering the part de facto captive.

This was achieved by obliging the supplier to transfer the title to industrial property rights or tooling to the vehicle manufacturer. Once these had become the property of the vehicle manufacturer, the supplier found itself unable to use such tooling or industrial property rights for producing parts that otherwise could have been sold directly to the aftermarket.

In this area, the new guidelines contain important clarifications. First, the European Commission conveys that an agreement between a vehicle manufacturer and a parts supplier is normally subject to competition law. Automotive parts suppliers mostly have own expertise which is necessary to develop and manufacture components. They are not merely an "extended workbench", which would need to rely on essential input from the vehicle manufacturer. In these cases, they are potential competitors as aftermarket parts suppliers, and the vehicle manufacturer can restrict their access to the aftermarket in exceptional circumstances only: Where a vehicle manufacturer provides a tool, or pays for it up front, the supplier may be prevented from using this tool to manufacture parts for any third parties (aftermarket or other OEM customers). In this event, the supplier will need to pay a royalty or purchase a second set of tools for IAM production.

If a vehicle manufacturer obliges its OE parts supplier to transfer the ownership of a tool, intellectual property rights, or know-how back to it, or if the vehicle manufacturer bears only an insignificant part of the product development costs, or does not contribute any necessary tools[4], intellectual property rights, or know-how, the agreement at stake will not be considered to be a genuine sub-contracting arrangement. As a consequence, the vehicle manufacturer will not be allowed to forbid its parts suppliers to sell parts directly in the aftermarket.

---

4   The Guidelines clearly state that where the vehicle manufacturer provides a tool, IPR or know-how to a supplier, this arrangement will not benefit from the Sub-contracting Notice if the supplier already has this tool, IPR or know-how at its disposal, or could reasonably obtain them, since under these circumstances the contribution would not be necessary.

2.3.3 Freedom to purchase parts and equipment

a) Independent repairers

As they do not depend on vehicle manufacturers, **independent repairers are free to purchase and to use any parts or equipment for the repair and maintenance of vehicles**, as long as these fulfil the legal requirements, notably those contained in the product safety and environmental legislations. Independent repairers may source "original parts", "parts of matching quality" as well as other quality parts from independent parts producers and independent parts distributors.

b) Authorised repairers

The legislation describes a repairer with a contractual relation to the vehicle manufacturer as "authorised repairer". This definition is somewhat discriminating — since, as such, the counterpart, the "independent repairer", is insinuated to be "unauthorised".

In practice, authorised repairers usually source spare parts from the vehicle manufacturers with whom they have an agreement. Nevertheless, in order to stimulate competition in the spare parts market, the new legislative framework continues to provide for the possibility of authorised repairers to source "original parts" or "parts of matching quality" from parts suppliers or independent parts distributors.

This freedom may however be subject to an obligation to source a minimum quantity of spare parts from the vehicle manufacturer. This obligation is nonetheless limited. As pointed out by the European Commission, in most cases vehicle manufacturers will enjoy such a position in the market that this minimum sourcing requirement should be as low as not to endanger competition in the market. In the past, the Motor Vehicle Block Exemption Regulation 1400/2002 provided that vehicle manufacturers could require their authorised repairers to source at least 30% of their requirements in spare parts for vehicles of the respective brand from the vehicle manufacturer or its authorised network.

This threshold does not exist anymore in the new legal texts. One general principle of competition law still remains though: the higher the market share of the vehicle manufacturer in the market for spare parts suitable for the repair and maintenance of vehicles of its own brands in a given national territory, the lower the percentage of minimum spare parts sourcing it will be allowed to impose on the members of its authorised repair network.

Since it can be taken as granted that regularly a vehicle manufacturer has a market share above 30% for the spare parts of a specific model of car, contracts on spare-parts distribution cannot be subject to the Block Exemption but must be submitted to an individual control.

Since authorised repairers may also have to carry out repair or maintenance services on vehicles of other brands, they also need to purchase parts from other sources. In this situation, they are to be considered as "independent/multibrand" repairers and therefore may source any spare parts from independent parts producers or spare parts distributors, as long as these fulfil legal requirements, notably those contained in the product safety and environmental legislation.

2.3.4 Access to the vehicle manufacturers' "captive" parts

a) For independent repairers

Some parts are exclusively produced by vehicle manufacturers themselves (e.g. chassis, engine blocks or certain body parts) or are parts on which vehicle manufacturers hold a valid industrial property right. These are only supplied to the aftermarket by the vehicle manufacturers themselves. However, access to these is indispensable in order to allow independent repairers to properly maintain and repair vehicles and to compete with the authorised repair networks. Therefore, the legal framework continues to state that a vehicle manufacturer may not prevent its authorised repairer from selling spare parts to an independent repairer requiring these for the repair or maintenance of a specific customer vehicle. However, a refusal of the authorised parts distributor/repairer to sell parts to its competitor may hinder the latter to carry out a repair job, thus forcing the car owner to take up the services of an authorised repairer. Such a refusal could be considered as an abuse of a dominant position, subject to general European Treaty rules on restraints of competition.

The possible access to captive parts via the authorised repairer does not represent an ideal solution, as independent repairers should be able to source any part, including "captive" parts, from the wholesale level (and not from their direct competitors) and at wholesale price in order to truly compete with the authorised repair network.

b) For independent parts distributors

The new competition law framework follows the same approach as the expired Motor Vehicle Block Exemption Regulation 1400/2002. It differentiates between motor vehicle sales channels, the trade in spare parts and the repair and maintenance services. As a consequence, vehicle manufacturers should offer to the members of their authorised network three separate

contracts whereby their contractual partner can carry out all three functions, two functions or just one of the three functions:
— distribution contract for new vehicles (official dealer)
— distribution contract for replacement parts ("authorised" parts distributor)
— contract for service, maintenance and repair ("authorised" repairer)

Concerning the distribution of the vehicle manufacturers' original spare parts, the vehicle manufacturers will usually opt for a distribution system with clear qualitative selection criteria. Therefore, if an independent parts distributor fulfils the qualitative criteria of the vehicle manufacturer (with regard e.g. to possible stock keeping requirements or the qualification of the personnel), he could be a candidate for an "authorised parts distribution contract".

Since "spare parts" by their nature either must fit or must match they cannot be replaced by "something different". That is why any restriction in their production and distribution carries the danger of monopolisation — there should not be any protection (i.e. design protection) or selective distribution systems allowed where there is no alternative to a specific product, like a spare part.

2.4 Service, maintenance and repair during the warranty period

2.4.1 The key concept

In its Explanatory Brochure on the MVBER 1400/2002, the European Commission had introduced an important clarification that independent repairers may carry out regular maintenance service and repair jobs during the warranty period. Despite this clarification many vehicle manufacturers continued to make warranty claims of vehicle owners universally dependent upon the condition that all services and repairs had been carried out by the authorised network, and with the exclusive use of the vehicle manufacturer's spare parts.

One of the major improvements in the new competition law framework in comparison with the expired Motor Vehicle Block Exemption Regulation 1400/2002 is the clarification by the European Commission that **vehicle manufacturers may not make the warranties conditional on the repair and servicing of a vehicle within their network, or on the use of their own branded spare parts.**

According to the new set of rules, consumers have the right to use any repair shop for non warranty work, during both the statutory warranty period (2 years in most EU member states) and any extended warranty period.

Of course, every operator is subject to statutory product and service liability. Thus, anyone who damages a vehicle as a result of negligent work or use of defective parts is responsible for it.

2.4.2 Recall actions, free servicing and warranty work

Within the warranty period, any defect originating from the car manufacturing process must be corrected by the vehicle manufacturer. Normally, the network of authorised repairers will execute the work on behalf of the vehicle manufacturer, and at its expense. In such cases paid for by the manufacturer, i.e. recall actions or free servicing or warranty works etc., the works must be carried out where specified by the manufacturer. Where it pays the repairer, the manufacturer may also determine which parts are to be used.

2.4.3 Insurance policies and warranty contracts

These rights to choose during the warranty period apply to warranties forming an integral part of the purchase of the vehicle. However, warranties which are in fact insurance policies, purchased separately, may not be covered. Leasing or financing contracts may also provide for additional limitations.

2.5 Access to technical information

With the adoption of sector-specific Guidelines, the European Commission has emphasised the importance of "Independent Operators". It has recognised that the independent aftermarket increases choice for consumers and keeps the price of repairs competitive by putting pressure on car manufacturers' networks.[5]

In order to truly achieve effective competition in the after-sales services, it is essential that all operators can get the technical information necessary to do the repairs and maintenance on increasingly sophisticated vehicles.

---

5 European Commission's Memo No. 10/217 of 27/05/2010 — Antitrust: Commission adopts revised competition rules for the motor vehicle sector: frequently asked questions.

To that end, the keystone of the new competition law framework is that **withholding technical information will be dealt with directly under Treaty rules on restraints of competition**.

Compared to the former Motor Vehicle Block Exemption Regulation 1400/2002, granting access to technical information is no longer viewed as a mere prerequisite for vehicle manufacturers wishing to enjoy an exemption from the normal competition rules. The new competition framework recognises that access to technical information, tools and training continues to be a prerequisite for effective competition in the automotive aftermarket.

2.5.1 Key definitions

a) Independent operators

The definition of independent operators is based on the definition which already exists in the Euro 5/6 Type-Approval legislation[6]. It includes independent repairers, spare parts manufacturers and distributors, manufacturers of repair equipment or tools, publishers of technical information, automobile clubs, roadside assistance operators, operators offering inspection and testing services and operators offering training for repairers. This list is however non-exhaustive.

b) The scope of technical information

On the issue of access to technical information, several technical European Type-Approval Regulations already contain key provisions on the access to vehicle repair and maintenance information for independent operators.[7]

The novelty brought by the European Commission to the new competition law framework is the cross-referencing between the type-approval legislation and the competition law rules. In other words, in order to know whether a piece of information should be made available to the independ-

---

6 Regulation (EC) No. 715/2007 on type approval of motor vehicles with respect to emissions from light passenger and commercial vehicles (Euro 5 and Euro 6) and on access to vehicle repair and maintenance information.

7 These are:
  — Regulation (EC) No. 715/2007 on type approval of motor vehicles with respect to emissions from light passenger and commercial vehicles (Euro 5 and Euro 6) and on access to vehicle repair and maintenance information;
  — Regulation (EC) No. 692/2008 which implements and amends Regulation (EC) No. 715/2007;
  — Regulation (EC) No. 595/2009 on type approval of motor vehicles and engines with respect to emissions from heavy duty vehicles (Euro VI) and on access to vehicle repair and maintenance information;
  — the ensuing implementing measures for the Regulation 595/2009 still to be adopted.

ent aftermarket operators, reference should be made to the provisions on access to repair and maintenance information in the type-approval instruments. Any information communicated to the members of the authorised networks should be made available to independent operators. This applies to the entire vehicle park of all self-propelled vehicles with 3 or more wheels.

Regulation (EC) No. 715/2007 contains a generic definition of technical information which gives a good summary of what "technical information for the repair and maintenance of vehicles" means:

> 'vehicle repair and maintenance information' means all information required for diagnosis, servicing, inspection, periodic monitoring, repair, re-programming or re-initialising of the vehicle and which the manufacturers provide for their authorised dealers and repairers, including all subsequent amendments and supplements to such information. This information includes all information required for fitting parts or equipment on vehicles;

In order to bring clarity on this matter, the European Commission also pointed out that the lists of items set out in Article 6(2) of Regulation (EC) No. 715/2007 and Regulation (EC) No. 595/2009 should also be used as a guide to assess what could be considered as technical information for the purposes of competition law. This list includes:

— unequivocal vehicle identification

— service handbooks

— technical manuals

— component and diagnosis information

— wiring diagrams

— diagnostic trouble codes (including manufacturer specific codes)

— software calibration identification number applicable to a vehicle type

— information provided concerning, and delivered by means of, proprietary tools and equipment

— data record information and two-directional monitoring and test data

Further to this clear reference to the Type-Approval legislation, the **new competition law instrument** also contains further specific examples:

— software

— fault codes and other parameters, together with updates, which are required to work on electronic control units with a view to introducing or restoring settings recommended by the supplier

— motor vehicle identification numbers or any other motor vehicle identification methods
— parts catalogues
— repair and maintenance procedures
— working solutions resulting from practical experience and relating to problems typically affecting a given model or batch
— recall notices
— notices identifying repairs that may be carried out without charge within the authorised repair network.

For the **parts identification**, the European Commission's Guidelines explicitly state that parts codes and any other information necessary to identify the correct car manufacturer-branded spare part to fit a given individual motor vehicle should be made available to independent operators if it is made available to the authorised network.

2.5.2 The technical information assessment "test"

a) The concept

The overarching principle under this competition law angle is that all the information for the repair and maintenance of vehicles made available to members of the relevant authorised repair network shall also be communicated to the independent operators.

If the lists and examples provided by the European Commission in the Guidelines bring clarity on what could be considered as technical information for the repair and maintenance of vehicles, it is non exhaustive. As such, if an item is not explicitly enumerated in the list, this does not mean that a vehicle manufacturer may withhold this piece of information.

The European Commission pointed out that technological progress in vehicle and in parts manufacturing implies that the notion of technical information is fluid. As such, if advances in vehicle technology engender new techniques in the repair or maintenance of vehicles or require new pieces of technical information, access to this information must be given to independent operators.

b) The test and the limits

The European Commission has elaborated a "test" in order to assess at any moment in time if a particular item of information should be made available to independent operators. Some information provided to the authorised repair network may not be considered as "true" technical information for "the repair and maintenance of vehicles" and could therefore be withheld by vehicle manufacturers. These limits cover purely commercial information (e.g. hourly tariffs of the authorised repairers) or the genuine information necessary for the manufacturing of spare parts or tools, such as the information on the design, production process or the materials used for manufacturing of a spare part. However, the Commission pointed out that in cases where the information can be used for a "double purpose" — such as information showing the interconnection of parts — the information should be made available as it is necessary information in order to maintain and repair a vehicle.

One important notion must be kept in mind though: withholding information shall not have an appreciable impact on the ability of independent operators to carry out their tasks in the market.

It is also worth noting that in contrast to the expired MVBER 1400/2002, the new competition law framework does not contain any reference to the possibility for vehicle manufacturers to withhold information by e.g. simply referring to the anti-theft or anti-tampering system of the vehicle or in general to "industrial and intellectual property rights" (IPRs).

2.5.3 The availability of the information

The way in which technical information is supplied is also important. The European Commission has emphasised that **access should be given** upon request and **without undue delay**, in **a usable form**, and **the price charged should not discourage access** to it by failing to take into account the extent to which the independent operator uses the information[8].

For new vehicles on the market, **vehicle manufacturers are asked to give independent operators access to technical information** at the same time as to its authorised repairers. They should not oblige independent operators to purchase more than the information necessary.

---

8   It is important to underline that for the vehicles type-approved according to the Euro 5 or Euro VI Regulations, the list of information contained in these respective legislations (including specific OBD information for the manufacturing of parts and tools) will have to be provided to independent operators even though these might not be communicated, in the strict sense, to the members of the authorised networks.

3. Comments by Carsten Reimann[9]

3.1 Electric vehicles in the new competition law framework

With the LEAF project Nissan is driving the first real revolution in the automotive industry since the Henry Ford Model T. This marks a shift in automotive history and of the modern society. The Zero Emission vision by Nissan and Renault is changing the direction of the market and will make our planet a better place to live. In the near future, a substantial share of the vehicles circulating around the world will feature an electric engine. Based on the expert conference at CEU San Pablo University in Madrid on 12 November 2010, this article looks at the legal framework for vertical restraints in the automotive sector after its latest review and how it will apply to electric vehicles. This will be done in two steps. Firstly, I will give a brief overview on the factual and political background of electric vehicles (EVs) and their mass-market introduction. Secondly, I will address the key questions from a competition law perspective.

3.2 Has the time arrived for EVs?

For many years, electric cars were stuck in a classic chicken-or-the-egg scenario for two reasons — the lack of demand and the lack of a mass-marketed product. Why would governments create the required infrastructure with no demand? Why would consumers create demand for a car they could not afford or could not use as a practical alternative to their regular car? Why would car makers invest to make electric cars when there was neither mass-market demand for them nor public-sector investments to create the required infrastructure?

It was a vicious circle. This situation is changing now. Zero-emission mobility is within our reach because of a powerful combination of technology and collaboration. The Renault-Nissan Alliance has developed the technology and has been involving more than 80 official public and private sector partnerships around the world to develop a complete sustainable mobil-

---

9 Attorney-at-Law and currently serves as Head of External Affairs at Nissan in Europe as well as Director of Nissan's Brussels Office. The views expressed in this article are those of the author and not necessarily those of Nissan. For helpful discussion and comments on this article I am most grateful to my Nissan colleagues Friederike Kienitz and Catharina Tauson-Denysiak and also to Arne Möller of Renault Germany.

ity system.[10] The first affordable 100% electric cars will be introduced in European markets in 2011. To start with, Renault and Nissan together will have four different models available.

But why are electric vehicles so important? The answer is simple — because EVs offer the best solution for achieving zero emission mobility. Electric cars have no tailpipe — therefore emit zero emissions. They have a lower CO_2 rating than any hybrid. At the same time, the electricity grid is cleaner than gasoline. And if renewable energy sources are used, the result is even lower emissions overall compared with oil-dependent cars.

When we started telling people in Brussels about electric vehicles in 2008, most still were non-believers and more or less sceptical. Many had heard about hybrids, some were still dreaming of running their cars on bio-fuel. Meanwhile, the paradigm has changed. According to independent market studies, there will be 10% of electric vehicles on the market by 2020. Even the German car manufacturers, some of whom announced to launch their first pure EVs as from 2013, have recently sent a prototype driving from Munich to Berlin with the message that electric mobility is possible.[11] If we look at countries like China, it is clear that the introduction of large-scale volumes of electric vehicles will happen, with or without us Europeans.

The EU Industry Ministers have understood the urgency and need of public intervention to get this innovative market kick-started.[12] At the Competitiveness Council in Brussels on 26 November they reached, *inter alia*, the following key conclusions:

— EU authorities need to use public procurement, existing funding tools and regulatory framework to speed up the market uptake of clean vehicles;

— A well-timed public policy sending the automotive industry a signal will improve European competitiveness in the global market for clean cars;

— European standardisation bodies must develop, as a matter of priority by mid-2011, a harmonised solution for the interoperability between EVs and the charging infrastructure;

— The adoption of innovations is driven by demand side incentives. A coordinated European approach to clean vehicle purchase incentives is urgently needed.

---

10 For details see www.nissan-zeroemission.com; www.electric-mobility.com.

11 See "Deutschland fällt beim Elektroauto weiter zurück", Wirtschaftswoche 22 Jan 2011.

12 See Common Declaration on Electric Cars — information from the Presidency, http://europa. eu/rapid/pressReleasesAction.do?reference=MEMO/10/608&format=HTML&aged=0&languag e=EN&guiLanguage=en.

The EU Council presented a joint declaration giving the electric vehicle introduction and industrialisation the highest priority in the European automotive industry: "The electric vehicle is not only a solution for efficient and sustainable mobility, but an important opportunity for the European automotive industry and connected sectors. We believe that the electric vehicle needs to be put at the centre of development and competitiveness prospects, linking research and development, innovation, industrial development and sustainability."[13]

Depending on how many governments follow this call and best in class governments like the UK provide consumer incentives in the early market phase, there still appears to be a realistic chance that Europe will keep up with the US and Asian countries.

3.3 Competitive assessment

3.3.1 Which rules apply?

Regulation 1400/2002 and the new Regulation 461/2010 refer to motor vehicles. There is no distinction between cars with internal combustion engines (ICE) and cars with electric drive. "Motor vehicle" means a self-propelled vehicle intended for use in public roads and having three or more road wheels. Electric engines also "self-propel" the car. Thus, electric vehicles fall under the new competition framework for the automotive sector.

Accordingly, like for gasoline cars, the repair and maintenance services for EVs would now be considered under the General Vertical Block Exemption. Following such a purely formalistic approach, the sale for EVs would still be regarded under the old Motor Vehicle Block Exemption (Reg 1400/2002) until 1 June 2013. This conclusion, however, seems questionable when looking at why the regulator decided to abolish the sector-specific rules and move to the general regime step-by-step.

The Commission on the primary market gave operators a three-year delay, during which time Regulation 1400 would continue to apply, in order to allow for the amortisation of investments dealers had made pursuant to that regulation.[14] As the first electric vehicles are currently being launched in Europe, there are no such grandfather investments made in

---

13 The Declaration on Electric Cars was signed by the following countries: France, Spain, Germany, Portugal, Ireland, Belgium, Bulgaria, Lithuania and Slovenia.

14 *Clark/Csiszar*, Motor vehicles — is there still room for sector-specific treatment as regards vertical restraints?, p. 2.

the past. Thus, there are no running business cases to protect, no former amortisations to pay off. On the contrary, the launch of a completely new type of vehicle and the pro-competitive effects related to it may justify the protection of totally different business cases. An EV dealer investing in special battery-related equipment will have a special interest to be able to recover these investments within a reasonable period of time.

Against the above background, car manufacturers can use selective distribution systems for electric vehicles. Quantitative selection is allowed for the sale of EVs depending on market shares. The arguments given to justify the delayed phase-out of the sector-specific regulations on the primary market do not fit in the context of electric vehicles.

3.3.2 What are the relevant product markets?

A relevant product market comprises all those products and/or services which are regarded as interchangeable or substitutable by the consumer by reason of the products' characteristics, their prices and their intended use.

The consumer will compare the benefits of ICE and EV models and then choose the car he finds the best fit for his individual mobility pattern and price he wants to spend on a car. Even if the product market segments are defined according to type of car (sports car, small car, SUV etc), ICE and EV versions will usually be available in most of those segments and always be regarded as interchangeable.

One may argue that driving range is an important factor determining consumers' choice of product. With the current generation of battery technology 100% electric cars like the Nissan LEAF allow a driving range of 175 km without recharging. A consumer who must often cover long distances between cities by car may therefore "exclude" such an EV from his list of product choices that he regards as interchangeable alternatives for his particular mobility pattern. However, even if a substantial group of consumers was in the same situation as in the above example, this does not mean that EVs would constitute a separate product market.

This is because driving range is just one among a number of other factors like environmental impact or technical specs of the car. Firstly, this consumer group may also prefer diesel cars to normal petrol driven cars as more appropriate for their long-distance mobility pattern. Yet no one has ever argued that diesel cars should be regarded as a separate product market. And secondly, 80% of the population in the world (for UK the figure is even at 90%) have a predominantly urban driving pattern which means that a driving range of 175 km will cover more than 90% of their individual mobility needs. This majority group will regard electric vehicles as a valid alternative to petrol-consuming cars. The other 20% described as long-distance drivers may still think of EVs as a second city car. Again, no one has ever argued that small cars which are "typical" city cars should be regarded as a separate product market.

In conclusion, electric vehicles may be seen as another segment on the overall product market for automotives. This becomes even more evident as some define — unlike at present — electric vehicles not only as 100% battery-driven cars but also as including hybrid variants.

3.3.3 Will there be a market for repair and maintenance services that is separate from that for the sale of new motor vehicles?

Based on the fundamentally different technological concepts, there are some special issues to be taken into account.[15] Electric cars have fewer moving parts so maintenance costs will be lower. Also, buying behaviour is likely to be different because for the first time the "normal" consumer can easily monitor his Total Cost of Ownership (TCO). Until now, operators of car fleets were the only ones really basing their purchase decision on the overall running costs of their vehicles. Life-time costs were less an issue for the private individual who is mainly looking at the initial purchase price. Even if the price-sensitive consumer is watching petrol prices in general, who is in fact making a bill adding the price of all the litres of petrol he will need in the next 5 or 10 years plus the maintenance costs on top of the initial purchase price?

EVs will allow all users, SMEs and also private persons, to closely monitor their driving patterns, power consumption and TCO. Electric vehicles are not simply traditional cars with a new drive but rather "battery-powered computers on wheels" more and more connected to external IT systems and grids. Finally, also opting for an energy arrangement, the consumer will look for a mobility system including the car and an energy supply contract. From a demand-side perspective, there are thus strong arguments for EV system markets.

Indeed reading in context some explanatory statements from the Commission confirms such a system market including motor vehicles, spare parts and after-sales services. Firstly, the distinction that the new framework makes between the markets for the sale of new motor vehicles and the

---

15   See US Department of Energy, How do gasoline and electric vehicles compare? http://www1.eere.energy.gov/vehiclesandfuels/avta/light_duty/fsev/fsev_gas_elec1.html.

motor vehicle aftermarkets is said to reflect the differing competitive conditions on these markets.[16] Secondly, this distinction is justified by the assumption that repair and maintenance as a whole represent a very high proportion of total consumer expenditure on motor vehicles which itself accounts for a significant slice of the average consumer's budget.[17] As seen above, this may not be true anymore for electric vehicles.

Thirdly, the Commission clarifies the question whether a market exists for repair and maintenance services that is separate from that for the sale of new vehicles: in some circumstances, a system market which includes motor vehicles and spare parts together may be defined, taking into account the life-time of the motor vehicle as well as the preferences and buying behaviour of the users.[18] One important factor is whether a significant proportion of buyers make their choice taking into account the lifetime costs of the motor vehicle or not.[19] Here the Commission is discussing the example of the fleet owner: Buying behaviour may significantly differ between buyers of trucks who purchase and operate a fleet, and who take into account maintenance costs at the moment of purchasing the vehicle and buyers of individual motor vehicles because the majority of the buyers and private individuals or SMEs do not have systematic access to data permitting them to assess the overall costs of motor vehicle ownership in advance.[20]

Even with no empirical evidence on consumer buying behaviour of EVs being available at the time it seems most likely that the Commission's example of the fleet owner will also apply for the private owner of an electric vehicle. As a consequence, there will be one single market for sales and after-sales services for electric vehicles. Such system markets would then allow manufacturers again to have sales and after-sales in one distribution contract with the EV dealer. There would be no franchisees doing only repair.

3.4 Conclusions

Electric vehicles will emerge as a new market segment. This will bring a number of new chances and opportunities. Not only technology and the

---

16 Sector-specific Guidelines, para. 11.
17 Sector-specific Guidelines, para. 15.
18 Sector-specific Guidelines, para. 57.
19 Sector-specific Guidelines, para. 57.
20 Sector-specific Guidelines, para. 57.

concept of the car as such will be more environmentally-friendly and innovative, but also business models, distribution channels and market players
will significantly differ. New after-markets and related markets in sectors
other than automotive will be the consequence.

Given multiple players from many sectors such as battery producers and
electric mobility operators (EMOs) selling "car electricity" and related
infrastructure, the newly emerging market environment will be highly
competitive. A sector-specific competition framework distinguishing
between sales and after-sales of cars is unlikely to reflect business reality.
Therefore it is very positive that the Commission is finally phasing out the
sector-specific rules of the old Motor Vehicle Block exemption.

The new framework will allow a cross-sector assessment which will be
required in the new markets of electric mobility solutions. As shown
above, there are some strong arguments for emerging systems markets on
which OEMs should be allowed to operate separate EV distribution networks right from the start. In fact, the competition law framework should
provide more freedom under the General Vertical Block Exemption as of
the launch of electric vehicles today and not only as from 2013 when the
last sector-specific rules are phased out for the sale of oil-dependent cars.

PART FOUR

NATIONAL ENFORCEMENT

CHAPTER X

NATIONAL EXPERIENCES IN VERTICAL RESTRAINTS: SPAIN

Joaquín López Vallés

Assistant Deputy Director of Industry and Energy. Investigations Division
Comisión Nacional de la Competencia (CNC)

1. Introduction

Vertical restraints are said to be dealt with at a national level. This assertion stems from the fact that vertical restraints are commonly used to govern the relationships between agents who distribute goods and services (manufacturers, wholesalers and/or retailers), and the fact that undertakings normally organise their distribution systems at a national level because of differences in consumer preferences and habits, and in regulations. It must also be borne in mind that vertical restraints are widely used by small and medium-sized enterprises (SMEs), which represent the majority of enterprises in the EU and generally focus their commercial strategies on their countries of origin. Consequently, vertical agreements do not always affect trade between Member States, and even when they do these are not always of Community interest for the European Commission. Therefore, the experiences of National Competition Authorities (NCAs) and national courts in relation to vertical restraints are an essential input for the European Commission as well as for other enforcers.

Three sectors stand out in Spain's recent experience in applying the vertical restraints regime as a result of the specific areas they relate to. They are the distribution of fuels for motor vehicles, the distribution of pharmaceutical drugs and motor vehicles. Some of these specific areas have been addressed in top cases at EU level but even so, national experiences provide a rich and varied perspective on the kinds of problems faced by the sector. We will discuss these issues in section II.

Experience also shows that NCAs and national courts have to deal with small cases. In the context of regulation that has suddenly changed from a formal approach to an effects-based one, small cases can raise specific issues, because competition enforcers sometimes pay excessive attention to formal aspects in vertical agreements rather than their actual and potential effects. We will discuss these considerations further in section III.

2. Recent Spanish experience in vertical restraints

The following chart highlights the most relevant cases regarding vertical restraints dealt with by the CNC[1] in recent years. Fuel distribution is undoubtedly the most problematic sector in Spain in terms of verticals, with cases relating to RPM and foreclosure effects deriving from non-compete clauses in the context of parallel networks with similar agreements. Other sectors with recurrent specific problems are the distribution of pharmaceutical goods (double pricing policies) and motor vehicles (discrimination against non-authorised dealers). In other sectors, relevant practices relate to resale price maintenance (RPM), exclusive distribution and non-compete clauses.

2.1 Fuel distribution

In Spain there are around 9,000 service stations selling fuel to motorists. Service stations are supplied by a single company, and are often also branded by the supplier: only around 15% of service stations are not branded by any supplier. Suppliers also own and operate service stations. The major supplier is Repsol, with a market share of around 40%, followed by Cepsa (around 17%), BP (7%) and GALP (7%).The competitive situation in mainland Spain differs from that in non-continental areas (the Canary Islands, Balearic Islands and the autonomous cities of Ceuta and Melilla)[2] at both supplier and retailer level.

There have been two main competition concerns in this market regarding verticals: the duration of exclusivity clauses (non-compete clauses) and RPM.

---

1   The CNC was created on 1.09.2007 as a result of a merger between the former Competition Service (now the Investigations Division of the CNC) and the former Competition Court (now the Council of the CNC). For the sake of simplicity, we will refer beyond this point only to the CNC.
2   Report on competition in the vehicle fuel sector. CNC, 2009.

MOST RELEVANT VERTICAL RESTRAINTS CASES IN RECENT YEARS IN SPAIN				
Date	Name	Sector	Matter of concern	Result
13/09/2010	S/0162/09 Semillas de girasol	Agriculture	Non-compete clauses	Commitments
18/06/2003	541/02 DIASA	Distribution of consumer goods	RPM	Filed
02/11/2004	578/04 Eko-Ama Mondáriz	Distribution of consumer goods	RPM	Infringement
31/05/2005	579/04 Asturcolchón/ Tempur	Distribution of consumer goods	RPM	Infringement
21/06/2007	612/06 Aceites 2	Distribution of consumer goods	RPM	Infringement
03/12/2009	S/0105/08 Corral Flamencas	Distribution of consumer goods	RPM	Filed
12/03/2007	614/06 Cervezas Canarias 2	Food and beverage services	Non-compete clauses	Infringement
19/02/2008	647/08 La Flor de Murcia/DAMM	Food and beverage services	Non-compete clauses. RPM	Infringement
30/05/2005	A325/02 Contratos BP Oil España	Fuel distribution	Non-compete clauses. RPM	Infringement
23/09/2008	2740/06 Total España	Fuel distribution	Non-compete clauses	Filed
29/09/2008	2739/06 Agip España	Fuel distribution	Non-compete clauses	Filed
29/07/2009	2697/06 Cepsa EESS	Fuel distribution	Non-compete clauses	Commitments
30/07/2009	652/08 Repsol/Cepsa/BP	Fuel distribution	RPM	Infringement
19/02/2010	2575/05 Disa Canarias	Fuel distribution	Non-compete clauses	Filed
21/07/2008	634/07 MDC / Haller	Industry	Exclusive distribution	Infringement
28/01/2009	2659/05 Rotores centrifugadoras	Industry	Exclusive distribution	Filed
06/11/2008	2801/07 Ssanyong España	Motor vehicles	Selective distribution	Filed
12/12/2008	S/0113/08 Ford	Motor vehicles	Discrimination against unauthorised dealers	Filed
17/04/2009	S/0054/08 Nissan	Motor vehicles	Discrimination against unauthorised dealers	Filed
04/05/2009	S/0075/08 Nissan Iberia	Motor vehicles	Selective distribution	Filed
23/06/2009	S/0125/08 Scania Hispania	Motor vehicles	Selective distribution	Filed
01/12/2009	S/0190/09 Citröen España	Motor vehicles	Discrimination against unauthorised dealers	Filed
05/03/2010	S/0070/08 Ancopel	Motor vehicles	Selective distribution	Filed
21/05/2009	2623/05 Pfizer/Cofares	Pharmaceutical	Double pricing	Filed
14/09/2009	S/0017/07 EAPC vs. Labs.	Pharmaceutical	Double pricing	Filed
17/02/2010	S/0038/08 FEFE VS Labs.	Pharmaceutical	Double pricing	Filed
23/10/2007	618/06 Logimail/Unipost	Telecommunications	Exclusive distribution	Filed

The current network of service stations extends across the length and breadth of Spain, and the existing network could be seen as a natural monopoly from both a national as well as a local perspective, in the sense that it would not be viable for a newcomer to replicate the entire network or any part of it in order to enter the market (although this does not mean that building new service stations may not be a viable competitive strategy in certain areas). Gaining access to the existing network of service stations is, therefore, crucial in order for competing suppliers to enter or expand their position in the market.

This makes the relationship between current suppliers and service stations all the more relevant. Apart from unbranded stations[3], service stations in Spain may be divided into five categories according to the ownership and management structure in place between the wholesaler ("company") and retailer ("dealer"):

— Company Owned Company Operated (COCO): Under this structure, the premises and land belong to the wholesaler, which also supplies and operates the station. It is unlikely that any newcomer could ever gain a foothold within this structure, since a supplier would not normally want to be served by a competitor.

— Dealer Owned Company Operated (DOCO): Under this structure, the premises and land belong to a third party, which lets them to a wholesaler that supplies and directly operates the station. It is unlikely that a newcomer could ever capture this structure either, since a supplier would not normally want to be served by a competitor.

— Company Owned Dealer Operated (CODO): Under this structure, the premises and land belong to a supplier, which lets them to a dealer who operates the station, which is served by the supplier. It is unlikely that a newcomer could ever capture this structure either, since a supplier would not normally want to rent the service station to a third party without the latter making a commitment to purchase fuel exclusively from the supplier.

— Dealer Owned Dealer Operated (DODO): Under this structure, the premises and land belong to a dealer, which also operates the station. Stations in this group could in principle be served by any supplier, including a new market entrant.

---

3 This classification is not exhaustive. See also Commission Decision of 12.04.2006 in case COMP 38.348 Repsol CPP and Resolution of the CNC of 29.07.09 in case 2697/06 Cepsa.

— Company Tenancy/Usufruct Dealer Operated (T&U): This structure is a hybrid between the CODO and DODO structures, under which the land and premises (or the land alone) belong to a third party, which establishes a tenancy or usufruct right in favour of the supplier. The supplier, in turn, rents the station out to a dealer, which operates it. This structure operates according to two modalities depending on the relationship between the bare owner of the land and premises (or the land alone) and the dealer. If these are not linked to each other, the structure is similar to a CODO structure and is not likely ever to be captured by a newcomer. However, if the bare owner and the dealer are linked to each other, the structure is more like a DODO structure, under which the bare owner/dealer might be served by another supplier, meaning the service station could in theory be captured by a new entrant[4].

Article 12 of Regulation (EC) 1984/1983, which was in force from the mid-1980s until Regulation (EC) 2790/1999 came into force, exempted exclusive purchase or non-compete clauses in service station agreements up to a maximum of 10 years, unless the supplier had let the service station to the dealer, in which case the non-compete clause could last for the whole period for which the reseller in fact operated the premises.

The latter exception led to complex ownership constructions, under which the owner of a service station or the land constituted a real right of tenancy or of usufruct on the land and/or premises in favour of the supplier, who in turn let the station to the dealer; which allowed for the exception to

---

4   These considerations on the relationship between the bare owner of the land and premises and the dealer follow the same logic than the exception provided for the exemption of non-compete clauses lasting more than 5 years under Article 5.2 of Regulation EU 330/2010, which reads:
   "By way of derogation from paragraph 1(a), the time limitation of five years shall not apply where the contract goods or services are sold by the buyer from premises and land owned by the supplier or leased by the supplier from third parties not connected with the buyer, provided that the duration of the non-compete obligation does not exceed the period of occupancy of the premises and land by the buyer". The Guidelines on Vertical Restraints explain the reason for this exception at §67:
   "The five-year duration limit does not apply when the goods or services are resold by the buyer 'from premises and land owned by the supplier or leased by the supplier from third parties not connected with the buyer'. In such cases the non-compete obligation may be of the same duration as the period of occupancy of the point of sale by the buyer (Article 5(2) of the Block Exemption Regulation). The reason for this exception is that it is normally unreasonable to expect a supplier to allow competing products to be sold from premises and land owned by the supplier without its permission. By analogy, the same principles apply where the buyer operates from a mobile outlet owned by the supplier or leased by the supplier from third parties not connected with the buyer. Artificial ownership constructions, such as a transfer by the distributor of its proprietary rights over the land and premises to the supplier for only a limited period, intended to avoid the five-year limit cannot benefit from this exception".

be applied and resulted in non-compete clauses lasting more than 10 years. Faced with this, the CNC's approach became progressively more restrictive: from case R 197/97 SHELL ESPAÑA[5], where the CNC stated that such complex ownership constructions were not artificial in cases where the supplier had accompanied them with significant investments in the station, to case 490/00 REPSOL[6], which found that the general period of 10 years' exemption under Article 12(1) of Regulation (EC) 1984/83 already took into account the investments made by the supplier and that systematic use of complex ownership constructions might constitute evidence of artificial elusion of the general rule. Finally, in case 520/01 DISARED[7], the CNC concluded that the exception to the general 10-year rule had to be interpreted in a restrictive manner. Eight years later, the European Court of Justice (ECJ) clarified in case C-260/07 Pedro IV that the exception to the general 10-year rule provided under Article 12(2) of Regulation (EC) 1984/83 admitted such artificial ownership constructions:

> "...Article 12(2) of Regulation No. 1984/83 must be interpreted as meaning that, for the purposes of applying the exception which it laid down, that provision did not require the supplier to be the owner of the land on which he had built the service station which he let to the reseller."[8]

These problems led to a clarification of the exception in Regulation (EC) 2790/99, which substituted Regulation (EC) 1984/83. Under Article 5 of Regulation (EC) 2790/99, non-compete agreements that were indefinite or lasted more that five years were not exempted unless the products were sold from land and premises owned by the supplier or let by the supplier to a third party with no relation with the dealer. In the Guidelines on Vertical Restraints that accompanied that Regulation,[9] the Commission clearly stated at §59 that:

> "Artificial ownership constructions, such as a transfer by the distributor of its proprietary rights over the land and premises to the supplier for only a limited period, intended to avoid the five-year limit cannot benefit from this exception"

This change meant that most of the agreements that had been exempted under the previous Regulation (EC) 1984/83 were no longer exempted,

---

5   Decision by the Spanish Competition Court of 12.09.1997.
6   Decision by the Spanish Competition Court of 11.07.2001.
7   Decision by the Spanish Competition Court of 31.05.2002.
8   Judgment of the ECJ of 2.04.2009 in case C-260/07, §60.
9   2000/C 291/01.

and this increased the number of cases before the CNC and the courts. In cases R 691/06 DISA[10], 2740/06 TOTAL[11], 2739/06 AGIP[12] and 2575/06 DISA CANARIAS[13], the CNC declared that certain long-lasting exclusivity agreements with service stations did not infringe competition law because of their lack of appreciability, in line with ECJ case law in *Delimitis*[14], given that the agreements in question made only a marginal contribution to the foreclosure effect of non-compete clauses. In case A 325/02 CONTRATOS BP OIL ESPAÑA[15], the CNC found that BP's agreements with certain service stations could not be exempted because they lasted for more than five years and contained hardcore clauses, namely RPM.

In 2006, the Commission concluded case COMP 38.348 REPSOL CPP[16] by means of undertakings[17]. Repsol undertook to grant bare owners of land or land and premises who had constituted a real right of tenancy or of usufruct over the land and/or premises in favour of Repsol, and who also operated the service station with a call option, the right to recover full ownership the station, for a price. This approach was subsequently also applied by the CNC in case 2697/06 CEPSA[18], in which Cepsa promised the CNC to grant bare owners that were also service station dealers a call option right to recover full ownership of the station, for a price. The main differences between the two Decisions were the means of price calculation. While the execution price in case 38.348 REPSOL CPP had a known ceiling, in case 2697/06 calculation of the final call option right price was left to an auditor.

As well as the problem of the long duration of contracts, the fuel distribution sector has also highlighted another matter of concern — the widespread use of RPM clauses. Fixed resale prices were found to exist and were prohibited in cases 490/00 REPSOL, 493/00 CEPSA[19], 520/01 DISARED, A325/02 CONTRATOS BP OIL ESPAÑA and 652/07 REPSOL/CEPSA/BP[20]. The problems with RPM have been twofold — the question of under

---

10 Decision of the CNC of 27.11.2007.
11 Decision of the CNC of 23.09.2008.
12 Decision of the CNC of 29.09.2008.
13 Decision of the CNC of 19.02.2010.
14 Judgment of the ECJ in case C-234/89 *Stergios Delimitis vs. Henninger Bräu AG* [1991] ECR I-935.
15 Decision of the CNC of 30.05.2005.
16 Commission Decision of 12.04.2006.
17 Article 9 of Council Regulation (EC) 1/2003.
18 Decision of the CNC of 29.07.2009.
19 Decision of the CNC of 31.05.2001.
20 Decision of the CNC of 30.07.2009.

what circumstances resellers were 'genuine agents' and the existence of fixed resale prices.

Under the vertical restraints regime, 'genuine agents' are considered to form part of the principal as regards commercial policy. Consequently, should a principal impose resale prices (or other resale restrictions) on its agents, there would be no infringement of Article 101(1) of the Treaty. This does not imply that the rest of the clauses regulating the relationship between the principal and the agent are untouchable by competition law (Guidelines on Vertical Restraints[21], §§18-21, and ECJ Judgement in case C-217/05 CEES[22]).

However, the concept of 'agent' in competition law is not the same as it is in other areas of law. The CNC examined the competition law requirements for being a 'genuine agent' in case 490/00 REPSOL. After comparing EU (risk-based) and Spanish (ownership-based) approaches in this respect, the CNC opted for the EU approach, based on the risks borne by the agent. This approach has been applied ever since.

Apart from the agency question, in some cases there has been controversy about suppliers fixing resale prices. In cases 490/00 REPSOL and 493/00 CEPSA, the CNC found that, although suppliers fixed resale prices, dealers could theoretically reduce these prices by reducing their commission. After an in-depth analysis, the CNC concluded that the functioning of point of sale terminals and the way provisional VAT payments were made (on the basis of the reseller's commission as fixed by the supplier) discouraged dealers from reducing sale prices at the expense of their own commission.

In case 652/07 REPSOL/CEPSA/BP, suppliers did not fix resale prices but recommended them. Nevertheless, the investigation showed that recommended prices were in fact fixed prices, since a range of factors reduced the incentives to cut the reseller's commission. An interesting aspect of this analysis is that these factors derived not only from specific circumstances relating to the vertical relationship, such as VAT declarations and the functioning of point of sale terminals, but also horizontal issues within the relevant areas of influence: recommended prices were set by suppliers with reference to the average prices in each service station's geographic area of influence, which therefore removed any incentive for the reseller to deviate from the trend. Since resellers knew that the same system was being applied by all their competitors in the area, any unilateral deviation from that price would result in lower profits for all, given the highly

---

21 2010/C 130/01.
22 Judgment of the ECJ of 14.12.2006.

standardised nature of the product, price transparency, mature and non-elastic demand, high barriers to entry, low degree of innovation and daily repetition of the game. Consequently the CNC declared that the bundle of vertical agreements on the part of the suppliers Repsol, Cepsa and BP with their respective retailers (service stations) reduced intra-brand competition and resulted in tacit price coordination between these suppliers, infringing Article 101(1) of the Treaty and its national equivalent.

2.2 Distribution of pharmaceutical medicines

By means of its Decision of 8.05.2001, the European Commission declared that the double medicines pricing system applied by GlaxoWellcome was illegal[23]. In view of the fact that the Spanish Government had subsidised and fixed maximum (industrial and final) prices for certain medications sold and consumed in Spain since 1988, Glaxo had established two different transfer prices to wholesalers, depending on the final destination of the medicines. The Commission found that the object of this system was contrary to Article 101(1) because it was aimed at preventing parallel trade and did not satisfy the cumulative criteria for the application of an individual exemption as provided by Article 101(3) of the Treaty.

This Decision was reversed by the Court of First Instance (CFI) in its Judgement of 27.09.2006 (case T-168/01), which stated that the system did not infringe Article 101(1) in its object, but it did so in its effect, and that the Commission had failed to rebut Glaxo's arguments on efficiency gains. Glaxo had submitted that parallel trade did not provide real gains for consumers because prices of imported medications aligned themselves with prevailing prices in the destination countries for Spanish medications. Preventing parallel trade, however, would see Glaxo's profits increase much more, and these would be invested in R&D, since competition between laboratories was now mainly driven by innovation. The ECJ[24] stated that the practice did infringe Article 101(1) of the Treaty by its very nature, but essentially supported the judgement of the CFI as regards its assessment of Article 101(3).

In the meantime, three cases were raised before the CNC regarding the possible illegality of similar pricing systems: cases 2623/05 PFIZER/

---

23 DO L 302, p. 1.
24 Judgment of the ECJ of 6.10.2009 in joint cases C-501, 513, 515 and 519/06 P.

COFARES[25], S/0017/07 EAEPC VS LABORATORIOS FARMACÉUTICOS[26] and S/0038/08 FEFE VS LABORATORIOS Y ALMACENISTAS FARMACÉU-TICOS[27]. In these three cases, the CNC concluded that there was no infringement of competition, because the laboratories in question did not establish dual prices but rather a single industrial price for each medicine, which was substituted by the intervention price set by the Government when the distributor showed that medicines had been sold in Spain.

2.3 Motor vehicles

The CNC has dealt with some cases regarding motor vehicles in recent years, none of which has been of singular importance. The main area of concern in these cases has been possible discrimination against independent repairers through retirement of the manufacturer's warranty (cases S/0054/08 NISSAN, S/0113/08 FORD and S/0190/09 CITRÖEN ESPAÑA), which has not been proven to exist or has not been found to be driven by the manufacturer. Other cases (2801/07 SSANGYONG ESPAÑA, S/0075/08 NISSAN IBERIA, S.A. S/0125/08 SCANIA HISPANIA, and S/0070/08 ANCOPEL) relate to the relationship between a manufacturer and a dealer being broken under Regulation (EC) 1400/02.

2.4 Other sectors

There are no common patterns in other sectors, but some cases are of interest for illustration purposes. Some cases, mainly in the distribution of consumer goods, relate to RPM practices: RPM was found to exist and was therefore sanctioned in cases 578/04 EKO-AMA MONDÁRIZ[28], 579/04 ASTURCOLCHÓN/TEMPUR[29], 612/06 ACEITES 2[30] and 647/08 LA FLOR DE MURCIA/DAMM[31]. In case S/0105/08 CORRAL DE LAS FLAMENCAS[32], RPM was found to exist, but the case was filed, while in case 541/02 DIASA[33] the evidence for RPM was insufficient.

---

25 Decision of the CNC of 21.05.2009.
26 Decision of the CNC of 14.09.2009.
27 Decision of the CNC of 17.02.2010.
28 Decision of the CNC of 2.11.2004.
29 Decision of the CNC of 31.05.2005.
30 Decision of the CNC of 21.06.2007.
31 Decision of the CNC of 19.02.2008.
32 Decision of the CNC of 3.12.2009.
33 Decision of the CNC of 18.06.2003.

The theory of harm in case 612/06 ACEITES 2 was supplier-driven RPM that was accepted by all distributors, each of which was aware of the supplier imposing RPM on other distributors. In this case, the negative impact of RPM derived from the supplier's leading position in the market and the tacit acquiescence of the distributors, in a situation of high distribution concentration (distributors party to the RPM agreements held a joint market share of nearly 70% in Spain).

In case 647/08, LA FLOR DE MURCIA/DAMM, RPM was supplier driven. The theory of harm was the supplier's strong position (market share in excess of 20% in Spain and higher in some regions) in the context of a market characterised by the existence of parallel agreement networks with non-compete clauses.

In the other cases, RPM was supplier driven, but there was no clear theory of harm to competition apart from the reduction in intra-brand price-competition, because neither the supplier nor the distributor held strong positions in their respective relevant markets and there was no evidence of either market concentration or parallel agreements. In case 578/04 EKO-AMA MONDÁRIZ, Mondáriz's market share was below 2% in Spain and below 15% in the region of Galicia, where it faced fierce competition. In case 579/04 ASTURCOLCHÓN/TEMPUR, Tempur's market share was 2% in Spain. Very interestingly, in case S/0105/08 CORRAL DE LAS FLAMENCAS, where El Corral de las Flamencas' market share was found to be below 1%, the CNC argued that RPM posed no harm to competition and filed the case. This case will be discussed in the next section.

In a case relating to the food and beverage services sector (614/06 CERVEZAS CANARIAS 2[34]), a series of non-compete clauses were found to foreclose access to the beer distribution market in the Canary Islands, and therefore were prohibited.

A final case, case 634/07 MDC INGENIERÍA/PRODUCTOS HALLER[35], is of interest before moving on to the next section. In this case, the CNC found that HALLER, a German manufacturer of urban waste collection containers was infringing competition law by preventing its exclusive distributors from engaging in passive sales. An appeal was lodged before the *Audiencia Nacional*, which studied HALLER'S arguments and concluded that the agreement was *de minimis*[36]. *This case will be discussed in the next section.*

---

34 Decision of the CNC of 12.03.2007.
35 Decision of the CNC of 21.07.2008.
36 Judgment of the *Audiencia Nacional* of 29.10.2009 in case 418/2008.

3. The *"de minimis"* dilemma

3.1 The de minimis principle

Article 101(1) of the Treaty prohibits agreements and concerted practices that distort or restrict competition by their object or effect. Case-law has established that only agreements that appreciably distort or restrict competition are covered by this prohibition. This means that agreements that do not appreciably restrict or distort competition are not prohibited, regardless of their object and/or effect. This is known as the *de minimis* rule[37].

The *de minimis* rule has its origin in the early case law of the European Court of Justice. In *Völk vs. Vervaecke*[38] *the ECJ held that*

> *"...an agreement falls outside the prohibition in Article 85(1) where it has only an insignificant effect on the market, taking into account the weak position which the persons concerned have on the market of the product in question".*

3.2 The de minimis rule at EU level

The Commission has issued specific rules for applying the *de minimis* rules to vertical agreements. These rules are contained in the Guidelines on Vertical Restraints (§§8-11) and the *De minimis* Notice[39]. According to these provisions, vertical agreements entered into by non-competing undertakings whose individual market share does not exceed 15% of the relevant market are presumed to be *de minimis* as long as they do not contain hardcore restrictions as defined in point 11(2) of the *De minimis* Notice[40]. Requirements for a presumption of *de minimis* in the case of

---

37 "Agreements that are not capable of appreciably affecting trade between Member States or of appreciably restricting competition by object or effect do not fall within the scope of Article 101(1)" (Guidelines on Vertical Restraints, §8).

38 Case 5/69 *Völk vs. Vervaecke* [1969] ECR 295.

39 Commission Notice on agreements of minor importance that do not appreciably restrict competition under Article 81(1) of the Treaty establishing the European Community (*de minimis*). Official Journal C 368, 22.12.2001, pp. 13-15. Hereinafter, the *De minimis* Notice.

40 *De minimis* Notice, §§7 and 11. Hardcore restrictions listed in point 11(2) of the *De minimis* Notice coincide with those listed in Article 4 of Regulation (EC) 2790/1999, which has been replaced by Regulation EU 330/2010 as of June 1, 2010. Since the wording of Article 4 of Regulation EU 330/2010 has changed slightly from the wording of Article 4 of Regulation (EC) 2790/1999, it must be noted that there may now be some inconsistency between the *de minimis* list of hardcore restrictions for vertical agreements (point 11(2) of the *De minimis* Notice) and the Block Exemption Regulation (BER) list of hardcore restrictions for vertical agreements (Article 4 of Regulation EU 330/2010).

vertical agreements between competing undertakings are stricter[41]. The 15% threshold is reduced to 5% where competition is restricted in a relevant market by the cumulative foreclosure effect of parallel agreement networks with similar effects on the market[42].

The *De minimis* Notice thus imposes a double condition for an agreement to be able to benefit from an automatic *de minimis* presumption: a market share threshold for both the supplier and the buyer (either 15%, 10% or 5%), and the absence of hardcore restraints in the vertical relationship.

In addition, the Commission is of the opinion that vertical agreements between small and medium-sized enterprises (SMEs) generally fall outside the scope of Article 101(1) because they are rarely capable of affecting trade between member states or of distorting or restricting competition[43]. The Commission points out that the latter is subject to the absence of hardcore restraints and cumulative foreclosure effects. However, even if an agreement between SMEs infringed Article 101(1), the Commission would not consider such an agreement to be of sufficient interest to merit launching formal proceedings[44]. It must be borne in mind that the lack of Community interest relates only to the Commission and not to National Competition Authorities (NCAs) or national judges, who will normally have to deal with any cases the Commission declines to investigate.

3.3 The *de minimis* rule in Spain

Article 1 of the Competition Act 15/2007[45] is the Spanish equivalent of Article 101(1) of the Treaty. It prohibits agreements and concerted practices that distort or restrict competition by object and/or effect[46].

---

41 Vertical agreements may also be reached between competing undertakings. In this case, the thresholds for a *de minimis* presumption are reduced to 10%, and the list of relevant hardcore restraints for the *de minimis* presumption is wider, also comprising those listed in point 11(1) of the *De minimis* Notice.

42 *De minimis* Notice, §8. The Notice indicates that, where agreements having similar effects cover less than 30% of the market, a cumulative foreclosure effect cannot be presumed, but there is no indication of whether 30% market coverage automatically leads to a foreclosure effect, and therefore a reduction in the thresholds. This is expected to be assessed on a case-by-case basis.

43 Guidelines on Vertical Restraints, §11.

44 Guidelines on Vertical Restraints, §11. The Commission might find Community interest in a case where the undertakings hold a dominant position in a substantial part of the internal market.

45 Ley 15/2007, de 3 de julio, de Defensa de la Competencia.

46 Article 1.1 of Competition Act 15/2007 is arguably wider in scope than Article 101(1) of the Treaty since it prohibits 'agreements', 'concerted practices', 'consciously parallel practices', 'collective decisions' and 'collective recommendations'. Hereinafter we will no longer discuss this difference between the two provisions and will use the term 'agreements' extensively.

Article 5 of the Competition Act 15/2007 states that practices prohibited under Articles 1 (agreements and concerted practices), 2 (abuse of dominant position) and 3 (unfair practices) that do not appreciably distort or restrict competition are of minor importance and consequently not prohibited. The concept of 'minor importance' is further developed in Articles 1 to 3 of the Defence of Competition Regulation (DCR)[47], which establish a stricter system than that resulting from the *De minimis* Notice.

Article 1 of the DCR ('*Conducts of minor importance with regard to market share*') provides a *de minimis* presumption for agreements between non-competing undertakings with market shares of below 15%, and agreements between competing undertakings with market shares of below 10%, both of these thresholds being reduced to 5% should such agreements contribute to cumulative foreclosure effects in the relevant markets.

Article 2 of the DCR ('*Conducts excluded from the concept of minor importance*') subjects the *de minimis* presumption of Article 1 to the absence of hardcore restraints in the agreement. For agreements between competitors, the list of hardcore restrictions is equivalent to point 11(1) of the *De minimis* Notice. But interestingly, the list of restrictions for vertical agreements that exclude a *de minimis* presumption is longer than the list in point 11(2) of the *De minimis* Notice, as the former also excludes agreements containing 'grey clauses' from the automatic presumption of *de minimis*[48].

Lastly, Article 3 of the DCR ('*Other behaviour of minor importance*') allows the Council of the CNC to declare a practice to be *de minimis* in an individual case, taking into account the particular circumstances of the case.

It must be noted that, prior to 2007, Spanish competition law was stricter with regard to agreements than Article 101(1) of the Treaty and did not provide for a *de minimis* exception. Article 1.3 of the previous Competition Act 16/1989[49] provided that

> "*The competition defence bodies may decide not to initiate or to stay the proceedings foreseen in this Act in the case of conduct*

---

47 *Reglamento de Defensa de la Competencia*, approved by Royal Decree 261/2008, of 22 February 2008.
48 Article 2 of the DCR excludes the automatic *de minimis* presumption to vertical agreements: with hardcore clauses (Article 2, sections 1, 2a), 2b), 2c), 2d) and 2f)), or
with non-compete clauses lasting more than 5 years (Article 2, section 2e)), or
where more than 50% of the relevant markets to the agreement are covered by parallel networks of agreements having similar effects (Article 2, section 4b)).
49 Ley 16/1989, de 17 de Julio, de Defensa de la Competencia.

whose relative unimportance prevents it from having a signifi-
cant effect on competition"

As upheld by the CNC in case 618/06 LOGIMAIL/UNIPOST, Article 1.3 of the Competition Act 16/1989 did not grant a *de minimis* exception to the general prohibition on restrictive agreements, but gave competition bodies discretional powers to prosecute practices:

"In EU law, the requirement that practices appreciably affect competition is a 'condition for the application' of the prohibition, whereas in Spanish law it is (under Competition Act 19/1989) a simple 'condition for prosecution' by the defence of competition bodies of practices prohibited by Article 1.1 of Competition Act 19/1989"[50]

This discretional capacity disappeared in the Competition Act 15/2007 and was substituted by a condition for the applicability of the prohibition (Article 5), in line with Article 101(1) of the Treaty.

3.4 Relationship between EU and Spanish de minimis regimes

Article 5 of Competition Act 15/2007 and Articles 1 to 3 of the DCR are closely connected to the application of the EU rules on vertical agreements. Firstly, by virtue of Article 3.2 of Regulation (EC) 1/2003, when an agreement has an impact on trade between Member States, it cannot also be found not to infringe Article 101(1) of the Treaty and equivalent provisions in national law. This implies that when an agreement affecting trade between Member States has no appreciable effects on competition under Article 101(1) of the Treaty, it cannot be found to have appreciable effects on competition under Articles 1 and 5 of Competition Act 15/2007 either. On the other hand, by virtue of Article 1.4 of the Competition Act 15/2007, the Block Exemption Regulations (BER) in force (such as Regulation EU 330/2010 and Regulation EU 461/2010) are *mutatis mutandis* applicable in Spain with regard to the prohibition set out in Article 1.1 of Competition Act 15/2007, even for agreements with no effect on trade between Member States.

---

50 Decision of 23.10.2007. The original in Spanish reads: "En el Derecho comunitario, la exigencia de que la conducta concertada afecte sensiblemente a la competencia es "requisito de tipicidad" de la prohibición, mientras que en Derecho español es (en la LDC de 1989) un simple "requisito de perseguibilidad" por las autoridades administrativas de competencia de conductas colusorias prohibidas por el art. 1.1 LDC" (FD 5°).

Therefore, although the procedural rules for *de minimis* assessment may differ at EU and national levels, they ultimately ought not to lead to different conclusions regarding what is and what is not *de minimis*. Nevertheless, as has been pointed out, the automatic *de minimis* presumption is stricter in Spain under Articles 1 and 2 of the DCR than in the EU under the *De minimis* Notice. This implies that the Spanish regime (and national regimes in general) must grant enforcers a margin for discretion that permits them to appreciate that agreements that do not comply with the automatic *de minimis* presumption (Article 1 and 2 of the DCR) do not have appreciable effects on a stand alone basis. This is what Article 3 of the DCR is intended to do.

At EU level, agreements that are not be covered by the automatic *de minimis* presumption can be divided into three groups: (1) cases where one or more of the parties to the agreement has a market share in excess of 15% (10% if they are competitors), (2) cases where there is risk of cumulative foreclosure effects and one or more of the parties to the agreement has a market share of more than 5% and (3) cases where market share thresholds are not surpassed but the agreement contains hardcore restrictions. According to the Spanish DCR, a fourth group should be added to these first three: (4) cases where the market share thresholds are not exceeded but the agreement contains grey clauses.

In practice, cases 1, 2 and 4 are dealt with similarly, and the primary matter of concern as regards the validity of agreements is not market share but the possible existence of grey clauses. From a practical point of view, it is pointless to draft a rule on situations in which agreements without hardcore clauses or grey clauses infringe Article 101(1) of the Treaty (or Article 1 of Competition Act 15/2007), given that parties will in any case benefit from the BER exemption where their market shares do not exceed 30%. Where market shares as defined in Article 3 of Regulation EU 330/2010 are in excess of 30%, vertical agreements will be assessed according to the Guidelines on Vertical Restraints, and additional rules on appreciability would be repetitive. Below 30%, agreements in cases 1, 2 and 4 not benefiting from the BER exemption will mainly fail do so because they contain grey clauses.

Case 3 follows a different approach to the other cases, since agreements containing hardcore clauses are presumed to restrict or distort competition by their object. *De minimis* has been applied in a very restrictive manner to such agreements. We firmly believe, however, that improving *de minimis* guidance for such agreements is necessary and might enhance efficiency in distribution.

3.5 The de minimis regime with vertical agreements containing grey clauses

The Guidelines on Vertical Restraints state that "There is no presumption that vertical agreements concluded by undertakings having more than 15% market share automatically infringe Article 101(1). Agreements between undertakings whose market share exceeds the 15% threshold may still not have an appreciable effect on trade between Member States or may not constitute an appreciable restriction to competition. Such agreements need to be assessed in their legal and economic context (...)"[51]. At this point the Guidelines refer to the judgment of the Court of First Instance (CFI) in case T-7/93 *Langnese-Iglo vs. Commission.* In that judgement, the Court clearly stated at §98 that

> "*It must be borne in mind that that notice [the De minimis Notice of 1986[52]] is intended only to define those agreements which, in the Commission's view, do not have an appreciable effect on competition or trade between Member States. The Court considers that it cannot, however, be inferred with certainty that a network of exclusive purchasing agreements is automatically liable to prevent, restrict or distort competition appreciably merely because the ceilings laid down in it are exceeded. Moreover, it is apparent from the actual wording of paragraph 3 of that notice that it is entirely possible, in the present case, that agreements concluded between undertakings which exceed the ceilings indicated affect trade between Member States or competition only to an insignificant extent and consequently are not caught by Article 85(1) of the Treaty [current Article 101(1) of the Treaty].*"

Therefore, vertical agreements between undertakings with market shares that exceed the thresholds of the *De minimis* Notice are not automatically thought to have an appreciable effect on competition[53]. An individual

---

51 Guidelines on Vertical Restraints, §9.

52 Notice of 3 September 1986 on Agreements of Minor Importance which do not fall under Article 85(1) of the Treaty establishing the European Economic Community (OJ 1986 C 231, p. 2).

53 The *De minimis* Notice indicates in this regard at point 2 that "In this notice the Commission quantifies, with the help of market share thresholds, what is not an appreciable restriction of competition under Article 81 of the EC Treaty. This negative definition of appreciability does not imply that agreements between undertakings which exceed the thresholds set out in this notice appreciably restrict competition. Such agreements may still have only a negligible effect on competition and may therefore not be prohibited by Article 81(1)".

examination must be made in each of these cases. The *De minimis* Notice is also clear in this regard:

> *"In this notice the Commission quantifies, with the help of market share thresholds, what is not an appreciable restriction of competition under Article 81 of the EC Treaty. This negative definition of appreciability does not imply that agreements between undertakings which exceed the thresholds set out in this notice appreciably restrict competition. Such agreements may still have only a negligible effect on competition and may therefore not be prohibited by Article 81(1)"*

As explained before, if there are no hardcore restraints, doubts on appreciability in cases where the parties have market shares in excess of the *De minimis* Notice thresholds, will arise when agreements contain grey clauses. Agreements without grey clauses will either be covered by the BER exemption if the parties' market shares are under 30% (Article 3 of Regulation EU 330/2010) or may be otherwise assessed under the guidance provided by the Guidelines on Vertical Restraints (it may also be that an agreement cannot benefit from the BER because of having been concluded between competitors that fail to satisfy Article 2 of Regulation EU 330/2010. In this case, the Guidelines on Vertical Restraints, combined with the Guidelines on Horizontal Cooperation Agreements[54], provide better guidance than the *de minimis* approach). A *de minimis* approach may be appropriate when examining agreements containing grey clauses between undertakings with market shares that are low but surpass the relevant thresholds for an automatic *de minimis* presumption.

As regards vertical issues, grey clauses as defined in Article 2 of the Spanish DCR cover (a) non-compete clauses lasting more than five years, (b) agreements having a similar effect to the existing ones in the market provided that they jointly cover more than 50% of the market. In both cases, and according to the Guidelines on Vertical Restraints, the main competition concern with grey clauses is that they may produce a (cumulative) foreclosure effect in the supplier's side of the market. In-store inter-brand competition may also be restricted. The Guidelines on Vertical Restraints refer to this adverse effect at §130:

> *"The possible competition risks of single branding are foreclosure of the market to competing suppliers and potential suppliers, sof-*

---

[54] Guidelines on the applicability of Article 81 of the EC Treaty to horizontal cooperation agreements (2001/C 3/02).

*tening of competition and facilitation of collusion between sup-
pliers in case of cumulative use and, where the buyer is a retailer
selling to final consumers, a loss of in-store inter-brand competition. Such restrictive effects have a direct impact on inter- brand
competition."*

At EU-level, the reference case law for analysing the appreciability of
the foreclosure effects of vertical agreements in the absence of hardcore
restrictions is the ECJ judgement in *Delimitis*[55]. *In this case, the ECJ was
asked for reference on a preliminary ruling on whether an individual
vertical agreement with a non-compete clause between a supplier and
a retailer was capable of (appreciably) affecting trade between Member
States. The ECJ concluded that assessment of this agreement's compatibility with competition rules had to be carried out in the light of its
legal and economic context. In order for a decision to be made that an
agreement has appreciable effects on competition, it must first be shown
that a new competitor's entry into the relevant market, or an existing
competitor's expansion, is seriously impeded or restricted by the existence of the cumulative effects of similar (networks of) agreements. Only
in this case, should an assessment be made of the extent to which the
agreement in question contributes to the cumulative foreclosure effect.*

In the *Langnese* case cited above, the CFI did not support the Commission's view that the *Delimitis* approach was subject to a previous examination of the appreciability of the effects of the agreement in question on
its own[56]. Subsequently, the case law seems to show that, in order to test
whether or not an individual vertical agreement has appreciable effects on
competition because of foreclosure effects, the *Delimitis* mechanics are to
be applied in all cases, in the sense that it must firstly be shown that entry
to and/or expansion within the market is restricted. Only if this is the case
is it possible to proceed to examination of the agreement in question.

The *Delimitis* doctrine has been applied in several recent cases in Spain,
in particular in the fuel distribution sector: cases R 691 DISA, 2740/06
TOTAL, 2739/06 AGIP and 2575/04 DISA CANARIAS. It is interesting to

---

55 Judgement of the ECJ in case C-234/89 *Stergios Delimitis vs. Henninger Bräu AG* [1991]
ECR I-935.
56 Judgement of the CFI in case T-7/93 *Langnese-Iglo vs. Commission*, §87. The Commission's
approach failed to explain how the first step could be taken without taking into account the
single agreement's contribution to the foreclosure effect in the relevant market. It appears
that in the first step, one should only pay attention to the market shares of the parties and
deliberately ignore the structure of the market and the possible existence of similar (networks
of) vertical agreements.

analyse and compare the criteria used in each of them, but first it may be useful to describe the fuel distribution sector in Spain.

Cases R 691 DISA[57], 2740/06 TOTAL[58], 2739/06 AGIP[59] and 2575/04 DISA CANARIAS[60] were all filed because of the lack of appreciable effects of the duration of purchase exclusivity in vertical agreements entered into by each of these suppliers and their branded service stations. The table below compares the criteria followed in each of these cases:

Case	Company	Bound stations (% of the market)	Company's market share	Company's examined agreements (% of the market)
R 691 DISA	DISA PENINSULA	80%	<5%	36 (<0.5%)
2740/06 TOTAL	TOTAL	80%	<1%	7 (<0.1%)
2739/06 AGIP	AGIP	80%	3.5%	4 (<0.1%)
2575/04 DISA CANARIAS	DISA CANARIAS	55%	42%	5 (1%)

In these four cases, the CNC applied the principles set out by the ECJ in *Delimitis*[61] and *Neste*[62], concluding that the agreements entered into by each of these suppliers could not make any appreciable contribution to the cumulative foreclosure effect in the market.

In R 691 DISA, 2740/06 TOTAL and 2739/06 AGIP, the CNC appreciated that it was difficult for a supplier to gain access to or to increase its presence in the fuel distribution market in mainland Spain, since 80% of the market was bound to existing suppliers by means of their ownership of service stations or of agreements containing lengthy exclusivity clauses, and entry or expansion through other means were unlikely. However, the conclusion was reached that none of the investigated suppliers contributed to a significant extent to that foreclosure effect, nor did the agreements in question. In this regard, the CNC took into account the supplier's market share (under 5% in the three cases), the number of service stations bound to the supplier in relation to the total number of service stations in the market (under 5% in the three cases) and the number of service stations that might be made available to other competitors in relation to the total number of

57 Decision by the Competition Court of 27.11.2007.
58 Decision by the Council of the CNC of 23.09.2008.
59 Decision by the Council of the CNC of 29.09.2008.
60 Decision by the Council of the CNC of 19.02.2010.
61 Case C-234/89 *Stergios Delimitis vs. Henninger Bräu AG* cited above.
62 Judgement of the ECJ in case C-214/99 *Neste Markkinointi Oy/Yötuuli Ky and Others*. 2000 ECR I-11121.

service stations in the market (under 1% in the three cases). The CNC also took into account the long lifetimes of some of the agreements (20 to 35 years) and the geographical dispersion of some of the service stations.

In 2575/04 DISA CANARIAS, the situation was slightly different, given that 45% of the market in the Canary Islands was in principle accessible to third parties (in mainland Spain only 20% of the market was accessible). In this context, the Council took into account the fact that, even though DISA CANARIAS' market share was 42%, the contested agreements amounted to only 1% of the market, meaning the accessible part of the market would rise from 45% to 46% if lengthy agreements were abandoned, a mere 2% increase in relative terms.

Cases R 691 DISA, 2740/06 TOTAL and 2739/06 AGIP also brought up an interesting issue. In each of these three cases, the contested supplier's market share did not exceed 5% and the agreements in question did not contain hardcore restraints as defined in point 11(2) of the *De minimis* Notice, so they would have been granted an automatic *de minimis* treatment under the Commission's *De minimis* Notice, but not under Articles 1 and 2 of the Spanish DCR.

3.6 De minimis regime with vertical agreements containing hardcore clauses

The Guidelines on Vertical Restraints state that "As regards hardcore restrictions referred to in the *de minimis* notice, Article 101(1) may apply below the 15% threshold, provided that there is an appreciable effect on trade between Member States and on competition. The applicable case law of the Court of Justice and the General Court is relevant in this respect. Reference is also made to the possible need to assess positive and negative effects of hardcore restrictions as described in particular in paragraph of these Guidelines"[63]. At this point the Guidelines refer to the judgments of the ECJ in cases 5/69 *Völk vs. Vervaecke*[64], 1/71 *Cadillon vs. Höss*[65] and C-306/96 *Javico vs. Yves Saint Laurent*[66].

In Case 5/69 *Völk vs. Vervaecke*, the Court considered that a hardcore agreement (an agreement with absolute territorial protection thus includ-

---

63 Guidelines on Vertical Restraints, §10.
64 Case 5/69 *Völk vs. Vervaecke* [1969] ECR 295.
65 Case 1/71 *Cadillon vs. Höss* [1971] ECR 351.
66 Case C-306/96 *Javico vs. Yves Saint Laurent* [1998] ECR I-1983, paragraphs 16 and 17.

ing restrictions on active and passive sales) would not be prohibited by Article 85(1) (currently Article 101(1)) if it had an insignificant effect on the market. At §5-7 of the Judgement, the Court stated that

> *"...an agreement falls outside the prohibition in article 85 when it has only an insignificant effect on the markets, taking into account the weak position which the persons concerned have on the market of the product in question. thus an exclusive dealing agreement, even with absolute territorial protection, may, having regard to the weak position of the persons concerned on the market in the products in question in the area covered by the absolute protection, escape the prohibition laid down in article 85(1)."*

The latter approach was confirmed by the judgement in Case 1/71 Cadillon/Höss, where the ECJ found that an exclusive dealing agreement could not be prohibited, even if it granted absolute territorial protection, if the parties to the agreement were weak in the territory covered by the exclusive dealing agreement. At §9, the ECJ said that

> *"An exclusive dealing agreement may escape the prohibition laid down in article 85 (1) because, in view of the weak position of the parties on the market in the products in question in the territory covered by the exclusive dealing arrangement, it is not capable of hindering the attainment of the objectives of a single market between states, even if it creates absolute territorial protection"*

These considerations were repeated by the Court in its judgement in case C-306/96 *Javico vs. Yves Saint Laurent.* At §17, the ECJ held that

> *"...even an agreement imposing absolute territorial protection may escape the prohibition laid down in Article 85 if it affects the market only insignificantly, regard being had to the weak position of the persons concerned on the market in the products in question..."*

From the foregoing it becomes evident that any vertical agreement, even one containing a hardcore restriction, must have appreciable effects on competition in order to be prohibited under Article 101 of the Treaty. Hardcore restrictions, however, deprive an agreement of the benefit of an automatic *de minimis* presumption under point 11 of the *De minimis* Notice, regardless of the market shares of the parties to the agreement.

This approach is consistent with Spanish regulations: hardcore restrictions make it impossible to apply an automatic *de minimis* treatment under Article 2 of the DCR. Nevertheless, Article 3 of the DCR explicitly allows the CNC to make a declaration of non-appreciability in a particular agreement, thereby creating a similar regime as that of the EU.

Unfortunately, compared with the *Delimits*-based doctrine in the case of agreements containing grey clauses, case law at EU level does not provide any clear reference points to help make decisions on situations in which individual agreements containing hardcore restrictions may be treated as *de minimis*.

The recent ECJ Order of 3.09.2009 is very relevant, in this regard, containing a preliminary ruling in the fuel distribution sector in Case C-506/07. The ECJ establishes that the fixing of retail prices by a supplier may not be prohibited under Article 101(1) of the Treaty if the agreement does not have the capacity to appreciably affect competition. The Court says that:

> *"A contract, such as the one at issue in the main proceedings, which provides for the creation of a right in rem, called a 'surface right', in favour of a supplier of petroleum products for a period of 25 years and authorises the latter to build a service station and to let that service station to the owner of the land for the same period as the duration of that right, and which contains clauses relating to the fixing of the retail price of goods and/or an exclusive purchasing obligation or a non-compete clause whose duration of application exceeds the time limitations laid down in Commission Regulation (EEC) No. 1984/83 of 22 June 1983 on the application of Article [81](3) of the Treaty to categories of exclusive purchasing agreements, as amended by Commission Regulation (EC) No. 1582/97 of 30 July 1997 and by Commission Regulation (EC) No. 270/1999 of 22 December 1999 on the application of Article 81(3) of the Treaty to categories of vertical agreements and concerted practices, does not fall within the prohibition laid down in Article 81(1)EC provided that it is not likely to affect trade between the Member States and that it does not aim to significantly restrict competition or have that effect. It is the task of the national court to determine whether that is the case by taking account, inter alia, of the economic and legal context within which that contract is situated."*

It is thus clear that RPM may also benefit from a *de minimis* treatment under particular circumstances (the 'economic and legal context'). But which circumstances are relevant for that purpose? For the purposes of a *de minimis* exception, the ECJ's Order in the GALP case (Case C-506/07) puts the RPM clause on the same footing as the long duration of the non-compete clause. Does it mean that RPM must follow a *Delimitis*-based approach in order to make it possible to verify appreciability?

We do not believe an automatic extrapolation of *Delimitis* is appropriated, as that approach was devised to assess a foreclosure effect, and hence one of the requirements is that access to the market be seriously restricted or impeded. The adverse effects of RPM have more to do with facilitating inter-brand and intra-brand coordination and unilateral effects by the supplier. Nevertheless, *Delimitis* may be of relevance in the sense that the adverse effect of RPM should be assessed by taking into account the existence of similar (networks of) parallel agreements covering a substantial part of the market.

A recent Spanish case, S/0105/08 EL CORRAL DE LAS FLAMENCAS, may clarify this point. In this case, the CNC concluded that resale price-fixing practices in a series of vertical agreements concluded by a manufacturer and its affiliated retailers did not have appreciable effects on competition and thus were not prohibited under Article 1 of the Competition Act 15/2007 (equivalent to Article 101 of the Treaty).

El Corral de las Flamencas is a clothes manufacturer which imposed resale prices on its retailers. The CNC considered that this was, by its very nature, a restriction of competition. However, it also felt it was very unlikely that this behaviour would be able to affect competition in the clothing market. In reaching its conclusion, the CNC took into account the position of the supplier in the relevant market (insignificant market share of less than 1% and geographically dispersed affiliated outlets), the position and number of competitors (the average brand in the market in question was said to be relatively small), the possible existence of cumulative factors (there were no parallel networks of agreements with similar effects) and the countervailing power of the company's affiliates (the supplier was found to have no significant bargaining power *vis-à-vis* retailers).

In case 634/07, MDC INGENIERÍA/PRODUCTOS HALLER, the *Audiencia Nacional* found in favour of the arguments of HALLER, against the advice of the CNC, and concluded that the restriction of passive sales to exclusive distributors was *de minimis*. The court based its conclusion on the supplier's position in terms of its market share (less than 5% in Spain and 4% in the EU) and also that of its distributors (which the CNC described as 'very small') in their respective markets, the limited effects of the practices examined, and the fact that the agreement involved licensing technology, in which the BER (Regulation (EC) 772/2004) was more permissive in terms of the possibilities for restricting passive sales than Regulation (EC) 2790/99.

3.7 Efficiencies of hardcore, community interest and legal certainty

A conclusion from the foregoing sections is that the *de minimis* rule is in principle applicable to any sort of (vertical) agreements, regardless of the kind of clauses they contain. However, there is an automatic presumption under certain conditions and also a non-automatic *de minimis* application. As regards hardcore restrictions, rules on non-automatic application of *de minimis* at EU level do not provide any real guide.

The recent Guidelines on Vertical Restraints not only explicitly recognise the fact that hardcore restrictions in vertical relationships may have positive effects and enhance efficiency, but also provide guidance on how and when they may occur. There is guidance on assessing positive effects or recognising concrete positive effects with regard to RPM (§225), resale restrictions leading to absolute territorial protection (or for a group of clients) (§61-62) and on restricting cross-supplies in selective distribution systems (§63) and dual pricing in the context of online and offline distribution (§64-65).

The efficiencies arising from suppliers controlling (re)sales may be higher in the case of SMEs and undertakings with weak positions in the relevant market(s). The reason for this is that the control of (re)sales may be linked to protecting the entry of such businesses into a market or their release of a new product or to protect expansion strategies. It may also be the case that such undertakings aim to use pricing policy to make up for their lack of a well-known brand image or to encourage distributors to spend money on purchasing large amounts of stock in order to promote sales efforts and specific investments.

Conversely, the negative impact of hardcore restrictions is obviously more limited in the case of small undertakings. Competition-related concerns deriving from vertical restraints can only arise if there is insufficient competition at one or more levels of trade, that is, if there is some degree of market power at supplier or buyer level, or both (Guidelines on Vertical Restraints, §6). It is therefore extremely unlikely that the way in which small undertakings organise their distribution networks and vertical relationships in general would be able to affect competition, even if they employ hardcore restrictions. This conclusion might be subject to the absence of parallel agreement networks with similar effects. However, even if parallel networks of agreements are in place, each undertaking's responsibility for that cumulative effect might be weighted according to the extent to which it has contributed to that effect (by analogy to *Delimitis*).

So there should be more scope for small undertakings to use hardcore agreements than there is between stronger competitors. The current regime, however, arguably discourages small undertakings from agreeing hardcore restrictions, even though such clauses would be more efficient than other non-hardcore clauses and would have negligible effects on competition. The use of a hardcore clause increases the likelihood of attracting complaints and the attention of competition enforcers, implying legal defence costs, which may be relatively higher for small undertakings.

Nor is there any settled case law on the issue of hardcore restraints. The Spanish case S-0105/08 *El Corral de las Flamencas* is arguably an exceptional case in the EU. Since each competition enforcer has a margin for discretion, it is not possible to guarantee that any other competition agency or judge would have reached the same conclusions when faced with the same facts. This is especially relevant in Spain, where, aside from the CNC and national judges, Autonomous Regions also have competition bodies that, although they do not apply Articles 101 and 102 of the Treaty, do apply their equivalents in national law. But the same problem might be found at EU level.

This last point also leads to the conclusion that recourse to a 'lack of interest' argument is only a means of transferring the problem to another enforcer, which may not be able to dismiss the case on the same lack of interest grounds. Some enforcers, such as the CNC, do not even have access to this recourse. National courts may not reject cases on the basis of 'lack of interest'.

In summary, the use of hardcore restraints entails high legal uncertainty for small undertakings, and may reduce their efficiency. The effects-based regime of vertical restraints contradicts this fact to a certain extent. Our impression is that the way to resolve this problem might be to reform the *De minimis* Notice, including the publication of specific guidelines. In the context of the reform of the vertical restraints regime, some respondents to the public consultation even called for a broader safe harbour[67] to be created. Regardless of what the specific solution may be, we feel it is preferable that it should come from the competition authorities.

---

67 European Advisory Group.

4. Conclusion

The CNC has had lengthy and varied experience in vertical restraints. At a national level, vertical issues normally involve small undertakings. Small undertakings normally entail a lower degree of complexity in terms of the scale of their distribution networks, but also more complexity in terms of investigation, given that vertical relationships are part of their normal business pattern, and are therefore more informal. Small agents are less concerned with competition rules and do not normally complain about the terms of a distribution agreement until the commercial relationship breaks down.

Vertical restraints between small undertakings are less harmful to competition, and this is true regardless of the nature of the clauses of the agreement. The ECJ has thus stated that hardcore clauses and grey clauses do not lead to an automatic prohibition of the agreement, since appreciability is a prerequisite for infringement of Article 101 of the Treaty. However, there is neither a safe harbour nor a helpful guide on appreciability in the case of certain practices, and this situation leads to legal uncertainty. As a result, certain vertical clauses that in some cases might enhance efficiency are underused. This situation might be reversed by means of a coordinated action by the Commission and NCAs in order to, at least, produce a set of rules for assessing appreciability in the presence of hardcore clauses and grey clauses.

Another reason that supports this last conclusion and proposal is that small cases always have to be dealt with. The Commission and some NCAs in the EU have the prerogative of deciding whether a case is of any real interest within their jurisdiction, and so one might argue that this is good way of dismissing actions against practices that do not really have the capacity to affect competition in the relevant market. We do not support this approach, however, because this way of acting does not solve the problem for NCAs that do not have the benefit of such a prerogative, provides no guidance for the enforcer, and leads to private litigation in small cases, since judges cannot make use of the 'lack of interest' resource. Without better guidance on appreciability, there may be a contradiction in the way that similar cases are dealt with between and within jurisdictions.

CHAPTER XI

NATIONAL ENFORCEMENT OF VERTICAL RESTRAINTS: GERMANY

XI.1 General Courts and some practical issues

MARKUS WIRTZ

Partner
Glade Michel Wirtz: Corporate & Competition

1. Introduction

Amendments to the German competition law in previous years have led to a far-reaching harmonisation with European competition law. This also applies to the provisions concerning vertical restraints. At the same time, national enforcement of vertical restraints has become an issue of increasing importance. The Federal Cartel Office (FCO) recently put a focus on vertical restraints which led to numerous searches, decisions and fines. From a practitioner's point of view, the need for legal advice has sharply increased — also catalysed by contradicting court decisions and legal uncertainty created by the FCO's enforcement initiative.

The paper consists of six parts: Following the introduction, the German law regarding vertical restraints will be presented in an overview. Parts three to six of this paper deal with important decisions by German courts, the protection of brands in selective distribution systems, category management, and the FCO's 2010 paper on vertical practices in the retail business. The last part contains the conclusions and an outlook for the EU as a whole.

2. Vertical restraints in German competition law

2.1 Development of the German competition law regarding vertical restraints

Vertical restraints are subject to the Act against Restraints of Competition of 1985 (GWB) as amended on 22 December 2007 by the *Preismissbrauchnovelle*[1]. The main difference with regard to vertical restraints between the latest amendments and the previous version of the GWB is that there are no longer different rules for horizontal and vertical restraints. Since 2005, both kinds of restraints have been treated in the same way by German competition law. The different treatment which had been in place for decades was changed to harmonise German with European competition law. By creating two central provisions — sections 1 and 2 GWB — for both horizontal and vertical restraints of competition, special provisions for horizontal and vertical restraints have been abolished. Before 2005, a vertical restraint generally required an order by the FCO to be legally prohibited. However, resale price maintenance had been prohibited quasi per se.

2.2 Applicable legal provisions

Sections 1 and 2 GWB are central provisions in German competition law. Yet, because of a dynamic reference to the European block exemption regulations in section 2 para. 2 GWB, these block exemptions apply in Germany — as well as in Spain — also in purely domestic cases which do not meet the threshold to apply European competition law (i.e. also in purely national cases).

Recent amendments of the GWB show the legislator's intent to harmonise German competition law with European competition law. The harmonisation of European and German competition law leads to an interpretation of the legal provisions being at least similar or exactly alike.

---

1   For details concerning this amendment see *Säcker*, WuW 2007, 1195, *Ritter/Lück*, WuW 2007, 698; *Ritter*, WuW 2008, 142; *Kahlenberg/Haellmigk*, BB 2008, 174.

2.3 Federal Cartel Office and competent courts

The task to protect competition in Germany is fulfilled by the FCO as well as by the Competition Offices of the 16 German states. The jurisdiction depends on the facts of the case: If the effect of an anticompetitive behaviour outreaches the borders of a state, the FCO is the competent authority. This result of the federal system is able to complicate proceedings and decisions, but practical problems seldom occur.

The FCO is integrated into the hierarchy of the federal administration, it is nonetheless an independent competition authority.

Challenging a decision of the FCO in front of a court reveals a speciality of German law. The German court system distinguishes between different kinds of jurisdictions, depending on the topic. Inter alia, it distinguishes between civil and administrative proceedings. Although the FCO is a public body and its rules of procedure belong to administrative law, its decision cannot be challenged in front of an administrative court but only in front of a civil court. The decisions by the FCO can be appealed to the Higher Regional Court — *Oberlandesgericht* — of Düsseldorf as the appellate body. Cases before the Higher Regional Court of Dusseldorf are dealt with by specialised competition senates. A further appeal on points of law is possible to the Federal High Court of Justice (*Bundesgerichtshof*).

Another speciality — especially in comparison with the CNC — is the FCO's discretion to pick up a case or not. In contrast to the CNC the FCO does not have to take action if a complaint is filed and does not have to issue a ruling concerning every complaint.

2.4 National enforcement in Germany

National enforcement of vertical restraints is an increasingly important topic in German competition law. Until the seventh amendment to the GWB in July 2005, vertical restraints were of little importance for the German antitrust enforcement agenda as they were regarded as less detrimental to competition than horizontal restraints. Before July 2005, vertical restraints except vertical price maintenance were valid and could only be prohibited for the future as abusive, a fact that left very limited or no room at all for damage claims. After harmonising the German competition rules concerning vertical restraints with the EU system, the FCO identified certain types of vertical restraints as a serious impairment of customer welfare and became more and more active in this area. Also, infringements of the rules on vertical restraints (section 1 GWB) today may lead to liability for damages.

According to its latest activity report, the FCO was specifically active with regard to resale price maintenance — whether legal, contractual, overt, disguised or indirect resale price maintenance — as well as restrictions concerning online sales. In 2009, the FCO decided several cases regarding Internet sales, exclusivity agreements and resale price maintenance. In January 2010, it started proceedings against a number of food retailers and producers of brand products based on suspicion of maintaining artificially high prices for these products through vertical arrangements.[2] According to the FCO, a focus is put on — besides resale price maintenance — hub and spoke cartels.[3] Hub and spoke cartels (also called "ABC cartels"[4]) are created from vertical relationships converted into horizontal cartels. Hub and spoke cartels include an indirect exchange of information between competitors. The exchange of information is facilitated by a third-party intermediary — this may be a common customer or common supplier.[5] The exchange of sensitive information leads indirectly to the disclosure of the pricing strategy of competitors allowing others to oblige e.g. their pricing. All undertakings taking part in this exchange of information — including the third party — are regarded as parties acting in concert with the objective to restrain competition. Recent examples of investigations of possible hub and spoke practices can be found in the UK (Replica Kit, Toys and Games, Dairy, Tobacco, Supermarkets), Belgium (Home and Personal Care Products), Germany (CIBA Vision, dawn raids in the food retail and drugstore, pet supplies and branded consumer products), France (Carrefour) and Switzerland (books). Not all cases were investigated as being hub and spoke cartels, but all of them included at least some elements of hub and spoke. In two UK cases, the British Office of Fair Trading fined several companies for price fixing of Hasbro toys[6] as well as price fixing for Umbro replica football kits[7]. Although these decisions were rendered in 2003, they are still the leading decisions with regard to hub and spoke. Both decisions were upheld on appeal; however, the UK Court of

2 Federal Cartel Office, Preliminary assessment of behaviour in negotiations between producers of brand products, wholesalers and retailers to substantiate the duties to cooperate, WuW 2010, 786.
3 Federal Cartel Office, Preliminary assessment of behaviour in negotiations between producers of brand products, wholesalers and retailers to substantiate the duties to cooperate, WuW 2010, 786, 790.
4 *Levy/Patel*, GCR 2010, Issue 9, 33.
5 *Levy/Patel*, GCR 2010, Issue 9, 33.
6 Case PN 18/03: Toys and Games, 19 February 2003.
7 Case PN 17/03: Replica Kits, 1 August 2003.

Appeal changed the prerequisites used by the Office of Fair Trading and demanded anticompetitive intent by all parties to exclude negligence or the lack of care.[8] The German FCO has not rendered a decision concerning a hub and spoke cartel yet. However, in the ongoing investigation of food retailers, drugstores, pet supplies and branded consumer products, hub and spoke is an issue being investigated.[9]

It has to be noted that the leniency programme by the FCO does not apply to vertical restraints. Thus, disclosing anticompetitive vertical restraints does not lead to a legally secure benefit for the disclosing undertaking, although the FCO has declared that it will honour cooperation by undertakings. An increased discovery as has resulted from the leniency programme concerning horizontal agreements is not likely. Undertakings in fear of disclosure by the FCO are more likely to put the anticompetitive practice to an end.

2.5 Competition policy for the Mittelstand — Sections 20 and 21 GWB

Despite a harmonisation with European competition law, section 20 GWB is a unique provision compared to the European competition law provisions.[10] It is based on Art. 3 para. 2 sent. 2 of the Regulation 1/2003[11] — the so-called German clause — which allows stricter national rules for the control of unilateral conduct. Similar provisions exist in France, Greece, Hungary, Ireland, Italy, Austria and Portugal. This provision inter alia protects small and medium-sized undertakings against larger undertakings which may not be dominating the market but which have market power relative to their suppliers, customers or competitors. Individual dependency is able to impair competition even if no market dominance is present.[12] These provisions are designed to protect competition as an institution by maintaining a level playing field and by enabling all market participants independent of size to take part in competition. Besides protecting competition, this provision also serves other goals, e.g., contractual fairness. These goals

---

8 Cases *Argos and Littlewoods vs. OFT and JJB vs. OFT* [2006], EWCA Civ. 1318, paras. 91 and 140.
9 See Federal Cartel Office, Press release, 14 January 2010.
10 For a detailed analysis of section 20 GWB see *Wirtz*, WuW 2003, 1039.
11 Council Regulation (EC) No. 1/2003 on the implementation of rules on competition laid down in Art. 81 and 82 of the Treaty.
12 *Hübschle*, in: Lange (ed.), Handbuch zum deutschen und europäischen Kartellrecht, para. 1042.

are being criticised as protecting small and medium-sized undertakings thereby stifling competition as historic market structures are conserved.

In addition to section 20 GWB, also section 21 GWB deals with unilateral conduct. Section 21 GWB prohibits boycotts and unilateral conduct that has the same effect as a prohibited agreement.

3. Selected decisions of German courts on vertical restraints

Before the German competition rules were harmonised with European competition law, the Federal High Court of Justice decided a few cases concerning resale price maintenance. When the decisions were rendered, resale price maintenance already was generally prohibited.

3.1 Case "four of the price of three"

In 1978, the Federal High Court of Justice had to decide a case where the producer of chocolate bars provided more content — "four for the price of three" — for eight weeks.[13] These boxes were sold to retailers for the same price as the boxes containing the usual number of chocolate bars. The additional content was printed on the box so that the customer was able to recognise the additional content in comparison with the usual product size. The success of the advertising campaign depended on selling both product sizes — the (previous) usual product size as well as the box containing one chocolate bar extra — at the same price. To achieve this result, the producer sold both box sizes at the same price to the retailer. If the different boxes were not sold at the same price, this would have resulted in a confused customer as the imprint indicating the additional chocolate bar created the customers' expectation to get the additional bar for free. Thus, the retailer was supposed to hand on the price advantage granted by the producer to the consumer.

The Federal High Court of Justice found a violation of competition law. By printing the increased content on the package, consumers were informed about the pricing of the two different box sizes. By selling the imprinted boxes, the retailers were forced to sell the product for the same price as the product with less content as the imprint indicated a price advantage

---

13 Federal High Court (BGH), NJW 1978, 2095 ("4 for the price of 3").

for the customer.[14] This advertising campaign resulted in a pricing restriction of the retailer. By implying no price change, the producer indirectly maintained the resale price for the product with more content. Although the retailers were free in determining the resale price for the usual box size, the court held the indirect price fixing for the larger box size as being prohibited resale price maintenance.

3.2 Case "one bar extra"

In 2003, the Federal High Court of Justice revisited this issue.[15] Subject matter was the Duplo bar, a chocolate bar sold as single bar or in boxes of ten bars. The producer of the bars sold eleven bars instead of ten for six weeks. During the accompanying advertising campaign, the producer advertised the additional bar in TV spots as "One bar extra — doesn't cost more". A competitor sued the producer because of resale price maintenance. The first instance court cited the above-mentioned case "four at the price of three" and found a factual restriction on retailers to freely determine the price. The Federal High Court of Justice "distinguished" the case which factually meant a reversion of the decision of 1978. The court required to take the duration of the campaign and its impact on distribution into account and denied an infringement of competition law.[16] The court affirmed a restriction of competition as the advertisements created factual pressure on retailers to stick to the previous price. The advertising campaign created the consumer's expectation to get an additional chocolate bar for free for a limited amount of time. This price advantage is able to result in an increased incentive to buy. Although no contractual restriction is present with regard to the box with eleven bars, a restriction is also possible by forcing the retailer to set a product at a specific price factually. The court stated that the freedom to set the price of the larger box size is nonexistent if the imprint on the box informing the consumer about the price advantage forces the retailer to set the price of the larger box size at the price of the usual box size containing ten chocolate bars.

However, the court denied a violation of competition law as the retailer's freedom to set prices had been restricted only for a limited amount of time and did not have an appreciable effect. First of all, the advertising campaign lasted for only six weeks. Secondly, the retailer had the same profit

---

14 Federal High Court (BGH), NJW 1978, 2096 ("4 for the price of 3").
15 Federal High Court (BGH), NJW 2003, 2682 ("1 bar extra").
16 Federal High Court (BGH), NJW 2003, 2682, 2683 ("1 bar extra").

margin as for the usual box size. Moreover, the retailer benefitted from an increased buying incentive. Setting a higher price for the larger box sizes would have eliminated an incentive to buy. The detriment not to be able to increase the price of the product is compensated by an increase of the sales volume as well as an increase of profits. Another benefit — not mentioned by the court — is an increase of inter-brand competition.

Today the harmonisation with European competition law may require an adjustment of the judicature of the German courts. With regard to the appreciability of a restraint, no new assessment of this issue has taken place by German courts yet. According to the decision by the ECJ in GALP, the supplier is allowed to set a maximum price or to suggest a price so that the retailer is able to freely set the resale price.[17] On the other hand, a clause is not exempted from Art. 101 para. 3 TFEU if the resale price is set by the supplier directly or indirectly. However, to find a violation, appreciability of a restraint of competition is necessary. In GALP, the ECJ denied a violation of competition law because of lack of appreciability.

The Guidelines on Vertical Restraints, by contrast, presume resale price maintenance to restrict competition and it is unlikely that this practice fulfils the prerequisites of Art. 101 para. 3 TFEU.[18] Furthermore, the guidelines discuss whether short time price campaigns within a franchise system or a similar system may be exempted.[19] This is at odds with the FCJ decision in "GALP" and the Federal High Court of Justice decision in "One bar extra", as the guidelines leave out the question of appreciability. However, the guidelines — in contrast to the decision of the Federal High Court of Justice of 2003 — take possible efficiencies of resale price maintenance into account for the first time which then have to be assessed under Art. 101 para. 3 TFEU.[20] Following the new guidelines of 2010 and the ECJ decision in "GALP" it is not unlikely that the Commission will take a more lenient approach towards resale price maintenance.[21]

Applying the guidelines will benefit cooperation for small and medium undertakings if their distribution system constitutes resale price maintenance but creates efficiencies at the same time. The main problem will be

---

17 ECJ, C-506/07 (GALP), Slg. 2009, I-00134 para. 33; see also *Möschel*, WuW 2010, 1229, 1231.
18 Commission, Guidelines on Vertical Restraints, 2000/C 291/01, para. 223.
19 Commission, Guidelines on Vertical Restraints, 2000/C 291/01, para. 225.
20 Commission, Guidelines on Vertical Restraints, 2000/C 291/01, para. 225.
21 *Buttigieg*, Journal of European Competition Law & Practice 1 (2010), 397, 402.

the legal uncertainty as resale price maintenance constitutes a hardcore restriction.[22]

3.3 Case "Subcontractor II" — ancillary restraints

The harmonisation with EU law also led to a new assessment concerning ancillary restraints. The Federal High Court of Justice changed the requirements for ancillary restraints by adopting EU law.[23] The case dealt with a non-competition clause between an undertaking and a subcontractor. Before the harmonisation, it was possible to enforce restraints like non-competition clauses in a subcontractor agreement if a legitimate interest had been present. Because of the harmonisation, a legitimate interest cannot be regarded as being sufficient to allow vertical restraints. Non-competition clauses restricting competition are only legally permissible if they constitute an ancillary restraint necessary to reach the main purpose of the contract.[24] The main purpose has to be neutral with regard to competition law. The new approach requires the necessity to facilitate the contract in question. Therefore, non-compete clauses need to be necessary concerning the scope of prohibited activities, duration and geographic reach. Here, the European Commission's notice on restrictions directly related and necessary to a concentration may serve as guidance.[25]

4. Internet sales and the protection of brands in selective distribution systems

4.1 Introduction

The continuing growth of sales via the Internet has an enormous impact on existing distribution channels. These ways of distributing goods or services online open up far-reaching opportunities for producers to market their product.[26] When updating the Guidelines on Vertical Restraints,

---

22 For an overview on the debate in the US and the EU see *Buttigieg*, Journal of European Competition Law & Practice 1 (2010), 397.
23 Federal High Court (BGH), WuW/E DE-R 2554; see also *Thomas*, WuW 2010, 177.
24 Federal High Court (BGH), WuW/E DE-R 2554, 2556.
25 2005/C 56/24.
26 *Franck*, WuW 2010, 772.

the Commission also focused on sales via the Internet which it tries to encourage.[27]

A current topic in German competition law is the admissibility of a prohibition to sell a brand product via Internet auction platforms. Producers and retailers have colliding interests: the producer wants to ensure advice and service by trained sales people. Distribution via online sales may take place without adequate service. Furthermore, a producer wants to protect its investments in advertising to build up a high-quality brand. Finally, the producer is keen on fighting free-riding which decreases its turnover while not decreasing its costs for trained sales people. An undertaking selling exclusively online benefits from the advice a stationary shop offers to its customers. In a case decided in 2003, the German Federal High Court of Justice held with respect to luxury products that a retailer solely selling online is neither able to present the products adequately nor able to give comprehensive advice.[28] Thus, it affirmed the necessity of establishing a stationary shop. On the other hand, the retailer is interested in using more distribution channels. The online distribution helps distributors to develop brick-and-click shops which sell online as well as in stationary shops. Moreover, distributors are interested in their freedom to determine resale prices. Establishing different distribution channels enables distributors to calculate different prices.

The prohibition to sell via Internet auction platforms has an impact on the competitive process. As a distribution channel is left out, intra-brand competition it decreased. The intra-brand competition benefits from new distribution channels as online sellers have lower costs than stationary shops with trained sales people. By prohibiting this distribution channel, it is impossible (or at least more difficult) for distributors to provide for lower prices. On the other hand, the prohibition may foster inter-brand competition as the customer is enabled to distinguish different branded products by its quality and the respective price. The protection of a brand can benefit a market by creating a product differentiation which enhances customer choice. By doing this, a market can be differentiated into products of different quality or brand image.

A selective distribution system helps the producer to control the distribution of its product. To establish a selective distribution system, the product in question has to show characteristics that result in the need of selective distribution. These characteristics are protection of a branded product,

---

27 Commission, Guidelines on Vertical Restraints, 2000/C 291/01, para. 52.
28 Federal High Court (BGH), NJW-RR 1000, 189, 190.

necessity of extensive customer advice and service or luxury products.[29] These criteria have to be applied objectively.

4.2 Recent decisional practice by German courts

A central point of discussion is which qualitative requirements a producer is allowed to demand from its sales partner with respect to online sales.[30] Producers of high-quality products might try to prohibit distributers from using specific distribution channels such as Internet auction platforms by using a qualitative selective distribution system which excludes online auction platforms generally. Recent decisions by the Higher Regional Court — *Oberlandesgericht* — of Karlsruhe (2009), by the Regional Court — *Landgericht* — of Berlin (2009) and the Regional Court — *Landgericht* — of Mannheim (2008) deal with the prohibition of online sales via Internet auction platforms.

These decisions specifically concern the question whether a producer can prohibit a distributor from selling applied products via Internet auction platforms such as eBay[31]. The products in question were branded school bags for children. The producer had established a selective distribution system and demanded its distributors to fulfil certain preconditions such as store size, store fitting, opening hours etc. Online sales were allowed if the website fulfilled certain criteria similar to the criteria set up for stationary shops. Shops which solely sold products via the Internet were not approved as distributors. Online sales via Internet auction platforms such as eBay were prohibited. The plaintiffs in all cases were retailers, approved by the producer, selling inter alia the producer's branded school bags in stationary shops and online. The producer of the branded products distributed the school bags to retailers, mail order businesses and also sold the school bags directly online. In all cases, the defending producer demanded from the plaintiff to stop selling the defendant's products using the auction platform eBay.

The decisional practice of German courts appears to be inconsistent: The courts came to opposite conclusions although the claims in all cases were

---

29 *Haslinger*, WRP 2009, 279.
30 *Haslinger*, WRP 2010, 279, 282; see also *Wiring*, MMR 2010, 659, 661; *Rösner*, WRP 2010, 1114, 1118.
31 See Regional Court of Berlin (LG Berlin), BB 2009, 1381; Higher Regional Court of Karlsruhe (OLG Karlsruhe), WuW/E- DE-R 2789; see also Federal High Court (BGH); NJW 1999, 189, 191; *Haslinger*, WRP 2009, 279, 282; Rösner, WRP 2010, 1114, 1121.

identical. All decisions were rendered in 2008 or 2009 and were subject to the old block exemption regulation on vertical restraints.[32] The decision by the Regional Court of Berlin declared the prohibition of using Internet auction platforms as void. The Regional Court of Mannheim as well the Higher Regional Court of Karlsruhe approved the prohibition of selling branded school bags via Internet auction platforms.

The decisions have been criticised for insufficient application of the standards set by the ECJ and for applying unclear criteria.[33] All courts referred to the decisions of the ECJ in *Metro I*[34] and *L'Oréal*[35], to set the standards for establishing a selective distribution system and to enable the assessment of restraints which are ancillary to the specific distribution system. According to these decisions, the criteria have to be objective and have to be applied to all distributors without discriminating any potential distributor. Examples of qualitative criteria are e.g. the professional qualification of the distributor and its personnel, the store fitting etc[36]. Further, it has to be shown that the characteristics of the product require a selective distribution system to ensure the preservation of the product's quality and the correct use of the product.

By applying these requirements, the courts reach different outcomes. The Regional Court of Berlin declared the prohibition of the use of Internet auction platforms as distribution channel as a violation of section 1 GWB. It held that the prohibition to sell via eBay constituted a restriction of competition. Qualitative criteria which have to be applied in a non-discriminatory way may justify a restriction. The court stated that the outright prohibition of Internet auction platforms did not qualify as a legitimate qualitative characteristic for the selection of distributors[37]. The Regional Court of Berlin did not apply the Vertical-BER, which is incorporated in German law and applies also to domestic cases via reference in section 2 para. 1 GWB; it denied the application with reference to the market share being higher than 30%. Thus, it concluded that a violation of section 1 GWB was present.

The decision by the Regional Court of Berlin has been criticised because the court did not assess an exemption according to section 2 para. 1 GWB (similar to Art. 101 para. 3 TFEU) without offering an explanation. Sec-

---

32 Commission, Guidelines on Vertical Restraints, 2000/C 291/01.
33 See *Franck*, WuW 2010, 772, 773.
34 ECJ, Case 26/76 (Metro I), ECR 1977, 1875.
35 ECJ, Case 31/80 (L'Oréal), ECR 1980, 3775 para. 16.
36 ECJ, Case 26/76 (Metro I), ECR 1977, 1875 para. 20.
37 Regional Court of Berlin (LG Berlin), BB 2009, 1381, 1382.

ondly, the court has been criticised as it did not regard the exclusion of sales via online auction platforms as a qualitative criterion.[38] By doing this, it did not transfer the standards for showcases set down by the ECJ in the Metro I case to respective criteria of online shops. These criteria include e.g. the overall picture of the website and the environment in which the products are presented.[39]

The Higher Regional of Karlsruhe as well as the Regional Court of Mannheim came to the opposite conclusion: Both courts transferred criteria such as size or quality of the showcase to corresponding criteria of websites. First of all, the courts recognised the need for expert knowledge as school bags have to fit the person who carries it[40]. Secondly, the courts affirmed that the producer marketed the school bags as upscale high-price products with a high marketing effort. The courts stated that the product did not need to be a luxury product to justify a selective distribution system[41]. Not only luxury products may require a selective distribution system but also other goods e.g. tableware, watches or press products.[42] Both courts regarded the general prohibition of online sales via eBay is a qualitative criterion for the selection of distributors. In view of the products in question, this ban was considered as legitimate and not to infringe Art. 101 TFEU. An exemption therefore was not required.

The decisions have been criticised for inconsistencies concerning the courts' arguments[43]. Neither the origin of the criteria nor the weight of the different criteria were stated by the courts. The decision by the Higher Regional Court of Karlsruhe and the Regional Court of Mannheim are said to lack a valid reason for affirming the necessity to prohibit sales of high-priced school bags via Internet auction platforms. The true reason, literature suggests, was that the Internet with its search engines contributed to an increase in free-riding. Selective distribution or other restraints set by producers are regarded as possible solutions to the free-rider problem[44].

On a different note, both courts did not stress the protection of a brand image as being decisive for their decision. It is disputed in how far vertical restraints to protect the reputation of a product are in line with section 1 GWB as well as Art. 101 para. 1 TFEU. In its Guidelines on Vertical

---

38 *Franck*, WuW 2010, 772, 774.
39 Commission, Guidelines on Vertical Restraints, 2000/C 291/01, para. 54; *Franck*, WuW 2010, 772, 774.
40 Higher Regional Court of Karlsruhe (OLG Karlsruhe), WuW/E- DE-R 2789, 2792 para. 54 pp.
41 Higher Regional Court of Karlsruhe (OLG Karlsruhe), WuW/E DE-R 2789, 2793 para. 56.
42 Higher Regional Court of Karlsruhe (OLG Karlsruhe), WuW/E DE-R 2789, 2793 para. 56.
43 See *Franck*, WuW 2010, 772, 775 pp.
44 Commission, Guidelines on Vertical Restraints, 2010/C 130/01, para. 107 lit. a.

Restraints, the Commission considered vertical restraints as being capable of contributing to the creation of a brand image[45]. These restraints can include standards to guarantee the quality of the product. In this respect, the reputation of a brand is beneficial to competition as it promotes product differentiation and enhances customer choice in terms of subjective customer preferences. The underlying argument is that although interbrand competition is weakened intra-brand competition is strengthened.

A fourth case, decided by the Higher Regional Court — *Oberlandesgericht* — of Munich in 2009, dealt with similar facts.[46] In this case, the defendant was the distribution company for an international undertaking producing sporting goods. The plaintiff was an association to protect competition. The producer's sales terms prohibit distributors to use Internet auction platforms. The plaintiff claimed that these terms were anticompetitive restrictions. This case has to be distinguished as no selective distribution system was present. As the defendant's market share was below 30%, the Vertical-BER applied. The court held that the prohibition of sales using eBay was no hardcore restriction within the meaning of Art. 4 (b) Vertical-BER.[47] The court found that online sales were not prohibited completely; furthermore, qualitative requirements concerning online sales were legally permissible as comparable to qualitative requirements for stationary shops. The court stated that customers using Internet auction platforms cannot be regarded as a unique group within the group of customers buying goods online, so that also no customer group restriction was present.

4.3 Consistent application by German courts?

The opposing court decisions reveal the need for an application of the rules in a consistent manner. The decisions by the Higher Regional Court of Karlsruhe, the Regional Court of Mannheim as well as the Higher Regional Court of Munich show a more consistent application of German and European competition rules. The question remains whether the decision of the Regional Court of Berlin will be an exception or whether more contradicting decisions will be rendered by the courts. A decision by the Federal High Court of Justice may help to resolve the opposing approaches and set a line for a consistent application of the competition rules in the future.

---

45 Commission, Guidelines on Vertical Restraints, 2010/C 130/01, para. 107 lit. i.
46 Higher Regional Court of Munich (OLG München), WuW 2009, DE-R 1068.
47 Higher Regional Court of Munich (OLG München), WuW 2009, DE-R 1068, 1069.

4.4 Conclusions for selective distribution systems.

A selective distribution system is not regarded as a restraint of competition according to Art. 101 para. 1 TFEU if selective distribution is required for the product and the restriction of online sales satisfies the brick-and-click test.[48] A restraint of competition is present if selective distribution is not required or the restriction in question is outside of selective distribution.[49] In this case, Art. 101 para. 3 TFEU and the Vertical-BER have to be applied. An exemption from Art. 101 para. 1 TFEU in particular depends on the market shares. The regulation is inapplicable if the market share of the producer on the sales market or the distributor on the purchasing market exceeds 30%. In this case, only an individual exemption is possible. For an individual exemption pursuant to Art. 101 para. 3 TFEU an in-depth assessment has to be undertaken. Thus, the "requirement" criterion in Art. 101 para. 1 TFEU leads to a different treatment between selective distribution systems and other forms of distribution.

This article suggests that it has to be questioned whether this privilege for selective distribution is justifiable. E.g. for fast moving consumer goods, having recourse to selective distribution may be theoretically possible. However, it is difficult to install and impractical as the absolute profit is small and the profit is made by selling large quantities. Besides, establishing a selective distribution system excludes distributors and reduces intra-brand competition. Therefore, it is suggested to revisit the "requirement" criterion. This criterion should not be purely subjective, meaning — from a producer's perspective — the need of presenting the product in an adequate manner. The test should be whether a vertical restraint is objectively necessary to protect the brand reputation of a product that is vital for customers' demonstrative consumption (e.g. luxury watches, luxury bags, other branded high price consumer goods) or because of guaranteeing quality (e.g. technical or safety products).[50] By changing the "requirement" criterion in Art. 101 para. 1 TFEU and applying it to all distribution systems, a brand is recognised as value to customers. Additionally, the protection of intellectual property rights would be fostered.

Secondly, this article suggests a new approach of the application of section 20 GWB and other national legislation in the EU concerning the control of relative market power in cases of distribution systems: to avoid

---

48 See Commission, Guidelines on Vertical Restraints, 2010/C 130/01, para. 54.
49 A restriction outside selective distribution which is exempted has been present in the case of the Higher Regional Court of Munich, WuW 2009, DE-R 1068.
50 *Franck*, WuW 2010, 778 p.

inconsistencies with European competition law, these "stricter national rules" should not be applied if Art. 101 para. 1 TFEU is not fulfilled or if the Vertical-BER applies. In the case of vertical agreements no unilateral action is present but an agreement which hinders the application of national law.

5. Category management

Category management is a tool to enhance efficiency within the producer-customer relationship.[51] Category management was established in the United States around the 1990s.[52] It is important for industry sectors where products are sold by large retailers. This especially applies to fast moving consumer goods. The consumer demands different branded products between which he or she is able to choose. This customer choice leads to high costs for organizing the different product assortments. Category management helps to manage these products. Retailers choose a producer as "category captain" or "category advisor" who is responsible for the assortment selection, the placement of products and the organisation of shelf space. The cooperation may include only the advice of a retailer or the complete outsourcing of the strategic decisions concerning the choice and organisation of products.[53] Category management benefits all parties, the producer, the retailer and the consumer. The retailer benefits from the producer's knowledge with regard to the different products as well as with regard to marketing. The producer benefits by advising the retailer, building a relationship and better understanding the retailer's needs.[54] The consumer benefits from a better choice of branded products.

To implement category management, categories of products are formed. As the categories are not limited to one customer but extended to the customer's competitors, the collection of information concerning all customers as well as cooperation between the category advisor and the respective customer is necessary to implement an efficient category management. The exchange of information is the basis and the objective of category management. Producers and retailers have practised category management for many years to increase the efficiency of their range of items.

---

51 *Wiring*, GRUR-Prax 2010, 332.
52 *Besen/Jorias*, BB 2010, 1099; *Wiring*, GRUR-Prax 2010, 332; the leading case in the US is *Conwood Company vs. United States Tobacco Company*, 290 F3rd. 768 (6th Cir. 2002).
53 See *Loest*, WRP 2004, 454.
54 *Wiring*, GRUR-Prax 2010, 332.

Agreements — which appreciably restrict competition — between undertakings operating on different levels of trade are prohibited according to section 1 GWB as well as Art. 101 para. 1 TFEU. However, these agreements may be exempted from the prohibition because their pro-competitive effects outweigh anticompetitive effects. Section 2 para. 2 GWB as well Art. 101 para. 3 TFEU allow an exemption based upon the Vertical-BER.

5.1 Implications for category management

Problems in this context are that especially new and innovative ways to increase efficiency in the producer-distributor relationship may create suspicion by the competition authorities. Three main problems show that category management is a fine line between efficiency and anticompetitive behaviour.[55] Firstly, the above mentioned exchange of information between the producer and its customers can be problematic from a competition law perspective. The exchange of information may enable the category advisor to gain insight into price structures and other sensitive areas which the retailer may not want to disclose. Even worse, as category management may include different customers who are competitors on the retail level, sensitive information may be exchanged which may restrict competition between competing retailers, such as information on pricing strategies, advertising campaigns etc. Secondly, category management may create a risk of foreclosure of other suppliers.[56] The category advisor may promote its own products to the disadvantage of competing customers. This danger may arise if the retailer is also the producer's competitor by selling store brands or if innovative newcomers try to get a food hold in the market.[57] The category advisor may thus exploit its knowledge to gain a competitive edge. Doing this, it is possible to foreclose a market as well as to reduce price competition and innovation. Finally, the risk of collusion between retailers — via the category advisor — and between suppliers — via a retailer — exists. The exchange of information may add up to anticompetitive agreements or concerted practices by competitors when using category management. This collusion is also called hub-and-spoke.

---

55 See Commission, Guidelines on Vertical Restraints, 2010/C 130/01, paras. 209 pp.
56 *Besen/Jorias*, BB 2010, 1099, 1101.
57 *Besen/Jorias*, BB 2010, 1099.

5.2 Category Management according to the Guidelines on Vertical Restraints

The new Guidelines on Vertical Restraints deal with category management for the first time.[58] The Commission acknowledged an increase in efficiency which can be reached by category management.[59] Category management agreements are exempted under the Vertical-BER if the respective parties' market share does not exceed 30% (on the sales market of the producer and on the purchasing market of the retailer). Above the threshold, an individual exemption is possible. The Commission is of the opinion that most category management agreements are unproblematic.[60] The Commission focuses on the efficiencies for producers, retailers and consumers.[61] Problematic areas of category management are the three above-mentioned issues.

5.3 The FCO's approach to category management

In general, the FCO accepts category management as an innovative way to create an efficient distribution system. However, the president of the FCO, *Andreas Mundt*, emphasised in 2010 that category management must not be linked to price maintenance.

5.4 Recommendations

It is not unlikely that category management will be scrutinised by the FCO and other competition authorities in individual cases in the future. The complexity of category management does not allow a prediction whether the FCO's enforcement practice will adopt a lenient or strict approach towards category management. A lenient approach may be present if no means of price-fixing or aspects of resale price maintenance can be found by the FCO. The many existing uncertainties concerning category management make category management more difficult and increase the need for legal advice and clearly structured agreements between the parties concerned.

---

58 *Wiring*, GRUR-Prax 2010, 332.
59 Commission, Guidelines on Vertical Restraints, 2010/C 130/01, para. 213.
60 Commission, Guidelines on Vertical Restraints, 2010/C 130/01, para. 210.
61 Commission, Guidelines on Vertical Restraints, 2010/C 130/01, para. 213.

The following points may lead to more legal certainty with regard to category management agreements: Firstly, category management needs written agreements. Although written agreements lead to more complexity and less flexibility, it also means legal certainty and may exclude personal responsibility by the management if something goes wrong in competition law terms in practice. Secondly, it has to be exactly determined in the agreement how the category is defined and what the category comprises, which information will be exchanged and who has access to information. Confidentiality is helpful to reduce the flow of information within the category advisor's undertaking which may otherwise lead to a horizontal restraint of competition if the information is passed on to a competitor.[62] It should also be determined who has access to information and how the return of information is organised when the project has come to an end. Moreover, the use of data which has been compiled jointly has to be clarified. "Chinese walls" may be required to ensure no exchange of information to persons not included within the confidentiality agreement.[63] A possibility is to establish so-called "clean teams" which only do category management so that they cannot use the information for operational activities.[64] Apart from a written agreement it is important to enforce the agreement and to assess the exchange of information on a regular basis. Statements by the category advisor have to be recommendations only which are not binding on the retailer.[65] This enables the retailer to preserve its freedom to decide on prices and other elements of competition with regard to the retailer's competitors.[66] An obligation to implement the result of the category management process must not be present. Additionally, the retailer has to have the possibility to verify the objectiveness of recommendations in order to make an independent decision. Otherwise it may be possible for the category advisor to manipulate the recommendations in a way favouring the category advisor's undertaking. Finally, it is essential to document the category management process.[67] This enables the retailer to monitor the category management agreement and may serve as proof of compliance with the competition rules in case of an investigation.

---

62 *Besen/Jorias*, BB 2010, 1099, 1101.
63 See *Wiring*, GRUR-Prax 2010, 332, 336.
64 *Wiring*, GRUR-Prax 2010, 332, 336.
65 *Besen/Jorias*, BB 2010, 1099, 1101.
66 The freedom of decisions has been stressed by the Commission, see Commission, Comp/M.3732 (Procter & Gamble/Gilette), para. 134 pp.
67 The documentation includes all communication between the parties, see *Wiring*, GRUR-Prax 2010, 332, 336.

6. The FCO's paper on vertical distribution practices in the retail sector

6.1 Overview of the FCO's paper on distribution practices

The FCO searched food retailers and producers of brand products in January 2010. The FCO suspects resale price maintenance as well as the establishment of hub-and-spoke cartels with regard to confectionary, pet food and coffee between producers of brand products and retailers.[68] In April 2010, the FCO published a preliminary assessment of the parties' behaviour in negotiations between producers of brand products and food retailers.[69]

In its publication, the FCO distinguished certain practices which themselves are anticompetitive. Furthermore, the FCO distinguished certain practices which only indicate an anticompetitive behaviour or which can be part of an anticompetitive behaviour. With regard to these practices, the FCO recommends undertakings to be careful when applying on these practices. The FCO does not analyse the purpose and effect of the different practices. Questionable practices include exchange of information about annual turnover, annual appraisal, intended future price increases, grey market problems, quality standards of downstream distribution systems or benchmark studies.[70]

6.2 Assessment of the publication of the FCO's paper on distribution practices

By merely dividing the behaviour into certain practices which clearly or possibly indicate an anticompetitive behaviour, the purpose and effect of the behaviour is not taken into account by the FCO. Neither is it possible to determine whether the combination of certain distribution practices is allowed or prohibited because the overall picture is missing. Additionally,

---

68 See Federal Cartel Office, Press release, January 14, 2010.
69 See Federal Cartel Office, Preliminary assessment of behaviour in negotiations between producers of brand products, wholesalers and retailers to substantiate the duties to cooperate, WuW 2010, 786.
70 See Federal Cartel Office, Preliminary assessment of behaviour in negotiations between producers of brand products, wholesalers and retailers to substantiate the duties to cooperate, WuW 2010, 786, 789.

the FCO explicitly states that any behaviour not listed in its publication is not automatically unproblematic.[71]

The recommendation to be careful when applying these distribution practices does not lead to any legal certainty.[72] A producer or retailer is most likely not willing to risk an antitrust proceeding or a fine. From a practitioner's point of view, the FCO did not add to creating a transparent scheme within which behaviour is allowed and which is prohibited as anticompetitive. Although the different clauses and provisions within vertical agreements have to be assessed in context, the publication by the FCO led to rather more legal uncertainty than before.

7. Conclusions

The recent amendments of German competition law show a major alignment of German law to EU law. The ongoing harmonisation leads to new questions with regard to the practical application of these laws, especially as far as similar cases in different states of the EU are concerned. When deciding new cases, the national competition authorities and courts have to take different aspects into account: The national case law and specific traditional legal approaches; special rules of national competition law (such as sections 20 and 21 GWB); decisions by the ECJ regarding Art. 101 TFEU as well as the block exemption regulations and finally decisions by courts of other European states with respect to the application of EU law or harmonised national rules. This leads to a better comparability of court decisions on the one hand; on the other hand it may entail the danger of contradicting court decisions and thus to legal uncertainty, especially for undertakings operating in several EU member states.

Different approaches by EU member states towards competition policy are able to increase differences in the practical application of competition rules. The danger of contradicting court decisions also arises in Germany as the above-mentioned cases concerning selective distribution systems show. Decisions by higher courts will be necessary to resolve these contradicting assessments; but also a more general exchange of views between the courts hearing competition cases is important. The European Competition Judges Forum is therefore a worthwhile initiative.

---

71 Federal Cartel Office, Preliminary assessment of behaviour in negotiations between producers of brand products, wholesalers and retailers to substantiate the duties to cooperate, WuW 2010, 786, 791.
72 See *Möschel*, WuW 2010, 1229, 1234.

Further harmonisation, not only of the competition rules but also of their practical application, may resolve many legal uncertainties. The Guidelines on Vertical Restraints are supposed to enhance the harmonisation of the practical application of the EU competition rules and the harmonised national competition rules.

Furthermore, a closer look by the competition authorities at efficiencies deriving from certain conduct may lead to a new assessment of some types of vertical restraints. While a restriction of competition may not be difficult to be found if any restriction of the freedom to act suffices, to reach a decision whether a restriction is anticompetitive, a more sophisticated assessment is necessary. This can be considered common ground today. In an individual case, this assessment includes the efficiencies being the result of a restrictive vertical agreement. Also, resale price maintenance may lead to increased competition.

The protection of the brand image as intellectual property and customer goodwill is an area of the antitrust law which still awaits some fundamental work to be done in academia and practice. Balancing the different legitimate interests between enforcing competition and protecting intellectual property rights requires taking manifold interests and their consequences into account. It is suggested in this paper to revisit the ancillary restraints doctrine and to apply the "requirement" criterion that may lead to the non-application of Art. 101 para. 1 TFEU not only to selective distribution systems, but to all vertical distribution systems for branded or technology products.

As a result of the increased enforcement activities of the national competition authorities in the area of vertical restraints, compliance with competition law becomes an increasingly important topic and the need for legal advice continues to grow.

XI.2 Vertical restraints in the recent practice of the Bundeskartellamt, Germany

Kai Hooghof

Head of Unit, German and European Antitrust Law
*General Policy Division of the Bundeskartellamt, Germany**

1. Introduction

The aim of this article is to present key proceedings in the area of vertical restraints in the recent practice of the Bundeskartellamt (or Federal Cartel Office, FCO).

It should be underlined that public enforcement in Germany — which falls under the competence of the Bundeskartellamt and the competition authorities of the *Laender*[1] — is well complemented by private enforcement. Indeed, in Germany, private enforcement in the area of vertical restraints plays a vital role. This has already been well documented.[2] From 2005 to 2007, the Bundeskartellamt initiated 25 proceedings involving vertical restraints.[3] For the same time period, a study on private antitrust enforcement in Germany indicates more than 50 private cases.[4]

To set the scene for the actual cases which have been addressed by the Bundeskartellamt more recently, I will first briefly describe the legal framework that applies to vertical restraints (part II.) and then outline the course of proceedings before the Bundeskartellamt (part III.). In the main part of this article (IV.), I will highlight key cases, before summing up in a

---

* This article *reflects the personal* opinion of the *author* and does *not necessarily reflect* the *views* of the Bundeskartellamt.

1 The Bundeskartellamt is competent to deal with a matter "if the effect of the restrictive or discriminatory conduct ... extends beyond the territory of a *Land* [Federal State]", in other cases the *Laender* authorities are competent for a particular matter.

2 For a good overview, see Peyer, Myths and Untold Stories — Private Antitrust Enforcement in Germany, 2010, available at http://ssrn.com/abstract=1672695.

3 For more information, see the Bundeskartellamt's Activity Reports, available in German at http://www.bundeskartellamt.de/wDeutsch/archiv/TB_Archiv/archiv_TBW3DnavidW2663.php.

4 See Peyer, *supra*, footnote 2, 50.

short conclusion (V.). The cases deal with resale price maintenance (RPM) issues and exclusivity issues in the energy sector stemming from resale bans and exclusivity contracts.

2. Legal Framework in Germany

The Bundeskartellamt — and the *Laender* authorities — act on the basis of the Act against Restraints of Competition (ARC)[5] which came into force in 1959. With the last major amendment in 2005, the ARC was further harmonized with European competition law, in particular as regards horizontal and vertical agreements. Section 1 ARC now very much resembles Article 101 (1) TFEU while section 2 ARC is based on Article 101 (3) ARC. Section 2 (2) ARC furthermore contains a dynamic reference to the EU block exemptions. Before the 2005 amendment to the act, sections 14 to 18 ARC (old) provided for specific rules for vertical restraints, which inter alia contained per se prohibitions for RPM in section 14 ARC (old)) and provided for ex post control of a number of vertical restraints such as exclusivity clauses, tying and resale restrictions (section 16 ARC (old). Also of relevance in the area of vertical restraints are provisions, which provide for stricter rules than those contained in the TFEU and EU secondary legislation.[6] In the context of this article, in particular section 21 ARC which applies to boycott measures as well as to situations in the stage before an actual anti-competitive agreement can be mentioned. For example, one undertaking induces another to violate competition law rules by way of pressure or the promise of advantages. In this case, putting pressure on the other undertaking is enough to constitute an infringement.

3. Proceedings before the Bundeskartellamt

The Bundeskartellamt[7] initiates proceedings on its own initiative (ex officio) or on the basis of complaints. Anyone may share observations with

---

5   Available in English at http://www.bundeskartellamt.de/wEnglisch/Legal_bases/Legal_bases W3DnavidW2625.php.

6   Cf. Article 3 (2) last sentence Regulation 1/2003, the so called "German clause".

7   Note that decisions — including decisions whether or not to open proceedings — are taken by the decision divisions. These divisions are in principle competent to deal with cases in specific industry sectors, with the exception of three decision divisions which are competent to deal with abuse and hard core cases in the energy sector and hard core cartel cases. For further information see http://www.bundeskartellamt.de/wEnglisch/GeneralInformation/Organisation.php.

the Bundeskartellamt; neither the complainant nor the complaint needs to meet any formal requirements. The Bundeskartellamt, in turn, does not have to take a formal decision on whether or not to react to a complaint or open proceedings; it has a wide margin of discretion.

The discretion of the Bundeskartellamt is limited by its *de minimis* notice[8] which broadly resembles the Commission's *de minimis* notice.[9] With respect to vertical restraints, it states that the Bundeskartellamt shall generally refrain from initiating proceedings if the market share of each of the undertakings involved in a non-horizontal agreement does not exceed 15 per cent in any one of the markets affected. In the case of a parallel network with similar effect that covers 30% of a market, the market share is 5%. The notice does not apply to restrictions which have as their object or effect[10] the fixing of prices or price elements or the restriction of products, sourcing or distribution of goods or services, in particular by means of sharing sources of supply, markets or customers.

In its decision whether or not to open proceedings, the Bundeskartellamt takes into account a number of factors such as gravity and impact of the alleged violation of competition law, the undertakings involved, the signalling effect of a decision on practices that are widespread, issues of proof etc. If the Bundeskartellamt decides not to initiate proceedings, it informs the complainant accordingly indicating that he has the possibility to pursue the matter in private litigation.

Two very different types of proceedings have to be distinguished. Firstly, the Bundeskartellamt may initiate administrative proceedings. Such proceedings are generally aimed at bringing to an end an infringement of competition law[11]. Furthermore, the cartel authority may declare binding commitments offered by undertakings which are capable of dispelling the concerns communicated to them by the cartel authority upon preliminary assessment.[12] In particular to clarify issues that are relevant for a number of undertakings or a whole industry sector, the Bundeskartellamt may decide that, on the basis of the information available to it, there are no grounds for it to take any action.[13]

---

8 Available in English at http://www.bundeskartellamt.de/wEnglisch/download/pdf/ Merkblaetter/0703_Bagatellbekanntmachung_e_Logo.pdf.
9 Available at http://eur-lex.europa.eu/LexUriServ/LexUriServ.do?uri=OJ:C:2001:368:0013: 0015:EN:PDF.
10 Here the Bundeskartellamt's *de minimis* notice is stricter than the Commission's notice.
11 Cf. section 32 ARC.
12 Cf. section 32b ARC.
13 Cf. section 32c ARC.

Secondly, in cases specified in the ARC[14], the Bundeskartellamt may also initiate administrative fine proceedings. This type of proceeding is very much based on rules for criminal procedure. In such proceedings, the Bundeskartellamt may impose fines against individuals and undertakings.[15]

4. Selected Cases

More recently, the Bundeskartellamt has in particular dealt with cases concerning RPM and, in the energy sector, with resale bans and exclusivity contracts.

As regards the RPM cases, it is interesting to note that these have raised considerable interest but also criticism in Germany. Some commentators have accused the Bundeskartellamt of following a line that, so it was said, was no longer pursued internationally.[16] This is surprising for a number of reasons: In the wake of the *Leegin* judgment by the US Supreme Court[17], the competitive effects and the question as to how to address RPM appropriately have been widely discussed.[18] The discussion has clearly identified possible competitive harm as well as efficiencies stemming from RPM and such situations in which one or the other is more likely. As with many antitrust issues, there is room for some uncertainty. Consequently, it is a competition policy decision whether potentially negative or positive effects should weigh more. In Europe, the answer clearly is that the risk of anti-competitive effects weighs more. Furthermore, anti-competitive effects are seen as more likely than potential efficiencies. This is reflected in the 1999 Vertical Block Exemption Regulation (VBER) and the corresponding Guidelines on Vertical Restraints (Guidelines), but also in the new VBER and Guidelines from 2010.[19]

---

14 Cf. section 81 ARC.
15 In the case of undertakings or associations of undertakings, section 81 (4) ARC states that "the fine must not exceed 10% of the total turnover of such undertaking or association of undertakings achieved in the business year preceding the decision of the authority".
16 See Caspary, Swimming against the Zeitgeist?, [2010] E.C.L.R., 125-130, Bach, Form-based Approach at its Best — German FCO Re-discovers Old Rules on Recommended Resale Prices, Journal of European Competition Law & Practice, 2010, 241-244.
17 *Leegin Creative Leather Prods., Inc. vs. PSKS, Inc.*, 551 U. S. (2007), available at www.supremecourtus.gov.
18 In this context, I will only refer to the OECD Roundtable on Resale Price Maintenance in 2008, available at http://www.oecd.org/dataoecd/39/63/GGTSPU-gg1.bundeskartellamt.bund.de-2308-3884119-DAT/43835526.pdf. Furthermore, it is worth mentioning that most recently, the American Antitrust Bulletin dedicated two volumes to "Antitrust Analysis of Resale Price Maintenance after *Leegin*" (Vol. 55, No. 1 Spring 2010 and No. 2 Summer 2010).
19 Available at http://ec.europa.eu/competition/antitrust/legislation/vertical.html. See in particular (the unchanged) Article 4 lit a VBER which states that the block exemption does not

From an enforcer's perspective, the experience in the cases that are presented below shows that RPM is indeed frequently used to maintain a higher price level absent of any efficiency arguments, e.g. the compensation of extra efforts by the retailer. This view is also reflected in the approach taken by competition authorities in other member states of the EU.[20]

As regards the US, it is also worth mentioning that commentators have meanwhile stated that the application of the rule of reason is not adequate.[21] Kirkwood, for example, has advocated the adoption of the European-style rebuttable presumption of illegality.[22]

4.1. CIBA Vision (2009)

CIBA Vision Vertriebs GmbH (CIBA Vision) is the market leader in the contact lenses business in Germany. In administrative fine proceedings, the Bundeskartellamt accused CIBA Vision of having illegally restricted the internet trade in contact lenses of its own brand and, furthermore, of having influenced the resale prices of internet traders in violation of Article 81 EC (now Article 101 TFEU) as well as section 1 ARC. In its investigation, the Bundeskartellamt found that Ciba Vision had entered into agreements with purchasers (partly by putting pressure on them) on the exclusion of internet trading. Other measures taken by CIBA Vision concerned so-called "price management" measures: CIBA Vision operated a surveillance and intervention system; several persons were in charge of monitoring and controlling the traders' sales prices in the internet. If the resale prices of individual traders were at a certain level below the non-binding recommended retail price (RRP), CIBA Vision staff would contact those internet traders and try — in many cases successfully — to induce them to increase their sales prices. CIBA Vision also maintained special cooperation relationships with key account internet sellers with high turnover and high

---

apply if the vertical agreement has as its object "the restriction of the buyer's ability to determine its sale price." The new guidelines explain in some detail the situations where RPM may lead to efficiencies, in particular in the introductory period of expanding demand, in respect of short term low price campaigns in specific franchise or similar distribution systems, also in some situations where additional pre-sales services are of value to customers, e.g. in case of experience or complex products. For more details, see Guidelines at paragraph 225.

20 One example is the recent *Tobacco* case (2010) in which the UK Office of Fair Trading imposed fines totalling £225m. See OFT press release at http://www.oft.gov.uk/news-and-updates/press/2010/39-10.

21 See, e.g., Kirkwood, Rethinking Antitrust Policy Toward RPM, Antitrust Bulletin, Vol. 55, No. 2 Summer 2010, 423-472. See also Varney, A Post-Leegin Approach to Resale Price Maintenance Using a Structured Rule of Reason, 24 Antitrust, 22 (2009).

22 Kirkwood, *ibid.*, 463 et seq.

prices. These sellers generally committed themselves not to sell products more than 10-15% below RRP. In exchange, CIBA Vision granted these sellers specific purchasing conditions and support with marketing measures. The above mentioned agreements in which CIBA Visions customers accepted not to sell contact lenses over the internet clearly restricted competition and violated Article 81 EC (now Article 101 TFEU). As regards RRP, it is true that the unilateral issuing of RPP is generally permissible.[23] However, if the supplier and its customer agree that the latter follows the supplier's RRP, the result is a fixed resale price. Such a fixed resale price may also result from seemingly unilateral conduct to which the supplier's trading partner tacitly agrees by following its price recommendation. Here, CIBA Vision had systematically identified and contacted traders which had not followed the RRPs. In the following talks the aim was to coordinate the trader's pricing policy and thus agree on the trader's future pricing. The results of the investigations showed that, as a consequence, traders had indeed raised prices so that there was an agreement or at least a concerted practice between CIBA Vision and its retailers in the meaning of Article 101 TFEU.[24] CIBA Vision's systematic price management measures resulted in a generally higher price level in the market vis-à-vis retailers. The Bundeskartellamt imposed a fine of EUR 11.5 million on CIBA Vision. While CIBA Vision disputed the accusation from a factual and legal point of view, it did not appeal against the decision.

4.2 Phonak (2009)

Whereas the decision in the Ciba Vision case was based on Article 81 EC (now Article 101 TFEU) and the corresponding section 1 ARC, the Bundeskartellamt's decision in the Phonak case was solely based on sec-

---

23 Cf. Article 4 lit. a VBER.
24 Cf. Court of First Instance (CFI), Case T-41/96, ECR [2000] II-3383 — Bayer/Commission, para. 70; Case T-208/01, ECR [2003] II-514 — Volkswagen/Commission, para. 34 et seq. See also Case T-67/01, ECR [2004] II-49, JCB Service/Commission, para. 128-130, where the CFI held that, in this case, the evidence was not sufficient to show that there had been agreements on fixing prices or that there had been elements of coercion to follow price recommendations. See also Court of Justice, C-2/01 P and C-3/01 P, ECR [2004] I-23 — BAI and Commission/Bayer, para. 83, where the Court stated that "... although the existence of an agreement does not necessarily follow from the fact that there is a system of subsequent monitoring and penalties, the establishment of such a system may nevertheless constitute an indicator of the existence of an agreement".

tion 21 (2) ARC.[25] Phonak GmbH (Phonak) was accused of having influenced in an anticompetitive manner the resale prices of its products.

Phonak GmbH, a subsidiary of Swiss-based Sonova Holding AG, is one of the leading manufacturers of hearing aids in Germany. Hearing aids are usually sold to end consumers via hearing aid retailers. In the Bundeskartellamt's view the sale of hearing aids was characterised by a lack of price competition, both at the production level and the retail level. This lack of competition resulted not least from the fact that there is insufficient product and price transparency for end consumers wishing to buy a hearing aid.[26] Margins in the market were very high and manufacturer's prices were generally much higher than in other European countries such as France and the UK.

In the Phonak resale price case, a hearing aid retailer had published its prices for hearing aids from all manufacturers on the internet. The retailer's prices for Phonak hearing aids were well below the lowest price applied in the market until then. As a result, other hearing aid retailers from across Germany complained to Phonak about the lower-price offers. Phonak, which provided price lists with RRP including price-floors and price ceilings, reacted by refusing to sell to the respective hearing aid retailer in order to induce him to raise his resale prices.

The Bundeskartellamt found that this conduct violated section 21 (2) ARC because the refusal to sell to the retailer constituted a disadvantage in order to enforce price recommendations, i.e. by pressuring the retailer to agree to charge prices not lower than the RRP. The action taken by Phonak had a competitive relevance beyond this individual case. Eliminating the only price-active internet-based provider of hearing aids was a means to maintain or re-establish the predominant (high) price level on the German market for the trade in hearing aids. Moreover, where price competition is already limited at the retail level, any further prevention of competition, in particular price competition by innovative sellers, is all the more severe. In

---

25 Section 21 (2) ARC states: "Undertakings and associations of undertakings shall not threaten or cause disadvantages, or promise or grant advantages, to other undertakings to induce them to engage in conduct which, under this Act or according to a decision issued by the cartel authority pursuant to this Act, shall not be made the subject matter of a contractual commitment.".

26 This finding resulted from merger proceedings concerning the merger project of Phonak and GN ReSound. The Bundeskartellamt's prohibition decision is available in English at http://www.bundeskartellamt.de/wEnglisch/download/pdf/entscheidungen/07_Phonak_e.pdf.   In 2010, on appeal, the decision was overturned by the Federal Court of Justice (BGH). See BGH WuW/E DE-R 2905-2921 — *Phonak/GN Store.*

the Phonak case, the Bundeskartellamt imposed a fine of EUR 4.2 million on Phonak, a fine which has become final.

4.3 Proceedings in the Retail Sector (2010)

The retail sector in Germany is currently undergoing a (further) consolidation process. Concentration in the sector is already very high — with the five biggest retailers accounting for around 90% of the market share.

In recent merger proceedings, the Bundeskartellamt investigated the retail markets in great detail.[27] The Bundeskartellamt found, in particular, that the popular dogma of fierce price competition in the retail sector is somewhat exaggerated: While it is true that competition with respect to certain key products (e.g. milk, sugar and butter) is indeed intense, it is unclear whether the same is true for more expensive, branded products. There clearly is much less competitive pressure exerted by so-called hard discounters on full-line supermarkets because the former do not carry certain products that other supermarket chains have in stock.[28]

Against this background the Bundeskartellamt thoroughly investigates planned acquisitions that come under German merger control. The Bundeskartellamt not only analyses competition effects on the supply markets but also on the buyer markets.[29] It has found that the big players on the retail markets play a pivotal role. The Bundeskartellamt will continue to work on analysing whether these undertakings have buyer power that has a negative impact on competition in the retail sector.

In this context, the Bundeskartellamt received information that manufacturers of branded goods and retailers selling confectionary, coffee and pet food had allegedly fixed end consumer prices. As a consequence, in January 2010, the Bundeskartellamt initiated proceedings and conducted inspections of numerous companies in the food retail sector, drugstore

---

27 See Bundeskartellamt, decision of 30 June 2008, Edeka/Tengelmann, available in German at http://www.bundeskartellamt.de/wDeutsch/download/pdf/Fusion/Fusion08/B2-333-07_Internet.pdf. See also press release in English, available at http://www.bundeskartellamt.de/wEnglisch/News/Archiv/ArchivNews2008/2008_07_01.php. See also decision of 28 October 2010, Edeka/Trinkgut. The decision will be available in German at http://www.bundeskartellamt.de/wDeutsch/entscheidungen/fusionskontrolle/EntschFusionW3DnavidW2649.php. See also press release in English, available at http://www.bundeskartellamt.de/wEnglisch/News/press/2010_10_29.php.

28 For more details, see the Edeka/Tengelmann decision, *supra*, footnote 27.

29 See the Edeka/Tengelmann and Edeka/Trinkgut decisions, *supra*, footnote 27.

sector and pet supplies sector, as well as of several manufacturers of branded consumer goods.[30]

The proceedings raised considerable interest and press coverage in 2010. In many statements, representatives of producers and retailers stressed that, in their view, certain practices in the sector led to significant efficiencies and were thus beneficial for consumers. In the retail sector, some argued, intense communication was necessary for sharing the risk between producers and retailers. Furthermore, highly competitive companies and retail markets, so it was said, guaranteed that consumers would not be harmed. The Bundeskartellamt, in turn, underlined that the legal situation was clear, both at a national and a European level. Furthermore, while there may indeed be practices which are pro-competitive or at least not detrimental to competition, other practices common in the sector may be directed at fixing retail prices and thus at eliminating the risk inherent in the business of independent retailers (as opposed to agents.[31] In particular if such practices are — as the Bundeskartellamt suspects — widespread in the sector, this would result in higher prices for consumers compared to a situation absent of price fixing agreements. A justification pursuant to Article 101 (3) TFEU would seem highly unlikely, in particular because the products at issue were neither product launches nor complex products where extra service had to be remunerated.

4.4 "Take or Pay" Clauses (2010)

In the context of its sector inquiry "Capacity situation in the German gas transmission networks" the Bundeskartellamt received complaints from an association of industrial energy consumers concerning anti-competitive clauses in energy supply contracts. In the course of its investigations the Bundeskartellamt found that certain electricity and gas supply contracts between energy suppliers and industrial customers include so-called "take or pay" clauses which oblige the customer to purchase a minimum volume of gas or electricity ("minimum take"). While the contractual obligation to purchase a minimum take is not objectionable under competition law the Bundeskartellamt found that it is inadmissible to simultaneously prohibit a customer from reselling his minimum take. In this case the customer is prevented from selling the volume of energy he does not require directly

---

30 See press release in English, available at http://www.bundeskartellamt.de/wEnglisch/News/
    press/2010_01_14.php.
31 Cf. Guidelines, paragraph 12 et seq.

to third parties or at the energy exchange. Such agreements restrict competition on the distribution markets and hinder trade with electricity and gas. To be specific, the resale ban allowed the energy provider to prevent its customer from entering into direct competition as an energy provider in a given network with the excess volume of energy. In the view of the Bundeskartellamt, the clause represents a hardcore restriction within the meaning of Article 4 lit. b VBER and is not exempted by either the VBER or Article 101 (3) TFEU. In the wake of the economic crisis, the resale ban was of great significance because the demand for gas and electricity, especially by industrial customers, has dramatically slumped as a result of the current economic crisis. The proceedings were concluded by commitment decisions because the energy suppliers concerned accepted to abandon clauses in contracts with their industrial customers, which prohibit the resale of minimum take volumes of gas and electricity[32].

4.5 Long-Term Gas Supply Contracts

In a test case in 2006 the Bundeskartellamt prohibited the long-term gas supply contracts of E.ON Ruhrgas AG[33]. The Bundeskartellamt's investigations have shown that a good 70% of the regional and local gas companies in E.ON Ruhrgas' network area have long-term contracts with E.ON Ruhrgas covering up to 100% of their gas requirements. A further substantial number of contracts stipulate the purchase of a minimum of 80%. Even without focusing on the network of a single gas transmission company such as E.ON Ruhrgas, the results of the investigations show that in Germany, 75% of all supply contracts with providers are concluded for supply quantities of more than 80% and long running periods. Third suppliers are thus deprived of supply possibilities for years. This combination of long contract periods, on the one hand, and a high degree of requirement satisfaction, on the other, leads to considerable foreclosure effects.

In its decision, the Bundeskartellamt prohibited E.ON Ruhrgas' existing long-term contracts with distributors which cover more than 80% of their actual gas requirements. These contracts were to be terminated at the lat-

---

32 The decisions are available in German at http://www.bundeskartellamt.de/wDeutsch/entsc-heidungen/Kartellrecht/EntschKartellW3DnavidW2636.php. See also press release in English, available at http://www.bundeskartellamt.de/wEnglisch/News/press/2010_07_07.php.

33 The decision is available in German at http://www.bundeskartellamt.de/wDeutsch/download/pdf/Kartell/Kartell06/B8-113-03.pdf?navid=37. See also press release in English, available at http://www.bundeskartellamt.de/wEnglisch/News/Archiv/ArchivNews2005/2005_12_13.php.

est by the end of the relevant gas year on 30 September 2006. In its decision, the Bundeskartellamt also prohibited the conclusion of new contracts with regional and local gas companies which run for more than four years and which cover more than 50% of the actual gas requirements, or which run for more than two years and cover more than 80% of the requirements. For reasons of proportionality, the prohibition concerning the conclusion of new contracts was limited in time until the end of the 2009-10 gas business year (i.e. until September 30, 2010). As a consequence of the Bundeskartellamt's decision, further gas transmission companies committed themselves to adjust their contracts. These commitments were declared binding by the Bundeskartellamt.[34] In 2009, the Bundesgerichtshof (Federal Court of Justice) confirmed the Bundeskartellamt's decision in the E.ON case.[35]

In order to determine whether further steps had to be taken in view of the aforementioned expiration date of the prohibition on 30 September 2010, the Bundeskartellamt has evaluated the impact of its decisions as well as general legal and factual developments on the gas markets in the past years which had an effect on competition conditions in the gas distribution sector.[36] The extensive evaluation of the market showed that the significance of long contract periods and high supply quotas had drastically declined and that the market is now characterized by different types of contracts, a wider selection of suppliers and greater bargaining power on the demand side. This illustrates that the Bundeskartellamt's decisions successfully stopped the anti-competitive practice of long-term exclusive gas supply contracts which foreclosed the market. With its decisions the Bundeskartellamt thus contributed significantly to a stimulation of competition in the gas supply markets.

---

34 The decisions are available in German at http://www.bundeskartellamt.de/wDeutsch/archiv/ EntschKartArchiv/EntschKartellW3DnavidW2637.php. See also press release in English, available at http://www.bundeskartellamt.de/wEnglisch/News/Archiv/ArchivNews2006/ 2006_11_27.php.

35 BGH (Federal Court of Justice), decision of 10 February 2009, KVR 67/07, WuW/E DE-R 1049-1058 — *Gasliefervertrāge.*

36 See press release in English, available at http://www.bundeskartellamt.de/wEnglisch/News/ press/2010_06_15.php.

4.6 Concluding Remarks

Reviewing vertical restraints is and will remain an important task in the Bundeskartellamt's practice. The Bundeskartellamt will continue to focus on restraints that have a significant market impact. In that respect, exclusionary practices by firms with a certain degree of market power as well as practices aimed at maintaining high price levels and margins without corresponding efficiencies should remain key issues in public enforcement.

CHAPTER XII

ENFORCEMENT OF VERTICAL RESTRAINTS IN POLAND: AN OVERVIEW [1]

JAROSLAW SROCZYNSKI*

Founding partner
Markiewicz & Sroczynski

1. Introduction

The entry into force on 1 June 2010 of the new EU Vertical Block Exemption Regulation (VBER)[2] and the Guidelines on Vertical Restraints[3] has become a good occasion to review the current status of the national legislations and practice across the European Union. Poland seems to be a noteworthy example. First, Poland is considered one of the leaders of the Central European competition law enforcement. Second, Poland's economy has survived the "end-of-decade" crisis largely intact. The prospects for 2011 are also rather optimistic.[4] Thus, the meaning of vertical transactions in Poland will be likely increasing as a result of new investments and development of the existing local distribution networks.

This paper outlines the regulatory framework applicable to vertical agreements in Poland and discusses selected local enforcement issues. It

---

* **Jaroslaw Sroczynski,** lawyer and economist, founding partner of Polish law firm Markiewicz & Sroczynski, advising in competition law. Founder and first director of the Antimonopoly Office in Cracow. National expert of the Polish competition authority in DG COMP. Participated in numerous Polish legislative projects, including unfair competition law, leniency regulation, technology transfer and insurance sector block exemptions, and consumer laws.
1 This paper was presented at the International Conference — Reviewing Vertical Restraints in Europe: Reform, Key Issues and National Enforcement, CEU San Pablo University, Madrid, 11-12 November 2010.
2 Commission Regulation (EU) No. 330/2010 of 20 April 2010 on the application of Article 101(3) of the Treaty on the Functioning of the European Union (TFEU) to categories of vertical agreements and concerted practices, OJ L 102/1.
3 OJ C 130/1.
4 See: data published by the Polish Information and Foreign Investment Agency (PAIZ), http://www.paiz.gov.pl/poland_in_figures.

is intended to provide a general overview of the assessment of vertical restraints in Poland, as well as against the new EU legislative background.

2. Legislation and enforcement

2.1 Regulations

2.1.1 Structure of regulations

It is worth recalling that the first law regulating competition was enacted in Poland almost two-and-a-half decades ago, in 1987. Subsequently, this law was adapted to the market economy introduced in Central and Eastern Europe in 1989 and was expanded to reflect the changes of the whole legal system. In particular, the antimonopoly regulator was created in 1990, namely the Antimonopoly Office, later renamed to the Office of Competition and Consumer Protection ("OCCP").

One of the most important landmarks was Poland's accession to the European Union in 2004, connected with the necessary harmonization of the Polish competition law with that of the Community. The current Polish Law on Competition and Consumer Protection of 16 February 2007 (the "Law"), which is in its scope applicable to vertical restraints, follows the pattern of Article 101 TFEU (former Article 81 of the EU Treaty). Thus, the structure of the regulation is three-fold: first, the Law contains a general prohibition of non-exhaustively listed practices, restraining competition by object or effect, second, it defines a *de minimis* exception applicable to transactions between undertakings of which at least one does not exceed the threshold of 10% market share, and third, it introduces a rule of reason fully consistent with that formulated in Article 101 Sec. 3 TFEU. In addition, the Law delegates the legislative powers to the Council of Ministers to exempt from prohibition specific types of restrictions, taking into account the benefits outweighing the anticompetitive effects of those restrictions. This delegation was effected in Poland by the pertinent block exemption regulation, described further on in this article.

2.1.2 Prohibited practices

In Article 6 Sec. 1, the Law contains a list of seven exemplary forms of the prohibited practices, without dividing them into horizontal and vertical. This means that all prohibitions fully apply to vertical restraints. The listed restraints are the following:

1) directly or indirectly fixing of prices and other conditions of sales or purchases;

2) limiting or controlling production or sale and technical development or investments;

3) sharing of sale or purchase markets;

4) applying to equivalent transactions with third parties onerous or not homogenous agreement terms and conditions, thus creating for these parties diversified conditions of competition;

5) making the conclusion of an agreement subject to acceptance or fulfilment by the other party of another performance, having neither substantial nor customary relation with the subject of such agreement;

6) limiting access to the market or eliminating from the market undertakings which are not parties to the agreement;

7) collusion between undertakings entering a tender, or by those undertakings and the undertaking being the tender organiser, of the terms and conditions of bids to be proposed, particularly as regards the scope of works and the price[5].

2.1.3 De minimis exception

As mentioned above, a *de minimis* rule (Article 7 of the Law) exempts vertical agreements concluded by undertakings whose market share is lower than the statutory 10% threshold. This provision raises several questions. The first question relates to the relevant time market issue, since the Law indicates the "calendar year preceding the conclusion of the agreement" as the proper period for establishment of the 10% market share prerequisite. This means that no account is taken of any market share changes between the date of the agreement and the last day of preceding year (or any other day or period of that year, which may serve better for the purpose of defining the market share). Therefore, this unnecessary formalism inscribed into the Polish *de minimis* rule, may open way for errors in rulings based on false positives or false negatives[6].

It is also unclear whether *de minimis* rule applies to individual undertakings only, or whether it should equally benefit group entities. For exam-

---

5   The restrains defined in points 1-3 are commonly referred to as "(vertical) cartels", in point 4 as "discrimination", in point 5 as "tying", in point 6 as "market foreclosure", and in point 7 as "bid rigging". The above practices may take form of agreements or their parts as well as all kinds of arrangements (concerted practices) between undertakings.

6   See: J. P. Sluijs, Network Neutrality Between False Positives and False Negatives: Introducing a European Approach to American Broadband Market, Federal Communications Law Journal, Vol. 62, 2010, p. 77; P. C. Carstensen, False Positives in Identifying Liability for Exclusionary Conduct: Conceptual Error, Business Reality, and ASPEN, Wisconsin Law Review, Volume 2008, Number 2.

ple, if the undertaking which signed the agreement has a market share not exceeding 10% but its parent company's market share exceeds 10%, can *de minimis* rule still apply? Opinions on this matter differ between commentators. According to one view, Article 7 constitutes an exception from the general rule of prohibitions and, as such, cannot be extended[7]. This means that only a single market share of the contracting undertaking should be considered. According to contrary views[8], if the parent company effectively shapes the business policies of the contracting undertaking, the group market share shall be taken into account.

The author of this article adheres to the view which, to some extent, combines the above concepts. First, treating the rule under Article 7 entirely and strictly as an exception seems to be too far-going. This would lead to a mechanical application of *de minimis* rule, departing from the functional interpretation. In turn, the economic-based approach to competition law largely depends on the functional understanding of the wording of legal provisions.[9] The function of *de minimis* rule is to create a "safe harbour" for undertakings whose market share is low enough not to exert any material effect on the market in result of concluded transactions. This circumstance can be considered only on the market relevant for the transaction, i.e. on the purely economic foreground. Second, an exception may not facilitate situations whereby it could be used contrary to the general rules of competition, including by circumventing the protective function of the Law (for example, through "delegating" an agreement which clearly restricts competition by a dominant company to a special purpose subsidiary with little or no market share).

The above leads to the conclusion that the exception under Article 7 is at the same time an indication that all "usual" classification tools should be applied. In other words, the transaction should be assessed from the point of view of its effect on the relevant product market. Therefore, not only the parent's market share should be considered, but also the market shares of other group companies, including sister companies and subsidiaries of the contracting undertaking. On the other hand, calculation of the 10% thresh-

---

7   See: A. Stawicki, *Ustawa o ochronie konkurencji i konsumentów, Komentarz* (Law on Competition and Consumer Protection, A Commentary) (ed. by A. Stawicki and E. Stawicki), Warszawa 2011, p. 278.

8   See: C. Banasiński, E. Piontek (ed.), *Ustawa o ochronie konkurencji i konsumentów, Komentarz* (Law on Competition and Consumer Protection, A Commentary), Warszawa 2009, p. 227; A. Jurkowska, *Ustawa o ochronie konkurencji i konsumentów, Komentarz* (Law on Competition and Consumer Protection, A Commentary) (ed. by T. Skoczny), Warszawa 2009, p. 443.

9   See, for example: M. Hughes, The economic assessment of vertical restraints under UK and EC competition law, European Competition Law Review 2001.

old should be confined only to the relevant market and not pertain to other markets. For example, if the vertical agreement has as its object the distribution of refrigerators, only the group market share in refrigerators should be counted and not in ovens, even though the parent company produces also ovens and exceeds 10% share in those products. In this manner, the exception would serve both the public cause, covering only those situations which are relevant from the competition point of view, as well as the entrepreneurial need for adequate legal certainty as to the scope of the available contractual freedom.

In the same, functional manner, one can tackle another shortcoming of the Polish *de minimis* rule, which is the lack of express reference to cumulative effects of multiple vertical agreements, that would together lead to an excess of 10% market share. Again, the final market share in the relevant market should matter and, if exceeded as a result of the conclusion of parallel agreements, the benefit of the exception should not apply.[10]

Finally, it should be mentioned that *de minimis* rule does not apply to cartels, including vertical cartels, a form of which are vertical bid-rigging cartels. The foregoing restrictions of competition (so-called hardcore restrictions) are qualified in the Law as prohibited under any circumstances.

2.1.4 "Rule of reason"

Another exception from the general prohibition of anticompetitive restraints is the "rule of reason" formulated in Article 8 of the Law. The prohibition of agreements referred to in Article 6 shall not apply to agreements which at the same time:

1) contribute to improvement of the production, distribution of goods or to technical or economic progress;

2) allow the buyer or user a fair share of benefits resulting thereof;

3) do not impose upon the undertakings concerned impediments which are not indispensable to the attainment of these objectives;

4) do not afford these undertakings the possibility to eliminate competition in the relevant market in respect of a substantial part of the goods in question.

---

10 The same approach has been adopted in point 8 of the Commission Notice on agreements of minor importance which do not appreciably restrict competition under Article 81(1) of the Treaty establishing the European Community (*de minimis*), OJ (2001) C 368. It is worth to mention that a threshold of 15% is applicable to vertical agreements under the above Notice. See also Article 6 of VBER, stipulating its inapplicability to parallel networks of similar vertical restraints covering more than 50% of a relevant market.

The wording (and meaning) of the Polish "rule of reason" is equivalent with its EU counterpart formulated in Article 101 Sec. 3. Since there in no "soft law" in Poland which would provide guidance as to how the conditions of Article 8 should be satisfied in order to benefit from the exception, the pertinent *acquis communautaire* should apply at hand[11]. Since the burden of proof of the circumstances defined in the "rule of reason" is shifted on the undertaking concerned, it will be in the interest of the undertakings to rely on the Commission Notices and EU court rulings. It will be also important to carefully examine the prerequisites of the "rule of reason", such as economic benefits of efficiency gains, since agreements attempting to be exempted under Article 8 cannot be pre-notified to the regulator. Accordingly, a risk of wrongful qualifications burdens exclusively parties to such agreements.

The above remark is all the more appropriate given that the "rule of reason" shall potentially apply to transactions where the parties' market shares will be usually high, at least exceeding 30-35%, or reflecting the parties' dominance on the relevant market.[12] Therefore, transactions benefiting from the "rule of reason" will not be, by their nature, free from any competition-related considerations.

It is disputable whether hardcore restrictions can be at all exempted under Article 8, in light of the derogation from exemption under the *de minimis* rule. The literal reading of the Law does not exclude the possibility of an exemption based on the "rule of reason", since Article 8 does not contain any equivalent of Article 7 Sec. 2, excluding hardcore restrictions from *de minimis* treatment. This means that, potentially, even a vertical resale price maintenance (RPM) practice could be exempted under the "rule of reason", provided of course that the strict test of Article 8 would be fully met.

On the other hand, such approach would lead to effects which are hardly acceptable, given the inner logic of the Law. In the case of the example of a vertical RPM restraint, it could be exempted even if the pertinent agreement was concluded between dominant or monopolistic companies, while it could not be allowed in relations between companies having only negligible market share, in accordance with the strict prohibition of Article 7 Sec. 2. It seems that the above result of the operation of the Law would be far from positive. Therefore, attempts were made in the jurisprudence and legal writings to define the proper demarcation line between the scope

---

11 Commission Notice, Guidelines on the application of Article 81(3) of the Treaty, OJ (2004) C 101. Also, point VI.1.3.2 of the VBER Guidelines will prove useful for interpretation purpose, expressing the most recent position of the EU authorities.
12 In Poland, a dominant market position is presumed when the market share exceeds 40%.

of prohibition of anticompetitive restraints and the (economically) viable exceptions to that prohibition. The above dilemma is obviously not only Polish-specific and reflects the discussion of the last decade in the EU and United States on how the economic approach to competition law should solve the loopholes of the form-based approach. [13]

The Polish regulator has taken the stance that the most serious violations of competition, including vertical cartels, cannot be exempted under the "rule of reason". [14] Legal commentators propose to use the distinction between restrictions by object and restrictions by effect as a tool for qualification. Thus, restrictions by object would not be exempted under any circumstances, including via the "rule of reason", while restrictions by effect would require prior analysis of their advantages and disadvantages for competition. The final assessment will have to take account of the balance between the positive and negative effects [15].

The author of this article again adheres to the functional and economic approach, enforced by the directions offered by the *acquis communautaire*, in particular, in the VBER Guidelines. Pursuant to paragraph 223 of the Guidelines, "*undertakings have the possibility to plead an efficiency defence under Article 101(3) in an individual case. It is incumbent on the parties to substantiate that likely efficiencies result from including RPM in their agreement and demonstrate that all the conditions of Article 101(3) are fulfilled. It then falls to the Commission to effectively assess the likely negative effects on competition and consumers before deciding whether the conditions of Article 101(3) are fulfilled.*" The approach of the Commission is quite clear: there is no room anymore for treatment of vertical hardcore restrictions as prohibited *per se*. In each case, even if RPM practices were applied, undertakings enjoy the right to demonstrate appropriate defences under the "rule of reason" and can attempt to clear the restraining agreement. The Commission may not refuse to conduct an analysis of case-specific circumstances. As a result, the prohibition must be economically grounded and the agreement cannot be rejected based purely on formal grounds of the wording of the law.

---

13 See, for example: Nicholas Norwood The Commission's "more economic approach" — implications for the role of the EU courts, the treatment of economic evidence and scope of judicial review [in:] Claus-Dieter Ehlermann and Mel Marquis (eds.), European Competition Law Annual 2009: Evaluation of evidence and its judicial review in competition cases, Hart Publishing 2009.

14 Decisions of the President of the OCCP Nos. DOK-107/2006 and RWA-37/2006.

15 See: A. Stawicki, *op. cit.*, pp. 219-222. See also: K. Kohutek, *Ustawa o ochronie konkurencji i konsumentów, Komentarz* (Law on Competition and Consumer Protection, A Commentary), K. Kohutek, M. Sieradzka, Warszawa 2008, p. 310.

The necessity to apply by the Polish competition regulator the EU interpretation standards follows directly from Article 3 Sec. 2 of the Council Regulation (EC) No. 1/2003 of 16 December 2002 on the implementation of the rules on competition laid down in Articles 81 and 82 of the Treaty.[16] Pursuant to the above provision, *"the application of national competition law may not lead to the prohibition of agreements, decisions by associations of undertakings or concerted practices which may affect trade between Member States but which do not restrict competition within the meaning of Article 81(1) of the Treaty, or which fulfil the conditions of Article 81(3) of the Treaty or which are covered by a Regulation for the application of Article 81(3) of the Treaty"*. This rule is known as the principle of convergence[17], the task of which is to attain uniform application of the rules of competition across the EU Member States. This means, in turn, that local interpretations may not lead to different treatment of the same agreement under national and EU laws. In particular, a vertical agreement compliant with EU protection standards should be admissible also when Polish rules of competition are applied. As a result, the manner in which the contradiction between form-based approach and economic approach to competition law can be solved is through gradual "blending" of the national and EU legal systems, for the purpose of achieving a commonly compatible hierarchy of assessment tools.

2.1.5 Block exemptions

Assessment of vertical transactions concluded by undertakings which do not exceed the level of 30-35%[18] market share is to some extent facilitated due to the block exemption regulation, issued by the Council of Ministers. The purpose of this regulation is to exempt certain groups of vertical arrangements from the general prohibition under Article 6 of the Law, taking into account the economic benefits prevailing over restrictions of competition.

The first vertical block exemption regulation was introduced in Poland in 2002. This first regulation expired in 2007 and was succeeded by the current Regulation of 19 November 2007. The 2007 Regulation will, in turn, expire on 31 May 2011. It will be replaced by a new vertical regulation as of 1 June 2011, a draft of which was already published on the OCCP's web-

---

16 OJ L 001.

17 See: KJ Cseres, *The Impact of Regulation 1/2003 in the New Member States*, The Competition Law Review, July 2010, Volume 6 Issue 2, p. 151; F. Amato, L. Armati, M. Merola, E. Morgan de Rivery, *Relationship between EC Competition Law and National Competition Law*, Concurrences No. 3-2009, p. 10.

18 The threshold of 35% can be achieved only temporarily.

site.[19] The draft was commented on in the process of public consultations and is currently on the path of the legislative procedure.

Both vertical regulations, i.e., the one which is still in force and the draft new regulation closely follow their respective EU counterparts. In particular, the first vertical regulation was based on the Regulation No. 2790/1999, which expired in 2010 and was a predecessor of the current VBER. The draft of the new Polish regulation almost entirely repeats the concept of the VBER; certain differences are of minor practical importance, being rooted mainly in the local law context. One difference worth mentioning is the lack of an equivalent in the new Polish regulation of Article 8 Sec. 2 VBER, providing that the block exemption shall remain applicable where, for the period of two consecutive financial years, the total annual turnover threshold is exceeded, in the case of vertical agreements between associations and its members or suppliers, by no more than 10%. On the other hand, the Polish draft regulation repeats the solution adopted in Article 2 Sec. 2 VBER, whereby a financial threshold of 50 million Euro annual turnover shall apply to individual members of associations, together with connected undertakings, in order to cover vertical agreements entered into by such associations by the block exemption.

It is particularly important to note that the new Polish regulation will follow the same solution as the one applied in the VBER, concerning the market share threshold applicable to exclusive supply contracts. In the VBER, this threshold was redefined as 30% share of both sides, i.e., the supplier and the purchaser. The current Polish regulation is not entirely clear on this matter and can be interpreted in two ways, i.e., as applicable to exclusive supplies only in relation to undertakings which both have market shares below 30% or as applicable already in a situation where the purchaser's market share is below 30%. The new regulation will eliminate this discrepancy.

The planned issuance of the new Polish vertical block exemption regulation follows the hitherto approach of the authorities to maintain a system of local secondary regulations, implementing the Law.[20] Even though the scope of the new Polish vertical regulation will be almost the same as its EU equivalent, it has an important role to play. Namely, it will remove legal doubts as to the qualification of vertical agreements concluded by undertakings with market shares between 10% and 30-35% which do not have

---

19 http://www.uokik.gov.pl/projekty_aktow_prawnych.php#faq1153.
20 In addition to the vertical block exemption, the Polish Council of Ministers issued also the following block exemption regulations: on specialization and research-and-development agreements, on technology transfer, and on the insurance sector.

an effect on trade between Member States but have an effect exclusively on the territory of Poland. In absence of a regulation specific to those latter cases, undertakings would not have the necessary legal certainty of whether the agreement will be block-exempted or whether it is necessary to use the "rule of reason" approach and methodology in order to confirm its compatibility with the rules of competition.

2.2 Fining guidelines

The President of the OCCP can impose financial fines for violations of the rules of competition, which obviously extends also to vertical restraints. Fines cannot exceed 10% of the undertaking's turnover achieved in the preceding financial year.

In 2009, the OCCP issued a set of guidelines concerning the imposition of fines for practices restricting competition. The fining guidelines constitute a body of soft law, with one-sided binding force applicable to the regulator. The guidelines can also serve undertakings as a tool of simulation of the probable amount of fines which can be imposed for particular violations. It should be noted that vertical restraints were qualified in the Guidelines in three different ways. Resale price maintenance agreements, in which the producer performs the role of a "supervisor", are treated as *de facto* horizontal cartels and are considered to be the "most serious" violations of the rules of competition. The other resale price maintenance agreements are treated as "serious" violations. In turn, those vertical agreements, which do not have as their object the pricing or reselling conditions, are considered to be the "remaining" violations and are treated in the most favourable way. This initial qualification is crucial for establishment of a base amount of the fine. Subsequently, various mitigating and aggravating circumstances are taken into account. It is worth noting that the role of a leader of the prohibited vertical arrangement or the use of retaliation measures in downstream market will results in an increase of fines. On the other hand, the final amount of fine will be established based on comparison of the scale of profits achieved from the illegal restraint with the whole turnover of the undertaking concerned.

It should be noted that the fining guidelines were received by the Polish courts with certain reserve, if not dogmatism. In the judgment of 19 August 2009[21], the Supreme Court ruled that an undertaking cannot positively rely on the calculation of fine in accordance with the guidelines,

---

21 III SK 5/09, in re: Marquardt Media Polska.

since the guidelines were issued only for the purpose of facilitating the enforcement of the Law, in absence of the normative base justifying their issuance. Finally, the Supreme Court stated that the guidelines do not bind in any way the courts deciding appeals from the OCCP's decisions. It is difficult to predict whether lower instance courts will now be encouraged to present a more flexible attitude to the fining guidelines. In spite of unavoidable limitations of this piece of soft law, the guidelines should nevertheless be perceived, especially from the undertaking's perspective, as very valuable input by the President of the OCCP in the process of better understanding of the competition enforcement practice.

2.3 Enforcement authority

In 2010, the OCCP celebrated its 20th anniversary. The OCCP is an administrative body, with its head office in Warsaw and nine regional branches in the main Polish cities. The President of the authority is appointed and dismissed by the Prime Minister. The OCCP has broad inspection powers, similar to those enjoyed by the EU Commission. Dawn raids and sequestrations of evidence are thus possible and not unusual.

The enforcement procedural system is a mixture of various procedures, including administrative, civil, criminal, and *sui generis* procedures stemming from the Law. The case handling process before the OCCP involves two phases: explanatory and administrative. Proceedings in complex cases extend to several months, sometimes it may take a year or two to decide a case. If necessary, the OCCP performs detailed market research, using its own resources or, sometimes, also external experts. In 2004, a department of market analyses was established within the OCCP's structure, similar to the introduction of the Chief Economist's position by the EU Commission.

The following table provides basic statistical data concerning the proceedings and decisions issued by the OCCP in vertical cases. The data for 2009–2005 indicates that approximately 10-20 decisions were issued per year, which corresponds to approximately 5-10% of all competition decisions of the regulator.

Poland: proceedings of the OCCP	2009	2008	2007	2006	2005
Number of antimonopoly proceedings:	176	109	248	361	328
Number of decisions:	107	104	141	202	144
Number of antimonopoly proceedings concerning **vertical agreements**:	22	30	21	30	26
Number of decisions:	10	13	7	22	9

Source: Annual Reports of the OCCP for the years 2005 — 2009.

The President of the OCCP can issue several types of decisions to under-takings who apply restrictive practices. If the violation still remains, a pro-hibiting decision will be issued. If the violation was discontinued, the deci-sion will declare illegality of the committed practice and confirm that it was ceased. The President of the OCCP can also issue a decision imposing an obligation which the undertaking must implement and which is aimed at elimination of the effects of anticompetitive practices. In the case of the above commitment decisions, financial fines are not imposed. The Presi-dent of the OCCP can also decide on interim measures or introduce an obligation of immediate execution of the decision.

Agreements which contain the prohibited, anticompetitive clauses are par-tially or wholly null and void.

2.4 Court review

Decisions of the OCCP's President can be challenged in courts. Appeals are handled in a two-tier court system. The first tier is the Regional Court in Warsaw, which has a special division called the Court of Competition and Consumer Protection, handling all competition cases in Poland. Appeals from judgments of that court are reviewed by the Court of Appeals in War-saw. Extraordinary appeals (cassations) are dealt with by the Supreme Court, provided they are pre-accepted for ruling in a review performed by a Supreme Court's judge.

The Court of Competition and Consumer Protection also authorizes the OCCP to make searches and sequestrations of objects serving as evidence in competition cases.

3. Examples of case law

The below brief selection of Polish cases pertaining to vertical restraints is limited by two circumstances: first, by the scope of this article and second, by the author's subjective assessment as to which cases (types of restraints) could be regarded as at the same time representative and inter-esting for a non-Polish reader who does not deal with Polish competition law on a daily basis.

3.1 Scope of application

An important general rule was established in the case re: Philips Polska[22]. The President of the OCCP terminated the antimonopoly proceedings, stating that vertical block exemptions shall apply to an alleged practice of discrimination. In the decision, the scope of the application of the vertical block exemption regulation was defined. The President of the OCCP confirmed that all clauses applied in vertical contracts, as long as they are not black-listed, must be regarded as admissible. This rule applies even if the object and effect of a given clause was clearly anticompetitive.

3.2 Resale Price Maintenance (RPM)

The most notable set of vertical RPM cases, initiated by the President of the OCCP in 2005 and continued through 2010, concerns price fixing arrangements between the three main Polish paint producers and their respective resellers, i.e., independent distributors and do-it-yourself chain stores (DIY). Each of the paint producers was found guilty of instigating its resellers to maintain prices for several so-called "driver" paint products on the same level as applied by competing resellers. The OCCP imposed fines totalling in some cases to tens of millions of Euros. The amounts burdening DIYs were particularly high, given the turnover values of those stores. In one single case, the fine calculated as appropriate for Castorama exceeded 55 million Euros[23]. However, this fine was not imposed due to Castorama's successful leniency motion. Interestingly, the OCCP did not investigate the horizontal origin of those similar, multiple cases of instigation, focusing only on the horizontal effect of the vertical arrangements.

3.3 Exclusivity

The OCCP demonstrated a flexible and economically grounded approach assessing exclusivity justified by special ownership rights, combined with intellectual property rights. In a case pertaining to the granting of exclusive broadcasting rights to Canal+ by the Polish Football Association, the

---

22 DOK Nr. 87/06.
23 DOK-4/2010.

President of the OCCP ruled that the exclusivity period of four years for broadcasting Polish league matches could be accepted[24].

On the other hand, the President of the OCCP banned exclusivity in relations between the incumbent railway cargo company and its customers. Multiple vertical restraints were jointly disqualified but were decided as a dominance case. No charges were made by the OOCP against the cargo customers who signed the exclusive contracts under significant market pressure[25].

3.4 Market foreclosure

The President of the OCCP prohibited an agreement between car manufacturer Fiat Auto Poland and its distributors, whereby the distributors agreed to sell cars to a terminated distributor only at retail prices[26]. The President of the OCCP qualified this vertical restraint as foreclosing access to the wholesale market to the distributor whose agreement was terminated.

3.5 Commitments

In exceptional circumstances, vertical price fixing arrangements can go unpunished, if the regulator accepts the parties' obligation to voluntarily terminate the violation. In a case against a producer of gutters Xella and its resellers, the President of the OCCP agreed that the parties to a prohibited agreement restricting the sales of Xella products below the purchase price would amend their agreements and eliminate the questioned practices[27]. The OCCP's approval of those commitments resulted in the lack of fines for Xella and its business partners.

4. Specific issues of Polish law

4.1 Vertical leniency

As mentioned in point 3 in connection with the "paint-DIY" decisions, leniency can be sought even in vertical cases. Formally speaking, there is no

---

24 DOK-49/06. See also: J. Sroczynski, *The Permissibility of Exclusive Transactions: Few Remarks in the Context of Exercising Media Rights*, Yearbook of Antitrust and Regulatory Studies, Vol. 2010, 3(3), p. 115.
25 DOK-50/2004; DOK-172/2005.
26 RKT-1/2004.
27 DOK-3/2008.

limitation of the scope of vertical leniency, since there is no legal distinction between horizontal and vertical arrangements in Article 6 of the Law. Furthermore, the pertinent provisions of Law which regulate leniency do not distinguish between vertical and horizontal violations. This solution is specific for Poland and does not exist in the EU law. To the best of the author's knowledge, full vertical leniency is also not offered under any of the national competition law systems of the Member States[28].

Legal commentators indicate that vertical leniency is rather unnecessary, in light of the lack of the same difficulties which justify this procedure in the case of horizontal cartels.[29] The main issue is the easier, if not even unrestricted access to evidence, unlike in horizontal collusions, which by their nature operate under cover. Vertical transactions always require some form of written evidence, such as agreements or invoices. Thus, the illegal actions of undertakings can be monitored and disclosed by the authority without the need to offer immunity for information which remains in the "public domain". Other commentators take a more favourable view towards vertical leniency, stressing the need for the President of the OCCP to apply this instrument in a careful manner, only in relation to the most serious violations of competition.[30]

Given the positive results of the vertical leniency program in Poland, such as disclosure of various vertical RPM cases by leniency applicants, and limited resources of the OCCP to inspect all the markets on a constant basis, the author is of the opinion that vertical leniency can play an additional, important role in competition law enforcement. However, in each case the President of the OCCP should verify whether the only reason of the leniency application is an attempt to cease illegal practices. In some situations, vertical leniency mechanism can serve as an additional source of achieving the administrative effect of nullification of such distribution agreements, which otherwise could not be easily terminated for specific contractual reasons and which contain clauses being at the same time anticompetitive and uncomfortable for one of the parties.

---

28 In the United Kingdom, vertical leniency can be obtained in cases of vertical RPM, if minimum or fixed prices were imposed on a reseller (OFT's guidance note on the handling of applications, December 2008, 803, point 9.11).

29 See B. Turno, *Ustawa o ochronie konkurencji i konsumentów, Komentarz* (Law on Competition and Consumer Protection, A Commentary) (ed. by A. Stawicki and E. Stawicki), Warszawa 2011, p. 1207.

30 S. Sołtysiński, *Z doświadczeń programu leniency w Brukseli i w Warszawie* (The experiences of the leniency program in Brussels and in Warsaw), [in:] C. Banasiński (ed.), *Prawo konkurencji — stan obecny oraz przewidywane kierunki zmian*, Warszawa 2006, p. 41.

4.2 Collective consumer interests

A noteworthy specialty of the Polish competition enforcement system is the active role of the Polish regulator in the field of consumer protection. The OCCP is one of the few European competition offices directly engaged in dealing with consumer matters[31]. Although consumer contracts constitute sale, and not resale relationships, it seems interesting to compare the legal powers of the OCCP's President in this area to those applicable to "regular" vertical restraints.

The Polish regulator can act in the general interest of consumers and initiate court suits as a plaintiff, challenging abusive clauses applied in consumer contracts. The OCCP maintains a register of those clauses, currently listing over 2000 examples from different business sectors. The OCCP can also issue decisions prohibiting violation of so-called collective consumer interests, taking form of application of abusive clauses in standard consumer contracts, committing unfair commercial practices, and so on. This area of enforcement is entirely administrative and most procedures are similar to those applicable to classical verticals, including an opportunity to escape fines through approved commitments. However, fines for anti-consumer acts can be imposed in the same amount as in the case of vertical restraints, i.e., up to 10% of turnover. A special set of guidelines on fining policies was issued by the OCCP in 2009.

A specific form of repression for violations related to the collective consumer interests is the obligation to remove effects of the violations. In particular, undertakings can be obligated to publish a special statement, admitting their commitment of the prohibited practice. Undertakings can also be required to publish the OCCP's decision on the undertaking's website or elsewhere in the mass media. It should be noted that violations of the collective consumer interests can be scrutinized by the President of the OCCP regardless of the market share of undertakings engaged in the prohibited practices.

5. Role of acquis communautaire / summary

5.1 Application of EU law and practice

In conclusion of this article, it seems necessary to devote a few comments to the role of *acquis communautaire* in the unavoidable situations

---

31 Other examples are Bulgaria, Luxembourg and, to some extent, France.

of "white spots" or discrepancies appearing between solutions adopted in Polish law on vertical restraints and in the EU law and jurisprudence. One should note that reference to *acquis communautaire* is frequently made use of by the President of the OCCP in decided cases and by undertakings appealing from unfavourable decisions. As mentioned above (point 2.1.4), the principle of convergence formulated in Regulation 1/2003 is a strong rule ensuring uniformity of enforcement practice across the EU. Important solutions were also adopted in Article 11 Sec. 1 of Regulation 1/2003, stipulating that the Commission and the competition authorities of the Member States shall apply the EU competition rules in close cooperation. Finally, Article 16 has a decisive role to play, regulating the uniform application of EU competition law. This provision is addressed both to competition authorities and national courts and requires that decisions issued by those institutions cannot run counter to the decisions adopted by the Commission.

From the point of view of enforcement of vertical restraints in Poland, it is particularly essential to ask whether and to what extent the Polish authorities will use the VBER Guidelines as an interpretation tool. We should keep in mind that there is no Polish equivalent of the EU Guidelines. However, the VBER Guidelines offer a broad platform for interpretation which can be applied in such enforcement areas, as resale price maintenance, Internet sales, agency agreements, intellectual property rights, effects of parallel networks, etc. Thus, it would be obviously beneficial if the VBER Guidelines were applied directly in cases decided in Poland. This would have a positive effect on the uniformity of EU practice in the field of vertical restraints.

If the President of the OCCP decides a case based on Article 101 TFEU[32], there is no reason that would prevent the regulator from a direct application of the VBER Guidelines[33]. On the contrary, the Guidelines should be always applied, as any other act of EU legislation, albeit constituting soft law. In cases decided exclusively based on Article 6 of the Law, the situation is more complex. The VBER Guidelines can also, of course, be used directly but the obligation to apply them is rooted not in the clear need to use the *acquis communautaire* in EU cases but in the necessity to adhere to "conforming interpretation" or, in other words, "pro-community interpretation" of Polish competition law.

---

[32] This is possible pursuant to Article 6 of Regulation 1/2003 and Article 10 of the Law.

[33] Although, as mentioned in point 2.2, the Supreme Court has taken a somewhat reserved stance towards the role of guidelines in competition law enforcement.

The need to apply "pro-community interpretation" stems from the principle of primacy of international law, expressed in Article 91 Sec. 3 of the Polish Constitution[34]. Most commentators approve the view that in discrepancies between Polish and EU law (which may well be referred also to unregulated areas), the first step made to remove such discrepancies should be an attempt to match or adapt the non-overlapping norms by way of appropriate interpretation of the local provisions[35]. This reasoning allows treatment of the VBER Guidelines as an obvious point of reference in decisions adopted by the Polish competition authorities in vertical restraints cases.

The scope of this article does not allow entering more deeply into the nexus between *acquis communautaire* and the local application of Article 6 of the Law to vertical cases. Therefore, only a brief remark, or *caveat*, should be made at the end of discussion on this point. One should note that the Polish Supreme Court approaches the issue of "pro-community interpretation" rather carefully and relates it mainly to interpretation of areas of law covered by EU directives. In the case of provisions of the Law regulating vertical restraints, the Supreme Court remarks that those provisions were not introduced in the process of implementation of any pertinent directives.[36] In result, according to the Supreme Court, judgments of EU Courts and decisions of the Commission can mainly serve (in cases which have no effect on trade between Member States) as sources of intellectual inspiration and examples of juridical reasoning helpful to understand certain notions applied in the interpretation of provisions of Polish law. This rather cautious approach of the Supreme Court suggests that Polish courts may treat the VBER Guidelines only as an auxiliary tool of interpretation, as opposed to a directly applicable act of *acquis communautaire*.

---

34 This provision stipulates that law which follows from agreements ratified in Poland (which constitute international organizations, i.e. the Lisbon Treaty), is applied directly, having precedence before national laws in case of a collision.

35 See: A. Kalisz, *Wykładnia i stosowanie prawa wspólnotowego* (Interpretation and application of EU law), LEX 61212; S. Biernat [in:] *Prawo Unii Europejskiej. Zagadnienia Systemowe.* (EU law. Issues of system.), ed. J. Barcz, Warszawa 2006, p. 291; D. Miąsik, *Solvents* to the Rescue — a Historical Outline of the Impact of EU Law on the Application of Polish Competition Law by Polish Courts, Yearbook of Antitrust and Regulatory Studies, Vol. 2010, 3(3), p. 15 *et seq.* See also judgment of ECJ in re: *Commission vs. Italy*, C 129/00.

36 See the quoted judgment of the Supreme Court, III SK 5/09. Also, the judgment of the Supreme Court of 9 August 2006, III SK 6/06 and resolution of the Supreme Court of 13 July 2006, III SZP 3/06, OSNP 2007 No. 1-2, item 34.

5.2 Concluding remarks

This brief overview of several substantive and procedural aspects of enforcement of vertical restraints demonstrates that in the course of the last two decades following the introduction in Poland of market economy, Poland developed a stable and well-thought system of competition law. Poland follows closely the EU developments in the area of vertical restraints and is currently in the process of adapting the local regulations to new ideas expressed in the VBER. The President of the OCCP presents a flexible approach to crucial enforcement problems tackled in the growing body of case law.

Undertakings can expect that assessment of vertical agreements in Poland will be compatible with EU practice in that regard. Harmonized laws and uniform practice serve the purpose of legal certainty, playing a crucial role in the process of business decision-making. In Poland, the level of legal certainty should be estimated as high, which benefits not only businesses and investors but also consumers, whose rights are well defined and better protected.

CHAPTER XIII

ENFORCEMENT OF VERTICAL RESTRAINTS IN THE NETHERLANDS

CONSTANTIJN BAKKER

Lecturer European Competition Law
International Business Department
Hogeschool van Amsterdam

1. Introduction

Until 1998, the Netherlands was considered to be a cartel paradise and indeed RPM (resale price maintenance) was, for example, not systematically prohibited. In this chapter, after a short overview of the history of Dutch competition law, the main characteristics of modern Dutch competition law will be discussed, in particular with regard to vertical restraints.

Although there are no problematic vertical restraints on the Dutch market, this chapter will discuss the decision of the Dutch Cartel Authority with regard to non-compete clauses in agreements with beer brewer Heineken[1] and the letter of this Authority regarding support systems in agreements between oil companies and their dealers[2].

1.1 History of Dutch competition law

The Dutch competition Act of 1956[3] (hereinafter: DCA) established a system, which empowered the Minister of Economic Affairs to prohibit "abusive anti-competitive behaviour", viz. behaviour that is contrary to public or general interest. The word "abusive" implied the use of specific criteria for establishing whether certain behaviours, such as systems of resale

---

1 Decision of 28 May 2002.
2 Letter of 6 March 2003.
3 In Dutch: "Wet Economische Mededinging".

price maintenance (RPM), are undesired. These criteria regarded. in the first place, economic desiderata, but enabled the authorities to take into consideration other desiderata as well, such as (from the perspective of 2011) sustainability and environmental protection[4]. Characteristic of this — so-called — *abuse system* was that the DCA did not produce any legal effects until specific behaviours were classified to be abusive. Hence, the law could only produce legal effects "ex nunc". Under the DCA regime, the Minister prohibited RPM with regard to a listed number of products. Hence, RPM remained allowed with regard to non-listed products.

Although the idea of judging the legality of anti-competitive behaviour on the basis of non-purely economic desiderata can be considered to be a very modern approach[5], the DCA was felt to have important disadvantages. In the first place, due to the fact that the Minister needed to prove the negative impact to the general interest of an anti-competitive system before he could prohibit it. Another problem was that the "ex nunc" approach did not offer the possibility of preventive measures with a view of in particular avoiding abuses of dominant positions. Last but not least, an important objection against the DCA was that its system did not correspond to the European system, which applied the so-called *prohibition system*, hence an "ex tunc" approach.

For all these reasons a new Dutch Competition Act[6] (hereinafter: NDCA) entered into force in 1998. This Act introduced a prohibition of cartels, which is modelled according to European competition law. The new Act has been amended several times, in particular in 2004 after the coming into force of EC Regulation 1/2003.

It is important that the NDCA established a Dutch competition authority: the "Nederlandse Mededingingsautoriteit" (hereinafter: NMa). Its powers are similar to the powers of the European Commission in the European field. The NMa, although it started its life in 1998 as an implementing body within the Ministry of Economic Affairs, was meant to become an independent administrative body, under the political responsibility of the Minister. The NMa received this independent status in 2005.

---

4   Cf. M.R. Mok "Marktwerking in discussie" in Tijdschrift voor Europees recht SEW, October 2010, pp. 399-403, page 400.
5   A prohibition system can also allow to take into consideration non-purely economic desiderata as justification for exemptions.
6   In Dutch: "Mededingingswet".

1.2 Main principles regarding (vertical) cartels in NDCA

Article 6 of the NDCA prohibits cartels in a way, which is modeled to the prohibition laid down in Article 101 TFEU. This Article, which very clearly prohibits RPM with regard to all products, runs as follows[7]:

1. *Agreements between undertakings, decisions by associations of undertakings and concerted practices of undertakings, which have as their object or effect the prevention, restriction or distortion of competition on the Netherlands market or on a part thereof, are prohibited.*

2. *Agreements and decisions that are prohibited under paragraph (1) shall be automatically void.*

3. *Paragraph (1) shall not apply to agreements, decisions and concerted practices which contribute to the improvement of production or distribution, or to the promotion of technical or economic progress, while allowing consumers a fair share of the resulting benefits, and which do not*

   a. *impose restrictions which are not indispensable to the attainment of these objectives, or*

   b. *afford the possibility of eliminating competition in respect of a substantial part of the products in question.*

4. *Any undertaking or association of undertakings invoking paragraph (3) shall provide proof that the conditions of that paragraph are met.*

It is remarkable that paragraph 3 of Article 6 NDCA[8] says that paragraph (1) NDCA shall not apply under certain conditions, whereas the similar paragraph 3 of Article 101 TFEU says that the provisions of paragraph (1) TFEU *may,* under the same conditions, *be declared inapplicable.* This difference in the two texts results from the fact that the European Commission in 2004 — after the coming into force of EU Regulation 1/2003 — decided to stop the granting of individual exemptions, although Article 101 TFEU was not amended to that new situation. In Article 6 (3) NDCA the Dutch legislator wanted to clearly emphasize that the NMa is no longer obliged to issue individual exemptions. As on the European level, this implies that

---

7 Translation by author. The unofficial translation in English which the NMa published on its website (www.nmanet.nl/engels/home/Legislation/Index.asp) does not show well enough the correlation between Article 6 NDCA and Article 101 TFEU, which exist in the Dutch versions of these provisions.

8 The current version of Article 6 NDCA came into force in 2004.

cartels may be exempted as a result of block exemptions. In this respect it is important to mention Article 12 NDCA, running as follows:

> *Article 6(1) shall not apply to agreements between undertakings, decisions by associations of undertakings and concerted practices of undertakings to which Article 81 (1) of the Treaty*[9] *is declared inapplicable, pursuant to a Regulation of the Council of the European Union or to a Regulation of the Commission of the European Communities.*

As a result of this provision, the block exemptions regarding vertical restraints issued by the European Commission, such as Regulation 2790/1999[10], also apply to vertical restraints on the Dutch market. This is independent from the question of whether these restraints may affect trade between Member States in the sense of Article 101 TFEU. The applicability of Regulation 2790/1999 necessarily involves the applicability of its Article 7, according to which the NMa may withdraw the benefit of the block exemption in respect of the Netherlands territory.

With regard to the interpretation of Regulation 2790/1999 by the NMa, it is worthwhile mentioning that the NMa issued guidelines[11] in 2001, explaining that it will normally apply Article 6 NDCA to conform to the "Guidelines on vertical restraints" of the European Commission[12].

Lastly Article 15 NDCA shall be mentioned. This provision allows the Minister to issue block exemptions under the same conditions as mentioned in Article 6 (1) NSCA and Article 101 TFEU. With regard to vertical restraints a Dutch block exemption was established regarding "cooperation agreements within the retail business"[13]. The difference with Regulation 2790/1999 is that it defines franchise agreements in some respects in a broader way. This Dutch block exemption applies exclusively to cooperation agreements, which do not affect trade between Member States.

---

9 Now: Article 101 TFEU.

10 OJ 1999, L 336/21. Replaced by Regulation 330/2010 (as from 1 June 2010).

11 NMa guidelines cooperation undertakings, OJ (Staatscourant) 8 June 2001, nr. 108, pp. 28-30, § 18.

12 OJ 2000, C 291/1.

13 Decision to exempt temporarily "samenwerkingsovereenkomsten detailhandel", OJ (Staatsblad) 1997, p. 704, which was extended for indefinite duration by Decision of 10 December 2008, OJ 2008, p. 542.

2. Non-compete clauses in agreements with Heineken

On 14 December 2000 beer brewer Heineken notified the NMa of its (standard) contracts with pub tenants and other members of the catering industry (hereinafter: "pub tenants").[14] These contracts provide for commercial or financial support to pub tenants in the Netherlands in exchange for exclusive purchase of Heineken's lager beer. Hence, the contracts contain a non-compete obligation by imposing trademark exclusivity. The duration of this non-compete obligation depends on the duration of the contract.

Some of these contracts have an unlimited duration, viz. the contracts granting to the pub tenant a security deposit, a loan or a cellar beer installation. Although these contracts are concluded for an unlimited period of time, they allow the pub tenant a term of notice of two months. There are also contracts that have a limited duration, viz. the lease contracts regarding premises of the brewer.

Regulation 2790/1999 does not apply to these contracts, since Heineken has a market share of more than 30%. Therefore the NMa needed to judge these contracts individually. However, after notification by Heineken, the NMa informally raised its objections to the contracts, which led the beer brewer to amend its contracts. Consequently, the exclusive purchase obligation was limited to *lager beer from the draught*. Moreover, Heineken committed itself to inform the pub tenants every year about the possibility of cancelling the contract.

In order to decide whether Heineken infringed Article 6 (1) NDCA, the NMa started to analyse whether the beer brewer has a dominant position on the relevant market[15].

2.1 Position Heineken on the relevant market

The NMa considers that the relevant market is the Dutch market for selling beer to the catering industry. On this market Heineken has a market share of ± 50-60%. Although such an important market share can be proof of a dominant position, Heineken does not necessarily dominate the market. There are three important competitors which have market shares varying from 5%-20%. Moreover, there is enough proof of actual competing against

---

14 Before 2004 it was possible to obtain, after notification, a declaration that Article 6 (1) NDCA does not apply or to obtain an individual exemption.

15 NMa Decision nr. 2036/91.

Heineken, even by competitors having a very small market share. This competition takes place by acquiring the sales outlets of the catering industry. Based on answers of different brewers, the NMa concludes that, on ± 50% of the market the acquisition of sales outlets depends on the possibility for brewers to offer financial and commercial support, apart from offering a good price and interesting reductions. This part of the market represents ± 60% selling beer to the catering industry. On the other 50% of the market, the decisive factors for acquisition of sales outlets are most certainly price level, possible reductions and brand preference. All brewers agree that there is intense competition with regard to acquiring these sales outlets.

Hence, Heineken has a strong position on the relevant market since 30% of this market is tied to Heineken as a result of the exclusivity clause. This is however no reason for the NMa to conclude that Heineken has a dominant position on this market.

2.2 Restriction of competition

According to the NMa, exclusive purchase obligations do not have as their objective to restrict or to distort competition. However, non-compete clauses can have anti-competitive effects. Therefore the effect of these clauses needs to be investigated for both the contracts of unlimited duration and of limited duration. This implies an analysis whether the brand exclusivity leads to (appreciable) restrictions of competition as a result of the duration of the contracts[16]. Moreover the NMa needs to investigate whether there are no other restrictions to cancelling the contracts.

2.2.1 Contracts of unlimited duration

The contracts granting security deposit, loan or cellar beer installation are concluded for an unlimited period of time. However, despite this endlessness of the contracts, they contain a notice period of two months for the benefit of the catering industry. Consequently, a pub tenant, who respects the notice period, can at any time cancel the beer tie. Heineken, on the other hand, is not permitted to cancel the contract, unless the pub tenant does not fulfil its obligations. Moreover, the beer tie regards only lager beer from the draught. Consequently, the pub tenant is allowed to sell lager

---

16 The NMa considers the duration of the contracts to be an important factor as a result of § 141 of the Guidelines on Vertical Restraints.

beer of other brewers in bottles and cans and draught beer of other brewers, provided it is not lager beer.

Hence, the contracts guarantee the pub tenant endless financial and commercial support, at least as long as he wishes it. Moreover, the beer ties in Heineken's contracts, as they are composed after the recommendations of the NMa, may produce less strict ties than the ones of its competitors. Heineken's competitors, having a market share of less than 30%, can — as a result of Article 5 of Regulation 2799/1999 — impose trademark exclusivity during a period of five years. During these five years the competitor, having used this opportunity, does not have to fear for any competition, not even from Heineken.

On recommendation of the NMA, Heineken committed itself to notify the pub tenants annually about the possibility of cancelling the contract within a delay of two months. Such notifications may stimulate pub tenants to enquire about alternative beer deliveries. The result of this enquiring may lead to renegotiating the conditions of the contract or to accepting offers of other brewers. This is why the NMa concludes that the contracts contain competition-stimulating incentives, which guarantee compensation for the unlimited duration of the contracts.

This does not necessarily mean that there are no other restrictions to cancel the contracts. Obstacles may exist with regard to refunding the loan or acquiring the cellar beer installation by another brewer. However, the contracts granting a security deposit or a loan can be cancelled without any obligation to pay a fine or another financial penalty. Hence, pub tenants are not prevented from repaying the outstanding part of the loan at any point in time. Under these circumstances the contract as a whole seems to be reasonable[17]. Also the contracts providing pub tenants with a cellar beer installation can be cancelled within two months. The pub tenant can take over the installation by paying the purchase price deduced with 10% depreciation per year. Thus, although the non-compete clause applies easily during 10 years, viz. the length of the depreciation of the cellar beer installation, the NMA considers that this is not going beyond what is necessary for the objective of the agreement[18].

---

17 The NMa refers here to § 156 of the Guidelines on Vertical Restraints.
18 *Ibid.* previous footnote.

2.2.2 Contracts of limited duration

With regard to the duration of the lease contracts the NMA refers to § 150 of the Guidelines on Vertical restraints to show that the Commission will consider it to be reasonable that the duration of the non-compete clause is linked to the duration of the lease contract. Hence, the NMA considers that the non-compete clause is not going beyond what is reasonable.

2.2.3 Conclusion

Due to the above mentioned reasons the NMa concludes that Article 6 (1) NDCA does not apply. According to Mok[19], the NMa was apparently of the opinion that, after the amendments to the contracts, there did not remain appreciable restriction of competition. However, in Mok's view, the amended contracts allow just more competition than the previous contracts and more competition does not necessarily justify the conclusion that there is no (appreciable) restriction of competition.

Mok certainly has a point. In its analysis of the facts, the NMa mentions that 90% of beer consumption in the Netherlands consists of lager beer and that beer selling in pubs consists mainly of lager beer from the draught.[20] This implies that the pub tenant is tied to Heineken for a large percentage of its beer sales. Moreover, according to Mok, the pub tenant cannot so easily cancel the contract with Heineken, because he must first obtain similar facilities from another brewer. This argument, however, seems not to be completely true. According to the NMa, Heineken has apparently lost more sales outlets than it has acquired during the investigated period 1998-2000[21].

3. Support systems in fuel distribution agreements

On 18 December 2001, the NMa announced its intention to declare inapplicable the European block exemption laid down in Regulation 2790/1999. It intended to do this with a view of prohibiting support systems that apply between oil companies and their dealers.

The Dutch market is characterised by a dense system of petrol stations along motorways, provincial roads and local roads. Petrol (Euro95, diesel

---

19 M.R. Mok "Kartelrecht I Nederland, de mededingingswet", Kluwer 2004, p. 284.
20 §16 of NMa Decision nr. 2036/91.
21 §93 of NMa Decision nr. 2036/91.

and LPG) is a homogeneous product. Moreover, petrol is not very sensible for price changes on this market: a price increase does not lead to less demand.

The market share of market leader Shell on the Dutch market is much higher than the share of market leaders in neighbouring countries. This is also true with regard to the share of number two (BP). Moreover, the threshold for newcomers is huge: almost no new locations are available and there are tough environmental requirements.

Price formation on the market of fuel is very transparent. All oil companies base their purchase price on the same international listing. Moreover, the oil companies publish a recommended selling price. There are only marginal differences with regard to the recommended selling prices of the different oil companies. With regard to distribution to an independent DODO[22] dealer, the oil companies in the Netherlands impose exclusive purchase obligations in their contracts with these independent petrol stations.

The big oil companies (Shell, BP, Esso, Totalfina and Texaco) apply a support system towards their dealers. These companies apply these support systems in a virtually identical way. The main characteristic of the systems is that the oil company decreases its prices towards dealer X whenever a neighbouring filling station decreases its consumer prices and therefore endangers the turnover of dealer X. The latter, obtaining this support, is obliged to pass on the price reductions to its customers. The oil company's support to the dealer will be terminated immediately after the competitor stopped with his price stunt. The NMa found out that the oil companies grant this type of support often and during long(er) periods. The consequence of the system is that it prevents dealers from decreasing their prices, since they know that a price reduction will not lead to increasing turnover, inasmuch as neighbouring competitors will be encouraged to decrease their prices as well.

In its letter of 6 March 2003 addressed to the oil companies, the NMa announced that there was insufficient evidence that a prohibition of the support systems would lead to lower consumer prices. First of all, the NMa established that the petrol market has a structure, which does not favour competition. This unavoidably affects the level of petrol prices. On the other hand, the NMa has observed developments on the petrol market, which in the future may result in greater competition. One of these developments is the increasing number of unmanned cheap petrol stations.

---

22 Dealer Owned and Dealer Operated.

Price fighter Tango has expanded its position (46 petrol stations), Shell became active on this market under the name Tinq (41 petrol stations) and Esso started to be active under the name Esso Express (10 petrol stations)[23]. Moreover, cheaper fuel became available for people having a "mobility pass" issued by consumer organizations[24]. Lastly, the auctioning of petrol stations along the motorways may lead to more dynamism along the main roads network.[25]

---

23 In its report of 6 august 2006 ("Petrol scan 2005/2006"), the NMa mentions that in 2005 serious price competition arose on the so-called underlying road network, but not along the motorways. With regard to the underlying network the number of unmanned petrol stations increased to 22%. This has led to ever-higher price reductions not only for the unmanned stations but also for the manned ones. Consequence of these price reductions is an ever-decreasing margin for the operators, causing that almost no petrol station along the underlying road network respect the recommended prices.
24 In 2006 the NMa concludes that these reduction cards have been overruled in the mean time, inasmuch as the standard reductions granted to non-cardholders developed at least to the level of reduction granted to cardholders (cf. NMa report of 6 august).
25 In 2006 the NMa concludes that the auctioning of petrol stations along the motorways did not seriously increase competition in the sense that it did not break open the market to new entrants (cf. NMa report of 6 august).

INSTITUTE of Competition Law
Antitrust databases and resources

The Institute of Competition Law is a think tank, founded in 2004 by Dr. Nicolas Charbit, based in Paris and New-York. The Institute cultivates scholarship and discussion about antitrust issues though publications and conferences. Each publication and event is supervised by editorial boards and scientific or steering committees to ensure independence, objectivity, and academic rigor. Thanks to this management, the Institute has become one of the few think tanks in Europe to have significant influence on antitrust policies.

Aim
The Institute focuses government, business and academic attention on a broad range of subjects which concern competition laws, regulations and related economics.

Boards
To maintain its unique focus, the Institute relies upon highly distinguished editors, all leading experts in national or international antitrust : Bill Kovacic, Mario Monti, Eleanor Fox, Barry Hawk, Laurence Idot, Fred Jenny...

Authors
2,200 authors, from 45 jurisdictions.

Partners
- Universities: University College London, King's College London, Queen Mary University, Paris Sorbonne Panthéon-Assas...
- Law firms: Hogan Lovells, Jones Day, Kinstellar, Vogel & Vogel, White & Case...

Events
More than 100 events since 2004 in Brussels, London, New York, Paris and Washington DC.

Concurrences Journal

Concurrences is a print and online quarterly peer reviewed journal dedicated to EU and national competitions laws

It has been launched in 2004 as the flagship of the Institute of Competition Law in order to provide a forum for academics, practitioners and enforcers. The Institute's influence and expertise has garnered interviews with such figures as Christine Lagarde, Doug Melamed, Bill Kovacic and Nicolas Sarkozy.

Contents

More than 4,500 articles, print and/or online. Quarterly issues provide current coverage with contributions from the EU or national or foreign countries thanks to more than 800 authors in Europe and abroad. Approximately 25 % of the contributions are published in English, 75 % in French, as the official language of the General Court of Justice of the EU; all contributions have English abstracts.

Format

In order to balance academic contributions with opinions or legal practice notes, Concurrences provides its insight and analysis in a number of formats:
- Forewords: Opinions by leading academics or enforcers
- Interviews: Interviews of antitrust experts
- Trends: 4 to 6 short papers on hot issues
- Law & Economics: Short papers written by economists for a legal audience
- Doctrines: Long academic papers
- Case Summaries: Case commentary on EU and French case law
- Legal Practice Short papers for in-house counsels
- International: Medium size papers on international policies
- Books Review: Summaries of recent antitrust books
- Articles Review: Summaries of leading articles published in 45 antitrust journals

Boards

The Scientific Committee is headed by Laurence Idot, Professor at Panthéon Assas University. The International Committee is headed by Frédéric Jenny, OECD Competition Comitteee Chairman. Boards members include Bruno Lasserre, Mario Monti, Richard Whish, Wouter Wils...

Online version

Concurrences website provides all articles published since its inception, and around 1,000 articles published online only, in the electronic supplement.

e-Competitions Bulletin

A unique database dedicated to case law

e-Competitions is the only online resource that provides consistent coverage of antitrust cases from 45 jurisdictions, organized into a searchable database structure. e-Competitions concentrates on cases summaries taking into account that in the context of a continuing growing number of sources there is a need for factual information, i.e., case law.

- 5,000 case summaries
- 1,500 authors
- 45 countries covered
- 22,000 subscribers

Sophisticated editorial and IT enrichment

e-Competitions is structured as a database. The editors make a highly sophisticated technical and legal work on all articles by tagging these with key words, drafting abstracts and writing html code to increase Google ranking. There is a team of antitrust lawyers – PhD and judges clerks - and a team of IT experts. e-Competitions makes comparative law possible. Thanks to this expert editorial work, it is possible to search and compare cases.

Prestigious Boards

e-Competitions draws upon highly distinguished editors, all leading experts in national or international antitrust. Advisory Board Members include: Sir Christopher Bellamy, Ioanis Lianos (UCL), Eleanor Fox (NYU), Damien Géradin (Tilburg University), Barry Hawk (Fordham University), Fred Jenny (OECD), Jacqueline Riffault-Silk (Cour de cassation), Wouter Wils (DG COMP)…

Leading Partners

- Association of European Competition Law Judges: The AECLJ is a forum for judges of national Courts specializing in antitrust case law. Members timely feed e-Competitions with just released cases.
- Academics partners: Antitrust research centres from leading universities write regularly in e-Competitions: University College London, King's College London, Queen Mary University…
- Law firms: Global law firms and antitrust niche firms write detailed cases summaries specifically for e-Competitions: Hogan Lovells, Jones Day, Kinstellar, Vogel & Vogel, White & Case…

Imprimé en France
FROC031542020620
24149FR00013B/226